AUSTRALIA

GOES

TO PRESS

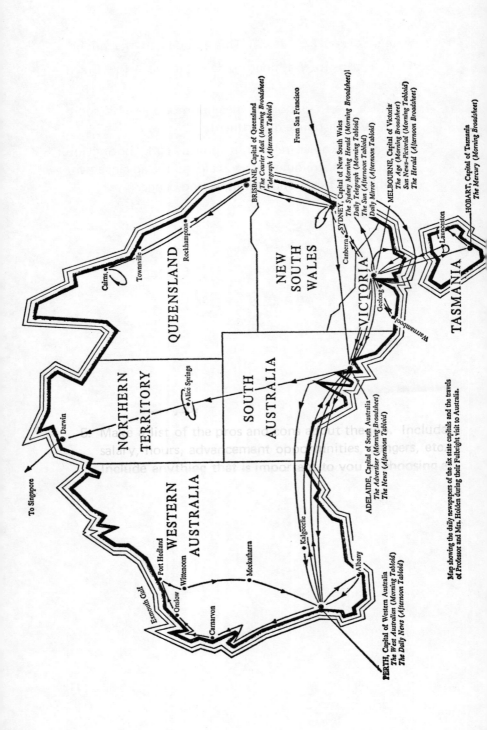

Map showing the daily newspapers of the six state capitals and the travels of Professor and Mrs. Holden during their Fulbright visit to Australia.

PERTH, Capital of Western Australia
The West Australian (Morning Tabloid)
The Daily News (Afternoon Tabloid)

ADELAIDE, Capital of South Australia
The Advertiser (Morning Broadsheet)
The News (Afternoon Tabloid)

BRISBANE, Capital of Queensland
The Courier Mail (Morning Broadsheet)
Telegraph (Afternoon Tabloid)

SYDNEY, Capital of New South Wales
The Sydney Morning Herald (Morning Broadsheet)
Daily Telegraph (Morning Tabloid)
The Sun (Afternoon Tabloid)
Daily Mirror (Afternoon Tabloid)

MELBOURNE, Capital of Victoria
The Age (Morning Broadsheet)
Sun News-Pictorial (Morning Tabloid)
The Herald (Afternoon Broadsheet)

HOBART, Capital of Tasmania
The Mercury (Morning Broadsheet)

AUSTRALIA
GOES
TO PRESS

by W. Sprague Holden

Professor of Journalism
Wayne State University

GREENWOOD PRESS, PUBLISHERS
WESTPORT, CONNECTICUT

Library of Congress Cataloging in Publication Data

Holden, Willis Sprague, 1909-
    Australia goes to press.

    Reprint of the ed. published by Wayne State University
Press, Detroit.
    Bibliography: p.
    Includes index.
    1. Journalism--Australia. 2. Australian newspapers.
I. Title.
[PN5510.H6 1977]   079'.94   77-8449
ISBN 0-8371-9689-2

Originally published in 1961 by Wayne State University Press,
Detroit

Reprinted with the permission of Wayne State University
Press

Reprinted in 1977 by Greenwood Press, Inc.

Library of Congress Catalog Card Number 77-8449

ISBN 0-8371-9689-2

Printed in the United States of America

This book is based upon research done during 1956–57 in Australia under the terms of a Fulbright grant. Some of the material has already been published as articles and essays in *Editor and Publisher, Journalism Quarterly, The Quill, The Masthead, Michigan Publisher, Nieman Reports* and *Public Relations Journal;* it is reprinted here with the permission of the publishers.

The photographs of newspaper pages were made by Joseph Klima, Jr., Detroit.

*Grateful acknowledgment is made to
the Ford Foundation for financial assistance
in making possible the publication
of this volume.*

Preface

A PERSISTENT CURIOSITY about Australia, beginning in boyhood, was the long ago genesis of this report. The more recent starting point was an occasion, a few years ago, when I wished to look up some data on Australian journalism. There was almost nothing in the otherwise well-stocked libraries of either Wayne State University (then Wayne University) or of the City of Detroit. This discovery approximately coincided with my eligibility for a sabbatical leave and with my wife's and my discovery of the Australian Fulbright program.

The eventual result was a thirteen-month visit to Australia. My Fulbright application, proposing "a study of the operation of Australian metropolitan daily newspapers," touched upon such points as "how news is gathered in Australia and how it is presented"; the play a newspaper gives local, state, national and international news; how papers are departmentalized; recruitment and training of young men and women for journalism; and other basic matters pertaining to newspaper publication. I proposed to "keep the inquiry on a comparative basis, as between the United States and Australia." Emphasis, I felt, should be on the news-editorial phases. They determine the character of a newspaper, and they are my special field.

Mrs. Holden and I lived in all six state capital cities, and Canberra, the federal capital, during our stay in Australia. I visited, usually every day for two or three weeks, fourteen of the (then) fifteen metropolitan dailies, interviewing more than three hundred newspaper people—including managing directors, editors, reporters, department heads and other key and subordinate personnel.

I did not, of course, ignore the business and mechanical departments. Invariably I visited them, interviewing department heads and exploring production methods, but the problems of reporting and editing commanded most of my attention.

I was a guest at dozens of news, editorial, photo, feature and other conferences. I accompanied roundsmen on their rounds in all seven cities. I met and interviewed a former Governor-General of Australia, five state premiers, dozens of government officials, labor and business leaders, plain citizens who were newspaper readers (and critics), heads of the numerous related activities in which Australian metropolitan newspapers are engaged and hundreds of other persons. I gained much valuable material from public and university libraries—notably in Melbourne and Sydney.

With one exception,* I was cordially welcomed and made to feel at home. Each paper I visited gave me the utmost in cooperation and assistance. I made many warm friends thereby. On one memorable occasion, I was asked to join a three weeks, sixty-man, "Northern Safari" into northwest Western Australia, a three thousand-mile automobile journey in company with leading newspaper editors and executives.

That event, sponsored by West Australian Newspapers Ltd., was designed to show eastern states newspapers some of the economic potentials of Australia's Far West. Besides sharing in that benefit, I found it an incomparable opportunity to become good friends with editors from eleven of the fifteen newspapers I was studying. The safari was undertaken in July, 1956, at the conclusion of my researches in Melbourne, our first long stop; thus the safari meant an assured welcome by new editor-friends later on in other capital cities.

This was the route we traveled and these, in order, are the papers I surveyed: MELBOURNE—*The Age, The Argus, The Sun News-Pictorial, The Herald;* BRISBANE—*The Courier-Mail,* the *Telegraph;* SYDNEY—the *Daily Telegraph, The Sydney Morning Herald, The Sun;* PERTH—*The West Australian, The Daily News;* ADELAIDE—*The News, The Advertiser;* HOBART—*The Mercury.*

The Argus is no longer published; it was closed down by its London owners in January, 1957, and its plant, equipment and other publications were sold to The Herald and Weekly Times Ltd. of Melbourne. I have included findings about it, even though it is dead;

---

* One metropolitan daily, the *Daily Mirror* (Sydney), is not included in this study because the proprietor, Mr. Ezra Norton, did not grant me the opportunity to do the necessary research. In December, 1958, Mr. Norton sold

for it represented a special phase of Australian journalism, and for 111 years held an honorable place therein.

Other factors, not discernible at a distance, were Sunday newspapers and similar once-a-week periodicals, of which Australia has many. Should the five Sunday newspapers produced by parent-daily companies be included? If so, what about the capital-city editions of *Truth*,** some of which are aimed at the Sunday field, and a multitude of other weekend publications produced by dailies and independent companies—all of them journalism?

The field had to be limited. I decided to include only the six state capitals, and their daily newspapers. This is not in any way to minimize the importance of other forms of journalism, all of which play roles of special significance. My decision thus to limit the study, and to assign to "metropolitan" a meaning that equates with the state capitals was dictated only by the allowable time for research and by limited space, and it was entirely arbitrary.

My Fulbright project was proposed and undertaken in the belief that it might shed a little light two ways—to acquaint Americans with phases of Australian journalism and to tell Australians a little about the U.S. and U.S. journalism.

No American who has not visited Australia can beguile his imagination into adequate concept of the warmth, the friendliness, the hospitality that is part of the visiting American's day-to-day experience there. Elsewhere in this work appear the names of the several hundred Australians whose assistance and counsel were all-important to my research. In the text, I have not used many names, for newspaper work is largely anonymous; and it is the methods and practices that I am chiefly reporting upon. Besides those listed in Appendix A are many more who were directly or indirectly helpful.

To each of these go my deep and abiding thanks.

April, 1961   W. SPRAGUE HOLDEN

Truth and Sportsman Ltd., publishers of the *Daily Mirror, et al.*, to a company associated with John Fairfax Ltd., proprietors of *The Sydney Morning Herald, The Sun, et al.* In May, 1960, the *Mirror* properties were acquired by News Ltd. of Adelaide.
** In all capitals except Perth. In November, 1958, shortly before Mr. Norton sold it, the Sydney edition of *Truth* became the *Sunday Mirror*. It continued as the *Sunday Mirror* after resale to News Ltd. in 1960 until May, 1961, when it was restyled and renamed the *Sunday Mirror News-Pictorial*. The Melbourne edition of *Truth* became *New Truth*.

Contents

1. GEOGRAPHY, POPULATION AND JOURNALISM . . . *Page 1*

The Land is Old – The Country is Young – Capital-City Journalism – The British Matrix – A Job for the Historian – The Whole Press

2. PROPRIETORS AND MANAGEMENT *17*

The Trend to Monopoly – Public Companies – Related Enterprises – And Some Unrelated – Paper, Profits and Personnel – Newsprint from Hardwoods

3. NEWS-EDITORIAL EXECUTIVES: THE HIGH COMMAND . . *27*

Tabloids with a Difference – The Editor – News Conferences – The Day's Editions – News Editor – Chief of Staff – Morning Dailies – Afternoon Dailies – Correspondence by Stringer

4. DEPARTMENTS OF THE NEWS-EDITORIAL DIVISION . . . *43*

Subbing, Chief Sub and Sub-Editors – The Chief Sub-Editor – The Sub-Editors – Subbing Problems – Leaders and Leader Pages – Pictures in the News – The Sports Pages – Football, Cricket, *et al.* – Horses and Punters – Women's and Social – Business and Finance – Motors – Libraries, Morgues and Block Rooms

5. ROUNDS AND ROUNDSMEN *83*

"Round" Means "Beat" – Police Rounds – Police Personnel – The Roundsman's Day – State Variations – Playing Police News – State Government and Parliament – Parties, Ministers and M.P.'s – Counsellors to the People – Town Hall Rounds

6. MORE ROUNDS *101*

News from Canberra – The Canberra Press Corps – Coverage of the Courts – The Industrial Round – Other Rounds – The Telephone Room

7. OVERSEAS AND DOMESTIC NEWS *121*

Australian Associated Press – Correspondents Overseas – Cable Editor – News from Asia – Cables in the Broad-

Contents

sheets – Cables in the Tabloids – News from the U.S. –
Teletype Room – Australian United Press – Queensland
Country Press – ABC News Service – Perth News Bureau

8. THE FEATURE PHASES . . . . *Page 145*

A Long Gamut – Editors and Staff – Timeliness – No
Columning Clutter – A Week's Run – Serials and Short
Fiction – All Kinds of Supplements – Young Readers –
Movies and Theatres – Books and Book Reviews – A
Tabloid Page of History – Comic Strips – Sunday Fea-
tures – Syndication – Trash *vs.* Solid Features

9. THE PRESS AND THE LAW *163*

A Thorough Grounding – Origins and Defenses – "A
Man Was Arrested . . ." – Seditious Libel

10. THE AUSTRALIAN JOURNALISTS' ASSOCIATION *171*

Birth of the AJA – Negotiations and Court Awards –
Details of Awards – Grading the Staff – Reporters'
Rights and Responsibilities – How AJA Works – Press
Council – Syndicated Imports – Golden Jubilee

11. CADET TRAINING FOR JOURNALISTS *185*

Best of Its Kind – Beginning with AJA – Cadet Provisions in Awards – Recruitment and Training – Classes,
Lectures and Exercises – On-the-Job Training – Diploma
in Journalism – Excellences and Deficiencies

12. LIFE-BLOOD: ADVERTISING, CIRCULATION AND PROMOTION *199*

The Business Office – From All Over – A Student of
Maps – The Papers Go Through – Promotion and Public
Relations – Toward the Potential Advertiser – To Get
and to Hold

13. CONCLUSIONS AND JUDGMENTS *209*

Aussie and Yank – Traditions and Shortcomings – Big-
ness Again – More Light from Abroad – Leaders Should
Lead – Where Are the Informed Critics? – The Press's
Public Relations – Today and Tomorrow

APPENDIX A. ACKNOWLEDGMENTS *223*

B. THUMBNAIL HISTORICAL SKETCHES OF FIFTEEN
AUSTRALIAN METROPOLITAN DAILY NEWSPAPERS . . *235*

C. AUSTRALIAN PERIODICALS *247*

D. Radio and Television 253

E. Professional Associations, Trade
Services and Publications 255

F. Authorized News Agent System . . . 261

Glossary 267

Selected Bibliography 277

Index 281

b) yes   b) Answers will vary.

ROBBERY AT THE SUPERMARKET (Pages 18-23)

Words to Know   1. b   2. c   3. a   4. f   5. e   6. d   7. h
8. i   9. g

Illustrations

following page 144

1. Australia's First Newspaper
2. Front Page of *The Sydney Morning Herald*
3. Front Page of *The Herald* (Melbourne)
4. Front Page of *The News* (Adelaide)
5. Front Page of *The West Australian* (Perth)
6. Cable Page of *The Age* (Melbourne)
7. Cable Pages of the *Daily Telegraph* (Sydney)
8. A Newspaper Poster

Tables

1. Area and population of the Australian states and territories and of their capital cities 3
2. Division of each pound spent by six newspaper companies 23
3. Police personnel of Australian states 86
4. Literary staff rates, Metropolitan Dailies Awards . . . 176
5. Cadet pay scale, Metropolitan Dailies Awards . . . 187
6. Column inches of advertising in metropolitan dailies for a typical month 200

I

Geography, Population and Journalism

The Land is Old

Every day, Monday through Saturday of each week, a few holidays excepted, printers touch buttons in the press rooms of the metropolitan newspaper plants in six Australian capital cities, and miracles commence. The sullen complaint of machinery roused from its static sleep becomes a murmur; the murmur gradually mounts to a roar. What Rudyard Kipling, who loved it, called "the loaded hour" has begun, and the great presses "devour their league-long paper-bale." The day's first edition is rolling.

A newspaper's new birth each day is an exceedingly complex process, of fantastic dimensions in relation to its usual life span of a few hours. It is as much a miracle in Australia as it is anywhere else on earth. For many hours beforehand, news from all over the great globe's 196,950,284 square miles—some from within and even some from beyond it—has deluged into the editorial offices of the metropolitan dailies. There the news has been edited and put into type. Morning papers may begin to print in mid-evening, but most of them roll first at about midnight. Afternoon papers publish first editions between mid-morning and noon. The number of editions varies up to a half a dozen, and may depend upon time of year or upon special circumstances.

Once the presses have worked their magic, responsibility passes to the distributors, for a newspaper is not a newspaper until it is read. In Australia, distribution is no easy task. The states are huge, distances are vast; and all populated, semi-populated and thinly-populated areas are the staked domains of capital-city newspaper circulation departments. The morning newspapers have a four- or five-hour advantage over the afternoons in the race to the reader. They are moved during the hours of sleep. Morning papers can be and are placed upon breakfast tables hundreds of miles away. By truck, train, airplane, motor bus—sometimes by school bus, milk truck or other unlikely conveyance—the papers travel to journalism's ultimate consumer.

Australian journalism, like so many phases of life in the only nation in the world that occupies a whole continent, has been conditioned by the physical nature of that continent.

Australia is one of the oldest land masses on earth. In certain areas its enormous, level gibber (stone-covered) plains and peneplains have known little or no disturbance from underneath for as long as one and one-half billion years. From above, weather has worked the continent over so vigorously and so long that in many places erosion has gone as far as it can go. Rain-producing mountains have been reduced, flattened or eliminated. And rainfall is one of the chief determinants of life on our globe.

Australia's land-mass is 2,974,581 square miles—only 47,419 square miles less than that of the 48 contiguous United States. One-third of Australia gets little or no rainfall and is desert. One-third gets a moderate annual wetting and is semi-arid. Over the last third the rainfall is adequate, or more than adequate, and that part of Australia varies from lush, beautiful farm and pasture land to tropical rain forest. Most of this last third extends along the eastern and southeastern coasts on both sides of the Great Dividing Range that stretches from north Queensland to Victoria paralleling the Pacific littoral, one hundred miles inland more or less. It dives under Bass Strait after its tallest upthrust into the Australian Alps, and reappears in the Central Highlands of Tasmania, the island state.

The Country is Young

The lush third's importance here is in what it has done to the British settlement of Australia since 1788 and by extension to journalism. An area and population listing of the six states and their capital cities tells part of the story:

TABLE 1.—AREA AND POPULATION OF THE AUSTRALIAN
STATES AND TERRITORIES AND OF THEIR CAPITAL
CITIES *

State or Territory	Area in Square Miles	Population (Est. March, 1960)	Capital City	Capital-City Population (June, 1959)	Percentage of State Population in Capital City
New South Wales	309,433	3,812,380	Sydney	2,054,800	57
Victoria	87,884	2,875,360	Melbourne	1,777,700	63
Queensland	670,500	1,450,314	Brisbane	567,000	39
South Australia	380,070	939,576	Adelaide	562,500	61
Western Australia	975,920	727,339	Perth	389,000	54
Tasmania	26,215	349,643	Hobart	109,200	32
Northern Territory	523,620	21,135	Darwin	8,620	40
Australian Capital Territory	939	51,642	Canberra	43,973	85
NATIONAL TOTALS	2,974,581	10,227,389		5,512,793	54

* Figures from Commonwealth Bureau of Census and Statistics.

The figures are not only remarkable but basic. In four of the
six capital cities—Sydney, Melbourne, Adelaide and Perth—live
more than 50 per cent of the population of their respective states.
Only Brisbane and Hobart, with less than fifty per cent, do not
conform to this population pattern. Darwin and Canberra are not
state capitals, and neither is large enough to support a metropolitan
daily newspaper.

Australia is growing rapidly. In the latter part of 1959, it welcomed its 1,500,000th immigrant since the end of World War II.
Its present population, slightly more than ten million, is not much
larger than that of Greater London. The capital cities are all sea
ports. If a map of Australia were superimposed on a map of the
United States, the geographical situation of the capitals and the
distances between them would be roughly comparable to these
U.S. cities: Washington—Brisbane; Charleston—Sydney; Tallahassee
—Melbourne; Miami—Hobart; New Orleans—Adelaide; and Los
Angeles—Perth.

The comparison makes it more evident where the great empti-
nesses of Australia are. Draw a line from Rockhampton, Queensland, southwest to Port Augusta, South Australia; include the island

state of Tasmania; draw another line across the southwestern tip of Western Australia somewhat north of Perth to a bit east of Albany —and within that enclosed 20–25 per cent of Australia's land area live something like 90 per cent of its people.

The effect upon journalism of this population distribution has been direct and continuing. In the huge capital cities huge newspapers have grown up. In the small outstate cities and tiny country towns, daily and other newspapers have developed commensurately. (See Appendix C.)

This, then, is the first great difference between Australian and U.S. journalism. No Australian state compares in population distribution with, say, the state of Ohio (8,000,000), which has a half a dozen cities ranging from 200,000 to more than a million and another score between 20,000 and 200,000. Consequently, in Ohio there are metropolitan, medium-sized and small-city newspapers. In Australia, there are only metropolitan and small-city.

The terms "metropolitan daily newspapers" and "capital-city journalism," as used in this book, require some exposition. In the *1961 NAARDS—Newspapers: Australian Advertising Rate and Data Service,* an annual compilation, 655 Australian newspapers are listed. By categories, they break down this way:

TOTAL	Daily Newspapers	48
"	5 Days a Week Newspapers	8
"	3 Days a Week Newspapers	29
"	2 Days a Week Newspapers	91
"	Weekly Newspapers	457
"	Fortnightly Newspapers	11
"	Monthly Newspapers	11
		655

Of the 48 dailies, as noted above, 14 are published in state capitals. But Hobart, capital of Tasmania, with a population of 109,200, is smaller than Newcastle, New South Wales (199,080), is about the same size as Greater Wollongong, New South Wales (118,090) and has only about 21,000 more population than Geelong, Victoria (88,160). More to the point, one of the two Newcastle dailies— *The Morning Herald and Miner's Advocate*—has a larger circulation than that of *The Mercury,* Hobart's only daily. By population and by newspaper circulation standards, Newcastle is therefore more "metropolitan" than Hobart. But Newcastle is not a capital city.

Canberra, on the other hand, not only is a capital; it is the national capital. But Canberra's population (43,973) is little more than one-third of Hobart's, and *The Canberra Times'* circulation is commensurately small.

The rest of the 51 dailies are neither capital-city nor metropolitan. Outside the big population centers, circulation of dailies drops sharply from six figures to five—more often, to four. New South Wales, the most populous state, has 17 suburban and country dailies. Of these, two have 15–50,000 circulation; four have 10–15,000; five have 5–10,000; and six have less than 5,000. The drop is either as great or greater in other states.

Inevitably each capital-city daily considers its whole state to be its special territory, in such matters as news coverage and circulation. Resultant problems are huge, as with Western Australia, a state larger in area than three Texases; or, as with Queensland, bigger than six Nevadas. A concentrated capital-city population may make news coverage and distribution of newspapers easier for that half of the state's population; but the difficulties are considerable in respect to the other half.

Another effect is upon opportunity for journalists. In the U.S., if a newspaperman is fired from his job, or if he does not like his boss, he can go to any of scores of other cities for new employment. In Australia, the journalist with a liking for metropolitan journalism has only fourteen dailies to choose from; and a number of these have interlocking management. In point of fact, he has to dislike, or be disliked by, only seven proprietors; and he can turn thereafter for a job only to the country's two-score small dailies or to its weeklies, or he must go to some other field entirely.

Capital-City Journalism

Each of the capital cities has a character and spirit all its own. Differences in climate, topography, history, economic and social milieu are matched, among their respective citizenries, by differences in attitudes, tempo of living, speech, manners and mores. All these, blended by time and circumstance, give each capital its special quality.

Yet, all six capitals are alike in certain respects; for they are all British-created cities, however thoroughly Australian they have become. They are endowed lavishly with parks and green recreation areas; each has its Botanic Gardens, tailored pridefully and exquisitely to bloom the year round. Public places are sites for massive monuments to wars, statesmen, events, explorations and occasional

men of letters. Each capital has its World War memorial conspicuously placed. Each capital supports a state symphony orchestra,
art and other museums, legitimate theaters, innumerable movie
houses (showing U.S. films almost entirely), a public library system
and other cultural institutions. Each has fine shopping centers, and
its own magnificent series of saltwater bathing beaches. Roads
lead from each of the six cities into pleasant suburbs and rich farm-
lands. If the traveler goes far enough, he comes to the bush, usually
green and eucalyptus-covered; and, still farther, eventually to the
outback, which is usually not. If he goes "beyond the black stump,"
he is into the "Never-Never," another name for the outback, which
is the dry, sterile-desert third of the continent, where rain almost
never falls. This is "the great Australian loneliness," inhabited only
by occasional aboriginal nomads, mobs of kangaroos, wallabies,
emus, goannas and other remarkable forms of animal life.

Life is pleasant and good in the metropolitan centers and about
their wide peripheries. Life can be hard and cruel in the outback,
with its long droughts and violent storms. Between these two extremes live ten million-plus Australians; and most of them are newspaper readers.

Australia—British Australia—started with and in Sydney,
with the First Fleet of 1788 under Captain Arthur Phillip; and
Sydney today is not only Australia's oldest city, it is her biggest, with
a population about equal to Detroit's. Sydney is also her most raucous,
her most diverse, her busiest, her most cosmopolitan. By their own
declarations, many Australians, especially Sydneysiders, believe "we
are more like you Americans than we are like the English." Sydney
is the busiest port of entry and departure for overseas travelers;
and something of the hustle and hurry of thousands of traveling
foreigners seems to rub off on Sydneysiders. They are also inclined
to be a little patronizing toward their sister-capitals—except for
Melbourne. There was much unhappiness in Sydney when Melbourne was chosen as the site for the 1956 Olympic Games, and
perhaps even more unhappiness later, because the event was such
a rousing success. However, a Sydneysider can always bolster his
assurance by remembering that Sydney has "The Bridge," the can-
tilever structure which leaps the narrows near Sydney Cove to bind
the north and south shores of Port Jackson, one of the most beautiful
harbors on the globe. The bridge may be an "overgrown coat-hanger"
to scoffers in Melbourne, but it is easily Australia's most famous
man-made landmark.

Sydney is also Australia's "best newspaper town," a phrase used here in a newspaperman's meaning, and not in the sense that the city has Australia's best newspaers. It has four dailies altogether, which is one more than Melbourne now has, and two of Sydney's are among Australia's best—*The Sydney Morning Herald* and the *Daily Telegraph*. If sin, sex, sensation and a lively concept of news are criteria, it has two more of the best—*The Sun* and the *Daily Mirror*. But if Sydney reminds the visiting American a little of New York and perhaps more of San Francisco, it will never lead the visiting Englishman to declare that its newspapers are like England's. There is no *Times* of London, no *Manchester Guardian* in Sydney; but neither is there anything as bad as London's *Daily Mirror, The News of the World* and other such journals that constitute so much of London's newspaper press. Sydney is Australia's "best newspaper town" simply because there is more going on there, and it has been going on longer. There is more excitement in Sydney, there are bigger news breaks than in the other five capitals. Sydney is the biggest member of the big league. Yet it is far from being a journalist's Utopia. No city of two million with only four newspapers and less than four proprietorships can be ideal for newspapermen. Indeed, one of the mysteries of Sydney journalism is why none of the four dailies comes within 100,000 circulation of the two top-circulation newspapers in Melbourne, which is a few hundred thousand smaller in population —and the difference, though somewhat smaller, was there even prior to 1957, when Melbourne had four dailies. Sydney is the last stronghold of personal journalism in Australia, in the sense that the proprietors, when anger dictates, often use their newspaper properties in the way enemy battleships use their big guns on each other.*

Melbourne is about half a century junior to Sydney, but it has lived intensely and colorfully through the years since 1835 when John Batman sailed up the Yarra River from Van Diemen's Land and announced with an ear for history and the quotation anthologies,

---

* This aspect of Sydney journalism may be illustrated by a recent incident. A reporter on a Sydney journal, comparatively new to town, had about decided to accept an offer for more money from another daily. He was summoned by his top boss to discuss the matter; to fortify himself, the reporter made a quick trip to the nearest pub. At the interview the proprietor came quickly to the point. He made a better offer, the young man accepted and the business part of the session was quickly over. "Tell me," said the proprietor, now in an expansive mood, "what do you think of Sydney journalism?" The detour to the pub made the young man brave, perhaps even eloquent. "Sir," he answered, "I think Sydney journalism with its three proprietorships is something like a zoo. A bloke has the choice of working in the tiger's cage, the lion's den or the snake pit." The answer was less analytic than striking, less just than colorful, less definitive than brave; but I have heard Sydney newspapermen argue that it was not wholly a triumph of alcohol over metaphor.

7

"This is the place for a city." Melbourne was a child of gold discovery in the 1850's, an era that exactly coincided with the California gold rush. It was the inheritor of the bitterness engendered by many rancorous interregional fights that preceded Victoria's separation from the parent New South Wales in 1851. It was once a rough and ruddy capital of a rough and ruddy colony; but in the time between, transformations have been wrought. If Sydney is the vigorous extrovert, Melbourne is the sedate matriarch, formal, precise, conscious of her fine breeding, very British in her attitudes. Melbourne was the Commonwealth's capital from 1901 to 1927 and will not let Sydney forget it. Sydney stays up all night, downtown and around King's Cross, its Greenwich Village-Telegraph Hill-Montmartre area. Melbourne has no King's Cross and goes to bed early. One week-night after seeing *The Age* put to bed, I drove home from downtown Melbourne; and after crossing Exhibition Street, I passed not a single human being, on foot or on wheels, in the seven mile drive to North Balwyn, where my wife and I were living.

St. Kilda Road, which leads to and from downtown Melbourne, is regarded by Melbourne as the finest boulevard east of the high roads of heaven. Collins Street, equally an object of local pride, with its grim-grey façades of banks, insurance companies and fine hotels; its shipping, wool and finance houses, and much of its way lined with green trees, somehow manages to look a little as if it had been serenely there a few weeks before time started. *The Age,* dignified guardian of Australian-British virtue and conservatism, fronts upon Collins Street, and is housed in a stolid building long in the throes of inner remodeling, that is straight Victorian up to its neo-Greek pediment, where Mercury is forever balanced on one foot at the peak. *The Herald* and *The Sun News-Pictorial* dwell under one roof on Flinders Street, overlooking the Jolimont railroad yards with the Yarra River and the Botanic Gardens beyond. As Australia's most successful newspapers, with their bold makeup and sprightly news concepts, they do much to suggest that Melbourne's somewhat self-conscious dignity is not stuffiness and that her conservatism is not always what it seems. Victoria is the state of the Eureka Stockade battle at the Ballarat gold fields in 1854, a blood-letting milestone in Australian labor politics and in the workman's emancipation fight. In Melbourne, near the sprawling Trades Union Hall is a monument unique in the world, three figure-eights capping a tall shaft—signalizing the birth of the eight-hour working day: eight hours for work, eight hours for play, eight hours for sleep.

Melbourne is the town where Ned Kelly, Australia's most famous bushranger hero, was hanged.

As a newspaper town, Melbourne rates well, despite only two ownerships for its three papers. The proprietor group includes many men who rose to authority as working newspapermen, and it pays no dues to a tradition of prima donna owners. *The Argus*, victim of an absentee-landlord decision, deserved to continue, though during the seven years of its last phase it seemed not quite sure what it wanted to be. From an arch-conservative newspaper, in makeup and editorial policies, it executed a 180-degree turn and became perhaps the flashiest paper in Australia, "a broadsheet edited like a tabloid," full of crusading turbulence that sometimes sent it riding off in all directions. It was winning its slow way in its new guise, when it was poleaxed from London; the corpse and the effects were sold to The Herald and Weekly Times Ltd. There may be a symptomatic truth in the epitaphic assertion that *The Argus,* transmogrified, was too racy for Melbourne's sedate tastes.

Brisbane, third of the capitals in order of population, is the dominant factor in the state of Queensland, which separated from New South Wales in 1859. Brisbane is Australia's tropical metropolis. It takes unto itself, as do the other state capitals, the principal brokerage, processing and transshipment of the state's wool, mining and other primary products, also much of its manufacturing. Brisbane, though often very warm, never gets cold. Queensland is Australia's Florida, as Western Australia is its California, in the holiday sense; and Brisbane, bordered by the neighboring resort centers of Surfers Paradise, Coolongatta, Tweed Heads and others, is Australia's Miami. Many city bridges bracket the meandering Brisbane River, several miles up from its mouth at Moreton Bay; and mountain ranges, including the Glass House Mountains, named by Captain James Cook in 1770 for their glistening peaks after rain, help to provide the city with a distinguished setting. Because of the heat and the white ants, or termites, most Queensland homes are built on stilts capped with metal plates, giving the streets an interesting upstairs look. Brisbaners live in the outdoors even more than their countrymen in the south, and life is more leisurely in the almost uniformly pleasant weather. It is not unusual to see workmen, barefoot and clad only in shorts, in or near the city; there is more sense of country-in-the-city in Brisbane than in either Sydney or Melbourne. Brisbane is a one-ownership town for dailies, and mostly absentee at that. In the morning *Courier-Mail,* a conservative broadsheet, and the afternoon *Telegraph,* a bumptious tabloid, it has samples of the extremes in journalism.

So does Adelaide, capital of South Australia, in the dowager morning broadsheet, *The Advertiser,* and in the afternoon tabloid, *The News. The Advertiser* likes things as they are; and is willing to rely on civilized exposition to keep them that way. *The News* can't wait for Utopia. It is brash and sometimes brassy, but it is as alert and forthright about injustices as any newspaper in Australia. Between the two, Adelaide is well served. The city's physical plan is unique in the continent-nation. The business district, only a few blocks square, is surrounded by a wide belt of green parklands which are play and recreation areas for the people who work in the city and live in the pleasant suburbs farther out. These suburban communities fan out toward the Gulf of St. Vincent on the west and toward the surrounding mountains, including massive Mt. Lofty, in other directions. Adelaide was laid out in detail before the first settlers came in 1836. Present dwellers are the fortunate legatees of their planning.

At the other end of the continent, Perth, capital of immense Western Australia and first settled in 1829, is isolated enough to seem like the capital of another country. Between Perth in the west and Sydney, Melbourne, Brisbane and Adelaide in the east, lie some of the hottest, cruelest, oldest and emptiest regions on earth. The east-west division—geographical, economic, spiritual and other—is so strong that in the early 1930's Western Australia unsuccessfully attempted to secede from the Commonwealth. There is little talk of division nowadays, but Perth's divorcement from her sister-capitals is still very real. A trip to Perth from Sydney is comparable to a trip from New York to San Francisco. For her part, Perth pays no great attention to her distant and bigger sisters, content to let them look upon her as the jewel of a city she admits to be. Perth possesses what Perthians affirm is the best climate in Australia—"the kind of weather that California thinks it has." The setting along the Swan River and against the backdrop of the Darling Range is superb, and an astonishing variety of adjoining country, from jarrah and karri forests in the southwest to million-acre sheep stations, ancient mountains and marrow-desiccating desert in the north and northeast, give Perthians a special kind of home environment. Perth's two tabloids, the morning *West Australian* and the afternoon *Daily News* reflect the Australian belief that morning papers should be "serious" and afternoons should "entertain." Both live under the same roof of Newspaper House and are owned by the same company, but competition is encouraged.

The isolation of Hobart, capital of Tasmania, is of a different and watery nature. "Little Tasy" is the way the mainlanders sometimes refer to the smallest of the six states. During the 1956 Olympic Games, there was embarrassment in high places, and annoyance south of Bass Strait, when Tasmania was inadvertently left off some of the official maps of Australia. Tasmanians usually do not seem to care, however, how they are regarded by their countrymen. Their attitude is often that if mainlanders haven't the wit to know what Tasmania has, that is their loss. Tasmania has quite a plenty. Hobart's sea-level situation below the overwhelming bulk of 4,166-foot high Mt. Wellington and athwart the wide Derwent River gives the capital a magnificent setting. Hobart is second in age only to Sydney. Tasmania was known as Van Dieman's Land when it was separated from New South Wales in 1829—the name was changed to Tasmania in 1853, three years before it was granted responsible government. The mellowing that time has given many of its solid freestone buildings and bridges—the oldest bridge, in nearby Richmond, goes back to 1823—is part of old Hobart Town's charm. The wild beauty of the Central Highlands and of the east and north coasts is only a few hours away by motor. So are the two other chief towns of Launceston and Burnie. The dry, raw outback of the mainland has its counterpart in the southwestern one-third of the island which is still largely untouched and unexplored by white men because of the impenetrable bush of the mountain lands.

Because Hobart has only one paper, *The Mercury,* a special relationship appears to obtain between it and its readers, a relationship not unlike that between a wise old uncle and a brood of nephews and nieces. *The Mercury* is intensely Tasmanian; it has been around much longer than any of its readers—more than a century. It has absorbed or survived all competitors, and its recently-acquired broadsheet dress, effected by purchase of *The Argus'* printing presses, signalized only one more change in its long history. *The Mercury,* a paper that is anything but mercurial, every day surveys Tasmania and things Tasmanian and finds them generally good.

The British Matrix

The British spirit, if not always the tradition, is alive and strong in Australia. New South Wales was Australia's first British name, and it came from Captain Cook's conclusion that the continent looked very much like Britain's Wales. Victoria and Queensland took their names from the same Queen-Empress. British place-names dot the state maps; the street names of the capital cities are a roll call of British kings, queens, statesmen, explorers, cities and towns. The forms of government in Australia are mainly British. Knighthoods, titles and other honors are conferred by the reigning monarch of England, who is also the Queen (or King) of Australia. "God Save" is the national anthem. Although Australia has complete political independence, and has great national pride, "to go home" still means, to many native-born Australians, to make the journey to England, even though they may never have been there.

Australian journalism has been shaped by its British origins no less than by geography and climate. Australia's first newspaper * was printed "By Authority" of the crown—as were the first in the American colonies. Australian journalism pursued a road to freedom from royal authority as hard as that of the Americans. It has had fierce struggles, first with the British royal, and later with Australian government, authority to maintain its freedom. It is restrained by British-model libel and contempt laws. During its colonial era (until 1901) orientation was almost exclusively toward England as the mother country.

Of the earlier time, Clive Turnbull, an Australian journalist, wrote that the Australian press "published pages of news extracted from English papers. . . . The dominance of European news in the early colonial press is frequently surprising to casual readers of old files who find Australian events, of which they would like to know more, subordinated to comparatively minor events in England. ** The introduction of cable communication changed all that; just as it changed the scramble to get into print—often with a special supplement—with the latest news, weeks old, brought by ship from London to Australia.

Styles in newspaper makeup followed British patterns, both during and after the reign of the solidly grey conservative newspaper with its advertisements on page one, little or no art, and its unadorned columns of small type under chaste label heads. When the change did come, it came to stay. It has not been many years since the last of the "broadsheets"—as Australians term their standard-size newspapers—exchanged advertisements for news on page one, and made other radical alterations. In its twenty-fifth anniversary edition (May, 1953) *Newspaper News* recalled that *The Daily Sun* (Sydney) began life in 1910 with news on its front page; that the *Daily Telegraph* (Sydney) changed from advertisements to news on page one after

---

* See illustration, following p. 144.
** "Journalism," in C. Hartley Grattan (ed.), *Australia* (Berkeley and Los Angeles: University of California Press, 1947), 320–21.

World War I; that *The Argus* (Melbourne) made the change in 1937, *The Age* (Melbourne) in 1941, and *The Sydney Morning Herald* in 1944.

Today there are few holdouts among the metropolitan dailies against circus and semi-circus makeup, splashy art and big heads. But however much there is of Northcliffe-Rothermere and of Pulitzer-Hearst in the present-day product, there is more that is Australian.

A Job for the Historian

The life of a newspaper is made up of parts of many lives; and the older a newspaper is, the larger is that part of its life that derives from its past. The dead belong to a newspaper and to its history—departed founders, proprietors, editors, reporters, writers and readers, known and anonymous, numbered in hosts. Continuity of publication creates what the psychologists and advertising people call an "image," and the image formed by a newspaper's past is a powerful influence upon its present fortunes.

The past components of Australian newspaper images cannot be brought together here, for history falls outside the purview of this book.*

Little has been published about the history of Australian journalism. The stories of a few individual newspapers have been printed, and a number of centennial editions of newspapers offer good raw material for a comprehensive work. When I asked the Public Library of Victoria, in Melbourne, for material on Australian journalism to be used as background for my study, the response was gracious; but it produced less than seventy-five items. Only a few books were included. Most of the matter was from magazine and newspaper files, pamphlets, brochures, printed lectures, special and centennial editions and the like. But all the items perused there and in other Australian libraries, all the publications listed in this book's selected bibliography, plus other material that escaped my scrutiny, still do not constitute an impressive literature of Australian journalism.

Australian newspaper people are reticent about themselves. Newspaper history is gravid with tales and chronicles that should be preserved to illuminate Australian history. If they are not they will be forgotten as the actors in them die. Almost no research is being done in the communications field. Little is known conclusively about

---

* In Appendix B will be found thumbnail sketches of fifteen metropolitan dailies, but these are in no sense a history of metropolitan journalism in Australia.

the country press, the magazines, the book business and more recently radio and the practically new-born TV. Nor will my study go much beyond the outlying underbrush in the great forest of Australian metropolitan daily journalism.

There is richness in the color, drama, struggle for survival, in the battles over public issues, in journalism's leading role in the building of a nation. To write the history of Australia's chief journals, past and present, would be, in large part, to write the history of Australia. Much of the story would parallel the story of U.S. journalism. There would be chapters on the "Published by Authority" era, when the Crown's Royal Governors, almost absolute monarchs in their own right, dealt roughly with a press determined to be free, were quick with imprisonments and fines for libel and contempt of court. North America's first newspaper, "Publick Occurrences," published in 1690, lasted only one issue and was shut down by the Royal Governor of New York. Australia's first newspaper, *The Sydney Gazette and New South Wales Advertiser,* was first "Published by Authority" of His Excellency, Governor King, March 5, 1803, and was printed by George Howe, a convict. Because of its official nature, it flourished: it was a weekly until 1825, a bi-weekly until 1827, a tri-weekly until October 20, 1842, when it suspended publication. It was Australia's only newspaper until 1810. But it was "official" and not free.

In the yet-to-be-written history of Australian journalism there would also be chapters on the growth of the capital cities; the change from early penal colonies to free and independent colonial status, and thence to eventual union in an independent federated nation; the exploration and settlement of the habitable areas of the interior.

There would be chapters on the press's role in such memorable events as the various gold rushes, in the Eureka Stockade battle at Ballarat, in the rise of the wool industry, in the fight against the squatters' resistance to the drive to "unlock the lands" for settlement, in the wars fought for England and for young Australia. There would be a weaving together of two basic themes for such a history: the newspapers' reporting and commenting upon the decisive events, and the effect of the press's influence upon those events.

Included, too, would be some significant words on the remarkable endurance of major newspapers. What other nation can say, with Australia, that about one-half of its leading dailies have passed their centennials? Or that only three or four—depending on how birth-dates are reckoned—are younger than the Australian Commonwealth itself?

The Whole Press

What exactly is the press of Australia?

It is a various thing, constantly changing. It is composed of newspapers, magazines, periodicals, fugitive pamphlets and publications. In this electronic age, it includes television, radio and motion pictures in their documentary and reporting phases. (See Appendixes C, D.)

The Australian press is statistically tabulated in *The Australian Advertising Rate and Data Service,* published annually and updated frequently; in the Australia and New Zealand *Press Directory,* published every two or three years. It is checked for circulation by the Australian Audit Bureau of Circulations, modeled after the U.S. Audit Bureau of Circulations. It is organized into many groups—news associations, proprietors, journalists, advertising specialists, circulation managers and others. It is reported in *Newspaper News* fortnightly and in its supplement, *Radio Television News,* both published by Newspaper News Pty. Ltd. of Sydney; and in the *Journalist,* monthly newspaper of The Australian Journalists' Association.

The press of Australia has a thousand voices. The press run of daily newspapers alone is about 3,600,000 or one copy for every three persons, a high per capita readership. New newspapers and magazines appear with a flourish of public relations trumpets, and anemic or old publications die without a whimper.

Like the press of other democracies, it is produced by a journalism that is free from government censorship or restraint. The Australian press is a profession, an art, a craft, a business, a quasi-public, privately owned institution. It is full of grandeurs and faults, sublimities and pettinesses. It is courageous and timid. It is fallible. It is indispensable to the successful on-going of a free people. The Australian press is acutely aware of its responsibilities though it does not always realize them.

2

Proprietors and
Management

The Trend to Monopoly

The trend toward monopoly ownership in metropolitan newspapers is a phenomenon of our times. It progresses in Australia under the same lash of higher costs in materials, labor and production and other economic pressures that are at work in the United States.

The 1905 Newspaper Press Directory of the British Empire stated that Australia had "close upon a thousand newspapers." Of these "over 300" were in New South Wales, 324 were in Victoria, 118 in Queensland, 46 in South Australia, 22 in Western Australia, 16 in Tasmania. The 1961 total, as noted earlier, was 655 for all newspapers.

Dr. W. M. Corden, writing in the June, 1956, *Meanjin,* states that in 1903 there were 21 daily newspapers in the capital cities owned by 17 separate proprietors. In the December, 1956, issue, while correcting a typographical error in the June article, Dr. Corden noted that in the 50 years after 1903, "while the population more than doubled, the number of newspapers fell by nearly one-third." By 1930, he continued, 20 daily papers in the six capitals were owned by 12 proprietors. The companies of Sir Keith Murdoch and Hugh Denison controlled 10 of the 20.

The peak had been passed seven years earlier, in 1923, when 26 metropolitan dailies were owned by 21 separate proprietors. The 1961 total of 14 metropolitan papers controlled by seven proprietors is a drop, from the peak, of nearly one-half in the number of papers and a reduction to exactly one-third in the number of proprietors. Yet circulations have continued to increase.

The lines of newspaper proprietorships in Australia are sometimes not clearly drawn. The Herald and Weekly Times Ltd. finds the word "chain" distasteful in reference to the five newspapers it controls, partly because different individuals, families and groups own minority interest in the various subsidiary companies; but it does not deny the control or the close association of the five. When Ezra Norton sold his Truth and Sportsman Ltd. holdings in January, 1959, to a group financed by John Fairfax and Sons Ltd., top Fairfax personnel moved into key posts on the *Daily Mirror* and other publications. Yet, R. A. Irish, chairman of the new Mirror Newspapers Ltd. (successor to Truth and Sportsman Ltd.) vigorously denied any ownership of shares or control by the Fairfax company. It was incidentally interesting that Irish was formerly a director of Associated Newspapers Ltd., a Fairfax subsidiary. But the question of Fairfax participation, ownership and control became academic in May, 1960, when the sale of the former Norton interests to Rupert Murdoch, managing director of News Ltd., Adelaide, and son of the late Sir Keith Murdoch, was announced. Murdoch's entry into Sydney journalism had been by way of the suburbs three months earlier when he bought Cumberland Newspapers Ltd., a company operating a chain of more than a score of weeklies in metropolitan Sydney. In response to this challenge, the *Daily Telegraph* and *The Sydney Morning Herald* became allies in a competing set of regional weeklies. The circulation and other phases of the battle—a two-way fight between the two sets of weeklies, a three-way among the dailies —were joined in earnest with Murdoch's acquisition of the Mirror properties. After a lull, Sydney journalism began to prove once more that its several dailies still had the old instinct for the jugular. And the daily proprietorships of Australia were now plainly down to seven after a few months of seeming to be eight.

Public Companies

All Australian metropolitan newspapers today are owned by "public companies," a corporate status indicated by use of the word "Limited" or its abbreviation after the firm's name. "John Fairfax Ltd.," for example, is the parent company of *The Sydney Morning Herald* and its related enterprises. This Sydney newspaper group was, in fact, the last major newspaper operation to change from "Proprietary" ("Pty."), an incorporated partnership limited to fifty persons;

or from "Proprietary Limited" ("Pty. Ltd.") a closely-owned firm in which liability for loss is limited to the business itself—creditors cannot touch members' personal assets. A public company issues shares and sells them to all comers, and the business is run by a board of directors who are responsible to the shareholders. A principal reason for shifting from "Pty. Ltd." to "Ltd." status is that a public company enjoys tax and other advantages. The change rarely means a new management or shift of control.

Many newspaper firms have operating companies subsidiary to the parent, or holding, company. John Fairfax Ltd., organized in 1956, for example, is the holding company for John Fairfax and Sons Pty. Ltd., which publishes *The Sydney Morning Herald;* for Associated Newspapers Ltd., which publishes *The Sun;* and Sungravure Ltd. which publishes *Woman's Day* and other magazines. O'Connell Pty. Ltd. was the company which, with the assistance of John Fairfax Ltd., purchased Ezra Norton's Truth and Sportsman Ltd. in December, 1958. A few months later the company name of Truth and Sportsman Ltd. was changed to Mirror Newspapers Ltd. Davies Brothers Ltd., of Hobart, is senior to Mercury Newspapers Pty. Ltd., Mercury Press Pty. Ltd. and Mercury Board Containers Pty. Ltd.

The larger the operation, with a notable exception or two, the more separate companies may be involved. One apparent exception is The Herald and Weekly Times Ltd., all of whose manifold Victoria-State operations are under the one company. But the company is parent to other companies in other states. Ultimate control of companies is lodged with the directors. Newspaper boards are small in membership—six persons is about average—and are usually made up of the largest stockholders or their representatives. The chairman wields the most authority.

The managing director is the executive head. He is chief liaison between the board and the production complex; in his hands rests responsibility for implementing board decisions and for showing a healthy annual profit. The title of the chief executive officer may vary, however. At News Ltd., in Adelaide, he carries the title of publisher —unusual in Australia for such high rank. In Perth, the managing editor is in top authority for West Australian Newspapers Ltd.'s two daily newspapers, two weeklies and other activities. John Fairfax Ltd. has a governing director and a managing director. Whatever his title, the executive head either exercises tight control of the enterprise and is a party to all decisions, big and little; or he delegates his authority, holding a loose rein. Australia has both types of newspaper executives.

The general manager, business manager, or simply manager, who may be next in command, occupies himself, as in the U.S., more with the business side of the firm than with the editorial, though he may have authority over all functions.

In Australia "all functions" may mean much more than newspapers.

Related Enterprises

The economics of publishing are so imperative that, although they are by no means the only companies so engaged, the metropolitan newspapers of Australia are also big magazine publishers, big book publishers, big job printers and big distributors of other publishers' products. Costly presses and expensive printing crews must be kept busy. Thus, a managerial executive may wear many hats. A few examples, some of them remote from newspaper work, illustrate the range and diversity of these related enterprises.*

And Some Unrelated

Consolidated Press Ltd., publishers of the *Daily Telegraph* (Sydney) wholly owns The Shakespeare Head Press which, in turn, owns a British book publishing house which supplies many of the books Australians read. Conpress Printing Ltd., a subsidiary, has great gravure presses which print *Women's Weekly,* biggest Australian magazine, and are kept busy between issues with other publications and with fine color job printing. The parent company distributes a long list of books and magazines, and has still other subsidiaries, including Modern Industrial Destructors, manufacturers of incinerators. It once purchased a laundry and used its floor space for storage room.

Davies Brothers Ltd.'s subsidiaries not only publish *The Mercury* (Hobart), but are commercial printers, carton manufacturers, process engravers, box makers, lithographers, bookbinders and designers, and they distribute other publishers' products in Tasmania.

Queensland Press Ltd. is parent company to Brisbane's Queensland Newspaper Pty. Ltd. (*Courier-Mail*) and Telegraph Newspaper Co. (*Telegraph*). These companies deal in newspapers, broadcasting and printing; and in book and periodical distribution.

* See also Appendix B for related publishing activities of Australian newspaper companies.

Among the many operations of The Herald and Weekly Times Ltd. of Melbourne is the equivalent of a big trucking firm. The company uses for distribution of *The Herald* 46 automobiles, 52 vans, eight trucks; for *The Sun News-Pictorial* 12 vans and 23 automobiles. Under its Colorgravure banner, the company publishes "Privilege Books" (How-To-Do-It, George Bernard Shaw's plays, a six-volume encyclopedia which sold 100,000 sets in six months, among others); and runs a book club with 64,000 members. The company has gravure job-printing, radio broadcasting, television, newsprint, paper reclamation, magazine and subscriber-insurance divisions and units. It operates the Australian Gallup Poll and maintains overseas and syndication offices, as do many other newspaper firms.

For job and other printing done on the side, layout and display-type services may be maintained by a newspaper company. *The West Australian* (Perth) advertising department assists customers on such orders. The same paper's parent company—West Australian Newspapers Ltd.—owns a trucking company, Bays Transport Service Ltd., which does outside and company hauling. Perth Newspapers Ltd., another subsidiary, once published *The Daily News,* but in 1953 the afternoon daily was brought into the parent company's tent, and Perth Newspapers Ltd. became custodian of the company's real estate.

In sum, Australian newspaper companies are concerned with much more than newspapers. Yet, if Australian publishing economics have been a dominant factor in creating this peculiar situation for the big dailies, it is not always to the liking of their executives.

I was told by a top executive who asked to be anonymous that sometimes Paper A buys Paper B (or special presses, or a magazine, a book publishing house, a radio station, a service, or starts an enterprise entirely new) not because Paper A needs it or even wants to acquire it or start it; Paper A simply wants to keep Paper B (and/or other items) out of the clutch of its bitter competitor, Paper C. This appeared to be a factor in the sale of Mr. Norton's Truth and Sportsman Ltd. publications.

This compulsion obviously is not always a motive in expansion and shifts. But it is never far away, and its presence has a direct effect upon Australia's newspapers. It may be one reason they are not better than they are. As one executive put it, "We're so busy protecting our paper, by buying up everything that might hurt it or compete with it to our disadvantage, that we haven't enough time or money left over to improve its quality."

A cynic might observe that this process has gone almost as far as it can go in three of the six capitals—Hobart, Brisbane, Perth —where monopolies are in control and where there seems to be little left to protect a newspaper from; or that, as to competition *within* the morning and *within* the afternoon fields, only Melbourne and Sydney have it in the morning, and only Sydney has it in both fields.

In many more places than not, the Australian metropolitan newspaper, like the American monopoly daily, is charged with the difficult task of being its own competition. In respect to the ultimate consumer, the situation recalls the dictum of a British statesman who declared that the person who subscribes to only one newspaper "is not a reader, he is a victim."

Whatever the causes—and of course they are complex—Australian capital-city newspapers do acquire some strange appendages and do achieve some odd mutations. It is little wonder that many executives of many talents are required to keep all enterprises running successfully.

Here, then, lies one more considerable difference between Australian and U.S. practices. It is the rare American publisher who takes on much besides newspaper publishing. He does not deal in books or magazines. The Hearst chain with its stable of national magazines, and the Newhouse organization with its recent magazine acquisitions, are among the few large exceptions.

Job printing, of course, is another matter. In the U.S., particularly for the small publisher, job printing is frequently the difference between staying in business and going broke.

Paper, Profits and Personnel

"Paper and people eat up nearly three-quarters of the money required to publish in Australia," said *Newspaper News* in its twenty-fifth anniversary edition. For the metropolitan papers the totals ran this way:

Printing paper took 39 per cent of the outgo; salaries and wages 32 per cent; cost of sales services 6 per cent; worker insurance, pension fund, etc., 1 per cent; taxes and duties 4 per cent; cables, teleprinters, postage, telegrams, general overhead 16 per cent, and brokerage and advertisement costs 2 per cent.

A group of six companies supplied *Newspaper News* with data to show how each of them divided, in shillings and pence, every pound spent:

TABLE 2.—DIVISION OF EACH POUND SPENT BY SIX NEWS-
PAPER COMPANIES.*

Newspaper Company	Wages	Paper Materials	General Costs	Taxation Dividends, etc.
Associated Newspapers	6s. 3d.	9s. 4d.	3s. 8d.	9d.
Advertiser Newspapers	5s. 5d.	6s. 5d.	6s. 2d.	2s.
The Age (Melbourne)	6s. 8d.	8s. 3½d.	4s. 1d.	11½d.
The Courier-Mail (Brisbane)	4s. 2½d.	8s. 7d.	5s. 6¾d.	1s. 7¾d.
The Herald and Weekly Times (Melbourne)	4s. 8d.	9s. 8d.	4s. 3d.	1s. 5d.
The West Australian	10s. 2d.	7s. 6d.	1s. 4d.	1s.

* The Australian pound is worth about $2.25. A pound is made up of 20 shil-
lings (20s.); each shilling is made up of 12 pennies (12d.).

Such matters are the special province of the general or business
manager, who must also keep sharp watch on newsprint. Much
newsprint comes, for most metropolitans, from the jointly-owned
Australian Newsprint Mills Ltd. at Boyer, Tasmania (q.v.), but the
rest must be imported. Because of the long distances imported paper
must be shipped, a company like West Australian Newspapers Ltd.
tries to keep at least a six months' supply on hand.

Even the smaller newspaper operations among the metropolitans
are big business. Davies Brothers Ltd., of Hobart, for example, reported for the year ending June, 1956, a total income of £1,222,300
(about $2,750,175) and net profits of £66,797 (about $150,292),
a slight increase over 1955. News Ltd., of Adelaide, showed a net
profit for the same year, after depreciation, taxation and other matters,
of £63,291 (about $142,404). Its competitor in Adelaide, Adver-
tisers Newspapers Ltd. for the same period had a total income of
£3,400,620 (about $7,651,395), and reported £124,600 (about
$280,350) in dividends paid and £80,589 (about $181,325) assigned to reserves. One of the giants, The Herald and Weekly Times
Ltd., of Melbourne, reported for the year 1955 a gross income of
£10,906,964 (about $24,640,669) and £574,588 (about $1,292,
823) for dividends and reserves.

In respect to payroll, newspapering in Australia is also big business, as three examples will attest. In 1956, Davies Brothers Ltd. employed 390 persons in all departments. A larger operation, Queensland Press Ltd., of Brisbane, employs in its subsidiaries 1,476 persons in all capacities. These are divided: 795 with *The Courier-Mail* and *The Sunday Mail* (produced in the same plant); 532 with the *Telegraph;* 68 with its radio stations; 75 with its printing services; 6 miscellaneous.

In Perth, at the other end of the continent, West Australian Newspapers Ltd. employs a total of 1,139 persons to publish its two dailies and its periodicals, to produce its job printing, and to perform its other functions.

Newsprint from Hardwoods

The long ocean distances between Australia and major newsprint-producing centers, dependency upon widely-spaced and sometimes unreliable shipping schedules, original costs and costs of freighting, were some of the factors which led Australian newspaper proprietors to seek ways to produce their own newsprint. The odds against success were formidable. A principal hazard was that Australia's forests are mostly hardwoods—and newsprint had never been made from hardwood. The fibre is too short.

How the difficult feat was accomplished is not within the scope of this work, but the fact of its success is: Australian Newsprint Mills, Ltd., in Tasmania, today supplies one-third of Australia's annual newsprint requirement of about 240,000 tons. In 1958, the ANM plant at Boyer produced 81,085 tons; and its entire output was contracted for a full decade ahead.

Australian Newsprint Mills Pty. Ltd. was organized in 1938, after independent inquiry and research begun a few years earlier, by the Herald and Weekly Times (Melbourne) and John Fairfax and Sons Pty. Ltd. (Sydney). The two newspaper firms started as equal partners. Since then, all of Australia's metropolitan newspaper companies have joined in as shareholders in this Tasmanian enterprise.

The eucalyptus logs that are Australian newsprint's principal ingredient begin their journey into paper on about 340,000 acres of the Tasmanian Central Highlands within the watershed of the Upper Derwent River and including the valleys of the Styx, Florentine and Counsel rivers. The huge trees are logged according to accepted reforestation principles, snaked out of the woods by bulldozers, trucked over the company's own roads to a stockpile at the little logging town of Maydena and subsequently sent by train to

Boyer, a country town a few miles above Hobart on the Derwent.

Logs vary from eighteen inches to nine feet in diameter. In the Boyer wood mill they are debarked, cut into seven-inch flitches (planks), then into four-foot billets. The billets are reduced by huge grinders to a wood mash, to which chemical pulp from New Zealand is added to brighten the dark mass. The resulting screened and washed "groundwood" is a liquid suspension containing only 0.6 per cent fibre. This "stock" passes onto a fast-moving endless wire cloth, which drains off the water. Driving rolls, vacuum boxes, absorbents and heated driers force it into its ultimate form—an endless roll of newsprint. The great sheets are cut into prescribed widths and lengths, rewound, wrapped and prepared for shipment. On company lighters they go downriver to ocean freighters.

Many other Australian firms make a number of other kinds of paper, from box board to the finest brands of printing stock. But newsprint production is a special matter. The Boyer product is of good quality in texture, printing surface and tensile strength. Research is constantly seeking means of improvement. The hardwood's chief difference from the softwood varieties of newsprint is a slightly darker cast.

ANM employs 1,100 persons. Its successful operation is a brilliant response by Australian enterprise to a challenge for which there was no easy answer.

3

News-Editorial
Executives: the
High Command

Tabloids with a Difference

Australian newspaper editors vary greatly in attitudes, practices and concepts of news. Some regard themselves as plenipotentiaries of a distant posterity, bound to produce a sobersides daily historical record. There are others whose re-discovery of the vendibility of recorded human aberration is a gladsome daily ritual. Each editor is an expert in his own way—it takes as much of a certain kind of skill to shout a lurid sex homicide effectively as it does to report, explain and interpret a federal budget or another West-East crisis.

"Tabloid" in U.S. journalism carries a raffish connotation that began in the 1920's. The connotation is not unknown in Australia. But if the word always equated with lurid journalism, eight-fourteenths of Australia's metropolitan daily press would be rubbishy rags; and they certainly are not that. The best of the tabloid editors, as one of them told me, "try to keep the objectivity of a broadsheet" —large, standard-size newspaper—by refraining from sensationalism and by trying to report all sides of a story. Wartime paper shortages brought the tabloid to Australia. Its continuance since then is a result of reader acceptance and the more economical production it entails.

The Editor

With few exceptions, the Australian metropolitan newspaper editor is a shirtsleeves, or working, newspaperman. He takes his top editorial responsibility seriously. His title as top man, though, varies considerably.

The Herald and Weekly Times Ltd. has an editor-in-chief and a deputy who rank next to the managing director in supervision of company activities. An editor is in charge of each of the company's two Melbourne papers, *The Herald* and *The Sun News-Pictorial*. The editor of *The Age* (Melbourne) is also a director of David Syme and Company Ltd. The editor of *The Sydney Morning Herald* has charge of leader pages and the book section, is co-equal in authority with the news editor (there is no managing editor). Both rank next to the general manager of John Fairfax Ltd., who reports to the managing director. The editor of *The Sun* (Sydney) has charge of leaders and features and the executive editor, his senior, is in charge of the rest of the paper. They also report to the general manager of John Fairfax Ltd. The editor of the *Daily Telegraph* (Sydney) is third in command, under the managing director and the editor-in-chief of Consolidated Press. The order of rank on the *Daily Mirror* (Sydney) is managing director, editorial director, editor-in-chief, acting editor-in-chief, editor. The editor-in-chief of *The Courier-Mail* (Brisbane) edits that paper and is senior to the editor of his company's *Sunday Mail*. Next in command to the executive editor of the *Telegraph* (Brisbane) is the editor. The editor-in-chief of News Ltd., of Adelaide edits *The News* and supervises the company's other activities. The managing editor of *The Advertiser* (Adelaide) is second in command to the managing director. No one holds the title of editor. Responsible to the managing editor (there is no managing director) on Perth's West Australian Newspapers Ltd., are the respective editors of *The West Australian* and *The Daily News*. The editor of *The Mercury* (Hobart) is third in the chain of command, after the managing director (who is also chairman of directors) and the general manager.

In the U.S. the term managing director is unknown. In Australia there are few managing editors. But no matter what the title, the executive in both countries, into whom the top editorial authority pyramids, has his troubles from above as well as from below. Said one of them ruefully: "If something's good, the reporter, the chief of staff, the editor all get their share of credit. The editor-in-chief gets none. But when something goes wrong, the managing director blames—guess who!"

The editor's day, whether it begins at about 3:00 P.M. for a morning paper, or at 6:00 A.M. or earlier for an afternoon, includes a series of conferences. There are also certain patterns he must follow, and they begin before he gets to the office. If there is a local opposition paper, morning or afternoon, he will have read the latest edition. He has heard the latest ABC newscast. By the time he arrives at his office, even if he has not already called in at least once to talk with his next in command, he has a comprehensive idea of the shape and dimensions of the news with which he must deal.

He will confer with his news editor (or, on a morning paper, with the night editor) who may run the news show later on. He will see the leader writers and choose topic and treatment for leaders. If the paper has an editorial cartoonist, the editor will choose, from a number of rough pencil sketches the cartoonist has prepared, the editorial cartoon for the day. Either before or after the main news conference he may sit in on a picture conference, though he may leave most of the picture choices to the news editor.

News Conferences

The main news conference gets the day into working tempo. News conferees may be three or four or a roomful of executives.

Present are the editor, assistant or associate editor, chief of staff, news editor, picture editor, cable editor, feature editor, leader page editor, the copy taster (q.v.) if any, sundry assistants and perhaps the sports and society or women's editor. The usual pattern is for the editor to preside and to call upon each person present, in turn, to review news developments in his special area.

The chief of staff summarizes all local and state news potentials —police, parliament, city government, human interest and general stories. The cable editor synopsizes overseas dispatches from the Australian Associated Press and special correspondents. The features editor reports on the stories planned for his pages. The sports editor talks of seasonal sports, upcoming events and coverage for the day's games. The news editor takes notes on all that is said, reports on Canberra possibilities and special events. Picture page and other pictorial needs are explored, with the picture editor reporting what is in the mill, what may be in prospect, and noting new assignments that develop from the conference.

From the presentation, a few matters of overriding news importance emerge. A decisive vote or debate looms in Parliament, the town council may be wrestling with the parking problem, a police hunt for a murder suspect is afoot, an important horse race is to be run that day, the cable editor is expecting a fat story from London, New York or Moscow. These are discussed from the standpoint of coverage, stories and pictures, and are evaluated for their newsworthiness. If the paper is crusading for a worthy cause the developing campaign is reviewed, with perhaps the chief reporter, if the paper has one, detailing its progress.

It is customary on some papers for reporting editors to bring along thin-paper carbons of their day's list of promising stories for distribution to their editor-colleagues. The news editor generally has had brief two- or three-man conferences with the cable editor, chief of staff, chief sub-editor, and perhaps with the editor, prior to the main news conference.

The advertising dummy for the day's editions has been delivered sometime earlier and page-by-page planning is well under way. Each day this process takes on overtones of a game and a battle. The game is to win a place for everything that is newsworthy. The battle is not so much with the advertising department (although there are exceptions) for it has spoken and there is usually no appeal from its verdict. The battle is more between divisions of the news department. How much space for hard news and features? For local, state and overseas? For pictures?

These questions are not all threshed out in the conference, but their outlines are stated and the way prepared for the game and the battle. Three copies of the ad dummy have been prepared—one for the editor, one for the chief sub-editor, one for the news or night editor. The editor has been told a day in advance the number of pages the issue will carry. In certain circumstances, pages may be added only in units of four because of press technicalities. On one hectic Friday, one editor said, the advertising department presented him with no less than nine different dummies.

At least one Australian editor thinks news conferences are a waste of time. He never holds them, maintaining that news selection and editing are a continuous task, not to be concluded until the paper has been put to bed. He regards his time in the office as one continuous conference.

The Day's Editions

When the conferences are finished, the editor may check over—"vet" is the Australian term—columnists' copy, letters to the editor, special features and other material. He plays the edition with a loose rein. He passes upon the leaders as they are written, the editorial cartoon as it is drawn. He is constantly available for counsel and decisions about the breaking news. Page proofs are delivered to him promptly. It may be part of the editor's task to keep the managing director up to the minute. In turn, the chief sub-editor or chief of staff or news editor keeps the editor informed about all developments. If Federal Parliament is in session, he may talk to his correspondents at Canberra as the day or night wears on.

First edition copies increase the tempo. Chief objective now is the edition for home delivery. It is the supreme effort of the day. The first edition is usually for "country" distribution; first-run papers have the longest possible interval in which to reach distant readers. For the second edition country news is swept out. On tabloids a dozen or more pages may be changed routinely, and the number may go on special occasions as high as 19 out of 26 double-page forms for a 52-page paper. On the *Telegraph* (Brisbane) the meeting to whip the second edition into shape is called "the break-up conference."

On an afternoon newspaper as many pages as possible are prepared for the stereotyper the night before publication. Early selection is made not only of news and features but of pictures for these pages. Such pages may be regarded as a "shakedown run," for they will be washed out by livelier stories for the home-circulation area printings.

The editor of an afternoon paper has less time to build for the final home-delivery edition than does his morning opposite number. There may be more and bigger news breaking during the daytime hours, but the morning papers have a longer interval in which to develop a top news story, particularly if it breaks, as many do, in the afternoon just before the P.M. paper's last deadline. Federal and state parliaments, for example, meet in the afternoon and evening, a custom which puts the afternoons under a constant disadvantage.

The Herald (Melbourne) publishes a City Extra at 12:35 P.M., a Home at 2:10; a Late Extra at 3:30; its Final at 4:25 P.M., with "fudge" chasers insertable from 30 to 55 minutes after the presses start to roll for each edition.

A fudge box is a column—or a half, a third or a quarter of a column—that runs blank on page one. Bulletins, sports scores and so on may be quickly inserted therein during an edition's run by use of a small stereoplate on an equally small roller that prints in the blank space. Fudge material usually is printed in red or blue ink.

Use of the fudge box enables a paper to print stop-press bulletins without replating. The practice is general throughout Australia, as it is in the United Kingdom, but has not been widely adopted in the U.S.

The Australian metropolitan daily is as subject to change as the U.S. big-city paper. This is the way one Australian daily did a face-lifting job after World War II, according to its editor:

> We changed its format and contents, its type dress and its concept of news. We reduced its solid news, particularly overseas news, in volume. We introduced a more popular slant. We increased the human interest content of stories. We sought out the unusual personal story. We pepped-up makeup, increased size of pictures and size of heads. We went in for campaign stories—graft, corruption, civic betterment. We told the story of little people, families without homes, their little joys and triumphs, their big defeats and their terrible tragedies.

That daily became, in his view, a paper of entertainment, changing from a paper of record. Now it endeavors to get "shock news" every day. The change has helped business greatly, he said.

With certain exceptions, Australian editors seem to place less stress on "now-ness" than do their opposite numbers in the United States. Australian editors will work as hard to keep on top of a rapidly-changing running story and will replate between editions if necessary. But there is not as much changing for change's sake.

Where an American editor may order leads rewritten and banner heads revised even though there's not a line of new material to warrant it, an Australian editor will tend to let both ride. This may seem a deplorable unwillingness to squeeze street sales to the last ha'penny, and a lack of initiative; but it saves much irritation for the customer who is not called upon to determine from a rewritten headline whether he is on top of the latest news or not.

In Australia, certain matters are much different from those in the routine of the U.S. editor. Here are a few:

All editorial employees, including cadets, get four weeks' leave every year. This means that staffs are seldom at more than eleven-twelfths of capacity.

All newspapers are completely unionized in all departments.

The absence of internal news-gathering agencies to serve the metropolitans means more correspondence arrangements with other papers, more stringers, more work for the Australian editor.

The emphasis put upon four kinds of football (none of them like the U.S. brand) in season and upon horse-racing the year around, makes the editor's weekends (Saturday is a race day and a football day) a special problem. This is especially true of afternoon papers which try to cover results of all sports contests in their final editions.

One top-level editor in a city where there was no competition for his paper, thought that competition "has brought out the worst, not the best," in Australian newspapers. He felt that if editors did not have to think about the opposition they would be able to develop better newspapers.

News Editor

The news editor may become the top editor during the period of most intensive activity. This is particularly so on morning papers where the editor puts in his main stint during the daytime hours. The news editor makes the decisions about page one, which may have a special sub-editor. He is in an across-the-desk relationship with the chief sub-editor, in whose charge are all makeup and edition changes on inside pages. Sometimes the man in charge is the night editor.

The news editor may be co-equal in authority with the chief of staff; or he may rank the chief of staff. Sometimes the news editor is senior to the chief of staff, chief sub-editor and all other department heads. There is no single pattern of authority. In at least one instance, on an afternoon tabloid, the posts of chief sub-editor and news editor were combined. This was done after a news editor had resigned and the chief sub-editor took over his duties. But he soon began to lean heavily on his assistant, so that in due course the two were dividing the duties of the two posts somewhat along the traditional lines.

On some papers the question of rank does not arise in the second echelon, as between news editor, chief sub-editor and chief of staff. "It's never been put to a test," said one news editor. "No reason for it to be!"

On the other hand, *The Sun* (Sydney) has no chief of staff. The news editor gathers the news of Sydney, of New South Wales and of Australia, evaluates it and passes it on to the chief sub-editor to prepare for publication.

The Sun news editor's day starts about midnight the night before, when a police roundsman, a photographer and a car driver begin the night's crime coverage. If he hasn't been awakened sooner, the early police roundsman calls him at 5:30 and summarizes what the morning papers are carrying, what the round has developed during the night and anything else he knows. The news editor is in the office by 7:30 A.M., and by then his best men have begun to operate.

A little after 8:00 A.M. he is in conference with the executive editor and the editor, and the day is well under way. This three-man administration has worked well for years, despite its exclusion of a chief of staff. The chief of staff's main job, directing the local reporters, still gets done, but it is done by the news editor.

This departure from orthodoxy takes a different form on *The Sun's* sister-publication, *The Sydney Morning Herald.* On that morning paper, as noted on an earlier page, the news editor is the top man in respect to the whole news-editorial operation except for the editorial page.

Traditionally, however, on nearly all Australian dailies, the news editor's most important responsibilities are to evaluate the top news, make sure all of it gets into print, and be the principal contributor to decisions regarding news play position, the art that accompanies principal stories and the kind of headlines the big stories get. A continuing concern is page one and what is done with it. His position in the table of organization is usually like this:

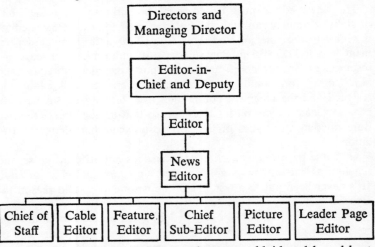

The news editor's task differs as between tabloid and broadsheet. Available space is the principal determinant.

After borders and flag are deducted, the Australian tabloid page has less than half the number of column inches contained on a broadsheet page. The broadsheet's page one is a large display case. There is room for the big news of the day and much that is not big. There is space to call attention to what is carried on the inside pages. There is opportunity for composing an attractive, balanced, even aesthetic arrangement of headlines, art and body type. The editors have ten or eleven columns in which to work.

The tabloid must capture readers with one or two—not more than three—units of interest on page one. Page one gets the "most" story on the tabloids. It may be the most interesting, most tragic, most pathetic, most unusual, most humorous, most horrible. One day a tabloid let run through all editions on page one a head-and-shoulders picture of a plain-looking woman who had reported to the police she had discovered a man hiding under her bed. The man had fled without touching her.

Nothing had happened; there was no story. Why such a play?

"We figured," said the news editor, "that it would make the old maids and the young girls shiver vicariously, and would pleasantly titillate all our other female readers. The men would wonder what fun the sneak actually had."

The story did not even make the broadsheets.

The news editor of another tabloid said that his concept of a good page one was: (1) An absorbing national or foreign story; (2) A good human-interest story; (3) A good sports story.

Perhaps this formula—if the term applies—is used more often in Australia than is that which gives over the whole front page to one sensational story. The news of the day, of course, determines the product; and four equally good stories breaking simultaneously must divide the page, whereas at another time, without such competition, any one of them might take over the whole page.

A printer on one of the Australian tabloids made a revealing judgment about page one makeup: "I like the way your U.S. tabs print posters on the front page." He meant the use on page one of a large label head, or a blown-up picture with little attempt made at printing anything else thereon. He meant that the U.S. tabloids which followed the practice were using the front page for advertising, not for news.

Tabloid reporting requires special skills, a number of news editors agreed. "In the tabloid, your reporter must summarize more," said one of them. "He hasn't the space to report as fully as does a broadsheet reporter. And when you summarize you can't escape giving opinion; your opinion is expressed in part by the things you choose to put into a severely restricted story and by the words you use to paraphrase or summarize. Often it's the difference between impressions about a speech and the speech itself."

The word "bold" recurred in one news editor's discussion of the news problem in tabloids. He looks for "bold" pictures, "bold" stories, "bold" writing. Essentially by "bold" he meant strong human interest and fresh treatment of the old news materials. "Bold" photos for a tabloid, especially for page one, are not easy to get, nor are they lightly chosen. Subject and quality of the particular shot draw earnest debate. How is the picture to be treated? How big to blow it up? Shall it be vignetted? If not, how much of the background stays? Where should it be played on the page? Shall the story run alongside, or will the cutlines alone carry the picture? There is seldom room for more than one picture on page one and it has to be the best available.

"Read me" stories, said another news editor, are always at a premium, for both broadsheets and tabloids.

Chief of Staff

Among his other duties, an Australian newspaper's chief of staff (C.O.S.) is boss of the reporters. He and his deputies are responsible for the gathering of all news that breaks in his area. And in Australia that area is very big. Sometimes it extends beyond Australia. It is not uncommon for a C.O.S. to send reporters to cover stories in New Zealand, New Guinea, Singapore, or even farther.

The C.O.S. on an Australian daily newspaper has no exact American counterpart. His responsibility resembles that of the U.S. city editor to a degree, but it is broader. An American city editor directs the local reporting staff. To an Australian C.O.S. such a news domain, the city plus the suburbs, is only a fairish beginning. In that he is responsible for all news within Australia, the C.O.S.'s job somewhat resembles that of the U.S. telegraph editor. Cable news, however, is not his responsibility. He has some of the U.S. managing editor's authority in contributing to decisions about grading, hiring, firing and pay scales.

Perhaps most interesting of all is the C.O.S.'s resemblance to the American state editor. In all the six states of Australia there is not one state editor. The reasons are, as noted elsewhere, that Australia's six capital cities rank by themselves in population and importance, including *news* importance; and that there are not many other major news sources because there are few big cities elsewhere. Only five provincial cities in Australia have more than 50,000 population and most of them are much smaller.

This is considerably different from, say, Ohio in the U.S. There the state editor of the Akron *Beacon-Journal* must be alert to news in five other metropolitan cities—Cincinnati, Columbus, Dayton, Toledo and Cleveland. But he has AP or UPI for automatic state coverage. By contrast, the Australian C.O.S., for news coverage outside his own city, depends upon bureaus, correspondents, stringers, the telephone and his own ingenuity.

This is no small problem. The *Year Book of the Commonwealth of Australia* (1959) reports 912 local government authorities in the nation, divided this way: New South Wales—236 cities, municipalities, shires; Victoria—203 cities, towns, boroughs, shires; Queensland—134 cities, towns, shires; South Australia—143 municipalities, districts; Western Australia—147 cities, towns, municipalities and road districts; Tasmania—49 cities and municipal districts. Besides these, there are scores of combinations among the local authorities for such area services as electricity, water, sewerage, health, transport, agriculture, pest-and-disease control. Toward each of them, some C.O.S. must maintain a watchful interest. They are one reason that a welcome addition to Australian newspaper staffs might be a Deputy-in-Charge-of-Distant-Domestic-News; or a state editor.

The lack of a C.O.S. on *The Sun* (Sydney) was noted in the preceding section. At the other extreme, the C.O.S. of *The Mercury* (Hobart) is responsible not only for general news reporting, but is in charge of pictorial, sports and women's departments as well.

All chiefs of staff on metropolitan dailies are supplied with deputies or assistants, whom they would find it difficult to do without. Each is at least a third hand; the best of them are a second brain. The deputy or assistant C.O.S. probably comes closer, spiritually and actually, to the American assistant city editor, than the C.O.S. does to the city editor. It is the deputy C.O.S.'s job to see that the news is well and truly gathered. What a capable sergeant is to an Army lieutenant, a good deputy is to the C.O.S.

The upper echelons of editorial command in Australia are generally male. A notable exception is the woman assistant to the chief of staff of *The Sydney Morning Herald*. In the mornings, she takes over, draws the roster, monitors radio newscasts, makes assignments.

From paper to paper the details differ, but these are functions and duties most common to chiefs of staff and their deputies:

The C.O.S. is solely responsible for news gathering within the metropolitan area, chiefly responsible for news gathering within the state, partly responsible for news gathering within and immediately without the geographical limits of Australia.

He allocates the duties of the reporting staff, supervises the various roundsmen's work, and makes assignments for news tasks which fall outside the regular rounds, well in advance whenever possible. He briefs the reporters and participates in news, pictorial and other conferences, reporting on news developments in his jurisdiction and helping to make judgments on news values and the play of stories. He rosters the editorial staff so that each person works a five-day week, with two full days off. He helps supervise the training of the cadets. Depending upon his paper's table of organization, he exercises direct, remote or no executive control over certain autonomous or semi-autonomous departments—e.g., women's, society, sports, turf, pictorial.

He maintains close liaison with other seniors—news editor, night editor, chief sub-editor, executive editor, etc.—in order that news decisions and orders may be carried out.

He has a hand in the preparation of special supplements or sections, especially if there is no supplements editor, and keeps in close touch with photographers and artists. He is responsible for keeping the duty book and other staff records, including sick leave, overtime, days off and holidays. He directs the work of correspondents and stringers in scores of outstate places, many of which are very lively news centers. He instructs them in news gathering as they need it and insures that they get paid regularly and fairly. (See below.) He is directly concerned in seeing that the award agreements between his management and the Australian Journalists' Association receive full compliance.

He may be responsible for the work of bureau staffers in other cities—e.g., Canberra, other capitals, provincial cities. On sectional news, the C.O.S. may become a field commander, marshalling his men to the coverage of a many-part story that breaks in several places simultaneously—a storm's havoc, a big fire or explosion, a riot.

The C.O.S. is an idea man. He must think up new angles to old news. One C.O.S. was almost successful in an attempt to telephone Princess Margaret. "I talked with one of her ladies-in-waiting," he recalled. A Melbourne C.O.S. telephoned Clement Attlee, in London, as Attlee was about to begin his Australia tour. "We will telephone anywhere on earth for a story," said another C.O.S.

Some chiefs of staff believe in extensive briefing; others do very little. Some do it at regular hours, usually at the beginning of the news day; others may do it irregularly, or by telephone. Because news does not punch a time clock, the job of C.O.S. is never done. On an afternoon paper his day starts before dawn, perhaps with a call from or to the police roundsman, his deputy or the chief photographer. If he is C.O.S. for a morning paper, his early morning sleep may be disturbed soon after he has begun it by news developments that will not wait.

Morning Dailies

The usual practice on a morning paper is for a deputy C.O.S. to come in about 9:00 A.M. and get the day started. He may compile afternoon and evening assignments; make some assignments to cover morning news; arrange for pictures; bring the futures book up to date; check on memos left by the C.O.S., news editor and others from the previous evening; type out the day's list of likely stories (eight carbons or more in some offices); roster the staff for next week's work days, with due note for staffers' holidays, days off and illnesses.

The C.O.S. himself arrives about 2:00 P.M. He has read the papers and heard the news broadcasts. His deputy briefs him up to the minute. Soon thereafter either the C.O.S. or his deputy makes the assignments for those reporters who have just come on duty. In mid-afternoon the first of his news day's conferences takes place—with pictorial; or perhaps it is a preliminary "natter" (talk) with the news editor. Formal news conferences, with the editor and other news executives, may fall anywhere between 4:00 and 7:00 P.M., depending on edition time and other factors.

By mid-evening the C.O.S. has his news task well in hand. Except for the police, all regular rounds are usually wrapped up. If state or federal parliaments are sitting, important news may still be coming from them; or from suburban councils, which often meet at night. A stray story here or there is still in the mill. But nearly everything is done that should be done. Except for story changes, the C.O.S. can ease up a bit after the first edition.

Afternoon Dailies

The C.O.S. on an afternoon paper follows somewhat the same schedule, though his news day, of course, is reversed. He must be up with the kookaburras. He faces a mid-morning or noontime first deadline. He may work no harder than his morning rival, but he must work faster and make his staff work harder.

By 7:30 A.M. he and his deputy have made assignments and covered all visible developing news. The next hour may be taken up with briefing and attending conferences. By 10:00 or 10:30 A.M., said a Melbourne C.O.S., "I like to have my part of the paper as nearly filled up as possible."

Meanwhile, the C.O.S. may have reports from police rounds, shipping, industrial or general assignment men sent out on interviews or human interest stories. He has fired queries and memos in half a dozen directions and has begun to reap returns from them.

Between-edition changes are usually more numerous on afternoon than on morning papers. The C.O.S. has been saving space for his best stories in the all-important home edition. He has other worries. Maybe the mobile picturegram unit, out on a story 150 miles away, has not been heard from. A Cabinet minister is in town but cannot be reached for a statement. A stringer in a distant township must be badgered into activity.

When the big edition has gone, anywhere from 1:30 to 3:00 P.M., the afternoon paper's C.O.S. can relax, or could if he did not have to think about feature stories and tomorrow's assignments and who's available and who isn't and about ideas for development from the futures book. His last task of the day may be getting the assignments for tomorrow into the duty book.

Correspondence by Stringer

In Australia, as in the United States, a good correspondent in a place difficult of access is a help in time of trouble. Correspondents are the C.O.S.'s responsibility. A map showing the situation of correspondents and stringers for Australian metropolitan dailies would include practically all of the outback country towns, down to hamlet size. Their payment runs to about 3*d*. or more a line, plus bonuses. Correspondents can make £30 or more a month for part-time work.

Coverage problems, said one C.O.S., "are terrible and are complicated by vast distances, poor transportation and sometimes worse communication." He was speaking of his own state, but he might have been speaking for all. Only in Tasmania and Victoria are distances manageable. Add the Northern Territory, the Territory of New Guinea and Macquarie Island near the South Pole, and the distance to the moon is not much more formidable.

A good stringer may not be beyond price; but most chiefs of staff will declare, at least privately, that he is worth more than he is paid. A sampling of newspapers will suggest the dimensions of the stringer network in each state.

The Mercury (Hobart) employs about one hundred part-time correspondents throughout Tasmania. It cannot follow the general practice of using the services of country editors because there are fewer than half a dozen weeklies in the state. A full-time staff of six journalists and two photographers, working under the direction of a bureau manager, is maintained at Launceston. In Burnie, third largest community in Tasmania, a part-time stringer covers area news. Teachers, postmistresses and town clerks act as stringers elsewhere.

The News (Adelaide) has stringers in all South Australian towns of one hundred or more population—about two hundred in all. They are carefully coached in the selection and writing of news stories.

Stringers in key places are expected to send in material every day. They are encouraged to take news photos; a man with a camera will contribute about twice as much news as one without. Outside of Adelaide the state's most important news sources are Mt. Gambier and Port Pirie. Although Broken Hill is across the border in New South Wales it is much closer to Adelaide than to either Sydney or Melbourne, and is commensurately a good news producer for Adelaide papers. *The News'* Broken Hill news source is *The Barrier Miner,* owned by News Ltd.

The Advertiser uses about the same number of correspondents in about the same places. Retainers are paid a dozen or more main news producers. They also receive space rates, the basis of pay for all stringers in Australia. *The Advertiser* distributes, as do other papers, a booklet of instructions to stringers. Called "The Advertiser Hints for Correspondents," it carries information about the paper's news needs and how they may be fulfilled. It also states what "we don't want": gift and card parties, birthdays ("except of persons of 90 years or over"), addresses by Parliamentary candidates, weddings and other trivia. It details sports and picture coverage, rates of pay and provides a calendar for upcoming events. It urges: "Phone it!" and concludes with a page of what to do "if in doubt."

The West Australian (Perth) also distributes a booklet, "Instructions to Country Correspondents," to its 160 correspondents. It divides news into three classes: news to be telegraphed or telephoned; news to be mailed; news that should not be sent. It outlines ways to transmit news of sports, elections, conferences; also pictures, and it documents other relevant matters.

The Sun News-Pictorial (Melbourne) has about two hundred string correspondents in Victoria and New South Wales; one is as far away as Port Moresby, New Guinea.

In Queensland an arrangement with the Queensland Country Press (q.v.) which serves eleven provincial dailies in the state, enables Brisbane editors to increase their effective stringer system by many times. A somewhat similar situation holds in New South Wales, Victoria and Tasmania. There the Australian United Press (q.v.) operates with and for about 110 country dailies, weeklies and other papers. On AUP circuits in the metropolitan field are *The Courier-Mail* (Brisbane), *The Sun News-Pictorial* (Melbourne) and *The Age* (Melbourne).

These two press associations are Australia's only internal news-gathering and news-disseminating services; and, as noted, they are associated with only a few of the metropolitans. The capital-city dailies, therefore, cannot, as do so many small dailies in the United States, fill up empty columns with wire copy.

This difference alone emphasizes the great importance of string correspondents to Australian editors; particularly to chiefs of staff, who supervise them.

4

Departments of
the News-Editorial
Division

Subbing, Chief Sub and Sub-Editors

"Subbing takes a very good man," said the Australian journalist. "Subbing," he explained, was short for sub-editing, originally an English term.

"Sub-editor" equates with the U.S. "copyreader." The "chief sub-editor" or "chief sub" equates with news editor, slot man or chief copyreader. To "sub" or to "sub-edit" is to prepare journalists' copy for the printer.

The Australian sub-editor corrects bad spelling, poor grammar, flaccid or faltering syntax. He excises verbiage. He sharpens, brightens, tightens. He writes headlines. He sets down orders to printers on head-type, body type, width measures, indents and other mechanical matters. Except for terminology, he operates in the same way, complete to pencil or ball-point pen, pastepot, shears and typebook, as the U.S. copyreader. Each one cuts, slashes, rewrites, interlines and alters bad copy into good, good copy into extra good, sometimes brilliant. In equipment, only the pins are different; instead of paper clips to hold a sheaf of copy together Australian newspapers favor small common pins.

Sub-editing is an art; it is practised best by journalists of maturity, for among the most important tools of the sub's craft are his news experience, his seasoned judgment and his fund of useless knowledge.

On these he draws to enrich copy. The sub is a paper's principal protection against libel suits. His work helps give his newspaper its individuality—and all papers are individual—perhaps even its character.

The sub-editors' room in an Australian newspaper plant is apart but not far from the reporters' room. It is adjacent to the teletype room and handy to the night or news or executive editor's office. It is dominated by a large table or desk which is sometimes shaped like the traditional U of the U.S. copydesk, but may be almost any shape—a boomerang, a kidney, an H, a square.

Some tabloids furnish typewriters to subs, because they must condense copy so rigorously and condensation often requires much re-writing. No chatter of typewriters disturbs the almost ecclesiastical calm of most of the broadsheets, however. For them, condensation is not so compulsive.

Other standard equipment in the sub-editor's room includes files of all editions of the home paper, of the nearest opposition and of exchanges, standard reference works (and sometimes a library), proof racks, copy trays. In a corner, on an unobtrusive table, will be found an electric plate, teapot and other tea equipment. Few departments of newspapers are without these last items. The tea-break is more immovably entrenched in Australian custom than the coffee-break in the U.S.

The Chief Sub-Editor

In charge of the sub-editors' room, or at least of the big desk, is the chief sub-editor. This responsible post may be a way-station to higher authority. Or it may be the highest to which a man may wish to aspire, so pivotal is it, so crucial to the success of the paper.

In the sub-editors' room of *The Age* (Melbourne) hangs a large portrait-photograph of a man who, from a distance, looks a little like a young King George V. But it is a royal photograph only in a newspaper sense. It bears this homage: "J. S. Stephens Chief Sub-Editor 'The Age' for Fifty Years (1885-1935) An Inspiration to his Staff."

The chief sub rules with a soft pencil for sceptre, an eye-shade for crown. If his paper is lucky, the wisdom of a Solomon, the historical acumen of a Thucydides, and the questioning mind of a Socrates is lodged in his person. This combination is more often desired than achieved.

The chief sub's senior—usually the news editor—may sit next to or across from him or may work in a different room. But around the chief sub, grouped to face him, are members of his staff, the sub-editors.

A basic sub-editing staff includes news editor, assistant news editor, chief sub-editor, six or more sub-editors, a cable sub-editor and his assistant. In the composing room is another sub, liaison man with the printers, who supervises page makeup. He checks cutlines, keeps page closings on a tight schedule, and does related tasks in exactly the manner of a U.S. makeup editor in the "back room." He is the peripatetic member of a sitting team whose organizational pattern may vary considerably from paper to paper.

Most of the capital city dailies have small, separate desks at which special sub-editors prepare cables, sports, women's pages.

One paper may have a separate desk for country news which runs in the first edition and is then washed out. Another paper may have a special sub for front page news. A third may assign special subs to interstate news, or to local copy. A fourth may have one sub who does nothing but check proofs as they come up from the composing room. Another may send all copy through a sub-editing staff that has no specialists, all subs processing all kinds of copy. A sixth may use special subs on opinion pages, features, and letters to the editor; others for the writing of captions and cutlines and the supervision of block-making (photo-engraving).

As the chief of staff is key man in the getting and writing of the news, the chief sub-editor is key man in its processing and its play in the paper.

Copy is brought to the chief sub from the reporters' room by copy boys and copy girls, or by a plant network of pneumatic tubes. Before he begins his day the chief sub knows the shape of the news. He keeps book on all that flows through his domain. He may dummy the whole paper, or perhaps only the news and feature pages in the middle or back of the book. He notes on each story what he wants in the way of a heading and its news play.

He keeps copy flowing to each sub-editor and he must keep to a rigid schedule of page makeup. On a tabloid this may mean a page every ten or fifteen minutes for a period of five hours, each page meshing with its opposite in the pattern of stereotype plates for the press run; i.e., in a 36-page edition, these pages being locked together—1-36; 2-35; 3-34; 4-33; 5-32 and so on to 18-19 as center truck.

The same kind of skill is required in Australia and the U.S. for page makeup; the goals of good composition and balance in all headline, advertising and art arrangement are identical. There is as much awareness and need for imagination in news play, use of type and in other phases of news-processing. As one chief sub-editor told cadets in a lecture, type is used either "vigorously" or "gently," according to the rating of the story. The lead story on each page rates the heaviest type, and others are scaled according to their play. There is variation of head sizes and judicious mixtures are made of italics and roman.

The competent chief sub plays his pages fluidly, ready to alter makeup to unexpected changes in the flow of news. He is alert to the human interest or humor piece which will brighten or help achieve balance in subject matter. He is in constant contact with the chief of staff about developing stories and running stories.

To the chief sub falls much of the responsibility for directing the day's paper to the desired ultimate excellence of the home-delivered edition. This crucial period is his hardest. He must work swiftly and competently, keeping all units and pages in mind as he evaluates the incoming against the already printed. His goal is the perfect paper. He never achieves it, for no editor ever does; but it must be as perfect as the available news materials and his skill and wisdom can make it.

Each chief sub has his own way of judging space requirements. He knows, of course, the size of the news hole before he begins work. But true skill at the job means the correct assessment of both the size of the diminishing hole, as the work day progresses, and of the volume and import of the breaking news. Some play it by instinct. One chief sub ignores the big news and pushes back-pages copy in the early hours. He fills up the less important news pages first and marks them closed, building to page one just before deadline.

The Advertiser (Adelaide) a morning broadsheet, employs a system of measuring that is all its own. Three times before the first edition rolls—at 7:30, 10:00 and 10:55 P.M.—all type that has been set, and all blocks (engravings) are measured against available space. This is done with a tape measure exactly five columns long. The total columns ready are added to estimated copy on the type setting machines, plus headline space. Another measure is made of the classified advertisements plus estimates of ads to come. These totals are deducted from the column-inch total for the whole paper. Thus the amount of space still available is calculated. At 10:05 the report may come, from the 10:00 P.M. count, that nine columns remain to be filled of a total of eighty-six.

A chief sub usually scans—or "vets"—all copy as it comes to

him. Some require that the edited story, with headline and directions to the printer, be returned by its sub-editor for a final check before it goes to the composing room. Others send it to be set without a second look, checking the story in proof later.

The Sub-Editors

Sub-editors' hours are staggered so that the beginning and end of the news day are adequately covered. On a morning paper a sub-editor reports in at 9:00 A.M. and prepares time-copy and feature material. At the other end of the day another sub-editor keeps the lonely lobster watch for important news breaks while the last edition is running in the early morning hours. He is called the "late-stop" man for stop-press news. He keeps a sharp eye out for "fudges"—bulletins that may be printed in the fudge box without makeover. There may be a second "late-stop" man for cable news.

The chief sub's directions to a sub about a story to be processed will include content of the lead, desired length, where cuts can be made with least harm, fonts and type-sizes, cross-headings and head.

Sub-editors frequently must weld together the components of a composite story. This is Australia's closest approach to U.S. rewrite; and the method unhappily takes over the disadvantages and none of the advantages. The sub-editor has nothing to work with but the story components themselves; he is removed from his news sources, and if the reporters who covered the event's various phases happen not to be in the office, he cannot query them about inaccuracies, ambiguities, missing points or obscure passages. Whenever possible, composite or sectional assignments are avoided; one reporter gathers the diverse material and writes it himself.

On afternoon papers, one or more sub-editors work, during the afternoon press run, on back-pages material for the next day. Because of early morning deadlines for the first edition as much as possible is done on it the day before. As many as fifteen pages of a thirty-two-page afternoon tabloid may be made up in this fashion. Much of this is washed out next day as the news builds toward the home edition.

Two or three Australian metropolitans use a "copy taster." This gustatory title indicates a sub who does little sub-editing, but through whose hands and under whose eyes pass every scrap of paper that is potential copy for the upcoming edition. He may be the only person in the office, or out of it, who reads all the news of the day in his home city. His purpose is to advise the news editor, chief sub and other seniors about play to be given the news that gets to print.

Subbing Problems

From being among the most conservative of English-language newspapers, with classified ads blanketing front pages and no special dress given to big news, Australian capital-city papers now rank among the most liberal and free-wheeling in respect to makeup.

The tabloids, with less front page space, try the hardest to sell the issue with an inky impact. But all the broadsheets are lavish with pictures on page one—some using four or more pieces of art. And bold headlines are usual. (See illustrations following page 144.)

Close attention is paid to pictures throughout the paper, most papers requiring at least one picture to each news page. Variety of heads and type faces is as great as in the U.S., though there are differences. Australian sub-editors do not regard label heads with disfavor, nor are they convinced about the virtues of the flush-left headline. A favorite among the broadsheets is the hourglass or "dumb-bell" head of three lines, top and bottom lines filled out, the middle one shorter and centered:

Menzies Flays	Evatt Assails	Bribe Inquiry
Labour	Menzies	is Still
for "Stalling"	for "Evasion"	Weeks Away

There are very few styles in newspaper makeup that do not find expression in Australian newspapers. This is particularly true of headlines. The filled-out line is generally preferred for large heads. Cut-in heads to wrap a picture, a map or chart are used a great deal.

Typing of copy and the dressing of the story lead differ markedly from U.S. practice. Without exception, Australian newspapers use copy paper that is half the size favored in most U.S. offices. It is eight by five inches. On each sheet no more than four or five lines are typed; usually the limit is one sentence to one page. Many U.S. newspapers use half-sheets but at least one American ex-newspaperman has never known a newspaper in his homeland to limit words per page so rigidly. Why is the method preferred in Australia? It enables the sub-editor, with a minimum of trouble, to rearrange the sequence of story if he does not like it. When each page carries only one sentence, rearrangement requires only a shuffle of the sheaf. Understandably, reporters do not like the practice.

On top stories the lead or "intro" (for "introductory paragraph" or "intro par") is set in big, black, bold type that a visiting American eye may mistake for a secondary or tertiary deck of the headline. On a tabloid, for an important story, this bold-face intro may be set the whole width of the page. It is usually as wide as the headline deck immediately above it.

Style books and their use vary greatly. Companies may publish a style book for use by all their publications, or for the newspaper alone. One venerable daily has no style book. "If it's in our paper, it's right," was the serene response to a query. One of the most complete and detailed style books is that of The Herald and Weekly Times, Ltd., used for all its publishing offices. Another style book has nine pages of rules and fifty pages of definitions and spelling of frequently-used words.

About newspaper expression, there is no dissent from the virtues of clear, clean writing. "Give us short words, short sentences, short paragraphs, clean copy," one style book orders. "Make yourself familiar with the rulings and principles which the remainder of this Style Book lays down." Says the *Daily Telegraph* (Sydney) Style Reminder: "We work on a tight, hard subbing style. We feature short pars, active voice and avoidance of adjectives and cliches. We insist on the active voice wherever possible, because it has a direct impact and makes for greater accuracy in reporting."

A tabloid with seven narrow columns to the page presents a special problem in headline writing. Some Australian tabloids reduce the size of head-type commensurately; but at least one, *The Sun* (Sydney), makes no concession to narrow width; instead it blows up the head-type and reduces the number of words in the head, e.g.:

JEALOUS OF HIS BABY	*Gov. official wife suicide* PAIR IN A DEATH CLASP	CAR CHECK HINT	HUGE CLAIM ON A SINGER
(1-col.)	(2 col.)	(1 col.)	(1 col.)

Sometimes the head will bite into half the length of a column in a page one story. *The Sun* also uses reverse white type on black backgrounds for certain blocks (engraved heads), running them black the first edition and grey the second, after there has been time to etch a half-tone.

The Sun saves precious seconds at edition times with an inter-communication system between the makeup sub in the composing room and the chief sub's desk. Typographical errors ("literals," in the Australian argot), pi type, transposed cutlines, missing lines and so on, can be called to the makeup sub's attention instantly; he can be told that a marker (correction) is on the way.

The type-book with which Australian sub-editors work constantly has all the headline fonts and all type-sizes in use in the shop. The count for a head is made exactly as in the U.S.; the only difference is preference for certain kinds of headlines over others.

Australian newspapers use perhaps more kinds of body-type than do U.S. newspapers. A column-long story may have five or six variations in size, face and kind. Except on short items, the leads are always set in type different from the rest of the story. Copyreading or sub-editing symbols are the same in both countries.

Many metropolitans look with no favor upon stories jumped from page one. "Run it down and cut it off," is the rule. Others will run a brief story on page one about a major event, with a guide line directing attention to inside pages for sidebar stories and other phases. Each will be a complete story within itself.

"Drop-on" equates with the U.S. "replate." A drop-on is not quite a new edition, but as it concerns the front and perhaps other pages, it is designed to freshen the paper with up-to-the-minute or special-area news.

In Australia, as in any land with daily newspapers edited to an editor's pride and a circulation manager's sales purpose, news-processing is the decisive and unsung department. Good reporters are never in as short supply as good news processors—whether they are called sub-editors or copy readers. Editors prize them with reason. And reporters sometimes dislike them. There are Australian equivalents of terms to describe the equivalent of the American reporter's view that copy readers run a "bleaching department" where all the color, drama and juices are taken out of stories. In both countries there are reporters whose work should seldom be touched, and there are copy readers (sub-editors) who believe that some change, *any* change on copy is an improvement; and to whom the urge to slash and slay and alter and rewrite is a drive greater than sex or hunger or survival.

However, when all else is said, a newspaper is only as good as its sub-editing or copyreading department. That is the reason that from opposite sides of the earth, on Australian and U.S. newspapers, the editorial moan is that no copy desk is good enough; it is the reason that the search goes on endlessly for the best maturity in newspapering that can be found.

Leaders and Leader Pages

Editorials are "leaders" in Australia, as in Britain. They are published on "leader pages" that show a range of differences, from newspaper to newspaper, as great as the differences between the editorial pages of the *New York Times* and the New York *Daily News*.

Two of Australia's fourteen metropolitan newspapers carry no regular leader pages—*The Sun News-Pictorial* (Melbourne), and *The Daily News* (Perth). They do, however, publish opinion pages that carry the by-lined views of commentators and letter writers; and they use occasional front page or run-of-paper editorials. The *Daily Mirror* (Sydney) had no leader page until News Ltd. purchased the former Norton holdings.

Two principal factors govern the kinds of leaders and leader pages that appear in the other twelve metropolitan dailies. One is the Australian tradition, discussed elsewhere, that afternoon dailies are less "serious," less dedicated to hard news and more concerned with features and entertainment than the morning papers. The second factor is the difference between the available space for leaders on tabloid and broadsheet pages. There is not much room for extended comment, or for development of a complex subject theme, in a tabloid column.

The leader page function is identical with that of American editorial pages. Australian leaders argue, explain, interpret, inform, amuse and entertain. They deal with municipal, state, national and international subjects. They use exposition, argument, interpretation and analysis. They employ wit, satire, burlesque, irony, indignation and alarm as the occasion requires. They know the uses of analogy, allusion, fable, contrast, repetition for emphasis and other devices of the competent writer. They admit no limitation upon subject matter.

As in the U.S., quality is variable. It ranges from the brilliant to the banal, with no paper performing consistently at either end of the gamut. Leader writers suffer from the same occupational complaints as their U.S. opposite numbers. Their restrictions and freedoms are similar.

Because Australia's privately-owned newspaper press is the same sort of quasi-public institution as the press is in democracies elsewhere, it acknowledges the familiar special responsibility of helping to create an informed and intelligent public opinion. The task of the leader writer is commensurate with this responsibility.

Perhaps more than American editors, Australians regard leader page features as supporting adjuncts to the leader columns. The whole page is often used to illuminate current issues. There is strong emphasis on "now-ness." On many papers, no leader page is considered ready to roll until the whole edition is about to be put to bed.

Editors plan ahead for special articles and other features, but they are also prepared to tear apart a carefully composed page to include new material to illustrate or give background for an important breaking story. Pages are often held open on morning papers so that a theater or music review may be included in the first edition.

Regularly-assigned leader writers on metropolitan papers vary in number from none to the seven-man staff of *The Sydney Morning Herald,* which includes the editor, four full-time writers, the financial editor (who contributes pieces on monetary and tax subjects) and an editorial cartoonist.

The Age (Melbourne), *The Advertiser* (Adelaide) and certain others have comparable staffs. The tabloid *West Australian* (Perth) has two full-timers. On some papers the editor does much of the leader writing. On *The Sun* (Sydney), the *Daily Telegraph* (Sydney), and *The Herald* (Melbourne) one man or two men write most of the leaders. Part-time leader writers are not uncommon.

Saturday brings a sea-change to many Australian leader pages. *The Advertiser* (Adelaide) and *The Age* (Melbourne), for example, produce in their Saturday leader columns prose that is more essay than editorial, more homiletic than topical. The *Daily Telegraph* (Sydney), on the other hand, ignores both current crises and ageless verities on Saturdays. Instead of leaders it publishes a column of humorous comment. *The Herald* (Melbourne) gives its leader page over to "The Herald Saturday Review," publishing "Topics of the Week" (a column of brief opinions on many subjects) and interpretive articles. *The Sun* (Sydney) runs no leader page at all on Saturdays.

Most, though not all, leader pages are the repository for letters to the editor. A number of papers, notably *The Sydney Morning Herald, The Age* (Melbourne), among others, devote special attention to this department, seeking to avoid by an emphasis on quality the effects of a sort of Gresham's Law of letters to the editor: bad letters (from crackpots, special pleaders, etc.) drive out good letters.

A favorite device, particularly among Australian tabloids, is so-called "50-50 letters." These are brief opinions of readers, edited to the bone. The name derives from a fifty-word limit on the letters and an attempt to hold to a fifty-fifty balance of pro and con on controversial topics. Advertisements appear regularly on many leader pages.

Because the practice of by-lined column writing has not caught on much in Australia, there are few pundits published on leader pages. And apart from state and Commonwealth Parliament correspondence, and reports from foreign capitals, there is little political columning on leader pages. Certain papers, however, publish daily anecdotal humor columns as counterweight to their more sober leaders.

Strange to American eyes is a daily bulletin, usually published on leader pages, under a "Vice-Regal" or "Personal" standing head. There, reminiscent of the official Court Gazette of London, are recorded the State Governor's daily engagements, and those of other high government officials. The Governor-General of the Commonwealth and the six State Governors are Australia's only Crown-appointees.

Australian leader pages are, of course, deeply concerned with politics at all levels. A visitor quickly learns that partisan names are not, however, always what they seem. The Liberals are the conservatives. Theirs is largely a businessman's, white-collar party, roughly comparable to our G.O.P. The Country Party is the political home of the farmer, the big rural landholder, the grazier and pastoralist—as the big sheep and cattle ranchers are called east and west respectively.

The Australian Labour Party has a long, colorful history and a militant tradition. It has succeeded so well over the years that it has achieved many of the goals that brought it into being in the nineteenth century. It has many factions and sundry splinter offspring, some of them sectarian. There are inter-union rivalries and schisms, and Communist-run unions are no rarity. In some state Parliaments sit representatives of these rebel groups, dissidents from the parent body, the ALP.

Other factors make understanding of Australian politics difficult for the visitor. The Australian Constitution is modeled after the American, but the Parliamentary form of government is purely English, down to the symbolism of the mace and the Speaker's wig.

Suffrage is universal, but the Upper Houses of five state Parliaments are chosen by a restricted electorate. The sixth state, Queensland, has a unicameral Parliament.

Eligible electors who fail to vote at elections are fined £2/0/0 (two pounds, about $4.50) if they can not produce a reasonable excuse. The free-wheeling Australian may vote for one party in state elections and for another in federal elections—and often does. Coalition governments are not uncommon at Canberra and at the state capitals.

A thorough grounding in Australian political history, both in the past and in the making, enables leader writers to carry on the Australian tradition of vigorous treatment of political questions. A free and unlicensed press, an end to convict transportation from England to Australia, miners' rights after successive discoveries of gold, responsible government for new colonies, land ownership, tariff protection and national federation are only a few of the basic questions that started the tradition early in the last century.

Labor politicians frequently charge that the newspaper press is anti-labor. It is good practical politics for them to do so; but when the chips are down in an election campaign, the charge is more valid. However, Prime Minister Robert G. Menzies, a Liberal, and state premiers and party leaders who wear the Liberal or Country Party label, are frequently keel-hauled or flayed by the metropolitan papers. The Australian press has as deep-seated a distrust of professional politicians as has the American, and for many of the same reasons. Bad trouble can develop. As recently as World War II, the chief censor for the State of New South Wales tried unsuccessfully to censor, then to prevent publication of the *Daily Telegraph* (Sydney), for daring to question the right of the Minister for Information, a member of the Federal Cabinet, to dictate what might be printed about certain wartime political matters.

Australian newspapers, like American, learned in a world war the delusion of isolation as a national policy. One consequence has been a heightened editorial concern with foreign affairs. Another is a demand for a new orientation, toward the Pacific countries and the United States, and less absorption in the affairs of far-away Britain and Europe. Most Australian editors today favor closer ties with the U.S. and as heavy an immigration as the country can assimilate. To survive, Australia must have more population; to that end, editors like to compare her with the United States during the great age of immigration of the nineteenth century.

Styles in leader-writing run a long gamut. There is much sharp, even brilliant writing, much effective exposition and sound argument. There is also pap, irrelevance and bias. When he sets about it, an Australian leader writer, like his American counterpart, can expertly fill a column with very little content or substance.

Production methods on leader pages are much the same as in the U.S. Early morning conferences for afternoon papers, mid-afternoon conferences for morning papers, decide subjects for discussion and writing assignments. Features for the page are prepared earlier. If the paper employs an editorial cartoonist, his sketches are passed upon at the conference. The leader page is locked up fairly early unless, as previously noted, news developments make last-minute changes necessary.

Some leader pages roar with spleen and vigor. Perhaps more than other papers, *The Sydney Morning Herald, The News* (Adelaide) and the *Daily Telegraph* (Sydney) are gadflies to complacency. The first two papers, significantly, were loud in their condemnation of the British-French attack upon Suez, whereas most of the Australian press tried to out-Eden Sir Anthony in support of it. The broadsheets generally prefer exposition to persuasion. Here the range extends from lucid analysis to firm stances squarely on the fence. Some papers say very little at great length. Others say a great deal quietly.

In the publishing of opinion, all Australian metropolitan journalism is divided into two parts: Sydney dailies and all others. Journalism in Sydney is rougher, tougher, more competitive if not more primitive, certainly more personal, than elsewhere. The boiling point of proprietors' temper is spectacularly lower than in the other capitals. The boiling is sometimes done on editorial pages. With three individualistic ownerships in Sydney, it is a nice question as to which proprietor is quickest on the draw, fastest with the blockbuster attack and the court writ. Name-calling on page one, on leader pages and in signed columns; court injunctions and suits, are part of the pattern.

Pictures in the News

"We like pictures with a gentle suggestion of sex," said the editor of one of Australia's most successful tabloids.

Between gentle (and sometimes ungentle) cheesecake and the solemn news picture of a moment in history there is a tremendous distance. The Australian newspaper includes them both. Pictures are rated high in readership by Australian editors. All major dailies invest heavily in cameras, darkrooms and darkroom materials, mobile picturegram (wired photograph) facilities, equipment for reception of overseas pictures sent by wireless and cable, contracts with picture suppliers at home and abroad, picture exchanges with other Australian newspapers and in all else necessary to the pro-

55

duction of fast, high-grade news photographs in a twenty-four-hour inward flow.

Not the least of the investment is in staff. It is testimony to the importance of the photographer that he occupies a separate section in the newspaper award. Further testimony to the same effect is that all metropolitan papers have picture editors. The clinching testimony is the product. Australia's news pictures are top quality.

The picture conference is held early each news day and is attended by the chief editorial executives of the paper. The picture editor has screened the several hundred shots the day has produced; and, from one to another of the surviving dozen or more the assembled editors move with the care of a committee of vintners considering samples of vintage wine. Different newspaper editors look for different qualities in pictures. But all of them look for excellence and reader appeal.

They may be choosing one or more pictures for each open news page, for front and back pages, for double truck picture pages, or for single picture pages. Australian editorial ingenuity gives them an enormous quantity of pictures from which to choose.

Each paper, or at least each newspaper company has its own photographers' staff. They range from half a dozen to more than forty individuals. They are available for pictures anywhere in their home state or beyond, though most work is done in the capital-city area. Each staff produces hundreds of pictures a day.

The Herald and Weekly Times (Melbourne) maintains a photography staff of forty-one persons, including cadets. *The Herald* employs ten, *The Sun News-Pictorial* twelve, and the rest work for other company publications. The company's publishing operations in a recent year used 36,712 photographs—one hundred a day.

Each metropolitan paper has at least a few dependable photographers who work on space rates, or who free-lance material in their home localities.

Each paper has arrangements with interstate papers for exchange of news photos. In general, morning papers exchange with mornings, afternoons with afternoons.

Each paper has its own arrangements with overseas picture suppliers, principally in the United Kingdom and in the U.S. This means, in effect, that the world is blanketed pictorially by the Australian dailies. From one to half a dozen electronically transmitted news shots are received each day, through government-owned Overseas Telecommunications Commission facilities or through the Postmaster-General's Office, by all fourteen dailies. They arrive either by radio beam or by cable. It is not unusual for a picture of a London, Paris, Washington or Moscow event to be hawked by newsboys on capital-city streets within a few hours, sometimes a few minutes, after the event has occurred.

In charge of all this activity is the paper's pictorial or picture editor. On the small paper, the pictorial editor may have sundry other duties. On the largest dailies, notably in Sydney, his senior may be pictorial or photography director, who has charge of all the picture-taking and picture-getting for the whole array of his company's publications. The *Daily Telegraph, The Sunday Telegraph, Women's Weekly* and other Consolidated Press, Ltd. (Sydney), publications are serviced by one department. So are *The Sydney Morning Herald, The Sun, The Sun-Herald* (Sundays) and other publishing units of John Fairfax, Ltd. Each of the newspapers in the Fairfax domain has its own picture editor, however. At the continent's western end the photography department of West Australian Newspapers Ltd. services two dailies, other W.A.N. publications and does commercial work as well.

The picture editor, who is sometimes a journalist, sometimes a photographer, is in charge of the photography staff, including cadets, and may be responsible for photo sales. He rosters the staff, assigns photographers to their daily tasks, supervises the cadets, directs the movements of the mobile picturegram unit, keeps materials in supply, screens and edits pictures, sits in on picture and editorial conferences, and is liaison man between the photo staff and the rest of the organization.

His men must be on call to all departments. Heaviest demand comes from the chief of staff for general-assignment pictures and from the sports department for seasonal work in football, tennis and cricket, and for year-round duty in horse-racing. But society, finance, police and other roundsmen use photos extensively, too. The picture editor supplies pictures offered for sale to interstate publications by the paper's syndication office.

A picture editor for an afternoon paper may start the day by listening to a 6:15 A.M. newscast, arrive in the office by 7:30, attend a picture conference covering the main news pages at 7:55, check page by page on pictures for the home edition at 11:30 and be ready for edition changes in pictures through 3:43 P.M. After that he prepares for the next day. A morning picture editor's routine is much like this, except there are fewer changes of pictures at night for new editions.

On afternoon papers, pictures for the back pages of the first edition are often selected the day before. On a typical day one tabloid may send through, late the afternoon before publication, as many as nine pages with thirteen blocks (half-tones), not including reversed blocks for heads.

If a daily staff is a Sunday paper's chief reliance for pictures, the staff is rostered and assigned accordingly, Friday and Saturday being the big production days for the Sunday stint.

As in the U.S., photos chosen for print go from the editors to the artists who re-touch, scale, crop, block-out, order blow-ups or reductions and set down other directions for the photo-engraver. The fastest time from picture to block (engraving) found in any capital-city newspaper shop was thirteen minutes. Another office said a rush job can be done in eighteen minutes.

The metropolitans find it cheaper not to use their own equipment to telephone pictures. The Postmaster-General's Department charges £1/17/6 (about $4.20) to wire a picture from Melbourne to Sydney. To send the picture with its own equipment, a Sydney or Melbourne paper would have to pay £10 ($22.50) for twelve minutes, plus a penalty rate of £5 ($11.25). The same differences hold throughout Australia for other points.

The European and U.S. offices of the capital-city papers pre-edit pictures before transmitting them by radio or cable. They can be transmitted through either New York or London. Most papers receive a minimum of one or two a day; sometimes the total is eight or ten. Nearly every plane arriving in Australia carries pictures for some Australian publication.

Among the principal suppliers of overseas pictures to the Australian Press are: U.S. Associated Press, U.S. United Press International, London *Daily Mirror,* British Central Press, Fox Photos, Reuters, Paul Popper, Photo Service and the overseas offices of the individual dailies.

As with news gathering and transmission, Melbourne is the key city for overseas photos. They arrive by wireless over the facilities of the Overseas Telecommunications Commission. They are simultaneously retransmitted to other capitals or drop copies are sent.

Sunspots can raise hob with overseas picture transmission. Distortions are not uncommon. Reception is usually good only after midnight. Winter is a bad time for transmission from London to Melbourne. Sometimes there is difficulty from nearer transmission points: from South Africa, Singapore or New Zealand.

On important overseas stories, Australian newspapers group together and share cost of pictures and coverage. This is done on big news breaks concerning the Royal Family and was done for such events as the Kelly-Rainier wedding, and the opening of a new British Overseas Airline Corporation flight service to Australia.

Photographs must be watched for libel and contempt of court penalties. The 1956 fines levied against *The Sun News-Pictorial, The Argus* and their respective editors for publication of a criminal suspect's picture are discussed elsewhere. All British newspapers are edited, text and pictures, in awareness of an uninvited editorial assistant, implacable British justice, closely watching over the editor's shoulder. At least one metropolitan editor has been warned that the next pictorial offense, his third, will bring him a jail sentence.

The taboos sometimes seem harsh. A man was cited by the state for having dirty premises. His yard and house were clogged with thousands of old newspapers and empty bottles. His defense was that the papers were his library and the bottles his burglar alarm. Newspapers did not use pictures of the mess because they would have been cited for prejudicing the case against the owner of the squalid litter.

Race track assignments recur regularly. On every race meeting day four photographers may be assigned to the job, along with the mobile unit for quick transmission of pictures back to the office. Custom demands race pictures from four different positions along the track.

Two assignments to the same news event may call for two entirely different sets of pictures. In celebration of "Apprentice Day" in Sydney, a parade was held. *The Sydney Morning Herald* and *The Sun* both wanted pictures. The *SMH* photographer got an orthodox record photo of the event—a line of boys marching. *The Sun,* preferring gimmicks and human interest, ran a shot of a small girl, thumb in mouth, watching the parade. Where the *SMH* used a shot of a boys' band huffing and puffing "Waltzing Matilda," *The Sun* man threw a couple of shillings in the line of march and got a picture of the young bandsmen's scramble for the coins. The two concepts signalize one of the differences between the staid Australian broadsheet and the sassy Australian tabloid.

Some papers encourage readers' interest in taking pictures. Spectacular storms, rains and other big weather stories have brought as many as fifty shots within an hour to *The Sun News-Pictorial* (Melbourne) which regards readers as an extension of its photography staff. A good picture will bring a guinea (about $2.40) or more. The highest price ever paid an amateur was £100 (about $225).

On some papers, picture morgues are the responsibility of the photography department; on others they are under the general librarian's aegis. As in the U.S., what to save and what to throw away is a constant problem. Ninety-five per cent of all that is saved may turn out to be worthless from a news standpoint, but the elusive answer to the difficult question is: Which is the newsworthy 5 per cent?

One of the brightest pictorial productions of Australian dailies is the center-pages double truck spread of pictures in *The Sun News-Pictorial* (Melbourne). Its achievements in good composition, balance, pictorial interest, unusual layout, skilful use of white space and vignettes have made it widely respected. Sometimes it will tell a picture story. Sometimes it will illustrate an event from several aspects. More often the pictures show a balanced variety of subjects. On Saturdays, *The Sun News-Pictorial* runs only world-news pictures on its center pages.

West Australian Newspapers Ltd. of Perth has a mobile picturegram unit available for use by both *The West Australian* and *The Daily News*. Two persons are reported dead in a motor smashup at Mt. Barker, two hundred miles south of Perth. Depending on the time of day, the unit transmits pictures to one or the other paper. The vehicle accommodates three persons comfortably; usually one reporter, one photographer and one technician go out on assignments.

During the short oil "boom" on Exmouth Gulf, in 1953, when Australia's first (and so far) only oil well was brought in, starting a wild burst of speculation in Australia's oil future, more than seven hundred pictures were sent south to Perth by picturegram from the nearest sheep station—Minilya—which had telephone connections with Perth.

In Australia, a picture may also be worth ten thousand words, but it takes talent, patience and energy to produce, edit and then use good pictures effectively. Australian newspapers spend thousands of pounds on news photography each year. The results indicate that it is well spent.

The Sports Pages

Sports are not the breath of life to Australians, but an immeasurable amount of Australian breath and living are expended upon them. There are such obvious international matters as Davis Cup matches, Olympic Games competitions, and Australia's phenomenal swimming and track records. There is also horse-racing; perhaps most of all there is horse-racing; e.g.—the Melbourne Cup. When that climax of Australian climactic races is run, on a spring day in November, Australia stops living for fifteen minutes. Melbourne becomes the capital of the universe. It's un-Australian to be born, get married, breathe, die, or think about anything else during the running of the Cup. There are about 2,500,000 radiograms (radio receiving sets) in Australia, and nearly a million television receivers. If there is one that isn't tuned to the Melbourne Cup race, it's because the tubes are blown.

Of the many factors that contribute to Australian adoration of muscular skill in competitive sports, two stand out. One is climate. In many places on the great continent the winters are so mild and the summers so cool that tennis and swimming are twelve-month sports. There are fifty-two Saturday race days, and almost as many race Wednesdays on the calendar. Football is the major autumn and winter (May to September) sport, cricket the spring and summer (November to March).

The second factor is betting, or punting. A better is a punter. Government sanctions, and draws tax revenue from, only race track betting, but the love, the irresistibility, of the wager is in the bone, blood and sinew of Australians; and the lotteries are one of Australia's biggest enterprises.

To satisfy Australians' insatiable hunger, the press devotes much money, talent, time and space to sports of all kinds. In addition to sports departments of dailies, there are other papers exclusively devoted to sports or which report and cover them in detail. Notable are *The Sporting Globe* (Melbourne), *The Sportsman* (Sydney), various editions of the weekly *Truth* and the Sunday newspapers of Sydney, Brisbane, Adelaide and Perth. Moreover, Australian sports specialists are not merely reporters, heralds and chroniclers of muscular events; they are high priests of a national cult.

Football, Cricket, et al.

There are many basic differences between American and Australian sports departments. One is the top command. Another is in the manner of reporting. A third is that on the largest Australian papers the turf department is autonomous and distinct from the sports department, just as the sports department is separate from general news.

The Australian metropolitan daily sports editor edits. He is not, like his American equivalent, a sports columnist and critic first and an editor later, if at all. He is not a byline performer. Outside his office, few know his name. He seldom writes or covers events. He assigns his men, watches the quality of coverage, plans layouts, supervises the sub-editing.

One sports editor described his role as "sort of a production manager." The term is apt, for sports is very much a show. If sports editors have a chief complaint, it is that instead of being able to take all sporting events to be their province, they are tied so closely to their desks that they seldom see a game, a contest or a race. All Australian sports reporters and editors serve the regular cadetship, which gives them good background and a working knowledge of all phases of the press.

A sports editor's authority may extend to coverage for more than his daily. The *Daily Telegraph* (Sydney) sports editor is also responsible for sports in other Consolidated Press publications; i.e., *Sunday Telegraph* and *Weekend*. Occasionally a sports editor will double in brass. *The Mercury* (Hobart) chief of staff acts as sports editor. A deputy chief of staff runs *The Advertiser's* (Adelaide) sports department.

Sports editors and writers are not only expected to be better seers than Nostradamus or an IBM mechanical brain. If they fail to prophesy correctly or are caught in an error, they are undermining the pillars of Australian society. A similar attitude is not unknown in the U.S.

Sports writing in Australia is prose without adornment. It is the Queen's English, written neat. Australian team names are as bizarre as American—Bulldogs, Magpies, Kangaroos, Wallabies, Tigers, Swans, Gorillas, Hawks, Saints, Dons—but there is no tradition of purple prose or bravura style. Australians greatly admire Damon Runyon, but there is no Runyonese on their sports pages; nor is any by-line individualism permitted in the manner of Grantland Rice, W. O. McGeehan, the early Westbrook Pegler, Red Smith, Joe Williams and other U.S. sport panjandrums.

Australia has sports columnists and experts, many of whose names or pseudonyms are household words; but as a rule they do not set up as Delphic oracles, Supreme Courts or yarn-spinners. Few are given either the space or the freedom which U.S. sports editor-columnists give themselves.

The Sun (Sydney) prints a different columnist every day, Monday through Saturday, alternating general sports, turf, trotting, cricket and tennis. The *Daily Telegraph* (Sydney) uses the work of five columnists who have a once-a-week go at trotting, boxing, general sports and racing. *The Sydney Morning Herald* has no daily sports columns, but runs them intermittently on general sports, turf, golf, cricket, and women in sports. More than one top-echelon Australian editor believes that too much news is saved by U.S. sports editors for their personal columns; it ought to be used in the news budget. Letters are solicited on some sport pages, so that the reader may indulge in a "grizzle" or a "whinge" about sports.

The personnel of a metropolitan sports department, including turf, is highly variable. On one daily, up to ninety people, including girl stenographers in the telephone room, and casuals (stringers) covering distant affrays, are engaged at peak hours in wrapping up the Saturday sports final.

The hard core of sports reporters, turf experts and sports sub-editors—for sports almost always has a sub-editors' table separate from the general news subs—runs between ten and twenty. On some papers, turf writers outnumber general sports reporters. Sports subs run from two to five to a paper. The total figures vary, of course, seasonally and through the week. Saturday's peak activity far outruns that of other days.

Subs have special problems with sports copy. Much of it is prepared by casuals, who are half-trained or untrained country correspondents, and putting it into printable shape is no easy chore. All kinds of persons serve as casuals—school teachers, bus drivers, barbers, chemists (druggists)—and results of contests are phoned in from the far points of the state.

Over-age and retired football, cricket and tennis players are often hired to cover or write pre-game dope stories about important matches. There is also quite a bit of "By So-and-So As Told to Such-and-Such."

Apart from racing, or turf, which requires highly skilled talents (see "Horses and Punters") sports writers develop specialties. Top reporters may do football in the winter, cricket in the summer. Others concentrate on tennis, athletics (track and field events), golf, swimming, bowls (bowling on the green), sailing, yachting, baseball, softball, field hockey, lacrosse, surfing, rifle shooting, basketball, dog-racing, dog field competitions, dog shows.

Lesser sports among these may be done by casuals. A football expert may do general reporting in the off-season. If a casual is given charge of a particular sport, tennis, say, he is expected not only to cover all newsworthy matches, but to report tennis news as it develops without office assignment or prompting.

Football in Australia resembles football in the U.S. in name only. There are four kinds, all of them harder, rougher, faster than gridiron football. All are played in shorts, sweaters, stockings and shoes, with practically no padding for protection against injuries. The four games are alike, also, in that they are swift, harsh body-contact matches, with long quarters and continuous action.

Australian Rules football is the top favorite in Victoria, South Australia, Western Australia and Tasmania, with some interest in New South Wales and Queensland. Rugby League football is the preferred game in the last two states. Soccer and Rugby Union, the other two, have their own followings.

Teams are professional or semi-professional and represent suburban municipalities of the capital-city. (Australian intercollegiate or interscholastic competitions are not regarded as major sports, and they get scant attention from the public prints). Melbourne may well be the most rabid football center. Two separate groups play Australian Rules football—Victorian Football League and Victorian Football Association. League football, senior in public interest, is played by the twelve teams of the VFL: Carlton, Collingwood, Essendon, Fitzroy, Footscray, Geelong, Hawthorn, Melbourne, North Melbourne, Richmond, St. Kilda, South Melbourne.

The Victorian Football Association with fourteen teams, has its fanatical supporters, but not as many as the VFL. Besides these twenty-six teams, there are forty to fifty other combinations, including the Bendigo League, a strong outstate group. In leagues, teams and play, Victoria is typical of the other five states.

To the sports editor all this means that during the long football season something like six League and seven Association games must be covered every Saturday. So rough is the play that twice a week during the season, after the Tuesday and Thursday practice sessions, a whole sports page may be devoted to stories about the injuries of players and their chances of playing the next game.

The tempo quickens as the season progresses, particularly if competition is close, much as with major league baseball pennant races in the U.S. The climax comes in the Grand Final, the play-off among the top four teams.

League football goes interstate every three years in the Australian National Football Carnival. The event lasts for two weeks and its competitors are drawn from a "strong" division composed of teams from Victoria, Western Australia, South Australia and Tasmania; and a secondary division made up of teams from Queensland, New South Wales, Australian Capital Territory.

Football has been played in Australia for at least eighty years, and its long endurance is often manifested in obituaries of newly-dead ancients who are described as football players of note in their younger

Departments of the News-Editorial Division

days. Upwards of 140,000 people may attend football games in one capital city at one time. This may seem small in contrast to 50,000 to 120,000 spectators in one baseball or football stadium in the U.S.; but Australia's entire population could be seated in 100 Melbourne Cricket Ground stadia.

For the League's Grand Final, played on Saturdays, fans sometimes arrive at the gates in mid-afternoon Friday, with blankets and radios, prepared to spend the night. In a recent year the Grand Final drew 106,000 partisan fans.

Attendance, however, is not the ultimate criterion. A "new-chum" (recent arrival from overseas) editor, noted that more people attended football matches than race meetings, ordered his sports staff to play up football and play down racing. He didn't realize, as one sports editor put it, "that every Australian is a punter for horses."

Another proprietor promoted a disaster because he did not understand what sports mean to Australians. He called in his editor, soon after taking over, and ordered him to throw out all sports. No horse racing, no cricket, no football.

Within three months there was no paper.

Cricket takes over when the football season ends. Football has at least a name in common with an American sport. Cricket, however, is as opaque to the visiting American as baseball doubtless is to Australians in the U.S. There are cricket leagues all over Australia, and about them, as their chroniclers, cricket writers speak their special language.

Some sports editors claim that cricket is "a dying sport" in Australia. If so, it is a long and vigorous death; particularly during the international "Test" Cricket matches. When Australia plays Britain's teams in Britain, games finish at about 3:30 A.M. Australian time because of the time difference, and the real devotee wouldn't think of going to bed sooner, particularly when "The Ashes" are at stake. The Ashes are a non-existent symbol of victory in Australian-British cricket competition.

Senior clubs of district cricket are named for the suburbs, as with football. There are twelve clubs in the district. They compete for a pennant and the winners play interstate champions for the Sheffield Shield, Australian cricket's "World Series." Like football, cricket is a semi-amateur, semi-pro sport.

American baseball is played here and there, but has not caught on generally. Australian boxing, once a great show which has produced some world-famous fighters, has suffered a decline, although the capital cities have occasional fights worth publicizing and reporting. Wrestling, as in the U.S., is a fitter subject for the drama critic than for the sports reporter.

Certain running races attract considerable attention. Notable is the Stawell Gift—Stawell is a Victorian country town—which offers a handsome prize to the fastest man entered. Winners have been known to augment the prize, by betting on themselves.

Australians stint nothing on their runners. During John Landy's ascendancy as a miler, one sports editor remarked that "Landy can have the front page every time he opens his mouth, if he wants it." Landy had the front page and Australian hearts on many occasions; on none more notably than when he stopped to help a fallen competitor in an Olympic Games trial early in 1956. The outburst of adulation on front pages and sport pages was typically Australian.

Women's sports get more printed attention than they did earlier. Australian women—their "Golden Girls" the papers called them—did much better than Australian men at the Melbourne Olympics. At least three major papers employ women as full-time sports reporters.

Surfing and volunteer lifesaving clubs are among the honored institutions of Australia—sort of a sporting aristocracy. Men of sixty and seventy boast of their decades of membership in a club. Competitions with other clubs, in beach rescues, boat launching, surfing and other skills, draw large crowds and are important sports events. Their beach parades, members dressed in gaudy "bathers" (swim suits) and skull caps are proud and colorful spectacles.

Night trotting began in Western Australia and has become popular elsewhere of recent years.

New South Wales and Victoria have no monopoly on athletes. A Perth editor estimated that there are 20,000 golfers, 20,000 bowlers and 20,000 tennis players in Western Australia. In Queensland there are an estimated 20,000 bowlers. There are 14 golf clubs within 20 miles of Brisbane, and 36 bowling clubs, not to mention 600 male basketball players and 3,000 tennis players.

School sports, such as they are, are reported on three levels: primary, secondary, university. In Brisbane, on Saturdays or Sundays, two columns of up-to-age-thirteen school games' results are often published in agate type. The primary schools play Rugby League and Australian Rules football, soccer, field hockey, basketball (girls), softball, tennis and cricket. Each school has an annual track meet; there are also metropolitan and state championship meets.

Australia has no tradition of business firms backing teams in industrial sports leagues. Teams are organized because people like to play, and they pay their own expenses.

Football, cricket and other associations also produce news off the field. Their business meetings must be covered.

Friday is a big day for sports in general as well as for racing. In part, this is because starting lineups for the next day's games are announced, the players who are "to get a Guernsey"—or start the game. Saturday, however, is the biggest day for Australian sports editors. So well are all functions organized and articulated that last editions of afternoon papers, rolling at 5:30 P.M., carry stories, summaries or scores of every major sporting event in the country. Games that last into the late afternoon or evening are written up play by play, with new intros (leads) for each edition.

The Herald's (Melbourne) may be the most impressive, because, as the only afternoon broadsheet, it can spread the results of contests over more white paper. Its sports final edition builds slowly. In the first edition are stock fillers which are progressively discarded as sports news comes in and the four edition times are met—at 12:30 P.M., 2:30, 3:30 and the last lockups at 4:25, 4:40 and 5:20 P.M.

The Daily News (Perth) sometimes doubles in size between its first and last editions on Saturday in order to be inclusive of all sports results. The last edition of the *Telegraph* (Brisbane) becomes a Sports Pictorial, with all but three pages of a twenty-four-page edition devoted to sports results, news pictures and features. Dailies backstopped by Sunday newspapers which are published by the same company know that their sister publications will also present detailed offerings.

One general result—true not only for Saturday's editions—is that the Australian sports page is heavily statistical; or perhaps it only seems more so than its U.S. counterpart. Some of the impression comes from the Australian manner of factual, unadorned reporting, but perhaps more derives from the need to cover all kinds of minor, distant sporting contests from the country towns of the state, because the only record of the played event will be found in the capital-city daily. Saturday golf scores, for example, may be collected from as many as thirty different courses.

Racing results from all over take up much of the agate tabulations. But a typical Saturday final edition would also include, depending on the season, results of contests in cricket, football, trotting, soccer, golf, shooting, fishing, sailing, cycling, rowing, tennis, school athletics, bowls, women's basketball, all of which have their devotees. Earlier editions carry the scores and plays of contests up to the moment of publication.

As with other news departments there are no legman-rewrite combinations in reporting sports. The reporter—at the race track, football field, cricket ground or wherever—organizes his notes, and either dictates word by word, or writes and then dictates, his complete story to a telephone-stenographer in the office. Perhaps 90 per cent of all sporting news comes into the newspaper office by telephone, local and long distance. As many as forty telephones may be used to receive the Saturday sport results for *The Herald* (Melbourne) and its companion paper, *The Sporting Globe*. The organized turmoil reaches its highest pitch just before deadline.

Perth newspapers on the other hand, have a time advantage of two hours over the eastern states. This is advantageous for Test cricket match scores from overseas as well as for Australian eastern states final scores and racing results.

Metropolitan papers do not hesitate to send their reporters far afield. The sports editor of a Brisbane paper said: "We send men as far as Adelaide for cricket and tennis, to Melbourne for racing and Australian athletics (track and field) and swimming championships, to Sydney for Rugby League, Rugby Union and soccer, and equally far for any sport, such as golf or fishing, if the event justifies it."

Horses and Punters

Fifty-two Saturdays out of the year are racing days somewhere in Australia. Wednesday is the second most popular day. Most states have additional special racing days; e.g., Queensland: New Year's Day (Jan. 1), Foundation Day (Jan. 26), Easter Monday (variable), Labour Day (First Monday in May), Queen's Birthday (June 4), Exhibition Day (August 15), Boxing Day (Dec. 26).

The Australian horse-racing population has been estimated at five thousand. The human, horse-betting (punting) population of Australia is something under ten million, but probably not much. For every punter at the track, there are three others who have done business with a bookmaker in the hope that he will make them a fortune. The great race courses are in the capitals, but no country town is without its race track. Even in the far outback, the smallest bulge-in-the-road town has its dedicated oval.

This is the reason that upwards of one hundred men are employed by Australia's metropolitan newspapers to report horses, jockeys, track conditions, finish prospects, results and judgments about Australia's most popular sport. Because racing is the only sport that produces news the year around, it is sometimes necessary for the sports or turf editor to get additional help from the chief of staff.

To the Australian punter the race course pounded by the horse on which his money is riding is the most important oval in the country, even if it is only an unfenced track in the outback. But the most visited and most bet upon are these:

New South Wales: Rosehill, Randwick, Warwick Farm, Canterbury Park (Sydney).
Victoria: Flemington, Caulfield, Moonee Valley (Melbourne).
South Australia: Victoria Park, Morphettville Fields, Cheltenham (Adelaide).
Queensland: Albion Park, Doomben, Eagle Farm (Brisbane)
Western Australia: Headquarters, Belmont Park, Ascot, Helena Vale (Perth).
Tasmania: Elwick (Hobart), Mowbray (Launceston).

There is also a whole galaxy of trots and dog race courses, all of which supply their quota of news.

Betting is too intricate a business for a foreign visitor to understand, much less explain, but "S.P." is a basic cabalistic sign. It means "Starting Price"—how much the horse will pay if it wins. It is the consensus of the animal's momentary worth collated from the best thought by turf scriveners, bookmakers, touts and punters.

Eloquent testimonial to racing's popularity is to be found in the "Form Guides" that blossom on Friday afternoons and Saturday mornings, and periodically during the week, in anticipation of race meetings. They are generally four-page tabloid lift-out sections and their whole concern is to apprise the studious punter of his chances of making money on a horse's nose. Each horse scheduled to race locally is given a thumbnail biography. Nearly every major paper in Australia publishes at least one form guide a week.

A typical tabloid guide will lead off with experts' selections at principal area tracks. Newspapers generally ignore the opposition, but not so in racing. Space is given not only to the selections of the editors' best thought about winners in each race, but to the selections of opposition turf editors. Each race is summarized by a consensus.

After the choices, complete listings are made for each race on the home track—horses, weights, jockeys, time. The inside pages may be taken up by the records of individual horses: breeding, age, trainers, how they ran at what dates, weight carried, and so on.

The amount of information published about individual horses in the form guides depends upon available space. Sometimes there is room for only the horse's last two races; sometimes for less than that. Shorter summaries of country and interstate races may complete the section.

All this is reported in a brand of horsy argot that is incomprehensible to the uninitiated. The jockey shorthand may be concluded with a cryptic judgment on the horse's chances. "Promising effort last time," "Has lots of speed," "Speedy, but this will test her," "Not hopeless," "Promising," or perhaps a devastating, definitive "No."

The West Australian (Perth) does not publish a local form guide as complete as those in Melbourne or Sydney; neither does *The Daily News* (Perth). One reason is that about 50 per cent of Perth betting is on the Melbourne races.

Reckoned somewhat like the gold in Fort Knox are the card-catalog summaries of all race horses that have any kind of an Australian record. These are usually the responsibility of one turf writer whose sole assignment is to keep them up to date. Since there may be as many as 500 race horses in the state at one time, and since there may be as many as 100 race meetings throughout the country on one day, each with new records to be noted, the dimensions of the record keeper's assignment are impressive.

On days that are not race-meeting days the turf writer is in circulation at the training tracks—usually at least three times a week. He is a kind of physician-priest, noting both the physical and mental health of his charges. A horse's sore foot, an indifferent training performance, a lost appetite, a moody depression, listlessness—all these may bear upon the placing of thousands of pounds at the next race meeting; so all must be noted and reported. The turf specialist watches time trials; he must have his pipelines open into scores of feed-box news sources; he must know trainers, grooms, jockeys and club officials intimately. He must never make a wrong guess about a race. His facts must come straight from the horses' mouths.

Much stress is laid on the actual time set in the horses' trial runs. At the track the turf editor checks with the casuals who are paid to supply him with information, moves about among the sheds, talking with trainers, jockeys and examining the horses. He collates the information, and from it may write the main racing story of the day. Racing stories lead the sports pages about three days a week.

Some turf writers adopt pseudonyms—"Cardigan," "Ebor," "Sunstar," "Malua"—so they can move about more freely without identification at tracks. Others write under their own names.

Racing is authorized by the State Parliaments. Privately-owned racing clubs are given franchises to operate. Only one track in a city may hold a meeting on a race day. Track betting is legal and the state draws a percentage of the take in a form of tax. Handicappers are employed by the individual racing club. The clubs have great power. They can rule a man off the track for life, or suspend him, for misconduct.

There are six provincial racing clubs within seventy-five miles of Brisbane. The Brisbane papers cover all Wednesday and Saturday race meetings throughout Queensland.

To an outsider, coverage of the races appears to be an excursion into metaphysics, magic, and second sight. The reporter and his assistants must note accurately the positions of a dozen or more horses at four points during the race—the start, half a mile from home, into the stretch, the finish—and identify each animal in the strip photos that are standard operating practice in the newspaper's reports of the day's racing.

A reporting team may work this way: One man covers all phases of the betting. A second watches the race, with close attention to the favorite's performance; afterwards he collects statements and comments from owners, jockeys, and others; also crowd color. A third man "calls" the race, following its progress from the press box with a binocular; two cadets take down the position of the horses at the four points. All this the writer collates into a story and dictates it over the phone to his office.

Afternoon papers can get pictures as well as stories onto the street within fifty minutes after the finish at local tracks. For such epochal events as the Melbourne Cup, papers from other states may send not only writers and photographers, but mobile picturegram units for instant transmission of race photos.

Despite the great interest, some sports editors believe horse-racing is losing its hold on Australians. One Sydney editor noted that Sydney has added half a million population in the last two decades, yet race attendance is no greater than it was in the 1930's.

Notably, racing service to readers has been diminished here and there, without cataclysm or even much outcry. The *Daily Telegraph* (Sydney) reduced from four to two its published shots of important races in progress, and no barricades were set up in Castlereagh Street. *The Sydney Morning Herald* cut the size of its Turf Guide from eight tabloid pages to four in 1956 and the planets continued in orbit.

Few things in life, however, are as certain as that Australians' passion for the ponies will continue to be strong and persuasive.

Women's and Social

Approximately one hundred women produce the women's department and social news of Australia's metropolitan newspapers. As members of the AJA, they serve cadetships, are graded and paid on equal terms with men journalists.

Women's departments are usually autonomous and self-contained. There are occasional divisions, some sharp, between women's and social news, although on many papers the two are an amiable amalgam. The social editress (the title is preferred to society editor) and women's editress—sometimes the same person—are responsible in their respective fields for news coverage and feature ideas, for cadet supervision and, more often than not, for sub-editing and layout. The exceptions for the two latter functions are papers on which a regular sub-editor cooperates or supervises.

Cadets may constitute about one-half the personnel of a typical department. Including only full-timers, departments number from two to eleven members. Most editresses come to their posts after serving as general reporters. One happy result is that Australian social and women's pages are not much afflicted with the oleaginous prose that characterizes many U.S. society pages. Part of the Australian training is to apply a general, and not a special, interest-gauge to all news. Stories are judged on their merits.

Moreover, on dailies which apportion a fair percentage of the news space to social-women's, the trend is toward news and features that will interest men as well as women: A woman horse-breeder, charity projects, the researches of women scientists, women in civic affairs. One top social editress said that she had told the managing director before she began, many years earlier, that she would work for him only if she could cut out the social "twaddle" and run a *news* department.

Subject matter on social pages is about what it is in U.S. newspapers. Engagements, weddings, dancing parties, charity functions, receptions, theater parties, arrivals, departures, graduations, teas, church groups' activities, club functions and other familiars are the biggest sources of society news. The state's Royal Show (similar to a U.S. state fair) held annually, tennis tournaments, cricket finals, special horse-racing days (e.g. Melbourne Cup), Australian and British holidays, diplomatic functions, fashion shows, jumble (rummage) sales are also grist to the social editress' mill. Social calendars and other routine features are published.

Because all capital cities are ports of call for ocean liners, much news and many features derive from ships' arrivals. Passenger lists of air lines and the guest lists of principal hotels are also closely watched for story potentials.

Quite different from American practice is the custom of announcing births, engagements, anniversaries and approaching marriages by classified advertisements. Paid death and memorial notices are familiar enough to U.S. readers, but not the others. In their classified sections, Australians may read:

"Forbes.—To Reg and Bonnie (nee Emsden)—a Daughter (Helen Mae) on 4th August" or ". . . have much pleasure in announcing engagement of their only daughter . . ." or *"Lunston-Crystal.*—On Saturday, Feb. 30, 9 a.m. the marriage of Millicent Anne to Patrick Joseph, at St. Jerome's Church. . . ." While these have nothing directly to do with the social-women's department, they frequently yield news tips worth developing.

Where it does not form a mixed grill with social news, the women's department covers a much broader but not less familiar number of special interests:

Women's organizations, food and cooking, personal and family problems, knitting (Australian women are prodigious knitters) and dress-making (*The Sun News Pictorial* of Melbourne sold 3,540 patterns in one three-week period), fashions (sketches and photos), child care, homemaking, interior decoration, vignettes of women in the news, gardening (where it isn't a separate department), health problems, occasional interstate and overseas correspondence, shopping guides, support of charities, other public appeals for money, teen-age concerns, questions and answers, stories on the Red Cross, hospitals, Girls Guides and other such organizations; features from the entertainment field, station life in the outback, inspirational contributions, horoscopes, phonograph reviews, seasonal foods, shipboard interviews, and a great range of general news and features about women.

Most papers follow a loose weekly pattern of recurrent subjects. Because Saturday is a popular day for weddings, for example, advance stories on Saturdays and accounts of weddings on Mondays are part of the pattern. Pictures of brides and of wedding parties bloom in profusion on these two days. The number of pages varies widely, from a single page on a slack day in a small daily, to twenty or more pages in a large Sunday paper.

On a typical Australian daily, the pattern of the week may run something like this, as to special features that spice run-of-mill news:

MONDAY. Stories and pictures of weddings, brides and grooms; personal problems column, calendar for the week. *The Advertiser* (Adelaide), *The Sydney Morning Herald, Daily Telegraph* (Sydney) publish no women's or society pages on Monday, after a large Sunday section.

TUESDAY. Cooking, shopping guide, homemaking, London story.

WEDNESDAY. Social roundup, recipes, patterns, knitting, shopping, inspiration article.

THURSDAY. This is the day for the biggest sections and spreads for both women's and social news. *The Sydney Morning Herald* publishes an eight-page separate section; *The News* (Adelaide), the *Telegraph* (Brisbane), the *Daily Telegraph* (Sydney) devote up to eight pages, sometimes even more, to the two departments. These papers present a full gamut of social and women's department items, with an occasional venture into movie, record and television-radio reviews.

FRIDAY. High fashion, recipes, overseas column, medical problems, Saturday brides.

SATURDAY. Wedding stories, pictures of brides, family problems, weekly review of social events, teen-age doings and rather solid features—Saturday is a strong day for features on dailies not associated with a Sunday paper.

Many newspapers build a following of readers around names that feature specialties. The name may be a real person, a pseudonym, or even a hand-me-down used by a number of editresses in succession. Mary Ferber on *The Daily News* (Perth), Sarah Dunne on *The Herald* (Melbourne), and *The Advertiser* (Adelaide), Margot on *The Mercury* (Hobart), Clare Crane on *The Sun News-Pictorial* are names well known in their respective circulation areas. Some papers play up individual staff writers and editresses; others do not.

Standing heads are used over recurring columns or features— Women's Doctor, Shopping Around, Talkabout, Diane Looks Around, Mouthpiece, Weekly Diary, Commentary, Sunspotter, Young Moderns, Women's Interests, Where My Pencil Takes Me, Readers Are Asking, Her Favorite Dress, Family Forum, Roundup suggest the variety.

Women's department members are a versatile lot. Each is expected to know how to perform all functions: cover news, write it, edit it, lay out pages, meet the public and so on. Editresses must wage constant war with news editors who want to encroach on their precious space, and they are inured to seeing their extra-good stories yanked from their pages to positions of more prominence. This is satisfying, of course, but often it leaves a problem of how to fill a page.

Makeup depends upon the kind of paper. Broadsheets have larger areas in which to lay out pictures and arrange stories. The writing must be tighter and more compact on tabloids. Some gossip is published in the name of news, and at least one by-liner writes prose that is collected with glee by her fellow-scriveners for its gooey and orotund inanities.

But she is an exception; and exceptions aside, the brand of performance in the field is creditable. Occasionally the observant reader must marvel at the expertise with which items are made to flower in almost impossible makeup situations. It is little wonder that Australian social and women's pages command a high readership.

Business and Finance

All Australian metropolitan newspapers respect news of an economic nature—which includes not only business, finance and industry, but stock exchange, agriculture, taxation, government regulation and related matters. No major paper is without a page or more dedicated to business-finance reporting; and, regularly, one or many such stories too big for routine treatment are printed on page one or elsewhere in prominent place.

Business-finance is a no-nonsense department. Because there is always more news than can be shoe-horned into the available space, feature stories and art are kept to a minimum. Statistics dominate the department, the writing is tight, hard news gets practically all the play, and the emphasis is on local events.

Staff may run as low as one part-timer—on *The Mercury* (Hobart) —and as high as seven—on *The Sydney Morning Herald*. The finance editor may do much or little reporting or he may concentrate on market and business analysis. But someone is always at the local stock exchange.

News handled falls generally into two large categories: (1) From the securities exchanges, other exchanges and markets; (2) From finance, agriculture and manufacturing sources.

In the first group, sales and price movements of stocks and bonds provide most of the news, and tabulated listings take a good part of each day's available space. Almost always there is an accompanying summary story. It tells what a select list of securities has done

that day, reports trends, and details other significant developments.
Principal attention of course, is on the local exchanges, but a
number of papers publish summaries from interstate. Overseas
stories, price indexes and summaries, especially from London and
New York, are published periodically.

There is often a summary of the local summary, divided into
"Rises" and "Falls" to give the hurried reader a quick picture of
the principal movements. Mining sales and quotations are listed
separately; likewise with quotations from the livestock, fruit, vegetable and other markets.

In the second category, almost everything else germane to the
economy is the business-finance department's province: dividends
declared, taxation and other business bills in parliaments; basic-
wage court decisions; business beginnings, mergers and failures;
annual reports, new share offerings, metals and mining. Many stories
are simply rewrites of company news releases, for firms are eager to
be noticed in the editor's limited space.

The big metropolitans reserve one, two and sometimes three
pages for business and finance. Among the other capital-city papers,
The Mercury (Hobart) puts most of its emphasis on a Wednesday
farming and financial eight-page center section, edited by a contributor. Daily stock exchange sales are typed up for publication
by junior staffers, the roundup including livestock sale prices at
Tasmanian abattoirs (stockyards).

On the west side of the continent, *The West Australian* (Perth)
daily business-finance department is conducted by an editor and one
assistant. Its sister paper, *The Daily News,* pays little attention to
business and finance news.

The exchanges of Australia—securities, mining, wool and others
—like exchanges elsewhere, somewhat resemble school rooms,
temples of worship and houses of bedlam, although they are constituted for quite a different purpose.

Two complete "calls" of listed stocks on principal exchanges are
made each day. Stocks are called in series. On the Sydney Stock
Exchange the categories are: Banks, Breweries, Coal, Gas and
Electricity, Hire Purchase (Installment Buying) and Finance, Insurance, Newspapers, Shipping, Trustee and Miscellaneous, which
includes about eight times as many securities as all the foregoing.

Few utilities and railroad stocks are listed, for most are government monopolies. The morning "call" includes everything up to the
letter "M" and the afternoon everything from "M" to "Z."

Afternoon papers may offer a complete story of the day's trading by their last edition, much as do U.S. afternoons. Close attention is paid market-leaders for their relation to trends—stocks of such big companies as Broken Hill Proprietary (the famous "B.H.P."), Imperial Chemical Industries ("I.C.I."), Colonial Sugar, British Tobacco, the big wool and stock brokers: Elder, Smith & Co.; Dalgety; Goldsborough Mort, Westralian Farmers, among others.

The stock market round is not only routine reporting of statistics. In periods of stress, stocks in Australia behave as stocks do elsewhere. No one who was there, a visitor is assured, will ever forget the Sydney exchange when Australia's first oil well came in. West Australian Petroleum Ltd. ("Wapet") brought it in, after long search, on Rough Range at Exmouth Gulf in the Northwest. The Sydney exchange went mad. Oil and oil-search stocks exploded. Brokers screamed, fought, rolled under tables. Disputes raged all over the trading floor. Australia's most serious deficiency in natural resources had been overcome; the event, everyone prophesied, marked the beginning of a new industrial era, lubricated by Australia's own oil.

That was in December, 1953. Eight years later the well at Rough Range was still Australia's only oil producer; and its output was too far away from the market and too inconsiderable to be commercially profitable.

Stock exchange statistical coverage is usually done by cadets or young staffers. Reporters for afternoon papers, who must work swiftly to meet edition press deadlines, use telephone, teletype, ticker and direct wire to get quotations and other news into the office. All exchanges offer swift mimeograph tabulations of transactions, minutes after calls are completed.

Finance editors pay close attention to all listed companies. Exhaustive files are kept on their stocks' price movements, balance sheets, annual statements, profit-loss tables and other matters. From these files, finance writers draw heavily for background on routine stories and for special uses.

One of the latter is "Broker to Client," a finance page feature of the *Daily Telegraph* (Sydney). In dialog form, "Broker" and "Client" discuss a selected company's history, financial and production records and prospects. To a similar purpose is "Investor's Notebook," a weekly column of comment by *The West Australian* (Perth) finance editor.

The stock exchange reporter must know local usage and custom; for example, that in Melbourne the drawing of a marble breaks a tie in the shouted bidding; and that in Sydney, a tie is broken by a throw of dice from a bottle.

The considerable rivalry between Sydney and Melbourne is reflected in business-finance news. Each city believes it is the most important economic nerve center in Australia. A transient would be foolish to express an opinion beyond the obvious one that each city acutely affects the other—and all others—in the sensitive area of stock-price changes and related financial matters.

Business and finance news is likely to share its page or spill-over pages with such a job-lot as weather, shipping, radio programs, comics and classified ads. There is some exchange of business and finance news among capital-city dailies, mornings to mornings, afternoons to afternoons. No economic activity is ignored. All papers give special notice to special-area interests. Many cover even the smallest markets. In Melbourne, for example, the Potato Board is called regularly for potato prices; the secretary of the Metropolitan Wholesale Merchants for onion prices; the Melbourne town clerk for fish prices at the Municipal Markets, and the stock yards for meat prices.

The wool market, to which all papers give special attention, is seasonal. It takes about a year to traverse the country, beginning in Queensland, for shearing, sales and other data, and ending in Western Australia. Sales begin in Melbourne in February and March. Wool exchanges and the large wool brokers, of course, are sources for most price information.

Business and finance pages are edited in part with the country reader in mind. The first edition of morning papers is especially important. A long story about wool for country readers may be cut to three paragraphs in the later metropolitan edition. Prices current for cattle, sheep, meats, fruit, vegetables, commodities in general are also important to country readers.

As Australia, the world's greatest wool producer, moves steadily toward more industrialization, the nature of the business-finance editor's job will change accordingly.

Motors

Besides routine motor news, most metropolitans carry a once-a-week story about new automobiles. This specialized feature is a report on tests by the motor editor. A broadsheet's feature may run as many as four columns, illustrated, and the periodic motors section itself, up to four or five pages. One Sunday paper publishes a regular "Detroit page."

In a sense, these new-car stories take the place of auto shows and new-model time in the U.S. press. Australia is the land of the small car and the old car. Owners lavish much loving care on their long-lived autos. Until General Motors-Holden showed Australians how tremendously a home-made car can prosper, Australia had only automobile assembly plants, and most cars were imported. But the new-car buff is also indigenous to Australia; and with scores of foreign cars to choose from, the purchaser needs some guidance. Hence, the new-car feature.

The motor editor usually devises his own tests and publishes his findings without help from dealers or manufacturers. He may report on as many as thirty cars a year. Much new-car news comes from Britain. U.S. imports are negligible because of prohibitive restrictions and costs. There are Sporting Car, Vintage Car, Veteran Car, MG, Morris, Renault, Simca, Volkswagen and other kinds of motor clubs. They hold gymkhanas to show off their four-wheeled loves.

The motor editor, who may be also more or less responsible for road condition news, gets much of it from the automobile club headquarters of his state, a group that functions much like the state divisions of the American Automobile Association.

The motor editor's job is usually combined with some other editorial function; he is generally chosen because he loves automobiles.

Libraries, Morgues and Block Rooms

Austerely, in freehand lettering, a single word is printed on a door off the main room of the reference department of the *Daily Telegraph* (Sydney). The word is "Clancy." Any literate Australian would know what the cryptic sign signifies. Behind the door is a room where surplus files—the "overflow" from the main room —are stored. The whole phrase, the title of a famous Australian poem by A. B. Paterson (who wrote "Waltzing Matilda") is "Clancy of the Overflow."

"Overflow" connotes a problem difficult to librarians everywhere: What to do with what cannot be put in the live files? As elsewhere, the problem is insoluble. As elsewhere, too, cross-filing and labels are big problems. There are sometimes unexpected file entries; none, though, to match the famous American story of Will Rogers' obituary being filed under "P" for "Part-Cherokee-Indian Humorist."

A morgue is a morgue in Australia, though it may not be called that. "Library" and "Reference Room" are preferred. Chief storage items are cuttings (clippings), photographs, flongs (mats) and blocks (engravings). One or two of the largest newspaper companies maintain a separate block room. Reference books, pamphlets, bound or microfilmed newspapers, current newspaper files, Hansard's (verbatim reports of Parliamentary proceedings) constitute other units. Sometimes filed materials are physically separate. The reference department of West Australian Newspapers Ltd., in Perth, is divided into library and reference sections under one director, with the cuttings section under another.

Basic structure and operation of most Australian reference departments are quite similar. The biggest job is clipping and filing. The company's own papers are invariably completely clipped, cross-indexed and filed, sometimes under a dozen subjects; so are the principal opposition papers. Because they are the Commonwealth's biggest cities, Sydney and Melbourne papers are the most thoroughly clipped. Not only photographs (and negatives) are filed, but frequently the printed pictures in the world's chief picture magazines, including the American *Life* and *Look*. Half-tone photos made from printed half-tone illustrations reproduce surprisingly well.

Among the notable aspects of individual newspaper reference departments are these:

The Courier-Mail (Brisbane) has a staff of sixteen in its library-morgue. It has microfilm of *The Courier-Mail* and its antecedents back to 1861, and it makes microfilms of documents for outside firms and persons. Individual staff assignments are to magazines, biographies, race records of all race horses, microfilm-microphoto, indexing, historical and extraction of Australian references from books.

About 325 magazines come to the combined library-reference section of Perth's *The West Australian* and *The Daily News*. On the shelves are *Who's Who's* from all over the world, biographies, guides, memoirs, Hansard's. About a thousand files are maintained on varied subjects. A special section is devoted to West Australia. A lending library of about 1,200 titles is maintained.

The Perth papers' editorial research department, which deals with current news, uses a color card system for indexing. The first card for a subject may be red; all others are white. Each section has a face sheet on which are recorded names and dates of everything in the large metal files for that section. "Accidents," for example, are cross-filed under "Western Australia," "Other Australian States," "Elsewhere." Under each of these three are types of accidents: "Motors," "Pedestrians," "Trains," "Water," "Aviation," and so on. All news cuttings are pasted on cards. A question-answering service to readers in this department is manned by cadets; thereby they gain experience in researching facts.

Along with other Australian dailies, *The Mercury* (Hobart) receives hold-for-release biographical material from Australian Associated Press, Reuters and other services. Divisions of its library-morgue are: Reference, Cuttings and Index; Photos, Blocks and Index; Newspaper and Magazines; Bound Volumes of *The Mercury;* Lending Library.

John Fairfax Ltd. maintains a huge library-morgue in its new building on Broadway. Most of the staff hold A.B. degrees. On the shelves are 50,000 reference works. A staff of 17 serves under a director, and between 60 and 70 per cent of the activity is indexing and filing. Its microfilms of *The Sydney Morning Herald* go back to 1831. A small-card cross-index file notes everything in the large envelopes in the cutting files. *The Sydney Morning Herald's* published news index, most complete in the country, is highly prized by all dailies, libraries and reference workers.

The Advertiser (Adelaide) maintains a biography file separate from the general file. A staff of seven runs the department. The finance and social departments keep their own files.

The News (Adelaide), besides its regular staff of five girls and a director, assigns a graded journalist to the library. It is his task to weed out dead material from the files and to maintain a daily log of important news events. This is printed later and added to the morgue files, month by month. Eighteen Australian papers are filed here for two months back. The three most-used periodicals, pictorially and for reference, are *Time, Life* and *London Illustrated News.*

If a reporter for the *Daily Telegraph* (Sydney) were assigned to do a background story on the Suez Canal a morgue attendant might hand him a folder, with the top sheet marked "Page 601." This would mean there were 600 earlier pages in the back files, arranged in chronological order as the story developed over the years. Suez would also be mentioned under "Conferences," for there have been many conferences on Suez; and under "Companies," for Suez is a company. Each file would have the same cuttings. All editions of Sydney's four dailies and three Sunday papers are clipped.

A second division at the *Daily Telegraph* is Reference, which includes all standard reference books, pamphlets, circulars, Royal Commissions' (investigating bodies) reports, police reports and Hansard's. A third division includes not only blocks (engravings), as the principal items, but the master file for everything, and complete electoral rolls. Because voting is compulsory in Australia, these rolls are invaluable for checking names and other facts about individuals. Each state has its own roll.

Australia's daily newspaper library-morgues are very much like those in the United States. They also are alike in a problem no library-morgue director has yet solved:

"How do you get people to bring back the material they borrow?"

5
Rounds and
Roundsmen

"Round" Means "Beat"

The Australian "round" is the U.S. "beat." In both countries the purpose of an almost identical system is the same. The "round" or "beat" system insures continuity, expert knowledge of a field and skill in transmitting the gathered news for publication. It also produces a sizeable percentage of the total news budget.

Rounds are reserved for a paper's most experienced reporters. A good roundsman becomes good from long years on the job; from his carefully constructed contacts and pipelines among the unknown and inconspicuous as well as among the highly placed; from his diligence and enthusiasm for his work.

In this he is no different from his American opposite number. Some of the rounds and some of the contexts within which the roundsman works are, however, quite different. Rounds vary from city to city, also in the way two or three may be combined in one reporter's daily tour of duty.

The *Daily Telegraph* (Sydney), for example, may combine shipping and Navy in one round; aviation and Army in another. Two or more roundsmen may cover the State Supreme, Coal Tribunal, Queen's Square, Federal and Bankruptcy Courts; another may cover Darlinghurst Courts and the High Court (Australia's Federal Supreme Court). Still other courts that must be covered are Inquests, Industrial, Traffic, Licensing, Central and Suburban. The news each round produces varies considerably and requires corresponding attention from courts roundsmen. A chief roundsman may be in charge of all courts coverage.

The West Australian (Perth) may combine in one round federal departments, Returned Servicemen's League (an important news source) and civil aviation. Its sister-paper, *The Daily News* (Perth) may assign a roundsman to weather and radio news, two men to local and police courts, another man to wills.

In Melbourne, one tour is called the Western Round because of its locus in Spencer Street in the west end of the city. It covers state railroads, State Gas and Fuel Corporation, certain other state and city offices, a number of labor unions, Chamber of Commerce and other associations. The federal round in Melbourne includes certain main government offices not yet moved to Canberra.

In Adelaide, between legislative sessions, the Parliament roundsman may do federal and state departments. Adelaide's North Terrace round includes the University, Art Gallery, Museum and other public institutions in the same neighborhood. The Melbourne Express round in Adelaide was once the principal source of news from newsworthy travelers in the pre-airplane era; today the round continues, but it includes the main hotels and the airlines as well as the railroads.

Parliaments are seldom kind to afternoon papers. They like to sit at night, on morning-paper time. And if they do commence earlier, they seldom get into stride before noon and home edition deadline for afternoons may be at 2:00 P.M.

As a consequence, afternoon papers expect little in the parliamentary line. Occasionally, though, they are well favored. In Brisbane, for three days hand-running in 1956 the afternoons took the play from the morning papers during a bitter parliamentary donnybrook over alleged malefactions in a government department. And in Adelaide, editors of *The News* recall the time when a parliamentary roundsman wrote nineteen stories between 2:00 and 3:15 P.M. and "fudges" for the fudge box after that.

The larger papers have radio-equipped cars; *The Sun* (Sydney), for example, has four, plus a walkie-talkie device. With this a roundsman on foot can talk to a colleague in the car and he in turn can dictate the story to a girl in the phone room at the office.

If a lottery is being drawn—big news for any Australian newspaper—one man may be stationed at the draw and another in the composing room for quickest possible conversion of numbers and winning names into type.

However, the principal rounds are the same in all six capital cities. They are police, state parliament, state government, town hall, law courts, industrial, aviation and military.

Some of these merit detailed attention.

Police Rounds

In the Police Administration building at Perth, Western Australia, hangs a Police Honour Roll plaque. It carries the names of thirty-four police officers who have died in the line of duty since the force was organized. The first entry is: "Capt. T. T. Ellis, Speared by Natives, November 11, 1834." The latest is the recent death of an officer at Meekatheera, W.A., in a motor accident. Fourteen of the thirty-four were murdered, manner of death tersely set down as "Shot," "Murdered by Native Tracker," "Murdered" and so on.

Implicit in the inscription are the unique circumstances under which much Australian law enforcement is accomplished. There is still occasional police duty to be done among the aborigines, and it is not without peril to officers; but there were no automobiles about in that early time to kill and injure the constabulary. The difference between the first and the thirty-fourth police death in Western Australia is a measure of the distance Australia has come since her eighteenth century beginnings.

A police story of sorts took most of the front page of the first paper ever published in Australia—*The Sydney Gazette and New South Wales Advertiser*. The lead story of Volume I, Number 1, dated Saturday, March 5, 1803, and printed by George Howe, convict printer, warned masters of ships bringing grain from Hawkesbury to Sydney that dumping excess grain overboard, damaging the grain, or wetting the cargo to make it weigh more, would bring them fines of five pounds that would go "to the Orphans Fund."

For more than a century and a half, from penal colony to free society, Australia's newspapers have published news of crime and of criminals, some of it horrendous. Newspapers in a democratic society have the responsibility of such publication. The purposes of publishing crime news are more or less identical in Australia and the U.S., but the methods by which news is procured and how it looks in print are different.

First off, state population patterns of big capital cities and thinly-populated rural areas make the work of the Australian police roundsmen both easier and harder than that of the U.S. reporter covering the police beat. It is easier, because most Australian crimes are committed, and most accidents, fires and other police matters occur in the metropolitan areas. It is more difficult, because when police news does break in the far reaches of a state, almost superhuman effort may be required to gather it in. No press association brings it automatically by teletype into newspaper offices.

One more difference between Australian and U.S. newspapers is basic. By far the greatest number of U.S. police stories concern municipal law enforcement. Police forces are branches of city government. In Australia, the principal law enforcers are the police forces of the six state governments.

Crime, accidents, fires, disasters—these are, as elsewhere, the stuff of most police stories in Australia, though not of all.

On the reasonable assumption that weather often kicks up a share of disaster, the police roundsman also may be responsible for the daily weather story. In certain cities where courts with jurisdiction over petty offenses are housed in or near police headquarters, the police roundsman does some court reporting.

Practically all police roundsmen include principal hospitals, ambulance and fire brigades in their daily calls. Bush fires and floods in season may come within the police round, and these terrible events have an annual news potential.

Police Personnel

New South Wales, with the largest population, has by far the largest police force. The scope of the police news problem may be suggested by relevant statistics from the *Year Book of the Commonwealth* (No. 45 [1959], p. 631):

TABLE 3.—POLICE PERSONNEL OF AUSTRALIAN STATES

		1957	
State or Territory	*Area in Sq. Mi.*	*No. of Police*	*Ratio Pop. per Police*
New South Wales	309,433	5,043	726
Victoria	87,884	3,709	728
Queensland	670,500	2,491	561
South Australia	380,070	1,234	708
Western Australia	975,920	970	713
Tasmania	26,215	507	647
Northern Territory	523,620	80	240
Aust. Capital Terr.	939	60	652

Total police personnel in Australia is 14,094. Women police are employed in all states. Ratio of population to police officers is about 689 to 1. Ratio of police personnel to area is about one officer to every 211 square miles.

All states except Tasmania employ "blacktrackers," full time or as casuals. These aboriginals, with their uncanny ability to follow trails invisible to white men's eyes, are used to trace missing persons or suspects "gone bush" in the outback. Ned Kelly, Victoria's most famous bushranger of the late 1870's, feared the blacktrackers set on his trail more than he did whole posses of white police.

The Roundsman's Day

The pattern of a typical day for an afternoon newspaper's police roundsman goes something like this:

He rises early. Between 6:00 and 7:00 A.M.—or even earlier— he has read the morning opposition, phoned police headquarters, listened to police radio, and checked with his night "offsider" (relief-man—if he has one), now going off duty.

His first stop may be at the principal city hospital—for a report on accident and violence victims. He may call at or telephone the fire brigades headquarters to check on the night's fires. In Australia fire companies are paid by government in part, by the insurance companies in part.

At the police watchhouse (jail) he learns what crime suspects have been booked and what fatal accidents have occurred. If he has not yet been to the press room in police headquarters he may go there now to phone in whatever he has learned. As with all Australian roundsmen, he writes his story before calling, or so organizes his material that he can dictate each story verbatim.

About mid-morning he goes for a conference to the office of the Criminal Investigation Bureau, source of the biggest news stories. The inspector in charge brings him and other reporters up to date on arrests and complaints.

Two or three stores have been robbed of sums up to £56. A football player is in bad shape after an automobile crash five miles out of town. A wife has been horribly bashed and battered; her husband, a man with a long record, has disappeared; the police are looking for him.

The roundsman gets most of the details of the bashing from the inspector. The rest he will pick up at the watchhouse or at the hospital where the dying woman has been taken. He thanks the inspector, goes back to the press room, organizes his stories and telephones them in.

During the morning he divides his time between checking other police offices and officials who may be visited in person—coroner, traffic, homicide, accidents—and in calling the rounds. He keeps in touch with the hospitals, fire brigade headquarters, country police stations and, if need be, the weather bureau. His deadline for the first edition is about 10:00 A.M. He continues to be busy until the last stop-press deadline is passed for the last afternoon edition.

Morning newspapers are more likely than evening papers to include, on the police round, trials for petty offenses. Most such cases are heard before noon or in early afternoon, when there is no deadline pressure on the morning paper roundsman.

The late pre-midnight-shift roundsman for A.M.'s is the man who gets the pressures. He must work under the gun to get the evening crime news into the office for first edition. The late evening hours of the morning-paper roundsman are, in good part, a repetition of the early morning hours of the afternoon-paper roundsman.

On the other hand, the morning paper's day-shift roundsman may see more of the sordid courtroom climaxes of the continuing crime chronicle than his opposition does. He sits in the press box and records disposition of cases of drunkenness, prostitution, vagrancy, petty theft and the like as they pass under the magisterial eye for judgment.

State Variations

Because of local conditions, problems of coverage vary from state to state.

In Brisbane, the roundsman must cover four main police stations—Central Criminal Investigation Bureau, Fortitude Valley, Woolloongabba-South Coast, and the Roma Street station. Besides these, he makes hourly checks with ambulance headquarters, the fire companies and the Brisbane Water Police. He must keep in touch with four police stations in the outer suburbs, and with others in Toowoomba and Ipswich.

His round extends from the New South Wales border to the Cape York Peninsula and into the Queensland outback. He may report for work and a few minutes later be in an airplane flying to Cairns, hundreds of miles north, to cover a story, or to Mt. Isa, which is even farther.

Despite the state's enormous area, Queensland's criminal traffic is relatively easy to control. Only three mainland routes lead into the state—from New South Wales via the coastal highway or the New England highway, and from the Northern Territory via Mt. Isa. On these and upon all air, rail and sea terminals, the police maintain watches to check interstate movements of criminals.

To a degree, the same is true of Western Australia, South Australia, Tasmania and the Northern Territory. Although Western Australia may be the biggest police jurisdiction in the world, and although it is divided into districts larger than many of the world's smaller countries, egress and ingress are limited to a few places. Its police force of 970 averages about one officer to every 1,000 square miles of country.

Most of South Australia's population lives between the Victorian border and Spencer's Gulf, in the southeastern one-fifth of the state. Besides the few seaports and air terminals, most points of entry are from Victoria and southwestern New South Wales, via Broken Hill.

Tasmanian police have only to watch the air and sea terminals.

Darwin and Alice Springs are the only two towns of any consequence in the Northern Territory (21,135 population). Most of the Northern Territory's police work is done around these two centers and among distant points in the outback. In the Petrov case, when the wife of Vladimir M. Petrov, defecting Soviet agent, effectively sought asylum in Australia while being forcibly transported home by Russian secret police, Darwin was the scene (April 20, 1954) of the world's most dramatic police-round story of the year.

New South Wales and Victoria, with the biggest populations, are the states with the biggest law enforcement problems. In Melbourne, the police roundsman is stationed in the Russell Street headquarters, principal police information center for Victoria. But he must keep in touch with five metropolitan and twelve outstate police districts. Across Russell Street is the City Courts building; and, next to it, the old Melbourne Gaol, where Ned Kelly was hanged in 1880, is now a police garage.

Sydney, as Australia's biggest city, makes the most police news. More reporters must be assigned to police rounds there than elsewhere. Apparatus for coverage must be commensurately elaborate. New South Wales has the largest police force, the most extensive enforcement network. All this, of course, is necessitated by a larger incidence of crime. And in the afternoon papers of Sydney, crime is frequently reported with more loving regard to the lurid details than anywhere else in Australia.

Police roundsmen often use the two-way short-wave radios installed in their own or office autos. Some, too, have mobile picture-gram (telephoned picture) units with which from far distances, they can transmit on-the-spot photographs of police stories back to the office.

In Sydney, the Metropolitan District is divided into four sections covering a radius of 30 miles—North, East, West and Far West.

The Sun, an afternoon tabloid, with fewer hours to operate in than a morning paper, covers Sydney police and crime news this way:

The night police roundsman calls the day reporter at 5:30 A.M. The four night police cars report in after their night shift is ended, at 6:15 A.M. The night roundsman checks their logs and queries them for details about the night's events. At 6:30, the night and the day roundsmen plan the day's coverage and the night man goes off duty.

The day man goes to the Central Intelligence Bureau at 7:20 A.M. The C.I.B. has police news from all over Australia. The roundsman reports at *The Sun* at 8:00 A.M. By 10:15 he is usually on top of the day's biggest stories in time for the first (10:30 A.M.) edition.

The Sun assigns three regulars and two juniors to its police rounds staff, plus two copyboys who answer the office phones and ring the rounds—up to 120 places in the four areas. Hospitals are called for news about victims of near-fatal and fatal accidents.

With the picturegram wagon—also called "the pie cart"—on distant police assignments may go another automobile; its job is to bring in the pictures if telephonic transmission fails. After the pictures are taken, a hookup with *The Sun* office is quickly arranged through the post office and the pictures are in the editors' hands minutes later.

The police headquarters, Central Intelligence Bureau, Courts of Petty Sessions, Charge Courts, cells, lineup and so on, are all in the same general area of downtown Sydney.

From the Detective Superintendent, Sydney roundsmen get a budget of news that may include murder, rape, breaking and entering, fatal accidents, robbery, stealing. Other places that must be checked regularly are the suburban police, Ambulance Transport Board, Fire Brigade Headquarters, Customs, Water Police, Harbor Patrol, Cliff Rescue Squad (a place called "The Gap" on Sydney Harbor's South Head overlooking the Pacific Ocean is favored for suicide attempts), the Consorting Squad (which checks on the movements of ex-convicts and known criminals), Mobile Scientific Unit, Ballistics Branch, Women's Police, Motor Squad.

Roundsmen are well-schooled in the qualities necessary for living harmoniously with the police. They know that policemen are fallible humans, that they respond best to reporters who respect confidences, who are straightforward in their dealings, and who are diligent in cultivating good personal relationships.

An American learns with surprise that only on rare occasions do Australian police carry firearms. They may have them on request and they are issued to police on night duty. But the American cop at a traffic post with gun in hip-holster—much less the American policewoman with an automatic in her handbag—have no counterparts in Australia. In this, Australian states follow English tradition. The reasoning is that fewer people are killed if guns are not part of standard law-enforcement equipment.

The police do not carry guns; criminals and hoodlums know it and consequently generally go unarmed. They know that if they carry guns and are caught, the book will be thrown at them. The reasoning seems valid. It isn't often that Australians read news reports of shooting affrays in their own country.

Like police reporters everywhere, the roundsman has many unpleasant, gritty moments. He deals with people in trouble. He sees humans at their worst, rarely at their best. Sometimes he faces personal danger. He must get stories from people who do not want him to have them, or who do not know what news is.

All these are reasons that a top flight police roundsman is highly prized by editors.

Playing Police News

The approach to police news by Australian editors is about what it is by American. They are perfectly aware that a good crime story builds circulation. If it is a "gee-whiz" instead of a "so-what" story they will give it everything they have; and they have a great deal.

For this, in addition to attracting more new readers and to making the old more interested readers, they earn the familiar charge that they unduly play up crime, and publish too many sordid details.

This is about as true and as untrue as it is in the U.S. Far more material is spiked, or fails to get written, than the public ever suspects. No Australian statistics are available about the proportion of published crime to non-crime stories; and they might prove nothing, or the wrong things, if there were.

If it is not particularly true that the Australian editor "gives the reader what he wants" of grue and blood and passion, it is demonstrably true that the Australian wants (i.e., reads eagerly) what he is given by the editors. If he did not want it, circulation figures would not rise when such stories are hawked by poster and headline.

To one American observer's knowledge, no Australian editor, fed up with the charges of sensationalism and over-emphasis on crime, has ever done what an American editor did long years ago. He published everything about crime that came across the copy desk or over the wires one day and it filled the paper completely.

Then he noted the obvious: that the usual amount of crime news available is about 5 per cent of the total published. He habitually spared readers upwards of 90 per cent.

In Australia—as in any land, including the U.S. where the police protect, instead of persecute, the public—the police reporter stands high on an editor's list of indispensable men. Papers could get along without almost all other reporters and editors and still publish news if the police roundsman stayed at his post. Police headquarters are nerve centers which record every smallest significant change in the peace and tranquility of their respective states. And from the smallest change to the largest—a child with his thumb caught painfully in the end of an iron pipe, the sowing of death and devastation by natural phenomenon or human malevolence—all are police rounds news stories.

State Government and Parliament

Few state capitals in the U.S. are the largest cities of their respective states. Albany, New York, is a dot on the map in comparison to vast New York City; the same is true of Springfield, Illinois, in relation to Chicago; Sacramento, California, in relation to Los Angeles; Harrisburg, Pennsylvania, in relation to Philadelphia, and Lansing, Michigan, in relation to Detroit. U.S. metropolitan papers' difficulties in covering home-state government news are consequently considerable.

Most metropolitan newspapers maintain bureaus in their home-state capitals; but this can never be as satisfactory as coverage on the home grounds. It is a futile piece of conjecture to estimate how much more U.S. citizens would know about their state governments, and how many more scandals would have been stopped before they got started, if more metropolitan papers lived next door to their state governments.

They do just that in Australia. The metropolitan dailies, in every instance, are within a short walk or taxi ride from parliament, premier, ministers and department heads; also as noted, all state courts from the least to the highest. Parliament and the ministerial offices constitute a regular round; often separate rounds; and when parliament is sitting, a small army of reporters can be loosed upon the state's affairs in a matter of minutes.

So many extra reportorial eyes and ears on Australian state government are the usual thing. This is a healthy condition as a deterrent to mis-, mal- and non-feasance in office. Extensive coverage creates increased reader interest; increased interest creates a demand for expanded coverage. It is a circular thing, self-nurturing, and to the citizenry's advantage.

Symbolism can be stretched too far, but it is worth noting that in all Australian Houses of Parliament the press gallery is situated at balcony level above members' seats and directly above and in back of the speaker's chair, in the usual British manner. This may not put the press above parliament in anything but a literal sense. But it suggests the press's role as alert watchman of the state and of the democratic process. Physically, the arrangement affords an excellent vantage from which to watch all that goes on below.

Each desk in the press gallery is assigned to a particular newspaper or news service; and it may have a light signal by which the roundsman may be summoned to the telephone.

Press rooms, with telephones and typewriters and other equipment, are situated off the gallery area, so that roundsmen can be in close contact with their offices and still not be away from their posts for more than a few minutes.

Parties, Ministers and M.P.'s

The federal and state constitutions in Australia much resemble those of the United States, but the forms of government are straight from Mother England. The party system divides principally among Labour, the party of the workers; Liberal, the party of the white-collar person, businessman and industrialist; and Country, the party of the pastoralist, grazier and farmer.

There are sundry small local and splinter groups which, in militant protest against some objectionable policy or person, divorce themselves from these main allegiances. The issue of communism in the labor movement is responsible for certain of these, although no communist holds parliamentary office anywhere in Australia and communism does not at present appear to be an acute political menace, or even problem. Sectarianism—Protestant *vs.* Roman Catholic—is also a factor in partisan schisms. Indeed, it is deeply entangled with the communism issue in a manner to baffle the foreign visitor.

Apart from main lines of class or special interest which determine partisan allegiance, the independent voter holds considerable power in deciding elections. In view of Australia's system of compulsory voting, that power may be decisive in close contests.

In four states, the lower house is called the Legislative Assembly; in South Australia and Tasmania it is the House of Assembly. In all states except Queensland, which has none because it uses the unicameral system, the upper house is called the Legislative Council. Terms and eligibility for holding parliamentary office vary, but most terms are for three years; with certain exceptions usually pertaining to property ownership, members are elected by popular vote. Most notable exception is New South Wales; the Council is elected by the members of the two Houses.

The head of the majority party, or of the most numerous party in a coalition situation, on the state level, holds the post of premier; in the federal government he is prime minister.

Cabinet officers of state and nation are chosen from the majority party membership in both houses, the number of ministers varying from state to state and from a dozen to more than a score. State ministerial posts, among others, are chief secretary, treasurer, agriculture and stock, labour and industry, health, child welfare, immigration, housing, mines, attorney general, public instruction, public works, water supply, forests, repatriation and deputy premier. But no state cabinet is exactly like any other in its organization and titles.

Each state government is headed by a governor, appointed by the reigning English monarch who, of course, is Queen or King of Australia and the other British commonwealths and dominions as well as of the United Kingdom. The state governors, like the Governor-General of Australia, who is also a Crown appointee, have great prestige and much influence but hardly any political power.

In respect to news, however, the most important person in state government is the premier. Next come his Cabinet ministers, the leader of the opposition, other members of Parliament, department heads and sundry other civil servants, following along in no particular order except that decreed by the temporary dominance of this or that phase of government in the news.

Actually, the top civil servant in each department is often a better fountainhead of news for the roundsman than the minister. The civil servant usually has been, and doubtless will continue to be, around longer than his senior; he therefore knows a great deal more about department business and history. But the minister, his boss, is always the quoted authority after appropriate clearance. This sort of arrangement is not unknown in the U.S.

The government roundsman checks the premier's agenda and appointments for the day; visitors are often sources of top-line stories. He sees all ministers daily. Special importance is accorded Cabinet meetings. There may be as many as thirty ministers, civil servants, department heads and other key figures a roundsman must seek out every day. Because the Cabinet is largely of one political persuasion, and because majority party caucuses decide what legislation shall be introduced—failure to pass a major bill may mean dissolution of the government—all party meetings are of basic importance. Nor can the splinter parties be ignored. Sometimes they hold the balance of power.

States' rights in Australia, a visitor learns, are as fissionable an issue as they are in certain regions of the U.S. In one perhaps unimportant sense, Australia is a nation against her will; for she entered federation after long decades of intercolony schisms and jealousies, and with many reservations among important groups. Sometimes the endurance of the old hostilities seems typified by the varying gauges of the state railroads.

One result of all this occasionally morose history is that some state events are more significant than national events. Since most state news is made on the parliament and government roundsmen's rounds, the fact is a measure of these roundsmen's importance.

Question Time opens sessions of Australian parliaments and it produces much significant news. Questions about all manner of state business are submitted in advance to particular ministers, including the premier.

The questions and the ministerial answers are printed in the assembly's journal which is distributed beforehand to the press as well as to members. Questions "without notice" may be answered from the floor or deferred for later reply. When Parliaments begin sessions at 2:00 P.M., questions and answers are about all that can make an afternoon paper's late editions.

Roundsmen are also supplied with printed matter relating to Question Time, notices of motions, orders of the day and other relevant material.

The Speaker, Clerk of the House and certain other functionaries wear wigs and robes, the regalia of the Speaker being the most resplendent. His power is great. He may "name" a fractious or intemperate member of the House and thus effect his expulsion from the floor. He may reprimand. He recognizes whom he pleases.

The mace is the symbol of the Speaker's authority derived from the sovereign people. Its place is at the far end of the long table that divides the government from the opposition benches. It is there only when the Speaker is in the chair; when mace and Speaker are not in place the House is not in formal session. As they enter or depart the Chamber, all members, other officials, roundsmen and visitors bow to the mace.

Roundsmen must combat the usual hazards of reporters everywhere who cover legislatures. There are M.P.'s, M.L.C.'s (Members of the Legislative Council), ministers and civil servants who: (1) Do not know what constitutes news; (2) Do not like publicity; (3) Dearly and unduly love publicity; (4) Have something they want to keep covered up; (5) Have a special interest that is not newsworthy which they seek to publicize in the press; (6) Have feuds to be furthered and who try to use the newspapers to further them; (7) Try to use "off-the-record" as a device for preventing publication of news; (8) Will talk anonymously but not in their own names when there should be such attribution; (9) Are not available when most wanted for news interviews; (10) Are too available when least needed; (11) "Leak" stories to favored journalists; (12) Regard journalists as snooping interlopers, and who look upon public business as their own secret, private domain.

Counsellors to the People

A good roundsman must have a smattering of knowledge about all manner of things; more so than in the U.S., for so much more of Australian business is government business.

The state governments administer the police forces, the railroads, the leasing of lands, much of the mining industry, much shipping and shipbuilding, power and light, other utilities, schools and many other basic activities which are seldom the direct responsibility of any U.S. state government.

Much that is not directly owned and operated is supervised by the state: markets, hours of business, the basic wage, price control, transport, housing, hire-purchase (installment buying) rates, food production, land settlement and many another activity.

A good roundsman develops his own system of pipelines into key places, and pipelines are as important to Australian parliament and government roundsmen as they are to newsmen covering government elsewhere.

Australian parliaments are extremely informal in debate. Heckling is a well-practiced art and its use is as different among individual M.P.'s as the differences between poniard and truncheon, scalpel and shotgun. Many a news story has been enlivened by inclusion of bits of the running commentary on the debate from across the aisle.

As in the U.S., it is not unusual for roundsmen to become valued counsellors and confidants of ministers and M.P.'s. Their long experience in reporting government, their accrued wisdom and intimate knowledge of public personalities and private lives, of procedural details and unwritten history, have helped more than one government official over difficult bumps and obstacles. Behind the scenes the roundsman makes news as well as reports it.

In the great central hall of the Victorian Parliament House at the head of Bourke Street, in Melbourne, the Federal Parliament of Australia sat during its first quarter century. Around the room, in an impressive stride of capital letters, runs this inscribed legend:

WHERE NO COUNSEL IS THE PEOPLE FALL BUT IN THE MULTITUDE OF COUNSELLORS THERE IS SAFETY.

Among the multitude of counsellors the newspaper roundsmen, who hold no office and who are not elected by popular ballot, add their considerable influence to the safety of the Australian people and of the Australian Commonwealth.

Town Hall Rounds

Municipal government in Australia is overshadowed by state government; but constant importance, of course, attaches to the problems of the central and the suburban cities of each capital. The place of decision is primarily in the town hall of each capital city; secondarily in the municipal buildings of the suburban satellite communities.

For each, that is, except Brisbane. Although Sydney is one of the largest metropolises of the Commonwealth of Nations, the City of Sydney proper covers only seven square miles. Melbourne's area is thirteen square miles, Adelaide's is four, Perth's is fourteen and Hobart's is eighteen. These five take their plan and form from London's City and its suburbs.

Brisbane is the only Australian exception. When it became a city in 1920 its limits were set, not at the central business-district boundaries, like those of its sister capitals, but to include the whole metropolitan area—385 square miles. It is perhaps the biggest local governmental unit in the British Commonwealth.

There are many smaller municipal governments, in each of the other five metropolitan areas, for the press to cover; and there is commensurately more in the huge municipality of Brisbane.

There are still other significant differences between the town hall round in Australia and the city hall beat of the United States. Neither police nor schools, as noted, come under municipal administration in Australia. Such area matters as water supply, streets and highways, utilities (although publicly-owned) and sewerage (many areas of the capital cities lack adequate sanitary and storm sewers) are removed from the authority of a single municipal government and come under separate jurisdictions, frequently district or area bodies set up especially to a given purpose.

Similarly with taxes. The revenue-raising authority is largely in the hands of the Commonwealth and state governments. Principal source of locally-raised revenue is taxes on property.

The *Municipal Year Book for the City of Adelaide* (1955–56) notes that the City Council "has authority by Statute to make by-laws (subject to the approval of the South Australian Parliament) for the suppression of nuisances and for all matters relating to good rule and government as regards the comfort, convenience and welfare of the citizens."

It notes further that,

> The principal Acts of Parliament affecting the citizens and the Council are the Local Government, Police, Health, Building, Fire Brigade, Municipal Tramways, Metropolitan and Export Abattoirs, Dog, Bread, Road Traffic, Food and Drugs, Gas, Electricity, Industrial Code, Impounding and Weights and Measures.

These are laws made and administered by the State of South Australia, principally, in effect, for the Adelaide community. However,

> The City Authorities control vehicular traffic, license motor cars, cabs, drays, and other vehicles plying for hire (except tram cars and omnibuses managed by the Municipal Tramways Trust . . .) lodging-houses, restaurants, hide and skin stores, stables, petrol-pumps, storage of explosives, news vendors, horse and carriage bazaars, signs, and street hawkers, and test weights, measures, weighing-machines and weighbridges.

Road, bridge and footway construction and maintenance are also the city's province; likewise parks, garden, recreation grounds, public baths, street lighting; and produce, fruit and vegetable markets. The City Council has representation on many a board of state-wide or national powers, as those powers relate to Adelaide.

In each capital city, the Lord Mayor and the Town Clerk are the civic roundsman's principal news sources. Council meetings supply a great deal of news; and perhaps even more comes from the deliberations and decisions of permanent committees. Adelaide's, for example, are: Works and Highways, Parliamentary and By-Laws, Traffic, Finance, Parks and Gardens, Public Health, Assessment Revision and General Purposes. The last consists of the whole City Council (six aldermen elected every three years and twelve councillors elected yearly), with the Lord Mayor as chairman.

The civic roundsman may have other responsibilities. In Adelaide the round includes the Chamber of Manufactures and the Chamber of Commerce. Suburban councils—about two dozen of them—which meet every two or three weeks, supply news items intermittently.

The pattern of Adelaide's municipal government is in general the pattern of the other capital cities. There are variations; but none materially changes the routines and responsibilities of the civic roundsman. The pattern of government and the public business of each capital city resembles that of the others; and the public business of all six is much like that of U.S. cities of comparable size. The Australian civic roundsman, like the city-hall reporter in the U.S., must be sure that nothing newsworthy escapes his attention.

In Hobart, *The Mercury's* civic roundsman regularly visits—besides the Lord Mayor and the Town Clerk—the City Treasurer, City Architect, Metropolitan Transport Trust, the Library, the Museum and the Post Office. He also calls upon the City Engineer, the Hydraulics Engineer and the Chief Health Inspector.

In Sydney, city officials have no authority over buses and trams, these being under the supervision of the Department of Transport of the State of New South Wales. But the Lord Mayor and Council (twenty aldermen) are responsible for city roads construction and maintenance, building standards, health standards (in conjunction with the state health commission), smoke control, building inspection and other matters.

The four principal committees of Sydney's municipal government are Finance, City Planning and Improvements, Works, Health and Recreation. On an area basis the Sydney County Council, for light and power matters; the Cumberland County Council, for over-all planning, and the Water Board for water supply, are important news sources. Sydney's forty-odd suburban communities are covered in less diligent fashion because they are lesser news producers.

A typical (Melbourne) City Council meeting finds the Lord Mayor presiding in long-robed, fur-trimmed splendor, lace at his throat, over the deliberations of perhaps a score of the thirty-three members (three from each of the eleven wards). In front of him sit the Clerk and a shorthand reporter. The august chamber is full of dark wood and dignity. The press gallery is at the Lord Mayor's left.

The day's Notice Paper contains the long agenda, with each committee chairman making reports which are received, debated and disposed of. In the gallery the roundsmen have a good notion, in advance, of what will be news and what will not. Much is routine, but now and again councillors clash and a story is in the making.

A good civic roundsman sometimes knows as much about what is going on in city government as does the Lord Mayor or even the Town Clerk. And the round will produce two or three good stories a day, or more, for his paper.

6

More Rounds

News From Canberra

Federation brought Australia into being as a new nation on January 1, 1901, after 112 years of colonial status.

Canberra, in the Australian Capital Territory (created as a compromise after bitter dissension between Melbourne and Sydney over a site), has been the seat of the federal government since 1927. Today, the population of the Capital Territory is still under 60,000, with about 90 per cent of it in Canberra. Area of the Territory is 939 square miles, of which the city of Canberra occupies about 25.

Canberra is a planned city. Its American designer, Walter Burley Griffin, who in 1911 won the competition for a Capital plan, projected it as a metropolis of several hundred thousand people. Because it is far short of that, Australians call it in jest, "seven suburbs in search of a city."

A good start has been made in the "search." The federal parliament is still housed in a temporary structure; a permanent, more resplendent capitol remains to be built. There are long stretches of emptiness between business and residential centers. From Red Hill, one of the peaks of the circumambient Australian Alps, many times more trees —eight million in all, exotic and indigenous, beautifully arranged and specially landscaped—are visible than government buildings or private homes.

But Canberra has beauty, charm, coherence, scope, serenity, room for growth. It is the capital of a lusty, growing nation. And covering the news from Canberra is a full-scale, year-round job.

Federal government coverage cannot all be done from Canberra, however. Dozens of agencies, departments and offices are situated elsewhere, principally in Melbourne, which was the federal capital from 1901 until 1927. Two world wars, among other reasons, prevented their full transfer to the new capital.

But Parliament meets in Canberra. It is the official home of the Governor-General of Australia and the Prime Minister. Key ministries and departments are there. Ambassadors, High Commissioners and other foreign diplomats maintain offices and residences there. National party policies are decided there.

Canberra is headquarters for the Commonwealth Scientific and Industrial Research Organization, spearhead of many a victory over grave national problems. It is the home of the Australian National University, with an Institute of Advanced and General Studies, the Commonwealth Observatory, National Mapping Service, Bureau of Mineral Resources, Australian Forestry School, Institute of Anatomy, the National Library, the Royal Military College, Harman Naval Station, the RAAF's Fairbairn Station.

Australia's foreign relations are determined and its national territories—A.C.T., Northern Territory, Trust Territory of New Guinea, Territory of Papua, Nauru, Norfolk Island, Antarctic Territory and Lord Howe Island—are administered there. Canberra is increasingly a convention city and national conventions often make national news. Through Canberra, by plane, train, bus and auto pass hundreds of newsworthy visitors on all kinds of missions.

In addition to all this news potential, Canberra correspondents are responsible for routine municipal coverage. "We have to be police roundsmen when there's a crime story breaking," said one veteran.

The chief concern of Canberra correspondents is the Federal Government, however—the two Houses of Parliament, Prime Minister, Cabinet and department heads. The life of a Federal Parliament is three years and the life of a government is only as long as it can command majority votes in the Senate (sixty members, ten elected from each state) and House of Representatives. The House has 124 members in all, 122 elected on a population basis from the six states; plus one each from the Australian Capital Territory and the Northern Territory, who can vote only on matters affecting their respective sub-divisions.

The Prime Minister is leader of the majority party or of a coalition of parties. His cabinet is composed of about a dozen ministers and ten junior ministers. Certain ministers hold more than one portfolio or post; all are subject to reshuffling. These are the offices as distributed during part of the life of the latest Robert G. Menzies Government:

Prime Minister, Treasurer, Vice-President of the Executive Council and Minister for Defence Production, Minister for Labour and National Service and Minister for Immigration, Minister for Commerce and Agriculture, Minister for External Affairs, Minister for Defence, Minister for Health, Minister for Trade and Customs, Minister for Shipping and Transport, Postmaster-General, Minister for the Navy and Minister for the Army, Attorney-General, Minister for National Development, Minister for Repatriation, Minister for Supply, Minister for the Interior and Minister for Works, Minister for Air and Minister for Civil Aviation, Minister for Territories and Minister for Social Services. Canberra roundsmen have much business with Cabinet ministers; sometimes even more with the civil servant executives and permanent employees of key departments. As on state levels, the official source of the news is the minister, and it is he who is quoted.

Cabinet meetings are closed to the press, but each yields its quota of news, usually big. Because the party in power almost always has enough votes to put through legislation, cabinet meetings and party caucuses affect decisions about legislation that may be all but ultimate.

A number of years ago a correspondent waited patiently and alone for an interminable cabinet meeting to break up. Labor was then in power. "Anything doing?" he asked the Prime Minister after the meeting finally ended. "As a matter of fact, yes," was the reply. "We're going to nationalize the banks."

The banks were not nationalized. Indeed the issue finally brought down the Government. But the correspondent, on that eventful day, had the news beat of the year.

The Canberra Press Corps

Correspondents' offices are on the same floor as the press galleries of House and Senate. They open off long corridors and are equipped with typewriters, telephones, desks, chairs and the all-important teletype machines with lines to the home office. During busy periods, the press offices resemble miniature editorial departments.

There are two seasons in Canberra coverage—Parliament sessions and the intervals between sessions. Thirty-three correspondents make their homes in Canberra. During Parliament sessions the number is approximately doubled. Chief point of their attention, of course, is the House of Representatives, whose membership is divided by states this way:

New South Wales 46
Victoria 33
Queensland 18
South Australia 11
Western Australia 9
Tasmania 5
Australian Capital Territory 1
Northern Territory 1
                            ———
                            124

From press galleries in another wing of the building somewhat fewer correspondents watch the proceedings of the federal Senate. Others keep tabs on the various ministers, some in the Senate but most of whom hold House seats. Australian politics are traditionally vigorous, individualistic, factional and frequently fractious.

Because of this, sharp watches must be kept upon party leaders. Splinter groups, rump movements, intransigence, defections sometimes seem almost more usual than party unity. Of all this the public must be kept informed.

The press gallery of the House consists of two rows of desks and chairs looking down upon the floor of Parliament. One row is directly above the Speaker's dais; the other runs the length of the House at the Speaker's left. There are places for fifty reporters and there is room for standees. The reporters' right to take notes is not shared by visitors in the public galleries.

The correspondents have their own permanent organization—the Federal Parliamentary Press Gallery, with a president and a secretary. The organization is responsible for the smooth running of the gallery, but has nothing whatever, of course, to do with the gathering of news by individual correspondents.

These newspapers have representatives permanently stationed in Canberra, many of them with upwards of a decade of service:

The Age (Melbourne) 2
The Advertiser (Adelaide) 1
The Courier-Mail (Brisbane) 1
Daily Telegraph (Sydney) 3
* *Daily Mirror* (Sydney) 2
The Herald (Melbourne) 2
The Sun (Sydney) 2

* Since the *Daily Mirror's* purchase by News Ltd. of Adelaide, *The News* (Adelaide) and *Daily Mirror* (Sydney) have operated a joint gallery reporting team.

The Sun News-Pictorial (Melbourne) 2
The Sunday Telegraph (Sydney) 1
The Sun-Herald (Sydney) 1
The Sydney Morning Herald 4
The News (Adelaide) 1
Telegraph (Brisbane) 1

Also with year-round representation are these news-gathering agencies:

Australian Broadcasting Commission 5
Australian United Press 3
Overseas Cable Service (Free Lance) 1
* Australian Press Services 1

Australian Broadcasting Commission, which has its own staff of reporters and correspondents all over Australia, covers Canberra as thoroughly as any newspaper. Australian United Press covers for provincial newspapers in the eastern states. Federal News Service is a free lance agency which services certain country newspapers. National News Service provides cover for selected United States, United Kingdom, Ceylon and Australia media. Overseas Cable Service reports for a group of South African, a few United Kingdom, and some Indian newspapers.

Of the Sunday and weekend newspapers, only the *Sun-Herald* (Sydney) and the *Sunday Telegraph* (Sydney) keep resident representatives in Canberra.

The *Daily Mirror* (Sydney) covers for the weeklies associated with it. The *Sunday Mail* (Adelaide) gets its cover from the *Sun-Herald* (Sydney), *The Sunday Mail* (Brisbane) from *The Herald* (Melbourne) and *The Sunday Times* (Perth) from *The News* (Adelaide).

Australian Associated Press is represented at Canberra only by stringers because its only responsibility toward internal newsgathering, as noted in another chapter, is to provide Reuters, in England, with an Australian cover. Reuters distributes its Australian news budget principally in the United Kingdom.

Largest of the combinations which work in association to gather the Canberra news is the Herald and Weekly Times Ltd. (Melbourne) group. This, of course, means *The Herald* (Melbourne), *The Sun News-Pictorial* (Melbourne), *The Courier-Mail* (Brisbane), the *Telegraph* (Brisbane), *The Advertiser* (Adelaide). Subscribing to and participating in its service during sessions of Parliament, although outside the group, are *The West Australian* (Perth) and *The Mercury*

* Mainly supplies features to the country press.

(Hobart) *The Examiner* (Launceston, Tasmania) receives a special service. Mornings and afternoons in this group work in separate schedules.

A longstanding arrangement finds *The Sydney Morning Herald* and *The Age* operating under the aegis of the AAP—a service apart from AAP's Reuter coverage. Until it died, *The Argus* (Melbourne) was a member of this group.

Beyond such formal, regularized relationships, newsmen in Canberra cooperate informally during rush periods, in the manner of reporters the world over. Nobody sanctions it. Everybody knows about it. Reporters from non-competing dailies who work the same shift exchange carbons of stories which broke at the same time and could not be covered by a single reporter. The only thing lost is the benefit of on-the-spot reporting. One such loose arrangement is known, austerely, as "The Club."

It should also be said that there is no member of the correspondents' corps who doesn't rejoice over an exclusive news beat and make the most of it for his paper.

In good part, Australia's federal Parliament favors morning papers, for its usual work hours are in the afternoon and evening. It meets four days a week—from 2:30 P.M. to 6:00 P.M. and from 8:00 P.M. to 11:00 P.M. on Tuesdays, Wednesdays and Thursdays; from 10:30 A.M. to 4:00 P.M. Fridays.

The short Friday workday assures M.P.'s a long weekend. It also gives the afternoon dailies their one news break of the week. On other days there is only the time from 2:30 to the final deadline—4:00 P.M. or earlier—for parliamentary news to make the late editions. On Fridays, the afternoon papers get copy from mid-morning on. However, the two Houses do not always stick exactly to schedule.

Because of the many other media activities of most Australian capital-city dailies, the Canberra newsman's duties go beyond news-gathering and filing.

Are pictures or stories needed for a magazine or periodical published by the home office? Does the boss want a Cabinet minister or an M.P. for a radio or TV appearance? Does a patron, an advertiser, a client or a friend of the paper want a favor done? Is a board member concerned about a bill before Parliament? There are many non-news missions to be performed.

A phone call or a teletype message to the Canberra correspondent will start wheels turning.

Question Time is well attended by reporters, for reasons plain to see. Because the Prime Minister is the chief target, the event is roughly the equivalent of the President's press conference in Washington, D.C.—although the Prime Minister holds press conferences as well. Question Time reveals important facts, trends, events, details. Reporters often plant questions with members in order to extract special information.

Sometimes answers by the ministers become important policy speeches.

A reporter's view of the House from a point above the Speaker's chair is inclusive of everything in the House, except the Speaker. The Prime Minister and his Cabinet officers occupy the front benches on the correspondent's right; in the back benches are the other Government members, in two parallel rows. Still others, along with members of sympathetic parties, occupy the benches at the curve in the room's far end.

To the left is the Opposition, its leaders sitting on front benches. Between Government and Opposition is a long table at the head of which are the berobed and bewigged clerks of the House. The Prime Minister and the Leader of the Opposition often sit at the sides of the table, facing each other.

At the far end of the long table, on a special stand, rests the mace, golden symbol of the Speaker's authority and of the formal sitting of the House. Closest to it are Hansard reporters, silent, effacing longtime functionaries of nearly every British parliament in the world, taking down verbatim reports. Hansard's equates with the U.S. Congressional Record.

At left rear are uniformed messengers who come at a member's summons. At the right is a glass-enclosed booth of the Australian Broadcasting Commission. Parliament sessions have been broadcast since July, 1946. Any Australian with a radio set and a listener's license can hear Parliamentary debates as clearly as if he were present.

The press gallery fills when the Prime Minister, the Opposition leader or some other important M.P. is slated to make a statement, or policy declaration, or to engage in the rough-and-tumble of debate. Informality and blunt speech characterize parliamentary proceedings; so does uninhibited heckling. Yet, most speeches are sharp and to the point. In the press gallery the Canberra corps takes notes in shorthand. When the vote comes, or a break in the proceedings, each correspondent hurries off to transcribe and file.

Australia, a young, vigorous country, likes its politics served raw and highly spiced. Religion is almost nakedly a participant in inter-party fights and intra-party schisms. Australian political parties are that peculiar compound of vaulting idealism, pure dedication, suspicious cynicism and arrant selfishness that characterizes democracies everywhere. The other side's motives are not only suspect, but diabolical; its record is not merely bad, it is mendacious, depraved, immoral.

A recent code of behavior specifically forbids members of the Australia House of Representatives from calling one another such names as assassin, cad, blood-drinker, cur, miserable body-snatcher, sewer rat, gasbag, ignoramus, political mongrel, lapdog or slimy reptile.

But as in the U.S., democracy marches on with firm stride in Australia. No one who has lived under the blinding light in which democracy conducts its affairs would have it otherwise. At the controls of the spotlight, in good part, directing its rays into dark places, is the journalist who reports government.

In a special sense there are no more important persons in Australia than the members of the Canberra corps of newspaper correspondents.

Coverage of the Courts

As in all democracies, coverage of the courts of Australia is a basic function of the press. Some of the capital dailies have staffs of up to a dozen roundsmen and casuals regularly engaged in reporting that lets no important case go unmentioned.

They regard this conscientious attention as part of the evidence that they are "Newspapers of Record." Special pages are reserved for straightforward, methodical accounts of court proceedings. "Law Lists" are published daily which note upcoming cases on dockets in each court.

The Sydney Morning Herald, for example, in its "Law Courts Notices Today" (cases to be heard), includes not only High Court, Supreme Court and others usual to all states, but Land and Valuation Court, Workers Compensation and Apprenticeship Councils. Under a standing head for "Divorce," rulings of "Decree Nisi" are summarized. News stories of court proceedings usually appear on a different page under a box head "Law Courts Reports." These are written in an orderly prose that makes no attempt at drama. Court stories are, of course, often published on page one.

In following much the same pattern in a smaller city, *The Advertiser* (Adelaide) divides coverage among a number of reporters. One roundsman may do the South Australian Supreme Court (one chief justice and six puisne, or associate, justices), which is the highest state court and is second only to the federal High Court. Three or four cases may be in progress in the Supreme Court at one time, all of them important. About seven hundred cases are tried by the Supreme Court annually, and most of them are newsworthy.

Another *Advertiser* roundsman may do local, industrial, bankruptcy and juvenile courts, because they are physically close to one another.

A third man does police courts, three or four of them usually being in session at once, trying minor offenses. All felony cases go to police court for first hearing.

Every Supreme Court case must be mentioned in *The Advertiser*. Of police court cases about 75 per cent see print. Suburban and country police courts and the local courts of the suburban communities are watched by casuals; sometimes they are covered by staff reporters. Perhaps 40 per cent of highway accident cases are reported.

A South Australian law not matched in all other states is a police act which limits to 50 lines of 13 ems in any one issue mention of cases involving immorality or indecency or unnatural conduct. This law is not always followed to the letter.

In all Australian courts, judges have the power to suppress anything they deem contrary to the public interest. They may bar press and public from hearing testimony. They may hear parts of cases in chambers.

Newspapers themselves withhold names of women victims in rape cases. In any sex case the name of the defendant may be suppressed right up until conviction in the Supreme Court, if the judge so orders. Euphemisms for "rape" and "adultery" and similar terms are not usually employed by the Australian press. There is little of this kind of absurdity, not uncommon in U.S. newspapers: "The victim's right leg, right collarbone, four ribs on the right side and skull were fractured, but police said she had not been assaulted."

The Sydney Morning Herald and *The Advertiser* are typical of the morning broadsheets in court reporting. Notable among the tabloids is *The West Australian* for its similar performance on a page about half as large. It lets no case of importance go unmentioned. "The Law Courts" is a standing head for a page of court news in *The West Australian*. Stories of major cases are followed by summaries of sentences for petty crimes, set in smaller light-face type.

Also notable among the tabloids is the *Daily Telegraph* (Sydney), which uses a standing head, "In the Courts," when there is sufficient news to justify it. Announcements of upcoming cases appear under "Courts, Ships, Mails, Weather" in small type toward the back of the paper. A veteran court roundsman checks over all copy—"vets" it—before it is turned in.

Among the broadsheets, *The Courier-Mail* (Brisbane), *The Herald* (Melbourne) and *The Age* (Melbourne) use court stories on a run-of-the-paper basis. The tabloid *Sun News Pictorial* (Melbourne) and *The Age* (Melbourne) publish "Law List—Today" as a standing head, as do other morning papers. On *The Age* a police roundsman covers minor cases in the city courts; a more experienced reporter covers the Law Courts Building round.

Exceptions noted above, the tabloids use court stories on no special page and in no special position, playing up those which best suit widely varying sets of news values.

Tabloids which equate news with entertainment, shock, sex or human interest, with less or no regard for "Newspaper-of-Record" quality may go sled-length on a court story. On Friday, October 26, 1956, for example, the *Daily Mirror* (Sydney) gave its entire front page to a story headed "10 Face Grave Morals Charge 'Obscene Exhibitions' Allegations." On Thursday, February 28, 1957, it similarly treated a story headed, "Found Wife Naked, Says Solicitor," publishing the pictures of the wife (clothed), husband and co-respondent on page one, with the first part of the story. Treatment and play of an identical news story will vary as widely in Australia as it can in the U.S., depending on the newspapers concerned.

Distance, of course, need have no bearing on the play given a court story. This newspaper axiom is as well-observed in Australia as elsewhere. A British physician, tried for murder, may dominate Australian front pages for days. So may a murder with society and political overtones in Italy.

Except for one link, Australian courts are entirely independent of the United Kingdom's judicial system. They are, however, closely modeled after the parent judiciary. There are federal and state courts and courts with special functions and jurisdictions, all carefully defined. The High Court of Australia corresponds to the United States Supreme Court; it hears cases appealed from decisions of the six State Supreme Courts, from the inferior federal courts, and sometimes directly from inferior state courts. The one remaining tie with England is the right of appeal in certain legal matters to the Judicial Committee of the Privy Council of the British House of Lords, the supreme British appellate court; and there is considerable feeling in Australia that even this link should be abrogated.

The state courts vary in name and in function. But there are the usual divisions between civil and criminal cases, misdemeanors and felonies. Inferior state courts are permitted to try certain minor criminal and civil cases; but after first hearing, persons held on charges of major offense are remanded to higher courts—usually the Supreme Court of the state—for trial or for sentence.

In the city courts which have jurisdiction over petty crimes and are scenes of first hearings, stipendiary magistrates sit on the bench. Neither judges nor barristers of these courts wear robes and wigs. There is a minimum of formality and outer show. They may try traffic cases, petty larceny, assault, bail jumping and similar minor offenses. They conduct hearings and bind over accused persons.

In Victoria, a burglary suspect caught in the suburban city of Kew would be taken to Melbourne's Watch House across from Russell Street Police Headquarters, brought into City Court and remanded back for trial in a Kew court. A major criminal case would be remanded to the State Supreme Court of Victoria. About half a dozen stipendiary magistrates sit each weekday in the city courts of Melbourne.

Court patterns vary from state to state. For example, Queensland has both police and stipendiary magistrates, Petty Sessions and Children's Court. Magistrates' courts can hear civil cases involving sums up to £600.

A special legal division, without equivalent in the United States, is the Australian system of industrial "awards." These are management-labor agreements presided over by federal and state courts set up to the purpose. Nearly every job in Australia, as to wages, hours and working conditions, is under the authority of such a court award. At intervals that may be from one to three years, employers, through their associations, and employees, through their unions, if they cannot agree on new terms, file logs of claims with these courts. These are, in effect, bargaining points concerned with wage and hour scales and conditions of carrying on the job.

The case is argued by barristers for each side, with one or more judges on the bench. The court's decision is binding on both sides. Intrastate industries' awards are made by state courts; interstate by federal. Even if the two parties to the agreement work out their differences without resort to open court argument, the court puts its seal of approval upon the result. Cases involving big industry and the basic wage ultimately affect thousands of workers.

These and similar types of litigation are best covered by reporters who are knowledgeable about law, economics, industry, labor and business. In these fields, the newspaper press of any nation is always capable of improvement.

In the higher courts of the Australian judiciary many of the British forms are followed rigidly. The judges wear robes and wigs. Barristers who argue cases wear less ornate ones. The accused stands alone in a dock. Upon entering or leaving the courtroom all persons, including roundsmen, must bow toward the bench.

A press bench or table or stall is provided, as are press rooms in the Law Courts Buildings. Next to the proceedings themselves, the clerk of the court is the reporter's most important and constant news source, although judges are neither more nor less accessible to the press than in the U.S.

The judge's power over his own courtroom and cases tried in it is absolute; and for offenders against his pleasure his contempt-of-court power waits ready for use.

The Australian newspaper press, as set forth in Chapter 9, has felt this power more than once. It is perhaps as necessary for editors to challenge the law by occasionally pressing their cause in situations involving the possibility of contempt citations as it is for the courts to invoke the contempt power. Courts and judges are no more infallible than editors; in the long sweep of time editors have often found it an historical necessity to combat the tyranny of the law, as embodied in arrogant judges.

The jurisdiction of the court begins at the moment of arrest. Nothing may be published that would assist in identifying the accused or that might prejudice his trial. The same principle of care and fairness applies to court proceedings.

A good law courts roundsman can be no novice. He must be a reporter of experience; of objective, fairminded attitudes. He must know law and news values, and he must be dedicated to the production of work that complies with exacting standards. The quality of court reporting depends entirely upon the quality of the reporter and of the paper for which he reports.

Australian newspapers report names in full in law courts stories. Reference is made, in first mention, not to K. K. Kevin, nor to Kevin K. Kevin, but to Kevin Kevin Kevin. In all later mentions the last name only is used. After the first use of a female's name the last name only is also used—e.g., Mary Smith Jones becomes simply Jones.

Sometimes the names of the judge and the opposing barristers are included in small-face type at the end of the story. In continuing cases, some papers conclude the story with the word "Proceeding" on a line by itself.

An excellent aid to court reporting, and widely recommended by newspaper people in Australia, is *A Guide to Australian Law for Journalists, Authors, Printers and Publishers,* by Geoffrey Sawer, professor of law at the Australian National University. Previously, at the University of Melbourne, Sawer was associate professor of law and lecturer in law affecting journalism. The *Guide* is published by Melbourne University Press (1949) and contains a foreword by George W. Beeden, at the time of publication General President of the Australian Journalists' Association.

Through the courts of Australia, as through the courts of other democratic nations, pass all manner of misfortunate persons, most of them present against their will, none guilty until so proved by authorized processes of law. No matter what the offense with which they are charged, or with which, as litigants, they charge others, they have one thing in common. They are all there in court that justice may be done.

Newspapers, through the eyes, ears, minds and hearts of their reporters, chronicle the proceedings. Perhaps harsh criticism of the press is justified for its sometimes lurid reporting of court cases. But by far the greatest number of reporters and newspapers do a conscientious, fairminded job. The excesses may even be a small price to pay—if, indeed, there can be any agreement as to what constitutes an excess.

The Industrial Round

The labor editor or labor reporter of the U.S. daily newspaper has a counterpart in the Australian industrial * roundsman. No major paper is without an industrial round and it is usually a full-time assignment.

A key to the industrial round's importance may be found in a verse over the front entrance of the Labor Trades Hall in Perth. Inscribed there is this quatrain:

> Be Workmen still, to Workmen true,
> Among Yourselves united,
> For only by the Workmen's hands
> Can Workmen's wrongs be righted.

Labor is much more concerned with politics, principally through the Australian Labor Party, or ALP, than U.S. Labor has ever been. Australian Labor grew strong politically mostly in self-defense. Labor Party roots go deep into Australian history. They trace to the beginnings of Australia as a group of free colonies, perhaps back even to the pro- and anti-emancipist struggle during the term of Lachlan Macquarie, New South Wales' far-sighted early governor (1809–22). Macquarie tried, with no conspicuous success, to have ex-convicts, who had served their terms, or who had been pardoned, accepted in the Sydney community of the early 1800's on an equal basis with free men who had no such taint.

* There are industrial reporters and industrial editors in the U.S., but they invariably are concerned with management news. "Industrial editor" is also the designation of the person who edits a management-sponsored employee publication for a large corporation.

Many milestones mark the rise of the ALP. Some of them were: the beginnings of the unions in such groups as the Australian Benefit Society, founded in 1838; the ending of the transportation of English convicts to Australia in the mid-century; the Eureka Stockade battle of 1854 at Ballarat, Victoria, which killed twenty-two men and helped to end an oppressive system of licensing gold miners; the beginning of responsible (parliamentary) government in the six colonies; the "unlocking of the lands" of the 1860's, which changed a system of favoritism to the squatters with huge landholdings, and gave the poor man a chance to buy small tracts and farms; the ultimate exclusion from Australia of Chinese, Pacific Islanders and other dark-skinned competitors in the labor market and the consequent beginning of the "White Australia" policy; the series of devastating marine and pastoral strikes of the 1890's; the triumph of the eight-hour day, commemorated by a remarkable monument near the Melbourne Trades Hall.

These and many other notable events underlie the political strength of the Australian Labor Party. Labor made its first formal bid for power in the New South Wales election of 1891, and won one-third of the seats in the lower house. In the first federal election after Federation (1901), the young ALP took eight of the Senate's 36 seats and 16 of 75 in the House. The second Australian federal government—that of Prime Minister Alfred Deakin in 1903—went into office with Labor's backing.

When Labor withdrew its support, the Deakin government fell; it was succeeded by the first Labor government in Commonwealth history. It was headed by John C. Watson and held office from April to August, 1904.

In 1910, Labor won a clear majority of both House and Senate. Andrew Fisher became Prime Minister. In an essay on "The Role of Labour" in *Australia* (edited by C. Hartley Grattan; University of California Press, 1947), Lloyd Ross, an historian of Australian Labor, wrote:

> With Fisher as Prime Minister, the Labour caucus elected a ministry composed of two miners, a wharf-labourer, a building-worker, a common labourer, a carpenter, a hatter, a compositor, an engine-driver, and a non-manual labourer. Said Lord Bryce, 'For the first time in history (apart from a movement of revolution) executive power passed legally from the hands of the so-called "upper strata" to those of the hard-handed workers. Australia and the world saw a new kind of government of the people, by a class and for a class.' (Page 244.)

Australia has had a number of Labor governments since then, notably during World War I, in the depression years beginning with 1929 and during World War II. Of Labor's political character, Ross wrote in the same essay:

> The Australian Labour Party is both socialist and reformist, revolutionary and Fabian. The emphasis is constantly changing, depending on such influences as the current record of Labour governments, the existence or absence of industrial unrest annoying to the general public, the character of the interparty struggles (with which the history of the Party is peppered), and the prevailing national mood. At times the movement will insist on its policy of nationalisation; at other times it will be content with slow, fractional reforms. Disunity on theory often leads to division and breakaways, but because the Party is the only mass progressive movement in Australia, unity is always regained eventually. Since socialists are always active inside the movement, they keep socialistic ideas current in the Party. Labour has yet to implement its socialist program, but no prominent member of the Party dares to argue publicly that socialist theory and objectives should therefore be discarded. On the contrary, the movement continues to support experiments with socialist legislation. (Page 251.)

Labor occupies the Opposition benches at Canberra today. But two of Australia's six states are administered by Labor governments. Each of the recently-deposed Labor regimes in Queensland and Western Australia had held office for many years.

Australia is one of the most heavily unionized nations in the world. In a 1958 labor force of 3,000,000 persons, 1,811,218—about 65 per cent of the men and 41 per cent of the women—were dues-paying members of 370 different trades unions. The Australian Workers Union, or AWU, is the national organization to which most workers in the pastoral (sheep and cattle raising), mining and other primary-producing industries belong. The Australian Council of Trades Unions is the national body with which hundreds of local unions are affiliated in all states. The Australian Labor Party, the political arm of the movement, is theoretically separate and distinct from all trades-union organizations, but usually its separateness is about that of a strong arm and a human torso.

Merely to state these matters is to suggest the importance of the industrial roundsman. Labor produces news in multitudes of ways and in many places—from statements of ALP policy in Federal Parliament by the Hon. A. A. Calwell, Labor Party leader, to (as recently) a story about a hatters union levying fines against members who went hatless to work.

Most labor stories are local to one state, meaning that most of their components occur within the capital city; to pinpoint it more precisely, most occur in the local Trades Hall.

In each capital city the Trades Hall is a key building, an imposing structure; it is headquarters for many, if not most of the state's trades unions. Within its walls important conferences and meetings are held, significant battles take place and policies and courses of action of far-reaching effect are decided. There may be found officers, staffs and records of many unions. Strike strategy is determined there and strike statements are issued from there; and it is there that schisms develop and are made articulate between various sections of Labor, notably between the Communists and the anti-Communists.

One such splinter movement in Victoria resulted in the dissidents being ordered—officials, staff and records—out of their Trades Union Hall offices. The order was disregarded; and in order to prevent eviction after hours, a man from the rump group slept in the bolted and barred office each night.

Because labor is such a constant fountain of news, the industrial round is no place for a novice. Besides the usual requirements of a good reporter, the industrial roundsman must, above all, have the confidence of the labor leaders with whom he deals every day. Newspaper-hating and newspaper-baiting is a long-established part of Australian labor's public relations pattern. Wherever this passes beyond the usual cliché and stereotype attacks upon "the lying capitalist press" and becomes active and virulent, a newspaper's industrial roundsman must be a diplomat as well as a journalist. Thus, an Australian labor leader may flay a paper mercilessly in public and vilify its proprietor in his speeches, yet—if the diplomacy is effective—still maintain cordial relations with that paper's industrial roundsmen. With this sort of thing, U.S. labor writers are not unfamiliar.

A roundsman who is trusted by union leaders is valuable beyond price to a newspaper; and he becomes trusted only through long years of demonstrating that he can keep confidences and that fairness and accuracy are primary tenets of his reporting canon.

Of about 60 unions in Adelaide, to cite a specific situation, 45 have headquarters in the Adelaide Trades Hall; upwards of 90 per cent of all South Australia's workers shelter under their aegis. The industrial roundsmen for Adelaide's two daily papers call at or telephone about 75 per cent of the unions' offices every day.

Similar patterns are followed elsewhere, with the Trades Hall always the chief center of the industrial roundsman's interest. In Sydney and Melbourne, where most federal headquarters of Australian unions are situated, roundsmen are frequently called upon to cover and develop stories of a national nature. Because of the close tieup between the unions and the ALP, industrial roundsmen are well equipped by background and experience to cover state parliament and government rounds. Many alternate during recurring slack news seasons for each. In speeches and in the printed word, labor leaders, without notable exceptions, publicly hate the Australian press. They attack it in season and out, not without cause, they declare. They charge that Australian newspapers are quick to analyze, criticize and/or condemn even such events and matters as the unions regard as of only "family" concern.

Another basis for Labor's "anti-Labor" indictment against the press is, they charge, that no matter how fair and objective the reporting of labor news may be; and no matter how many favorable discussions and commendations labor may have won in newspaper leaders during previous months, the papers generally end up at election time, supporting candidates who are opposing the ALP nominees.

On the other hand, I found union leaders and Labor politicians quite ready to declare privately that labor receives at least a reasonably fair treatment in news coverage. This was true of officials high in the ALP, of state Labor ministers, and even of Communists who hold office in certain unions they have tried, usually unsuccessfully, to take over.

Many Australian labor leaders have learned how to use the press to their own purposes. They know how a front page blast from them will take away the edge of an editorial damnation inside the paper. They are not, therefore, greatly concerned about the paper's expressed opinion of them, and their private feelings are not always in consonance with their public views. This is not to say, obviously, that the newspapers are secretly well-beloved by labor, for they are not.

Apart from the political aspects, Australian labor news is much like that in the U.S. The key matter here, though, is that the political aspects cannot be thus separated. A Labor premier of New South Wales or Tasmania can speak as the chief political official of the government for all the people of his state. But he also generally speaks as the political head of a political party, with the Opposition well in mind. During a prolonged shearers' strike the premier of the state most concerned did nothing effective about it with the most efficient expertise, presumably because he was a Labor politician as well as premier. Situations like that may produce very big news indeed.

Quality of reporting labor news is about what it is in the United States. Roundsmen are generally as determined as American reporters to be fair, to present opposing views in stories concerned with anything from a mild dissension to a national blood-feud.

There is a similar spectrum of quality. "We tend to go for the glitter," said one industrial roundsman. He meant that drama, conflict, charge and counter-charge were the ingredients his paper preferred. But there is plenty of the other kind of coverage—reporting in depth, backgrounding, fair analysis and perceptive interpretation. It should be that way. A majority of the readers of Australian newspapers are Labor partisans, union members or members of workers' families.

A brief report on labor news coverage and industrial roundsmen's routines is no place for full dress treatment of the Australian labor movement. To a large extent, the history of Australia is a history of the working man, his failures and his triumphs. It must suffice here that he has been, is, and will continue to be the source of much important news in the Australian press; and that as long as this remains true the newspapers will continue to need the wisest, most experienced and devoted industrial roundsmen they can develop.

In the main, that is the kind they have.

Other Rounds

There are other rounds on Australian dailies, and any of them at any time may flare into importance as a news producer.

Paper A may have a regular or intermittent round for inquests, depending on the incidence of crime. Most dailies assign a man to supervise the broadcasting of news over radio and television stations with which they are affiliated. Paper B may decide the suburban cities of its capital need one or more roundsmen's attention each day. Paper C may combine military air force and/or naval with civil aviation and keep a roundsman busy. The University rounds may take the services of a full- or part-time roundsman. Railways and tramways are not an unusual combination.

Shipping, agriculture, state lottery when the drawings come up, the General Post Office (as Australia's biggest business), health, religion, foods, produce markets, commodities, business offices of primary producers and manufacturing associations and real estate, are some of the other rounds among the fourteen capital-city papers.

Perhaps the best way to sum it up is that, apart from the principal rounds, the pattern is that there is no pattern; and that just as the Australian round equates with the U.S. beat, so do the two systems resemble each other.

The Telephone Room

"Do you mean to tell me," declared an astonished Australian editor, "that your rewrite system doesn't result in stories which are grossly inaccurate? How can a man talk a story into a telephone from notes, and expect somebody at the other end to write his story accurately for him?"

Excepting only the American newspaper's indifference to shorthand, adeptness at which is required of all Australian journalists, nothing in the editorial phases of U.S. journalism drew more questions than the use of legman-rewrite teams.

There are no rewrite men on Australian newspapers, not even in Melbourne or Sydney, where newspaper competition is hottest. However, the general absence of competition within morning and afternoon fields is not the reason for failure of the rewrite system to be adopted in Australia. In the old days competition was often fierce and relentless and the chief reason for rewrite's existence—to beat the opposition onto the street—was as present in Australia as in the U.S. In those old days, editors were as anxious to score beats on big stories as they are today; perhaps more so. But rewrite never caught on.

The reasons remain a mystery that my survey could not solve. Perhaps the editor's question, reported above, contains a clue. Perhaps Australian editors knew in advance the legman-rewrite system would not work, so they never tried it. Or if they did, perhaps their fears were justified. One can only guess.

It may be noted here that the system Australian papers use instead of rewrite is not without flaw. That system is straight dictation, down to the last punctuation mark; and disparities in two or more journals' account of the same event, the same speech, the same interview, are as common in Australia as elsewhere. The reason for the differences is not in the means of transmitting; the reason is found in the differences between reporters.

Each newspaper maintains a special telephone room in which sit a staff of girls equipped with headphones and typewriters whose job is to type the stories that are dictated to them by roundsmen on their rounds, reporters on general assignment, sports writers covering athletic contests, correspondents and stringers with important news to be got into print.

The reporter may write out his story first, ring his office and read it slowly to a telephone girl while she types it out on the machine in front of her. Or the reporter may, if he is good enough, dictate it from notes.

Neither way allows for or permits exercise of any editorial judgment on the part of the typist. In the U.S. the final story may not always exactly resemble the story the legman envisioned as he talked his notes to his rewrite partner; but this is not to say that the Australian story is always better. Two reportorial heads possessed of sound news judgment and drilled in accuracy may be better than one.

The girls are extremely accurate. The reporters go slowly, spelling out every name, using A for Alice, B for Bob, C for Charley, and emphasizing every punctuation mark, sentence end and paragraph break.

The telephone room of an Australian daily on deadline for its sports final on Saturday afternoon is a busy place, indeed. So is it busy on other fast-breaking, many-segmented stories. A fair judgment might be that the test of a system is whether or not it works. The U.S. legman-rewrite team and the Australian telephone-room systems appear to work about equally well.

7

Overseas and
Domestic News

Australian Associated Press

Because of her geographical isolation Australia has a special and difficult problem in the gathering of foreign news. Since World War II she also has had a special reason for getting all of it she can, and as swiftly as possible. Japan's drive southward toward the Australian continent demonstrated that she is uncomfortably close to a number of nations in need of space for their expanding populations.

News from all over is, therefore, of real concern to every Australian. By radio, cable, air mail and ship, thousands of words pour into the country every day. Pictures are received by the same means. Australians want to know what goes on among their friends, and they must know what goes on among those who are not their friends.

In respect to all that, perhaps the most important spot in Australia is a suite of rooms at 390 Lonsdale Street, Melbourne, Victoria—the offices of the Australian Associated Press, chief source of foreign news to the metropolitan dailies.* AAP is a cooperatively-owned news service that receives from abroad a continuous flow of world news, twenty-four hours a day, and dispatches it to its member-owners.

These members publish fifteen daily newspapers: SYDNEY— *The Sydney Morning Herald, The Sun, Daily Telegraph;* MELBOURNE—*The Herald, The Sun News Pictorial, The Age;* BRISBANE—*The Courier-Mail, Telegraph;* ADELAIDE—*The Adver-*

* The Australian Associated Press moved there in August, 1959, after nearly a quarter of a century in an upstairs suite at 377–379 Little Collins Street, Melbourne.

tiser, The News; PERTH—*The West Australian, The Daily News;* HOBART—*The Mercury;* BURNIE (Tasmania)—*The Advocate;* LAUNCESTON (Tasmania)—*The Examiner.*

Five members that publish Sunday newspapers—these being *The Sun-Herald* and *Sunday Telegraph* (SYDNEY), *The Sunday Mail* (BRISBANE); *Sunday Mail* (ADELAIDE); *The Sunday Times* (PERTH) all use AAP service. Among the metropolitan dailies, only the *Daily Mirror* * (SYDNEY) is not a member of AAP.

About seventy provincial newspapers throughout Australia buy a basic coverage from AAP, through arrangements with such internal press agencies as Australian United Press and Country Press of Queensland.

About 30,000 words a day, 10,000,000 words a year, at a cost of more than £300,000 annually, are sent into Australian newspaper offices over AAP's 4,000 miles of leased teleprinter wires. AAP deals almost solely in news from abroad. It supplies no intra-Australian news. In this, it differs from U.S. press associations, which bring domestic as well as foreign news to subscribing members. From Australia, AAP sends only a compact daily budget of news to Reuters, in London, for editing and distribution to Reuters members.

AAP began life in 1935. Earlier, Australian papers were served basic foreign news by two organizations, the Australian Press Association and the Sun-Herald Cable Service. The first primarily served morning, the second, afternoon papers—New Zealand as well as Australian. First step towards AAP was taken when the two groups agreed to eliminate their costly double transmission of basic news from overseas. Thereafter, "Comnews" was sent to a single Australian address, and retransmitted by press telegram to the members of both groups.

In June, 1935, the two agencies pooled staffs and resources. First AAP chairman was Sir Keith Murdoch. Administration was vested in a four-man board including two joint managing directors drawn from among the newspaper proprietors. In organization and operation, the model for the new AAP was the cooperatively-owned U.S. Associated Press, although there is no other connection between the two newspaper groups. Policy was spelled out in a "Memorandum of Association":

> This Association of Australian newspaper publishers for the collection and distribution of general news shall be devoted to the ob-

* Since News Ltd. acquired the former Norton properties, *Mirror* papers have used United Press International.

jective of supplying the Australian public with the most accurate and most searching information of all world activities and thought without any tendency toward or opportunity for the exercise of political partisanship or bias.

The home office was established in Melbourne under a secretary and an Australian manager. Branch offices were opened in London and New York. Contracts for use of their complete news files were drawn with Reuters, the U.S. United Press, *The Times* of London, *The New York Times*.

AAP's London and New York offices condensed and edited mountains of words and sent their own file to the head office in Melbourne, where it was retransmitted to member papers.

Later, the Board of Management was expanded to six proprietor-members, including two joint managing directors.

Managing editor, at Melbourne, was and is Duncan Hooper. London editor was W. E. Parrott; New York editor was A. W. V. Kind. Secretary was B. J. Carr. AAP's longtime manager was A. Watkin Wynne, from its inception in 1935 until his retirement in the mid-1950's.

Throughout more than two decades, the fundamental structure of AAP has remained the same; but service has grown in many directions. Its yearly flow of words is about five times greater than it was in 1935. Its coverage has been expanded.

Besides original news sources listed above, its daily file now draws also from the U.S. Associated Press and from additional British newspapers.

Perhaps most notably it began a new relationship with Reuters in 1947. This was a partnership, based on a shareholding in Reuters by Australian Associated Press. AAP supplied Reuters with Australian news, and received from Reuters a more comprehensive world coverage, especially in the Southeast Asia and Pacific areas where AAP and Reuters collaborated in reporting. As a part-owner of Reuters, AAP subscribed to the Reuter Trust, with a representative on the Board of Trustees. It also had a seat on the Reuter Board of Directors. At the same time a similar partnership was arranged between Reuters and the New Zealand Press Association, a cooperative news agency similar to AAP. The Australian and New Zealand news interchange was improved by this agreement.

AAP-Reuters correspondents now cover southeast Asia from Singapore, Bangkok, Djakarta, Hong Kong, Kuala Lumpur, Saigon, Tokyo and other points. Still other correspondents cover the Pacific islands and other Pacific news sources. The closer relationship with Reuters and the New Zealand Press Association through AAP strengthened the service of all three.

AAP operates separate radioteletype channels from London, New York and Singapore. The periods of time during which news is transmitted from these three overseas cities total twenty-five hours per day. London and New York, of course, are the main sending centers and account for by far the greatest part of this transmission time.

London is clearing house for European news; also for news from Africa, British West Indies, the Middle East and as far into Asia as India. New York is the center for news relating to the American continents. Countries in the Pacific area account for a fair amount of toll traffic. News is received in Melbourne by radio teleprinter, radio telephone and cable.

In London, New York and Washington, the AAP shares Reuters news offices. The radio beam from London to Melbourne is the longest in the world in respect to distance, commercial nature and volume of words. New York transmits to Melbourne via San Francisco.

The AAP's London office occupies a small part of the enormous editorial rooms of Reuters in Fleet Street. This is an operation so big that news is sent by teletype from one part of the floor to another, to avoid a confusion of copy boys running in all directions.

A bad run of weather conditions can disrupt transmission to Australia. In July, 1957, during one of the busiest weeks of the year, when AAP sent to Melbourne 6,000 words on Wimbledon tennis alone, sun spots delayed transmission for three hours. When such emergencies arise, AAP transmits to Melbourne through Cable and Wireless Ltd. of London.

In Australia, all wireless, cable, telephone and telegraph equipment and services are leased from the Overseas Telecommunications Commission (a federal government instrumentality with Melbourne offices now conveniently next door to AAP) or from the Postmaster-General's Department of the federal government. Private concerns are not permitted to own such communications facilities.

Forty teletype printers in Australian newspaper offices are linked with the Melbourne office printers or are held in reserve for emergencies. Much of the daily news budget, on its receipt in Melbourne, is punched out on tape, which then is fed through automatic teleprinters for retransmission to member-papers. Tape, of course, reduces the margin of error. AAP's claim is that a news bulletin can be on the desk of the chief sub-editor of each member-paper within two minutes after it leaves either London or New York.

Of AAP's total personnel of eighty, about thirty are employed on the communications side as teleprinter operators. About one-half of AAP's full-time employees are stationed in Australia, the other one-half overseas. The Melbourne office is under the direct supervision of the AAP managing editor.

AAP is a non-profit organization. Costs are prorated among member-papers, after income has been balanced against expenses. The population of the area in which a newspaper circulates determines its financial contribution. Thus small papers are not penalized.

AAP prepares a continuous news budget which is picked up by morning dailies beginning in mid-afternoon and running until after midnight; by afternoon dailies during their remaining half of the news day. Service is news only; it includes neither pictures nor feature stories. Time copy and hold-for-release obituary biographies are sent out regularly to subscribers, however. AAP supplies news neither to business firms nor government agencies, although commercial radio stations are among its customers.

AAP coverage is the basic news. No metropolitan Australian newspaper relies solely upon AAP for its foreign coverage; most of them maintain their own correspondents in foreign news centers. Background interpretive and special articles are supplied by syndicates, by the special services of the larger newspaper combines and by the individual newspaper's own resources. Australian metropolitan dailies could depend entirely on AAP for foreign news, but not one does.

No special services are supplied by AAP. All members receive the whole news budget. There is no regional rewrite or cutdown service, as with USAP. This means considerable surplusage, for news values vary from area to area. Queensland papers, for example, give priority to all world news about sugar production, for Queensland produces nearly seven million tons of crushed sugar cane annually. Sugar news holds a low priority in the other five states. Yet AAP cannot stint on sugar news simply because Queensland is a minority of one. Queensland papers will use it; the rest, if they wish, may spike it.

What is true about sugar is true about other matters. A major problem in every Australian sub-editors' room is, therefore, not the getting of enough news, but the sorting of a flood of it, that it may be reduced to publishable proportions.

Cable editors' estimates on day-to-day use of overseas dispatches, from AAP and other sources, vary widely. AAP purposefully oversupplies its members; but practically everything gets used, in one form or another.

Transmission of news to Melbourne from overseas has gone through three stages. At first, all dispatches came by cable. With the beginning of radio, transmission was by cable mixed with a little radio. Now, news is received almost entirely over leased radio channels. Exorbitant cable charges of the past have been replaced by the Commonwealth press rate of one penny per word.

Communication is two-way between the Melbourne headquarters and all subscribing papers. An intricate system of lights in the Lonsdale Street editorial offices instantly warns of any break in transmission.

The AAP network of world-wide instantaneous communication is as far away from the system of gathering overseas news in the mid-1800's as the typewriter is distant from the clay-tablet writing of the Phoenicians. In its editions of December 21, 1955, celebrating the move to its new home on Broadway, *The Sydney Morning Herald* recalled the pre-cable days:

> Before cabled messages came to newspapers in 1872, *The Herald* used extraordinary measures to get the news first as it arrived from England in ships.
> *The Herald* had a special boat built and a crew standing by day or night ready to move out through the Heads as far as Coogee to board ships and obtain all the newspapers in the ship.
> Its representatives boarded incoming vessels at King George's Sound, Albany [in southwestern Australia], prepared messages during the run across the Bight, and delivered them at Glenelg to a horseman who galloped to the telegraph office at Adelaide.

Boat races and headlong haste overland to get to newspaper offices the all-important English newspapers from inbound ships were like similar scrambles in the U.S. in pre-cable days. All that exists now only in the history books. Today AAP news coverage is fleet and world-wide. It is apparently as objective and impartial as good news judgment, experience, probity and human fallibility can make it. It may even be, as one Australian cable editor declared, that "a sparrow can't have the pip anywhere on the great globe without AAP knowing about it. Of course," he added thoughtfully, "it must be a newsworthy sparrow."

Government has no shackles on AAP. It is untainted by politics or special interest. Its job is to tell the world's story every day to Australians. The distance and difficulties involved are enormous; some are unique. Yet each year its service is improved and expanded. Australian Associated Press does the gigantic job with competence.

Correspondents Overseas

In addition to AAP and other press associations, Australian metropolitan newspapers receive quantities of wordage from other sources, including their own correspondents, stringers and space writers, and from syndicates and newspapers in other lands.

Australian newsmen must be among the most peripatetic in the world. Veteran journalists in their forties or beyond who have not been abroad are almost the exception. This is the generation which went off to World War II. Still, to a visitor the tradition of distant and frequent travel seems a built-in part of Australian newspapering.

It is almost a phase of a reporter's education that he spend some time in the United Kingdom, if not to work in London's Fleet Street, at least to visit what so many Australians—including thousands who have never been to the British Isles—refer to as "home." Sports writers go to England to cover international tennis at Wimbledon, Test Cricket at Lord's; political reporters are sent to prime ministers' conferences and other Commonwealth events.

The United States is hardly less well known by Australians. Many traveled the U.S. during World War II and others were stationed there. One suspects that the nineteenth century Grand Tour of Europe has been superseded for Australian newsmen by a swing around the world with London, New York, Washington, Los Angeles and San Francisco as regular way-stations. Most who visit the U.S. seem to know more about New Orleans than they do about Chicago, St. Louis or Detroit. The pattern is East and West Coasts, either one first, then a swing through the South.

Every major Australian daily newspaper has a news and/or business office in London, most of them in Fleet Street. Although there is always the dependable AAP for basic news, editors prefer their own correspondents' work for background, fill-in, or for more detailed reports of all events with an Australian regional or capital-city aspect. Correspondents also contribute regular stints about Commonwealth and British government affairs, sports, theater and music, seasonal activities and so on, many of these being in the form of a "London Diary," or a once- or twice-a-week omnium gatherum.

These are the London office addresses of Australian capital-city dailies:

85 Fleet Street (Reuter Building)—*The Sydney Morning Herald, The Sun* (Sydney), *The Mercury* (Hobart). (Also Melbourne Herald Cable Service.)

107 Fleet Street—*Telegraph* (Brisbane), *The Advertiser* (Adelaide), *Daily Telegraph* (Sydney), *The Courier-Mail* (Brisbane), *The Herald* (Melbourne), *The Sun News-Pictorial* (Melbourne).

110 Fleet Street—*The West Australian* (Perth), *The Daily News* (Perth).

132 Fleet Street—*The Age* (Melbourne).

34 Ludgate Hill—*The News* (Adelaide).
Red Lion Court—*Daily Mirror* (Sydney).

Still other Australian publications maintain London offices, according to Whitaker's Almanack, 1960, or else share them with parent or related publications. Among these are *The Chronicle* (Adelaide), the *Sunday Mail* (Adelaide), *The Examiner* (Launceston), *The Weekly Times* (Melbourne), *The Bulletin* (Sydney), *Truth* (Sydney), *The Sun-Herald* (Sydney).

On the western shore of the Atlantic, principally in New York and Washington, are stationed other far-wandering journalists. Australians are accredited to the Press Galleries of the United States Congress from: Australian Newspapers Service, *The Sydney Morning Herald, The Sun* (Sydney) and Reuters-Australian Associated Press. In New York, the Australian Associated Press, the Australian Broadcasting Corporation, Australian Newspapers Service, Consolidated Press and its *Daily Telegraph* (Sydney), the *Daily Mirror* (Sydney) and the *Truth* weeklies and *The Sydney Morning Herald* are listed in the United States *Editor and Publisher Year Book* as maintaining correspondents' offices. Certain staffers of the foregoing are also accredited to the United Nations.

International Press Institute frequently draws Australians to its overseas conferences. Correspondents from individual dailies are sent to neighboring Indonesia, to Malaya, Burma, Pakistan, India, and farther afield into Japan and Communist China. When the Suez assault broke, the *Daily Telegraph* (Sydney) had one of its veteran war correspondents flying to Egypt in a matter of hours.

Not one cable editor or reporter with whom I discussed the matter failed to wish Australian coverage of the Far East were better. World War II showed how immutably Australia is anchored by geography to the Orient, no matter how spiritually, ethnically and otherwise she belongs to the West. Criticism of Australia's failure to maintain better Far Eastern coverage ranges from a mild wish for improvement to scathing denunciation.

An economic reason for the difficulty was stated by Sir John Williams at the annual meeting of the AAP in December, 1957. The Commonwealth Press rate of 1*d.* per word does not apply in the Far East. "To send one word of news from Djakarta to Australia, for instance, costs 10*d.* Australian currency. From Bangkok the charge is 2*s.* 5*d.* Charges of this kind can discourage even the strongest newspapers. For others they make direct reporting of events in some Pacific countries impossible." (*Newspaper News,* January 10, 1958.)

Economics, however, is not the whole reason. One cable editor said, "To learn what's happened, thumb through our files for 1946 to '49 or '50 and see what foreign news we published; then compare it with what it has shrunk to today. Then take a long look at the amount of space we now devote to horse-racing."

The debate, along with the reasons and the answers given on all sides, is inextricably bound up with the perennial—rather daily—editorial problem: what the public wants, gets and ought to have.

One conclusion is that no paper, anywhere, including Australia, ever offers enough of what the public ought to be given.

Cable Editor

"Cable editor" is a title rarely used in U.S. newspaper offices. Only a few metropolitan dailies employ such editors. Cables and all other foreign news come along in the ruck of the general telegraphic file. The telegraph editor edits the news from abroad along with the news from the other American states.

Contrarily, Australian newspapers have no "telegraph editors" or "wire editors," the chief of staff being generally responsible for national Australian news. Thus, the Australian cable editor's job coincides with that of the U.S. telegraph editor's only as the latter deals with foreign news.

Indeed, a few Australian metropolitan dailies have no cable editor. Specializing is discouraged; cables are passed about to any sub-editor. Most papers, however, do have cable editors, some with staffs of three or more sub-editors, who sit apart from the main sub-editing horse-shoe desk, so they may work better as a unit.

Cables of course supply a large volume of page one news. Even the most parochial of tabloids, rigorously faithful to the human interest, the sports or the police-round story, will surrender its show-window page to international crisis. Let Suez explode, the U.S.S.R. aim a haymaker at the U.S., or Downing Street face up to calamity, and front pages are not big enough to meet the news emergency. World War II was reason enough for Australian cable editors to have a built-in sensitivity to international crisis.

How is overseas news judged?

The question drew many responses from cable editors: "Like any other news." "On its merits." "How good a story is it?" "It's got to stand up competitively."

A sense of responsibility toward "important" hard news from overseas varies as widely as do the newspapers and the men who edit them. "We publish everything we can get," said one cable editor. "It's got to be even better than local stuff," said another.

How much cable news gets onto newsprint? Five per cent, said one cable editor. Twenty-five out of hundreds of AAP items in a night, declared another. Up to 100 per cent, said a third. Thirty-five per cent. Five to 10 per cent. "Too much has to be spiked." Ten per cent was a "high" estimate on still another paper.

Supplementary material from abroad may or may not pass through the cable editor's hands, depending on its nature. Interpretive stories, weekly letters, background stories, "situationers" from Reuters and elsewhere, are usually the province of the features editor. Much is used on the Saturday magazine pages or on leader pages. Not infrequently, hard news from overseas is rewritten to incorporate background material from the morgue. Royalty gets a far bigger play in Australia than in the United States, and not only British royalty.

AAP and other news services send out, at the beginning of each news day, a list of upcoming stories for guidance of news executives. A boon to cable editors was the penny-a-word rate instituted a few years ago. It ended need for the use of "cable-ese," that tortured and compressed gobbledygook invented to save money. No longer do overseas dispatches from AAP employ such monsters as *offstart, onpress, criticaller, interestingest, Fridayward, upbring, Britgovernment, cordialest, outstraighten*—all in the interest of making one hybrid word serve for two or more. Cable news is now received in formal English, complete with all the articles intact.

In volume, about 52 per cent of overseas news comes via London, 36.3 per cent comes from New York, and about 11.5 per cent from other sources, mainly Pacific area news centers.

Cable news is not changed as much between editions on morning papers as it is on afternoon papers. There is not the need to appeal to the street-corner buyer with hourly sensations from abroad. Morning papers frequently end up with two-thirds of their first-edition cable news intact in the final.

News From Asia

Among top-echelon editors as well as among cable editors I observed a general dissatisfaction with Australia's coverage of Pacific news. One executive called it "appallingly bad," and said he was working to remedy the condition. He wanted more stringers and more travel in the Pacific by competent staff writers. One bar to getting his wish is implied in what Sir John Williams had to say about news transmission costs, in his 1957 address quoted above.

There are, of course, excellent reasons for a continuing expansion of Pacific area coverage. There are, perhaps, equally good reasons that a better job has not been done.

For the first, Australia is thousands of miles away from the main bodies of English-speaking peoples with whom she has most spiritual community. To the north are millions of Asiatics, with whom Australians must live in amity or not at all. It would appear imperative for Australians to know them intimately and to be up-to-the-minute on Asian politics.

The other side is more complicated. News is difficult, sometimes impossible, to get from many Asiatic areas. The "bamboo curtain" of censorship is usually down in China. News-column limitations are a problem. Foreign news must compete with domestic. The small percentage of cable news that appears in print underlines this rather mechanical difficulty.

Finally, there are the cable editors themselves. Editing is a matter of constant choices: this story over that, how much to blue pencil out, what to spike—this story from Peiping or that from London? The pull is toward London. Peiping gets noticed, but a cold in a royal head at Buckingham Palace may get more news play than a démarche by the People's Republic of China.

However, one of the admirable qualities about newspapers is that they cannot remain the same. Cable news space may have declined from its wartime and postwar volume, but coverage grows slowly better, when it might well grow worse. AAP is expanding its services. In his 1956 annual AAP chairman's report, Sir John Williams had stressed that word-volume had increased tenfold in the agency's twenty-one years of life; and had said that particular attention was being paid to the problem of increasing Asian news.

If attitude is all-important, then the outlook is fairly good for more extensive coverage of Asian news by Australian newspapers.

Cables in the Broadsheets

The broadsheets, in general, do better with foreign news than the tabloids, although most dailies of both sizes reserve special pages for its presentation. (See illustrations following page 144.)

Page size is most of the reason for the different approaches. Broadsheets have up to twice as much space in which to present cables—an undeniable advantage. Thus, there is not such an imperative to slash, spike or boil. The cable editor of a tabloid appears to be usually more interested in human interest stories than in hard news. Obviously too, broadsheets carry far more page one cable news than do the tabloids.

The broadsheets make this disposition of overseas hard news, apart, of course, from page one stories and special correspondence:

The Age (Melbourne) puts its biggest play of cables on page four, with an occasional grouping of short items under a "World News in Brief" standing-overline heading. *The Herald* (Melbourne) puts most of its overseas stories on pages two and five. Special attention is paid to Herald and Weekly Times foreign correspondents. *The Sydney Morning Herald* saves page three for cables. *The Advertiser* (Adelaide) usually puts its shorts—"Cables in Brief"—on page four, with major overseas news on early odd-numbered pages. *The Courier-Mail* (Brisbane) groups its foreign news on pages four and five, sometimes employing also eight and nine. *The Mercury* (Hobart) assigns no special pages to world news, but tends to print top overseas dispatches as lead stories on back pages.

Cables in the Tabloids

In the tabloids—with only half-sheets on which to display the news, and unpredictable advertising to complicate the problem more than twice as much as with a broadsheet—cable editors meet their daily space problem in this manner:

The Sun News-Pictorial (Melbourne) concentrates its cable news on page four. "World Roundup" is a standing head used over "good, light stuff," much of it from the U.S.—stories about film stars, weddings and divorces of prominent people. *The Sun* (Sydney) makes its cable news competitive with all other news, on a run-of-the-paper basis. It was believed that more elasticity and variety would be obtained without the use of a separate page or section. The *Daily Telegraph* (Sydney) allocates two pages—usually six and seven—to overseas stories, then edits the two differently.

The left-hand page of the double spread usually carries the general head, "News of the World." Stories are grouped under standing label heads: "United Kingdom," "Japan," "Korea," "America," "Canada," "France," and so on.

News headings are restricted to the lead stories on the two outside columns. One- or two-word labels are cut into the lead sentences of other stories. Stories are edited to the bone, into about 30 per cent of their original wordage. Dispatches may be used from a dozen countries. Also, each day boxed groupings of brief special items are published under such heads as "People," "The Odd," "Today in Science." One one-column vignetted photo—usually a head shot—is run on the left-hand page.

The *Daily Telegraph's* second cable page carries half a dozen stories with conventional headings. The lead story may exceed a column. The paper publishes U.S. United Press International dispatches as well as AAP and special correspondence. In the course of a year, perhaps 20 per cent of all page one lead stories in the *Daily Telegraph* are foreign news.

The *Daily Mirror* (Sydney) uses a single page of cable shorts. Brief items are grouped on an inside page under the general head, "World News in Brief." Most are one-paragraph. *The West Australian* (Perth) puts most of its cable news on pages two and three, using for the short items a "World News in Brief" standing head. *The News* (Adelaide) puts its main foreign news on or near page ten, letting it fill later pages, often with "More World News on Page—" directions to guide the reader. *The Daily News* (Perth) uses page three as its principal cable news page. Short items are grouped under one head. Important overseas stories lead other pages. The *Telegraph* (Brisbane) publishes most of its overseas news on two or three consecutive pages near the middle of the paper.

Photos as well as text require special handling in the tabloid page. One device employed to break the greyness, with maximum effectiveness in small space on cable pages, is single-column vignetted headshots. Boxes—"rules-all-around" or "RAR"—are also an aid to makeup on cable, as well as other, pages.

News from the U.S.

One broadsheet cable editor said that 30 to 50 per cent of all cable news his paper published originated in the U.S., principal news sources being Washington, New York City, Hollywood, though not necessarily in that order. Almost any big story from these American news centers will get notice, often front page play, in Australia's major dailies. But mere publication is not the whole point. W. Macmahon Ball, Professor of political science at the University of Melbourne, is one of Australia's most astute social critics. Before World War II, he wrote in *Press, Radio and World Affairs* (Melbourne University Press, 1935) that "America breaks into the Australian eye only on dramatic occasions—there is no narrative of news to give background." That is the heart of the matter; sometimes background and context are more important than the actual event.

What is the situation today? No evidence can be conclusive, but the comments of three more cable editors are pertinent to the question, if they are not symptomatic.

One cable editor opined that today there is more news of the U.S. published in Australian papers than in English; an index, he declared, of the increasing importance of the United States to Australia. The cable editor of a tabloid said that, in dispatches from the U.S., he looked for rural, backwoods slants; he likes to play up country and small-town tragedies, the odd, the amusing; ergo, the unimportant. Of the 1956 Eisenhower-Stevenson presidential campaign, a third cable editor said, "there wasn't one story worth printing." Except for the outcome, the hard-news aspects, he believed, were not of much interest to Australian readers.

The shortcomings of the daily newspaper as purveyor of stories-in-depth are a perhaps well-frayed tale. Mechanical and human fallibility and space limitations are the villains. To put events of crisis and tragedy into their largest contexts may not be a newspaper's particular responsibility. It is at least arguable. Is or is not the job done when the immediate phases of the event are reported without attempt at depth? Newspapers are not encyclopedias or socio-economic treatises. So run the pros and the cons.

Australian papers are neither better nor worse than the rest of the English-writing press in respect to this problem. To illuminate the point, an American may cite two instances concerning U.S. news.

The running chronicle of integration in Southern schools was played prominently in Australia from the first U.S. Supreme Court decision. Stories about Negro students trying to enroll in white Southern universities, Negro transportation strikes, the use of troops to prevent riots in various Southern cities were duly transmitted by the AAP and other overseas agencies.

But seldom was the larger context apparent—the background origins of the trouble, or the "good" side of the story: the forty-odd states where there was no trouble; the amicable Negro-white relations in Northern schools where no integration was necessary because there never had been segregation. That was not news.

The other event was Washington's role in the 1956 Suez crisis. At best, the cabled stories slurred over the basic fact that President Eisenhower was standing firmly, not as an enemy of Britain and France but *with* the United Nations as the only possible agency to deal with the crisis. At worst, he was painted as an Anglophobe and a bosom pal of Nasser. The implication, if not the outright charge, was that he was intent upon humbling England and France, his country's closest friends and allies; and upon destroying Israel, a nation to which the United States had been midwife if not parent.

If the context had been broadened a little, the President's horns would not have been quite as long and pointed, and his tail not quite as devilish as the Australian press let them and it be painted. Then Australian readers would have better understood what the President sought to do: to make the U.N. custodian of the world's peace, arbiter of its martial quarrels; even to keep it from destruction.

Perhaps the larger context "was not news." Notable exceptions were *The News* (Adelaide) and *The Sydney Morning Herald,* which deplored the wild assault on Suez.

Practices like these are not unique to Australian papers. United States and English dailies do no better in similarly frenetic situations. Moreover, it is a fair question to ask how many U.S. readers—or editors, for that matter—can properly differentiate between the politics of Mr. Menzies and Mr. Evatt; or even say positively who they are. Or to ask how many Americans know the names of the Australian states and their capital cities?

Teletype Room

The teletype room of a newspaper appears to have a life of its own. It is a corner of robot land where the clean impersonality of machines supersedes human function. Flick a button and they go to work, with slow rhythmic chatter telling sombre tales of men, women and governments; of ships and shoes and sometimes sealing wax; once in a while sad stories of the deaths of kings. Attended or unattended the machines jerk out their printed chatter on endless rolls of paper, the world's autobiography today. They will talk on paper until they are shut off.

Australian teletype rooms look alike, more or less; they are compact, functional, from an identical mold; with machines placed at intervals on desks or shelves along the walls. There are three kinds of machines: for receiving only, for sending only, and for receiving and sending.

All are rented from the Postmaster-General's Department, which controls all communications in Australia. Telex, an important adjunct, is a system whereby the P.M.G. can arrange a hookup for direct teletype communications between two or more newspapers in different cities; this cuts down sending time and eliminates the need for retransmission.

Newspapers that supply radio stations with news, or which require several copies of dispatches for their own purposes, use carbon-papered rolls of paper in their receiving machines.

Teletype rooms are often staffed by women, who transmit whatever dispatches are to go to other newspaper offices, and keep incoming copy moving toward the editorial department. Some machines are turned on only for stated periods during the news day. Usually one machine is kept in reserve for emergencies.

The Postmaster-General's Department services all machines. Generally there is a direct line to P.M.G.'s repair service department.

Dailies have direct communication, by teletype—and some by a system of pneumatic tubes—with the local General Post Office, for the quick receipt and dispatch of press messages.

Many teleprinters are equipped with tape-perforating units to cut down on manpower and errors of retransmitting. Machines are sometimes installed during the annual Royal Show in each state for quick intercommunication between the paper and its Showground office.

In the listing below, all teletype machines receive and send messages, unless otherwise noted. Machines are also used by other publications owned by individual dailies.

ADELAIDE:

The Advertiser uses five machines: two AAP—one for receiving only; two Herald and Weekly Times (Melbourne)—one receiving, one sending; Telex.

The News uses five machines: two AAP; Parliament Press gallery in Canberra; *Barrier Miner* (Broken Hill, N.S.W., owned by News Ltd.); Telex.

BRISBANE:

The Courier Mail uses six machines: two AAP; two Herald and Weekly Times (Melbourne)—one receiving, one sending; Parliament Press gallery in Canberra; *Sydney Morning Herald.*

The Telegraph uses seven machines: two AAP; *The Sun* (Sydney); two Herald and Weekly Times (Melbourne); Parliament Press Gallery in Canberra; Telex.

HOBART:

The Mercury uses three machines: AAP; Launceston Bureau; Melbourne Bureau.

MELBOURNE:

The Age uses five machines: *Sydney Morning Herald;* AAP; Parliament Press Gallery in Canberra; AUP; a supplemental unit.

The Herald and *The Sun News-Pictorial* share a common wire room with nine machines: AUP for receiving only; Overseas Telecommunications Commission for Herald and Weekly Times Ltd. foreign correspondence; another O.T.C. which relays stories to *The Advertiser* (Adelaide), *The Telegraph* (Brisbane), *The Courier-Mail* (Brisbane), *The Daily News* (Perth) and *The West Australian* (Perth); two AAP; two supplemental AAP; Parliament Press gallery in Canberra; one held in reserve.

PERTH:

The West Australian and *The Daily News* share a common room with five machines: two AAP—one receiving only; two Melbourne —one for Perth News Bureau and the two papers' representatives in Melbourne, one for receiving only; *Kalgoorlie Miner.*

SYDNEY:

The Sun and *The Sydney Morning Herald* share a common wire room with twelve machines: *Sun News-Pictorial* (Melbourne)—receiving only; two Parliament Press gallery in Canberra; two AAP from Melbourne—receiving only; Newcastle Bureau and relief machine; AAP from Canberra; *Telegraph* (Brisbane)—receiving only; Radio Station 2 UE—sending only; Melbourne Herald and Weekly Times; two Telex.

The *Daily Telegraph* uses seven machines: AAP—receiving only; two U.S. United Press International, the second for Radio Station 2 UW; Melbourne bureau; Parliament Press Gallery in Canberra; two reserve machines.

Daily Mirror—no information obtainable.

A newspaper's bureau in another capital city uses teletype communication which usually does not go through the wire room of the paper in which the bureau may be housed. Best exemplification of this is in Melbourne where The Herald and Weekly Times building shelters bureau offices of eight newspapers, among others, in four other Australian capital cities.

Australian United Press

Unlike the U.S. Associated Press and the U.S. United Press International, the Australian Associated Press and The Australian United Press are not competitors. Moreover, neither has any connection with the U.S. press association of similar name.

The AAP, as already noted, brings in overseas news for the big Australia dailies. The AUP collects domestic news for distribution to the Australian "Country Press," an omnibus term that includes all non-metropolitan newspapers, daily and otherwise. The AUP merits attention in this study because it includes some metropolitan dailies in its service, and retransmits a budget of AAP news to non-metropolitan papers. It also supplies a small budget of Australian news to a British agency.

The AUP was founded in 1932, a merger of smaller agencies. It is a cooperative enterprise, composed of nineteen dailies and thirty-seven tri- and bi-weeklies and weeklies in New South Wales, seven dailies in Victoria, and two dailies in Tasmania. Pony wire service or its equivalent to other non-dailies brings the total up to about 110 member papers. Offices for collection and transmission of news are maintained at Sydney, Melbourne and Canberra. Many stringers are employed in small towns. An interlocking service arrangement with the Queensland Country Press (see below) associates eleven other dailies with AUP.

Member papers also collect and transmit news for the agency. Costs are prorated among the members. A Central Board composed of three members each from New South Wales and Victoria, two from Tasmania and one from Queensland, determines policy. State boards decide local matters. Board members are elected by share-holding newspapers.

The three news offices of AUP operate exactly like those of daily newspapers, except that they publish no papers. Six AUP staffers go to Canberra from Sydney and Melbourne when the Commonwealth Parliament is sitting. They join three men who are there the year around. Sydney transmits twenty-four hours a day, seven days a week, for morning and afternoon papers. Melbourne, with only morning papers on its circuit, transmits from 5:30 P.M. to after midnight.

Rounds are covered in the big news centers. In Sydney, an AUP staff of 23 men is assigned to police, civic, state, industrial, federal, political, finance or general assignment, or to serve as sub-editors. Part-time roundsmen cover aviation, military and lesser news sources. A chief of staff, a news editor and three sub-editors serve under the Sydney managing editor. Another managing editor for Melbourne heads a staff of fourteen news gatherers and sub-editors. There are five circuits from Sydney for New South Wales and Queensland. The Melbourne office transmits on one circuit to Victorian and Tasmanian papers. Canberra's file during Parliamentary sessions goes to all members. AUP maintains no regular news photo service.

The business office at Sydney is manned by a secretary, an accountant, six teleprinter operators and office boys. Cadets are assigned to AUP offices, and the Court Award * under which AUP (and AAP) operates is similar to that of the metropolitan dailies.

A service is supplied to the Northern Territory's few papers. AUP does not go into South Australia, for there are no country dailies there, nor into Western Australia, where there is only one, *The Miner* (Kalgoorlie).

Two of Melbourne's three dailies—*The Age* and *The Sun News-Pictorial*—receive AUP news. *The Herald,* an evening paper, receives none. Part of Melbourne's and Sydney's task is to receive, edit and transmit a budget of overseas news to member papers from the Melbourne office of AAP.

The Melbourne AUP office transmits about one hundred stories a night. A "cut-down" system is in operation at the main sending centers.

Queensland Country Press

Queensland Country Press resembles the Australian United Press, with which it is loosely associated. It is a group of eleven Queensland

* See Chapter 10, p. 171.

and one New South Wales country dailies between Cairns and Murwillumbah, N.S.W., a distance of more than 1,000 miles. Headquarters are in *The Courier-Mail* (Brisbane) building. Every day over four circuits—southwest, central, south coast and north—goes a budget of up to 6,000 words for the dozen provincial-daily members. Overseas news is cut down from a budget of 4,000–8,000 words purchased from the AAP. There are reciprocal news arrangements, not only with AUP, but with *The Courier-Mail*.

General news is sent at intervals—6:10 to 6:40 P.M.; 8:10 to 8:45 P.M.; 9:15 to 10:30 P.M.; 11:10 P.M. to 12:25 A.M. from 12:45 until the wire closes. Between these transmitting periods, member papers send their local stories, convey messages and special stories. In Northern Queensland sugar is important news; in the Darling Downs area sheep and wheat are dominant; in Rockhampton, cattle.

Queensland news comes first with member papers. Like other members of the Australian provincial press, they leave much of the task of informing Australians about foreign news to the metropolitan dailies.

ABC News Service

Australian dailies pay the government-owned and -operated Australian Broadcasting Commission's news broadcasts the compliment of close monitoring. On Paper A a stenographer takes notes for a *précis* to be sent immediately to the news editor or chief of staff. On Paper B the news editor himself pulls a set of earphones from a desk drawer and gives close attention to the ABC newscast. The papers do not like ABC to score beats on them.

It is little wonder. Australians are strongly conditioned to radio listening, and radio news has a vast following. ABC news is on the air nine times daily over the whole continent. It employs a staff of 173 journalists. It has 850 part-time country correspondents. On June 1, 1947, when it first set up shop, its staff consisted of only a score of news persons.

Of ABC's sixty-six national stations, two are situated in each capital city, and in Canberra; Alice Springs, Darwin and Port Moresby have one each, and all the others are regional or country stations. (See Appendix D, page 253.)

Newspaper News for May 16, 1958, called ABC's "the largest news service in the Commonwealth," and quoted ABC's description of itself as "the biggest landline network in the world." The news service is financed from "just under half a million of the ABC's annual income of over £4,000,000 [about $9,000,000] of listeners' license fees." Headquarters are in Sydney.

ABC maintains a staff of ten persons in London, one in New York, two in Singapore and there are stringers in Indonesia, Burma and India. Cable services from Reuters, U.S. United Press International, Exchange Telegraph and Press Association go into the London office of ABC, where dispatches are rewritten for radio and are recabled to Sydney. The U.S. United Press International also feeds directly into ABC from its Australian bureau in Sydney. In 1957, ABC began news telecasts in its Melbourne and Sydney television stations.

ABC's head office is manned by thirty-seven journalists and twenty-one typists from 4:00 A.M. to 11:30 P.M. daily (and around the clock when necessary), seven days a week. Five categories of news —national, state, regional, short wave and overseas—draw a total of about 150 news bulletins a day of five to fifteen minutes.

Charles Moses, general manager of ABC, told *Newspaper News:*

> The Commission's charter calls for a news service aiming at a degree of objectivity not called for in other organizations. And its sense of news values is not expected to follow that of ordinary journalism.
>
> The editorial staff is directed to give a balanced presentation of events and to see that first things come first. For instance, a murder is unlikely to be given news precedence over items of world or national importance. In the selection and presentation of news, we expect our editorial staff to leave final issues of judgment to the listener, and to give equivalent prominence and wordage to all sides where there are conflicting points of view.

To this *Newspaper News* added:

> The ABC News Service claims to be so different from news supplied through newspapers and commercial radio-TV services that it can scarcely be said to compete at all. It claims also to place the news emphasis on the constructive social news of the community and to avoid sensationalism.
>
> For instance, the ABC will give priority of position in a regional bulletin to the opening of a new school rather than to an automobile accident in which three people have been killed. Nor does the ABC News Service report all murders, crimes and accidents. It ignores sex crimes altogether unless there is some special social significance in the occurrence to which attention needs to be drawn.
>
> The ABC claims to set a high standard with its news service because it is not competitive and does not therefore have to be producing news to whet the appetites of the people. As a result of its policy of eschewing the more exciting daily occurrences, the ABC bulletins report many things which ordinary newspapers and commercial station radio news services do not cover.

Commercial stations—and newspapers—understandably envy ABC News its freedom from competition, its ability to keep free from sensationalism and its absence of compulsion to show an operating profit. Moreover, it was a battle between ABC and the newspapers that was partly responsible for its establishment.

M. F. Dixon, the Commission's first news editor (in 1936) told the story in *Meanjin* for March, 1955. The story is too long to be retold in detail; but it began when the newspapers granted ABC permission to broadcast the news they had gathered, and then placed severe strictures on its use—for example, wrote Dixon, one restriction was that "world news must not be broadcast until at least an hour after publication."

So ABC began to build its own service, encountering difficulty at each step. By the outbreak of World War II its success in scoring news beats "made the newspapers angry and aroused their political supporters to decry our efforts on the ground that an ABC news service could be nothing more than a mouthpiece for the government of the day." But persistence, impartial reporting and a constant drive for improvement of service at home and abroad finally won the day.

"The Broadcasting Act was amended," Dixon relates, "directing the ABC to set up its own news-gathering organization immediately. A year of intensive work followed." More full-time and part-time staffers were hired. The London bureau was expanded and "tape machines from British United Press and [U.S.] Associated Press [were] installed. On June 1, 1947 the first ABC News Service news was broadcast.

"It was," says Dixon, "an instantaneous success." Commercial stations presently began to subscribe to the service. The newspapers slowly gave up their opposition to it. So well has it functioned since it began that Dixon can say that "A government-controlled service subject to whatever party happened to be in power would never be accepted by the people of Australia, but a service owned by the people and run solely in their interests is bound to endure."

This big and efficient news operation cannot be ignored in a report on Australia's metropolitan dailies; for perhaps at this moment, a stenographer in a busy Australian newspaper office is monitoring an ABC newscast, or a news editor is reaching into his drawer for his headphones.

Perth News Bureau

Perth, capital of the mammoth state of Western Australia (as big as the combined areas of France, Sweden, Germany, Finland, Norway and Poland), is Australia's far western outpost on the Indian Ocean. Perth's population of about 400,000, and its place as the heart of

Western Australia's economic, social and political life, make it an important news center. But its geographical situation 1,400 miles west of the nearest eastern states capital—Adelaide—makes the problem of news transmission and reception something quite special.

Perth's two dailies, *The West Australian* (morning) and *The Daily News* (afternoon), owned by the same company, receive AAP's regular budget of overseas news. They maintain bureaus and have correspondence arrangements in all important Australian news centers, principal transmitting points being Melbourne and Canberra. Some of these special arrangements are discussed elsewhere. But unique to the great continent is the method of gathering and sending to eastern states newspapers a daily news budget from Western Australia. This service is called Perth News Bureau of West Australian Newspapers Ltd.

Quartered in Newspaper House, with *The West Australian* and *The Daily News,* Perth News Bureau supplies news to eight eastern morning, and four afternoon dailies, to five Sunday newspapers, to AAP and AUP; and, through them, to other agencies. The Bureau transmits from 8:15 A.M. to 11:00 P.M., every day of the year. The News Bureau was begun in 1953. Previous to that time, stringers and special arrangements between individual newspapers had brought most Western Australian news eastward. That year a basic structure and operation were worked out, and they have been in force ever since.

The News Bureau manager is assigned morning-paper journalists from *The West Australian,* evening-paper from *The Daily News,* for the daily routines, and from both papers on Saturday for Sunday-paper news transmission. There is much reciprocal service, news from the east exchanged with the two Perth papers' production without charge; and assessments for those papers with whom there is no reciprocal agreement.

Perth cadets receive some of their training in the News Bureau, principally in news selection and news transmission. News Bureau personnel are taught that speed in transmission of big, hard news is essential; that rewriting for the wire should stress people, not abstractions; that the News Bureau may be the principal factor in telling Western Australia's story to the rest of Australia and to the world; and that the News Bureau's responsibility for accuracy and completeness of coverage is absolute.

Service goes out automatically. Few requests come in for special coverage, but all that are received get immediate attention. Most of the stories go directly only to Melbourne. There carbons are automatically punched out on teletypewriters upon receipt and the stories are distributed to Melbourne papers and to correspondents stationed there, or are retransmitted at once to other News Bureau clients.

A big "W.A." story will make every daily newspaper—metropolitan and country—and every newscasting radio station in the country. The News Bureau develops as many of its own stories, with its own assigned personnel, as possible, but much is rewritten from *The West Australian* and *The Daily News.*

Human interest and time-copy stories are sent out by air mail. The USUPI, and USAP and *Agence France Presse* are supplied with news on request. Reuters gets a special service. Press telegrams as well as teletype are used to move copy routinely. Stories are sent in formal English, with no resort to cablese.

The teletype closes daily at 11:00 P.M., Perth time (which is 1:00 A.M. in the east), but Press forms marked "URGENT" are sent around the circuit for anything later that is big enough to warrant special notice. A story breaking in time for Saturday afternoon papers is rewritten once for Sunday papers and a second time for the Monday editions of morning dailies.

Material from each of the two Perth papers is kept separate, and News Bureau personnel are enjoined against talking about exclusives not yet in print; so that neither *The West Australian* nor *The Daily News* will inadvertently learn, through the News Bureau, any of the other's secrets.

SYDNEY GAZETTE,

And New South Wales Advertiser.

PUBLISHED BY AUTHORITY.

Vol. I. SATURDAY, MARCH 5, 1803. Number 1.

It is hereby ordered, that all Advertisements, Orders, &c. which appear under the Official Signature of the Secretary of this Colony, or of any other Officer of Government, properly authorised to publish them in the SYDNEY GAZETTE, AND NEW SOUTH WALES ADVERTISER, are meant, and must be deemed to convey official and sufficient Notification, in the same Manner as if they were particularly specified to any one Individual, or Others, to whom such may have a Reference.

By Command of His Excellency the Governor and Commander in Chief, WILLIAM NEATE CHAPMAN, Secretary.

Sydney, March 5th, 1803.

General Orders.

REPEATED Complaints having been made of the great losses sustained by the Settlers at Hawkesbury, from the vexatious conduct of the Boatmen by whom they send their Grain to Sydney, the following Regulations are to be observed.

Every person sending grain from the Hawkesbury to Sydney in an open boat, or a boat that is not trust-worthy, the Magistrates are directed to take no notice thereof.

If on proof it appears that the Master of a Boat receives more grain than the vessel ought to take with safety, the Master shall make good any quantity he may throw overboard, or otherwise damage, lest the freight of that part, and, on conviction before two Magistrates, forfeit 5l. to the Orphan Fund.

If it shall appear to the Magistrates that grain coming round to Sydney has been wetted, that it might weigh heavier or measure more than the quantity put on board, the Master will, on conviction, forfeit 5l. to the Orphan Fund.

The Commanding Officer of the New South Wales Corps will direct the Corporal of the Guard on board the Castle of Good Hope to read the General Orders that are marked off in the Extracts to be furnished with, to the Corporal, and the Party that may relieve him; the said Orders are also to be read to the Guard on board the Supply Hulk.

By Command of His Excellency W. N. CHAPMAN, Sec.

Government House, Feb. 21, 1803.

THE Receiving Granaries at Parramatta and Hawkesbury, being filled with Wheat which is spoiling, no more can be taken in at those places until further Orders, except in payment for Government Debts, and the Wheat Investments lodged in the Public Stores.

Wheat will continue to be received into the Stores at Sydney, until further Orders.

Wheat will be issued to the Civil, Military, &c. until further Orders; except to the detachments and labouring people at Castle-Hill, Seven-Hills, and other Out Posts, who will receive Flour, as they have not the conveniency of Mills.

By Command, &c. W. N. CHAPMAN, Sec.

Government House, Feb. 24, 1803.

THE GOVERNOR having permitted Mr. Robert Campbell to land 4000 Gallons of Spirits for the domestic use of the Inhabitants, from the Castle of Good Hope; it will be divided in the following proportion, viz.

For the Officers on the Civil Establishment, (including Superintendants and Store-keepers), 1000 Gallons

For Naval and Military Commissioned Officers, 1000 Gallons;

For the Licensed People, 1000 Gallons;

To be distributed to such Persons as the Governor may think proper to grant Permits to, 1000 Gallons.

The above to include the Civil and Military Officers at Norfolk Island.

By Command, &c. W. N. CHAPMAN, Sec.

Government House, March 4, 1803

ADDRESS.

Innumerable as the Obstacles were which threatened to oppose our Undertaking yet we are happy to affirm that they not unsurmountable, however difficult the task before us.

The utility of a PAPER in the COLONY, as it must open a source of solid information, will, we hope, be universally felt and acknowledged. We have courted the assistance of the Ingenious and Intelligent:—We open a channel to Political Discussion, or Personal Animadversion:—Information is our only Purpose; that accomplished, we shall consider that we have done our duty, in an exertion to merit the Approbation of the PUBLIC, and to secure a liberal Patronage to the SYDNEY GAZETTE.

JOHN JAQUES TAYLOR, At the Back of the General Hospital, Sydney, RESPECTFULLY acquaints the PUBLIC, that in consequence of the reduction that has lately taken place in the Prices of many Articles of common Consumption, &c. is enabled to make an Abatement in his Charges, and that all Orders with which he may be honoured shall be carefully and punctually executed.

Page 1 of Vol. I, No. 1 of Australia's first newspaper. *The Sydney Gazette and New South Wales Advertiser* was published from March 5, 1803, until October 20, 1842; its first editor-publisher was George Howe, a convict. The "Published By Authority" label indicates the official sanction of the colony's governor. Reproduced by permission of the Mitchell Library, Sydney.

Oldest metropolitan daily newspaper in Australia, and perhaps the most dignified, *The Sydney Morning Herald* usually gives the top center spot on page 1 to a large picture, a smaller photograph appearing at the bottom of the page. The day's top story is usually played on the left side. Stories are permitted to run to some length; the make-up shown here is quite typical for the ten columns of the 16½ by 23½ inch broadsheet page. Heads are inverted pyramid or hourglass. A brief fudge box is reserved for late news. *SMH's* individuality is exemplified by "Granny's" column, "Column 8," which is actually in column 10.

With the biggest circulation in the Australian afternoon field, *The Herald* (Melbourne) dresses its page 1 boldly for street sales. Big Gothic headlines, including one white-on-grey halftone; four pieces of art, nearly a score of stories, a fudge box printed in red and five advertisements contribute to a circus-makeup effect. Note absence of flush left heads. Page is 16½ by 23¾ inches, ten columns wide.

The News (Adelaide) uses a number of familiar tabloid devices to attract readers' attention. Besides the cheesecake on this page 1, circus makeup is enhanced by large black headlines, leads (intros) set in boldface larger than the body type, boldface paragraphs in the texts of stories, use of eight stories below the fold and a "Stop Press" (fudge box) printed sideways in red ink. Page measures 11¾ by 16½ inches and is seven columns wide.

The West Australian (Perth) is evidence that tabloids, as well as broadsheets, can be conservative in makeup. Some leads (intros) are set in boldface, as is the Australian custom, but they are not blatant. Neither is the boldface three-line head on the lead story. Head type is exclusively Gothic, even in the white-on-black halftones. With one exception, cross-line subheads are body-type boldface caps. The page size of 11¾ by 18½ inches, is longer than that of most tabloids. The six columns are each slightly less than two inches wide.

Because of the importance of foreign news to an Australia isolated by geography and distance from other nations of the West, foreign news is of special significance to Australian readers. *The Age* (Melbourne), a broadsheet conservative in makeup, reserves page 4 for overseas stories that do not merit more prominent play, and runs one-paragraph items under a standing head, "World News in Brief." Ten columns are printed on a page 17½ by 23½ inches.

The tabloid *Daily Telegraph* (Sydney), with a more difficult editing problem because of its size, reserves two pages for cable news of less-than-page-one importance. Brief items are printed on the left hand page under label heads denoting country of origin, with only an occasional head or one-word designation. "People," "Today in Science," and "The Odd," denote special subject matter. On the page opposite appear longer stories and one continuation jumped from page 1. Page is 12 by 15½ inches, seven columns wide.

Australian newspapers and magazines use posters like this, displayed on news stands and in front of the shops of authorized news agents, to advertise their top offerings. Newspaper posters, printed on special presses, are delivered with the day's consignment of papers. The two-color poster shown here measures 17½ by 26 inches and proclaims an important story in *The Age* (Melbourne).

8

The Feature Phases

A Long Gamut

Feature material in the Australian metropolitan daily press runs the gamut from thoughtful prose on serious subjects to cheesecake and garbage. The leader (editorial) page may carry a long interpretive feature about Australia's immigration program, Russian imperialism or United Kingdom or United States foreign policy. Back among the classifieds lurk crossword puzzles, astrological advice, comic strips. On other pages may be picture spreads, Australiana, human interest yarns, vignettes of history, handyman hints, political and foreign correspondence, science, wild life, religion, nature, gardening, architecture, health, medicine, automobiles, reviews of films, books, art, radio-TV, ad infinitum. There is almost nothing that may not appear as feature material. Except for the straight entertainment units, much is timely and tied in with the day's news.

One reason for the extensive use of features in the dailies is the small number of Sunday newspapers. (See Appendix C.) But neither these newsprint periodicals, nor such publications as *The Western Mail* (Perth); the farm, stock and labor weeklies, and a few specialized Saturday newspapers answer the need.

Neither, for all that, do the weekly and monthly magazines that proliferate so vigorously in Australia. The magazines of largest general circulation are edited for women. Although they are widely read by men as well as by women, and although there is a publication for every taste, there still remains a vacuum for special articles and features. This vacuum the dailies strive to fill.

Both the daily magazine pages and the weekend magazine sections of the big dailies resemble those of American newspapers. Most obvious difference, of course, is in page size and the way it dictates use of space. One broadsheet can print more than twice as much material as a tabloid page.

Editors and Staff

Thus the feature editor—he is often called features editor—is an important functionary. Each capital-city daily has one, either full-time or part-time.

The range of his responsibilities is varied. On Paper A, his domain is "everything except the news desk, sports, society and the leaders." On Paper B, it is only the weekend magazine. On Paper C, features are handled by the chief of staff. On Paper D, he wears the title of assistant editor. On Paper E, responsibility for particular features—supplements, magazine, pictures, leader page articles and so on—is divided among several persons.

Feature editors work closely with chiefs of staff and with their senior editors. The fewer special writers a feature editor has for full-time use, the more he depends upon the reporting staff for local material.

The *Daily Telegraph* (Sydney) has six full-time feature writers, two part-time, under a full-time feature editor who works closely with the editor and the editor-in-chief. *The Herald* (Melbourne) reserves a large room across from the main editorial department for its feature writers—three or four regulars sharing it with the music critic, the drama critic and columnists. The feature editor of *The News* (Adelaide) has no special staff, yet his paper carries proportionately as much locally-produced feature material as any other capital-city tabloid. It is the work of about a dozen senior reporters. The feature editor of *The Courier-Mail* (Brisbane) is in charge of leader page features, Saturday's magazine page and society page features. He draws about 60 per cent of all material used from *Courier-Mail* reporters and special writers.

The feature editor generally does his own copy-reading (sub-editing). He may edit the Letters-to-the-editor column. He works closely with staff artists on layouts and on preparation of photos and other art work.

The feature editor is charged with producing pages or sections designed to suit as many reading tastes as possible. The world—and these days the space infinitely surrounding it—is his oyster. He looks for pearls everywhere. No precise formula for features is used in any Australian newspaper office, but the orthodox ingredients, not excluding the classic "S" trio—sin, sex and sensation—are much in evidence. These are: biography, history, background, exposition, mystery, travel, romance, adventure, "inside" stuff, royalty, Hollywood, glamor, sports, Cinderella and Prince Charming and so on.

The verbal material is liberally mixed with big illustrations, including cheesecake, and is dressed up with bold headlines and typographical devices.

Timeliness

The feature editor can never safely forget that he is competing not only with today's news in his own paper and in the opposition's, but with other media. Television is not the least of these. But perhaps the most formidable competitors are weekly and monthly magazines.

Because the magazines crowd their deadlines with last-minute topical stories and news pictures, the newspapers retaliate by trying to match them in depth-treatment of subjects and in full-bodied feature material. Good background on a man, woman or situation newly-propelled into prominence is expected from the feature editor at a moment's notice.

In London a prime minister resigned suddenly. An Australian afternoon tabloid got the bulletin at 6:45 A.M. In addition to extensive spot-news coverage, the paper's first edition appeared at 11:10 with a full page background story about the resignation. By 9:00 A.M. the story was written, edited, given headlines and the layout arranged. Engravings were ready by 10:00. All was in place in advance of the deadline.

This is done, when necessary, not only on feature pages, but on the leader page. One day word of a crisis in the Dutch royal family junked leader page features as the page was torn apart. A story about Queen Juliana and Prince Bernhard went to press alongside the day's leaders, while on page one a banner head proclaimed trouble in the Netherlands.

If the feature editor has charge of the leader page (except for the leaders themselves), he may supervise the transformation of the page that occurs on Saturdays on some dailies. (See Chapter 4.)

No Columning Clutter

One of the excellences of Australian journalism, in the feature division, is that newspapers are not cluttered, as are so many American, with a rash of daily columns dealing with the asinine, the frivolous and the nauseating. Nor are there any widely-syndicated pundits who will solve all national and international problems for the editor at a few shillings per column.

The evidence is strong that Australians prefer their analyses of events and men, even their chitchat, to be home-written and not imported. There is frippery and nonsense in the Australian press, but it is Australian and there is not as much of it as Americans get from Hollywood, Broadway, café society, Washington, tin pan alley, Las Vegas, Miami and other cultural centers.

The anecdotal-humorous columnist is firmly a fixture; no major daily is without his product and his product is always local. A few specialists ply their trade in such basic fields as politics, foreign affairs and economics, but generally they write for only one paper.

Thus, Australians pay the frightful price of having no Australian counterparts of Drew Pearson, George Sokolsky, the brothers Alsop, Walter Winchell, Westbrook Pegler, Marquis Childs, Fulton Lewis Jr., Earl Wilson, Louella Parsons or Hedda Hopper.

Except for the work of regular correspondents, few overseas commentators are published. Walter Lippmann, Robert Ruark and Billy Graham are among the few Americans given place, and each of these runs in only one or two papers. Because of the strong Commonwealth tie and agreements with United Kingdom news sources, more British commentators on foreign affairs than American are used.

On the other hand, quantities of general material—special articles, pictures (color and black-and-white), cartoons, books, other serial matter and other features are purchased from abroad. Most of it originates in the United Kingdom and the United States. London and New York correspondents are charged to look out for usable stuff; and there are contractual arrangements between many Australian and foreign newspapers.

Because so many Australian newspaper proprietors are also book, magazine and job publishers, the syndicate offices, which all large papers maintain for purchase and sale of material from and to outside sources, are busy places. (See page 157.)

A Week's Run

Many a feature is the work of one person, and is published regularly on certain days of the week. In the composing room of *The Advertiser* (Adelaide) for example, a sign, conspicuously posted, suggests both the diversity and the pattern of such material:

ONCE A WEEK FEATURES

MONDAY. In the Church. Talking Shop. Trevor Smith (London Letter). Melbourne Letter.

TUESDAY. Perth Letter. For Our New Citizens (News and notices about and for immigrants). Abattoirs (Meat packing house prices) and Markets. Motor Section (Autos) and Vegetable and Fruit Prices.

WEDNESDAY. Facing Up With Fatch (Humorous topical verse by Max Fatchen, staff writer). Sydney Letter. Building and Real Estate. Around the Shops. RSL Activities (Returned Servicemen's League).
THURSDAY. Brisbane Letter. Sheep Prices. Readers Are Asking (Questions and Answers). Vegetable and Fruit Prices. In Your Garden. Motor Cycling. For Our New Citizens. Wireless Notes. Films in the Suburbs. Toc H (War Veterans Organization). Weekly Rainfall. Lawyer's Diary (Answers to legal questions from readers).
FRIDAY. Hobart Letter. LCL Activities (Politics: Labour, Country and Liberal Parties, the three principal political divisions). Guide Notes. Scout Notes. Weekend Fishing. Don Iddon's Diary (New York letter).
SATURDAY. Facing Up With Fatch. For Our New Citizens. News from the Churches. Record Reviews (Phonograph). Radio Talks of the Week. Religious Views and News. Book Reviews. Magazine Pages. Books and Authors. Political Comment. Canberra Comment. Fruit and Vegetable Prices.

Another typical pattern is that of *The Age* (Melbourne) which has special features each day: Daily—Magazine Page; Monday—Building Page; Tuesday—Motoring Page; Wednesday—Fashion and Record Pages; Thursday—Radio and T.V. Weekly Program Supplement; Friday—Gardening and "Junior Age"; Saturday—Literary Supplement.

Most newspapers follow some such weekly routine, with individual daily features showing a wide range.

Serials and Short Fiction

Publication of books in serial form is one of the oldest uses of feature material in Australian journalism. *The Bulletin,** that rugged and remarkable weekly begun in 1880, brought many new authors to the light of first publication; and so did other magazines. However, many an Australian classic first took printers' ink on the newsprint of daily newspapers. One of the more notable was *Robbery Under Arms* by Rolf Boldrewood, first published in 1880 in *The Sydney Mail,* then an adjunct of *The Sydney Morning Herald.*

To this day, *The Sydney Morning Herald* continues its fiction discoveries in its literary competitions. The 1957 winners were (first place) *The Middle Way,* by John McGhee, a story of the Australian business world, and (second place) *The Sunlit Plain,* a tale of skin and hide-buyers in the dry, hot outback, by H. D. Williamson.

Among previous major award winners (up to $2,000) have been *The Harp in the South* by Ruth Park; *High Valley* by Mr. and Mrs. George Johnston; *You Can't See Around Corners* by Jon Cleary;

* Purchased in 1960 by Australian Consolidated Press and merged with *Observer* early in 1961.

Sowers of the Wind and *The Ridge and the River* by T. A. Hungerford; *I Camp Here* by Mrs. E. M. Job; *Gold in the Streets* by D'Arcy Niland and *Return Via Canterbury* by Barbara Jefferis. Poetry and short stories are included in *The Sydney Morning Herald* literary competitions. Prizes are awarded from a fund of £30,000 set aside by the proprietors "to stimulate development of Australian Art and Literature."

During the thirteen-months' period of this study, major Australian dailies served up several full-length reprint tomes or condensations thereof. Among these were Sir Winston Churchill's *History of the English-Speaking Peoples, Journey Into Space* by Charles Chilton, Lord Alanbrooke's World War II Memoirs, David Howarth's *We Die Alone,* Howard Brown's *Thin Air,* a mystery story; J. M. Scott's *Sea Wyf and Biscuit,* Petrov's *Empire of Fear* and Gen. Courtney Whitney's book on General Douglas MacArthur.

Serials have been used to impressive effect. Christmas, height of the hot summer, is the circulation fall-off season for newspapers. It is between school terms. People go holidaying and drop their newspaper subscriptions while away. During one of these slack periods, *The Sun News Pictorial* (Melbourne) added 55,000 above its usual slack-season figure, by serial publication of an exciting piece of fiction.

Short stories are published in all dailies, either regularly or sporadically. This practice, too, is of long duration. The Oxford University Press World's Classics collection, *Australian Short Stories* (1951: London, New York, Melbourne) covering a span of half a century, includes fiction pieces first published in *The Argus* (Melbourne), *The Sydney Morning Herald* and *The Sun* (Melbourne). Both reprints and new stories are published by Australian dailies today.

All Kinds of Supplements

Supplements proliferate in the metropolitan papers. They appear sporadically and are usually tied in with advertising. Refrigeration, camping, air transportation, tourism, Boy Scouts, anniversaries, new buildings, historic occasions—almost any field, business or activity that uses advertising is a potential subject for a supplement.

Some supplements are superb. Some are produced without regard for advertising. Many perform a real public service and are worth preserving as reference material. Others are only too plainly slapdash jobs, with the money motive blatant.

The *Daily Telegraph* (Sydney) is one of only a few papers with a special supplements editor and a staff of writers.

Supplements editors sometimes feel strongly that they are given too little time by the advertising department to build material for a supplement. An editor may also feel that his stories, tailored to fit the ads, are regarded by the business office only as a necessary nuisance to the supplement's income-producing purpose.

In its twenty-fifth anniversary issue, *Newspaper News* spoke of supplements publication extending back to the 1920's. It declared that "the supplement field has hardly been scratched and there is every prospect that the current revival of this form of presentation may stimulate its development and lead to many surprising innovations in the next decade."

During the twenties, it continued, many supplements "were based on the booming constructional activity of the period. Every new skyscraper, block of flats, bridge and factory" was occasion for a supplement, "backed by the advertising of firms which had taken part in the construction."

By 1952, they were back in full swing after a wartime disappearance. "Newspapers used them to increase revenue and hold circulations; advertisers found them more useful than ever to push sales at a time when trading conditions were difficult."

Most are published in tabloid size today. "Biggest money spinners . . . have usually been in retail shopping, furnishing, construction and homemaker fields. Big industries like radio, motors, electrical goods, sportsgoods and theatres have also benefited from supplement promotions."

Nowadays, the article concluded, principal non-advertising supplements that appear regularly are "complete one-issue novels, turf guides, weekly news reviews, women's supplements, Sunday and daily comic sections." In sum, "Dailies which have built up solid circulations on their reputation for spot news coverage have found supplements useful to develop general home readership and to attract the attention of the business world."

Australian newspaper executives occasionally wonder in print whether supplements-for-advertising have not been overdone. Meanwhile, supplements keep on appearing in the Australian newspaper press. Not as extra sections of Sunday papers but as editorial matter supported by directly related advertising, supplements are far more a firmly affixed adjunct to Australian dailies than to American.

Young Readers

Young readers receive special attention from Australian dailies. Editors run special features for children and some maintain special departments by which they seek to build a lifelong reading habit for the newspaper. *The Age* (Melbourne), for example, runs a "Junior Age" department every Friday.

"Young Sun," which daily fills a page of *The Sun News Pictorial* (Melbourne) is one of the more impressive. Much of it is written by the young readers and it publishes their art work. Subject range is wide, with much attention given to science, Australian history and lore, etiquette, how-to-do and how-to-make. Primary target is the teen-age set. Occasionally a whole page of letters from young readers is published.

Movies and Theatres

Film reviews are part of the expected journalistic pattern since movies are still very popular despite the strong impact of television. About 90 per cent of the films shown in Australia are U.S. made. Reviews appear in nearly all capital-city dailies, although *The West Australian* and *The Daily News* (Perth) are exceptions. Both dailies dropped film reviews some time ago. James E. Macartney, managing editor, reasoned that most movies were of a monotonously predictable pattern; therefore, reviews were not worth the newsprint required to print them. The decision occasioned wounds and no casualties. Moviegoers became used to figuring out the type of movie from the ads. However, movies of an off-beat nature, or a special interest continued to be given notices.

The entertainment departments of nearly all other major papers publish movie reviews and news in flood. Most Australians are as familiar with the home life, family life, love life and movie life of their heroes and heroines as is the average pap-fed, glamor-struck American movie fan.

The legitimate theatre, of course, gets special attention. No paper is without its drama critic; and some of the critics, for competence, could move in the most exclusive critical circles anywhere, and feel quite at home.

In respect to the theatre, Australia is in a position not unlike that of the U.S. hinterland. It is no ferment of drama activity. Mainly, it takes what Broadway and the London stage offer. But Australia's great distance from both the U.S. and England means, among other things, that the best, and the second-best get onto capital-city stages; and that Australians are spared the worst.

Many seasons are spiced, moreover, with something new in Australiana. It may be, as in the mid-1950's, *Ned Kelly,* by Douglas Stewart, a drama of the Australian folk-hero; or *The Summer of the Seventeenth Doll,* Ray Lawler's exciting story of Queensland sugar-cane-cutters on holiday in Melbourne. Or something like the birth of the Elizabethan Theatre Trust, a subsidized venture in theatre altruism. With each success, the newspaper critics have something new to hail, and each failure gives them something new to dissect, analyze and mourn, before burial.

Books and Book Reviews

Books are foundries for the forging of ideas in any civilized society, and newspapers are heavily obligated to be interested in ideas as much as they are in news. Indeed, the biggest news is often ideas and the people who hold them.

The Australian press—newspapers, magazines and the radio—is generous with space given to books, authors and to literary discussions. Few capital-city dailies are without at least a once-a-week corner, column or section. Book reviews and news are regularly broadcast. Australian editors, obviously, do not expect a book page or column or section to "pay for itself in advertising," the excuse which many American newspaper publishers and editors use for giving scant attention to books.

Especially notable are the book pages of the *Daily Telegraph* (Sydney), *The Herald* (Melbourne), *The Courier-Mail* (Brisbane), *The Advertiser* (Adelaide), *The News* (Adelaide) and *The Mercury* (Hobart). Perhaps foremost among them are *The Age* (Melbourne) and *The Sydney Morning Herald*. Every Saturday, these dailies produce, with dignity and éclat, two of the biggest daily editions in Australia. They are heavy with classified advertisements, features and news, roughly in that order by volume. The 40 to 50 (of about 64) pages of classifieds are their monetary treasure; but the literary pages are their pride. Discussions and reviews are not confined to books. An issue may review as many as a dozen works of fiction and nonfiction, and may "notice" others. But the supplement and adjacent pages carry articles and essays of timeless interest, which deal with almost any subject under the sun, Australian and British preferred. The papers provide two of a limited number of platforms in Australia where a writer may develop a theme with some leisure and elbow room. Wit, grace, eloquence, the turn of a phrase and other often-neglected writing qualities are invited.

The Australian literary editor farms out the incoming volumes to staffers and to outside reviewers, accepts occasional unsolicited contributions, edits and lays out the section with its reviews, special pieces and columns—of which there are three or four, including drama, radio and other arts.

A few other literary sections occasionally come up to *The Age* and *The Sydney Morning Herald* in quality and diversity, but none would seriously challenge the top London literary supplements. In respect to the whole product, however, Australian book reviewing is of good quality—sometimes of superlative.

A Tabloid Page of History

In a discussion of the rise of features in Australian newspapers, A. H. Chisholm, in his article on "Newspapers" in *The Australian Encyclopedia,* had this to say:

> More substantial features have included, and still include, the life-stories of notable (or notorious) persons, fictional serials, and special articles of many kinds.
>
> In the early 1940s a Sydney evening newspaper of the "brisk" type, *The Daily Mirror,* experimented by giving each day a whole page to an article on an historical or semi-historical subject (with at times a story of crime interpolated), and rather to the surprise of the promoters, when these were discarded there were so many protests that it became necessary to re-introduce them. Subsequently the editors of various other metropolitan papers, realizing that well-written articles of the kind exercise popular appeal, have adopted a similar policy. An incidental consideration is that this development disposed of the impression that such articles were suited only to periodicals or Sunday newspapers.

The *Daily Mirror's* "culture page" is sold to others. In Melbourne it appears in *The Herald* as "Byways of History."

Comic Strips

The long shadow of "The Yellow Kid," which in New York of the 1890's started it all, extends to the cities of Australia. Comic strips are as firmly a part of Australian journalism as black ink or lottery results. They are published not only in the big newspapers, but in the small ones, in magazines and as comic books, that ultimate flowering of the comics art-form.

Because of its population distribution, Australia is not an especially happy hunting ground for the comic-strip artist. Six major papers—one to each capital city—are about the most he can hope for among the metropolitan dailies; for first-run rights are, of course, exclusive in each circulation area.

In point of fact, only one strip enjoys that special place. "Blondie" (or "Dagwood" as it is occasionally titled) by Chic Young, appears daily in six capital-city papers. Apparently the frustrations of the harassed Dagwood are not solely American, but universal.

Two strips are available to readers in five capitals—"The Potts," of English origin, and "Bluey and Curley," Australian. Like "Blondie," "The Potts" is a family type of strip. Bluey and Curley are indigenous cobbers who go to the races, spark the girls and generally reflect the Australian male's interests comically.

"Pop," "The Heart of Juliet Jones," "Wally and the Major" (Australian), "Us Girls" (single panel: Australian) appear in four capitals. "Twin Earths," "Suzy," "Little Eve," "The Saint," "Martha Wayne," "Joe Palooka," "Li'l Abner," "Mandrake the Magician" each have place in three capital dailies.

Thirteen other comic strips appear in two papers each and thirty-six more appear in only one. Besides these sixty-four, still other strips are published in the Sunday newspapers, weekend weeklies and in scores of smaller newspapers and magazines.

Perhaps most remarkable of all is the presence of Pogo in the *Daily Telegraph* (Sydney). The Okefenokee idiom of the dreamy Georgia possum and his incredible chums most certainly baffles some Australians. But the *Daily Telegraph* management spares them only in the untranslatable sequences that deal with presidential campaigns and other unexportable or esoteric U.S. phenomena. In perhaps a reciprocal gesture, Walt Kelly occasionally admits to the swampy strip some wonderfully vocal Australian fauna, notably a bandicoot and an old man kangaroo.

The date of the introduction of the first blown-in-the-bottle daily comic strip to Australian journalism is beyond the purview of this study. But an average of eight strips to a major paper—*The Mercury* (Hobart) carries only three, the least of any in Australia—suggests that Australian editors seek to advance readership by pictorial humor and adventure as well as by other means.

Sunday Features

Australian Sunday newspapers run heavily to features of all kinds. Comic sections are included in all of them, although only *The Sunday Mail* (Brisbane) prints comics in color. Other Sunday papers tried color, but returned to black-and-white because editors felt the cost was too high for the return. The comics are used lavishly—more than a score in some papers. They are generally the same compote of U.S., British and Australian strips that characterize the daily comic pages.

Sunday papers run from thirty-six to ninety-six pages. A typical issue of a tabloid divides roughly in this manner:

First twenty pages carry general news of local, state, interstate and overseas origin; leaders, comment columns, editorial cartoon, review of the week; Canberra, London, other overseas and political commentary; a great deal of advertising, including many full pages and double trucks.

A feature section might follow. It would offer such material as reviews (books, theater, movies, art, phonograph records), fiction; feature stories on an infinity of subjects, much of it Australiana; illustrated material, including crossword puzzles.

A determined play is made to publish complete sports sections, with results of Saturday's games, matches, meets and other competitions from all over Australia. The strongest emphasis, of course, is on horse racing from principal tracks, locally and from nearby states. Other sports, more seasonal than racing, come to prominent notice in turn. Football, cricket, trotting, tennis, golf, bowls and all other popular Australian sports, even pigeon racing, get at least a statistical summary.

Somewhere will be found a church page, an automobile page, a garden page, perhaps a handyman or do-it-yourself page, a small homes or architecture page, an amateur photography page, a nature page, a children's page. There will be a business-finance round-up; real estate sales; a corner for chess or bridge; comment on bird and animal pets, perhaps some seasonal material.

Sports, comics, features, women's and social, magazine, may be published as lift-out sections in multiples of four pages. The only broadsheet, *The Sunday Mail* (Brisbane), includes a four-color tabloid "The Sunday Mail Magazine" which presents comics, fiction, cartoons, Australiana, quizzes, astrology, gardening and a children's section. The magazine is printed in mid-week and sent out early to news agents. Much of the material for it is produced in Sydney.

The search for lively features is constant. Much is bought from overseas and from interstate syndicates. In its magazine, *The Sunday Telegraph* (Sydney) publishes a "Today" section, which reprints stories from *Time* Magazine. Another page summarizes gossip columns of the United Kingdom and the U.S., a practice with other papers. *The Sun-Herald* (Sydney) publishes "Fact," a round-up of short features from all over the world.

A typical women's and social section will contain, besides the usual social items, a double truck or more of news pictures, a shopping guide, a serial story, featured columnists, cooking, astrology, beauty, medical advice, budgeting, pets, knitting.

Sunday is such a big day for the distaff side that venders of women's special needs highly regard the Sunday advertisement's pulling power.

Or perhaps, it is the other way around—the advertisements make it a big day. In any event on Sunday there is much editorial space to fill.

Syndication

With certain exceptions, newspaper syndicates in the U.S. operate independently of individual newspapers. Salesmen go from newspaper office to newspaper office all over the U.S. selling their products to editors. Most home offices are in New York City. In Australia, however, syndication is done, with certain exceptions, through a department of a daily or its parent company; but two ways, not one. All papers buy *and* sell material on a syndicate basis. The biggest business is recorded in the offices of The Herald and Weekly Times Ltd., of Melbourne, for five dailies and associated publications; John Fairfax Ltd., for *The Sydney Morning Herald, The Sun* (Sydney) and associated publications; Consolidated Press Ltd., for the *Daily Telegraph* (Sydney), *The Australian Women's Weekly* and associated publications; West Australian Newspapers Ltd., for *The West Australian* (Perth), *The Daily News* (Perth) and associated publications.

Yaffa Syndicate is one of the few Australian agencies not connected with a daily; its association is with *Newspaper News*. Both were founded by the same man, the late David Yaffa. Many book-length serials and other fiction and non-fiction pieces are sold by Yaffa Syndicate. Another independent is Press Feature Service.

Australian syndication offices are headed by a chief editor and staffs of up to a dozen persons. Their principal task is to examine the incoming flood of material from overseas with an eye to buying for the needs of their own publications. A second function is to promote resales to periodicals in other circulation areas. A third responsibility is to offer for sale in other circulation areas—and often in other countries—material produced in their own organization.

Australia's small population and its comparatively few outlets for editorial material are the principal reasons that her syndicates are adjuncts to newspapers. For an exclusive feature, there is a maximum possibility of only five metropolitan-paper sales, apart from one's own use of it, for mornings do not buy what evenings have used and vice versa. In general, dealings are between morning and morning, or evening and evening papers.

The Herald and Weekly Times Ltd., for example, buys overseas material, first, for its Melbourne publications—principally *The Herald, The Sun News Pictorial* and *The Sporting Globe*. Then it offers its purchases to these dailies: its three other associated papers, *The Advertiser* (Adelaide), *The Courier-Mail* (Brisbane) and the *Tele-*

graph (Brisbane); and to *The West Australian* (Perth) and *The Daily News* (Perth). This loose association is known as the Melbourne Herald Cable Service. To this group, the syndicate also offers material produced in Victoria for use by its own publications. If a story has a New Zealand angle it is offered to three New Zealand dailies.

A syndicate editor reads advance proofs of special material produced in his own office for possible sales elsewhere. He fires off tearsheets to prospective buyers as swiftly as possible. Reciprocal arrangements are common. The Herald Cable Service may send to *The Sydney Morning Herald* group the material it has, and be offered in return matter exclusive to the Sydney group. Similar arrangements are in force between Consolidated Press Ltd. of Sydney (proprietors of the *Daily Telegraph*), *The Courier-Mail* (Brisbane), *The News* (Adelaide) and other papers. The Consolidated Press syndication department works closely also with *The Herald* (Melbourne), a primary sales target; for a sale there almost automatically assures sales in three states.

Material from overseas includes books of fiction and non-fiction, news and feature photos (black and white, color, wired), articles by famous persons, correspondents' columns, panel cartoons, comics, crossword and other puzzles, columnists' work, sports features, promotion devices, and many another type. Books are often purchased for serializing, and the rights sold interstate to help defray the purchase price.

Much business comes to the newspaper syndicates from the country press. Blocks (cuts), mats and stereos are distributed to local, suburban and provincial papers.

Most Australian metropolitan dailies, whether they maintain thriving syndicates or not, have tieups with overseas publishing houses. The Herald and Weekly Times draws from *The Express, The Daily Mail, The London Standard,* all of London; and *The Herald Tribune* (New York). Consolidated Press buys from, among others, King Features, Superior Features, United Press International, Ben Roth, in New York; from Reuters, Press Association, London Planet, in London. As with the other companies, John Fairfax Ltd.'s overseas offices do much screening of material to send to Australia: from Paul Popper, Camera Press, Daily Express, in London; from *Newsweek, Look, Life* for Australian rights in New York; *Paris-Match,* in Paris. The list of sources is more typical than definitive, for purchases and sales are fluid and are made according to the available material.

Comic strips are a special syndication problem, for they are as highly regarded as circulation-builders as they are in the U.S. The paucity of first-rate comic strips of Australian origin is a matter of concern to many journalists, especially to members of the Australian Journalists' Association, who constantly call for fewer imports of all syndicated material and plump for a more vigorous cultivation of native talent.

There is no dearth of strip and editorial cartooning talent in Australia. One need only to recall that David Low is a native Australian, and to think upon the great galaxy of pen-and-ink artists that the country has produced. Joliffe's wonderful "Witchetty Tribe" is humor that could come from nowhere but Australia. Rigby (cartoons) and Ward (text) on *The Daily News* (Perth) formed a remarkable team. Molnar in *The Sydney Morning Herald* and editorial cartoonists on other papers carry on the tradition. But in the comic-strip field only one of the *Daily Telegraph's* (Sydney) eight strips is Australian and only two of the *Sunday Telegraph's* twenty-two strips are home-produced—"Ginger Meggs" and "Captain Yonsson." Biggest stable of Australian comics is to be found at The Herald and Weekly Times. Five strips are produced there: "Wally and the Major," "Bluey and Curley," "Us Girls," "The Potts" and "Ben Boyang," which appears elsewhere as "Gunn's Gulley." When *The Argus* (Melbourne) was alive, it was home for "Herman Wizzer" and "Speewa Jack." *The Sun-Herald* originates "Fatty Finn," "Frisky," and "Family Man"; and *The Sunday Mail* (Brisbane) is home paper to "Uncle Joe's Horse Radish."

Australian strips are marketed wherever buyers can be found. Besides in Australia, they are published in India, New Zealand, England, France, Norway, South Africa and Latin America.

American strips sometimes need alteration. Dollars and cents must be changed to pounds, shillings and pence. The word "bum," not tolerable, must be changed into "tramp" because of quite a different Australian meaning. Other words must be watched.

Special events create a sharp demand for syndicate service. When Australia's lone oil well was brought in on Exmouth Gulf there was a big increase in eastern states' demand for pictures and features about Western Australia's empty North. The various Royal Tours of Australia create huge demands for special cover. The story and pictures of the Russians' attempt to force Mrs. Vladimir Petrov aboard their homeward bound plane at Darwin, in April, 1954, set some kind of record. The 1956 Olympics at Melbourne sent syndicate sales booming.

A crimp is put on many sales because of the national magazines and periodicals published by the metropolitan dailies. An article, story or picture which runs in *Woman's Day, The Australian Women's Weekly, The Sporting Globe, The New Idea* or in any other publication owned by a capital-city daily, cannot, of course, be released to competing media nationally or locally. However, material from such national publications is regularly sold overseas, to South Africa, India, Malaya and elsewhere.

Australian journalists of the upper echelons who go abroad keep a weather eye out for new sources of good material; and overseas literary agents frequently sell to Australian syndicates serial rights of new books. Highly perishable topical material from New York can reach Sydney by air freight within three days.

Not actually a part of syndication, but related to it, and sometimes under syndicate office supervision, is the photo sales department. U.S. newspapers sell their news pictures to the public, but few if any do it on the scale practiced by Australian newspapers as a routine matter.

The picture-sales office is almost always on the street level, for handy access to passersby. In the window are displayed blow-ups of pictures recently taken by staff photographers. Any picture that has appeared in the paper may be obtained even if it is not in stock at the moment.

The demand for certain subjects is enormous. A Royal Tour will bring an avalanche of demand. Sales are huge for pictures of Johnny Ray, Frank Sinatra, Betty Hutton and other U.S. entertainers who tour in Australia. One picture of Queen Elizabeth II sold 2,000 copies in six months. Sports sales alone are fantastically big. One paper sells enough photos to pay the salary of its entire photography staff. The Royal Show of each state held annually brings a big demand for a wide range of Show subjects. One of the smaller dailies takes in about £70 a week in photo sales during a "quiet" period. The *Telegraph* (Brisbane) took pictures of assembled children of twenty-seven different schools and sold £120 worth at one school.

Trash vs. Solid Features

Differences in the use of features among Australian major dailies are more of degree than of kind. Indeed, the material Australian feature editors publish is generally the sort of thing preferred by their American counterparts. Strong local, state or regional and national interests balance about exactly, from place to place.

The Australian morning papers use less frivolity and entertainment and more solid stuff than the lighter-hearted afternoons. But the most staid of them—meaning *The Age* (Melbourne), *The Sydney Morning Herald, The Advertiser* (Adelaide), *The Courier-Mail* (Brisbane), *The West Australian* (Perth) and *The Mercury* (Hobart)—do not pass up cheesecake *qua* cheesecake, or neglect wholly the hypotenuse, two sides and three angles of sexual triangles. On the other hand, the most raffish of the dailies occasionally comes up with sober analyses of U.N., the federal budget or some complicated national problem that might not be out of place in *The Times* of London.

There is trash; and one could wish there were less of it. And there is irresponsibility. In scores of conversations with Australians, I found a widespread desire for fewer sins in the name of circulation and for more solid stuff in the name of responsibility.

If enough Australians want that, they will get it.

9
The Press and
the Law

A Thorough Grounding

Cadets (beginners) who seek a Diploma in Journalism are given a thorough grounding in Australian and British law, particularly that pertaining to the public prints. Cadets not working toward a diploma are required to attend lectures in their respective offices on the general subject.

Libel and contempt of court are the subjects most important to the young reporter, with libel in the first place. Court coverage is generally for the mature and experienced journalist, but the greenest cadet can put his paper into legal jeopardy through a slip of his typewriter. In Australia as in the U.S. the greatest source of potential libel suits is inaccuracy. A wrong identification can put the paper on the defensive against charges of libel *per se*.

Origins and Defenses

Laws against defamation are spelled out by the Australian states. The classic prohibitions against holding up persons to ridicule, contempt, hatred; against impugning a person's character, injuring his ability to earn a living, or attacking his professional integrity, all derive from the British criminal code, as do U.S. laws. In the same manner, Australian laws vary somewhat from state to state.

Civil libel cases are between private persons. Criminal libel cases may be prosecuted by either a private prosecutor or by the Crown; they deal with aggravated malice of attack, with possibilities of breaching the peace, and with aggravated or unreasonable abuse of high government officials.

Defenses against libel actions in Australia are about what they are in the United States. *Truth and public benefit* is one defense, although there is a wide and debatable no man's land between the certainties and otherwise of what constitutes "public benefit." *Fair comment and criticism* is another, providing that the comment is based upon demonstrable fact, does not invade privacy, and is truly fair—more debatable ground. *Absolute or qualified privilege* extends to the work of most formally constituted government bodies, agencies and authorized officials acting in their official capacities. *Counter-attack in self-defense* is admissible as a defense.

Comment on court actions must be limited to completed cases. Reasonableness, temperateness and fairness are basically important. Papers are responsible for everything printed in them, including "honest" mistakes and literals (typographical errors).

As noted elsewhere, contempt of court in Australia is different, in extent and meaning, from contempt of court in the U.S. The reason is that Australian courts take jurisdiction at the moment of arrest, and are zealous about protecting arrested suspects from "trial by newspaper." Suspects must not be identified in any way before their first appearance in court. With certain exceptions, a judge may ban any reporting of a case while it is in progress; but all prohibitions are ended after the case is concluded. Decorum is strictly enforced in court, and the judge is the sole judge of indecorousness. Reporters, like all visitors, must bow to the bench upon entering and leaving a courtroom. Criticism of courts, the decisions of judges and juries, and of the judges themselves, is permitted as long as it is sober, constructive, objective and relevant.

Obscenity is defined and prohibited by statutes that differ from state to state. Queensland and South Australia have the most rigid codes. The Queensland Objectionable Literature Act, administered by the Queensland Literature Board of Review, has brought many a publisher into court. The powers and zeal of this Board are suggested by the decision of the Full Bench of the High Court of Australia (the highest national tribunal) in a case involving the allegedly objectionable nature of material published in a number of "romantic" pulp magazines.

A three-to-two decision reversed a decision of the Queensland Supreme Court which had upheld the conviction of three magazine publishers.

The *Daily Telegraph* (Sydney) of November 8, 1956, quoted this from the majority decision:

Whatever sensations are aroused by the narrative must be short-lived, for a story seldom occupies more than a dozen pages. . . .

But publications of the kind here in question seem to be quite outside the scope of the Act.

What they contain is an affront to the intelligence of the readers, but hardly a threat to their morals.

The stories are extremely silly, the letter-press is stupid, the drawings are artless and crude, and the situations absurd.

But we are not concerned with the damage done to the intellect, or for that matter to the eyesight of the readers of these foolish periodicals.

Our duty is to apply our judgment to the question whether, regard being had to the nature of the literature, to the persons and age groups among whom it is distributed, and to its tendency to deprave or corrupt them, it is objectionable, or that it unduly emphasises matters of sex, or is likely to be injurious to morality or to encourage depravity.

An examination of the literature is enough to satisfy us that the proper judgment upon the literature is that it is not "objectionable" within the definition upon any of these grounds.

Newspapers' publication of trial testimony, even in the most sensational sex cases, gets lenient treatment from the courts. The litigation, in late 1956, over a university professor's dismissal is an example. Suing for back pay and reinstatement, the professor found himself in court combatting the University's contention that he had had an affair with one of his female students. The detailed accounts were published with impunity as verbatim and summary testimony. The newspapers' field day—quite a "trial by newspaper" it was—received not so much as a disapproving frown from any court.

Because of the Australian copyright laws, and because news itself cannot be copyrighted, reporters are required to rewrite, with due attention to a change in form of expression, any item that may be lifted from another publication. As in the U.S., this type of open "larceny" is freely practiced by opposition papers against one another. Occasionally, however, a paper decides its opposition has gone too far, and it protests; on even rarer occasions, papers have been taken to court for such transgressions. As Geoffrey Sawer says in his *Guide,* "The moral is: never reproduce, always re-write, and devise some significantly new 'angle' for the re-write."

Reporters for Australian newspapers have few special rights not enjoyed by other citizens. A journalist can be denied entrance or put out of premises by proprietors. Reporters have been punished for refusing to reveal sources of information to government bodies: the situation is as parlous in Australia as it is in many states of the United States.

"*A Man Was Arrested* . . ."

Police reporting requires a close acquaintance with newspaper law and court practice, for it is even easier in Australia for a reporter to engage his paper in a costly contempt-of-court judgment or actionable libel than it is in the U.S. More than one Australian paper has felt the punitive hand of a court for going too far.

In 1956, *The Sun News Pictorial* (Melbourne) and *The Argus* (Melbourne) paid out fines of more than £200 for publishing news photographs of a young man being taken to be booked on charges of violent assault upon a young woman. It did not mitigate the offense that the suspect was later convicted and sentenced to a long prison term. Nor did *The Argus* save itself by obliterating the youth's features with a large white X. Pre-trial publication of the photographs, the court declared, was prejudicial to the defendant. Similar judgments dot Australian journalism history.

The pertinent legalism is that in Australia the court takes jurisdiction the moment an arrest is made; it does not delay, as in the U.S., until the prisoner is brought into court. Thus, each crime story of scope and substance becomes a calculated risk to the Australian editor.

One result of this stern judicial attitude is that there is less chance for "trial by newspaper" between arrest and the actual court proceedings than in the U.S. However, what appears in print *during* a sensational trial can equal anything the yellower sections of U.S. journalism can serve up. Privilege for the recorded court testimony takes down the bars. It makes all the difference *when* an editor publishes details of a crime story. An effect, curious to U.S. readers, is the pattern of reporting arrests that Australian papers must follow.

A most atrocious murder may have been committed and a suspect caught with the death weapon in his bloody hands. Yet his name cannot be mentioned or any clue given to his identity. If his picture is published, the newspaper—as indicated above—is in real trouble. The last paragraph of the story, inevitably reads something like this: "Later a man was arrested by police and taken to gaol where he was charged with a crime."

The withholding of names from print has still another effect. In stories of dramatic arrests there is very little purple prose reporting the antecedent conflict between police and wanted person. It is difficult to dramatize an anonymity.

Somewhat after *The Argus - Sun News Pictorial* case, a murder trial was concluded in Melbourne. The defendant was pronounced guilty and sentenced to life imprisonment. During the trial, of course, his name was privileged and could be published. But in all Melbourne daily newspaper offices, at trial's end, the decision was not to run the convict's picture with the story.

The reasoning was that the law allowed him twenty-eight days in which to file an appeal. If he did so, the court might conceivably find that his appeal had been prejudiced by publication of his picture at the time of verdict or sentence. Within the same period, pictures of a suspect in a New York kidnap-killing were freely published in Melbourne. The Victorian Supreme Court jurisdiction does not extend to New York.

A paper may not be immune when it publishes a picture of a wanted person—not even if it does so at the request of the police. Recently, a capital-city paper printed such a picture and the community was thereby informed about the wanted person's appearance. Plainly the police desired help in finding him. The fugitive was duly caught, tried and convicted. There was no move by the court to punish the paper for this publication, but the risk was there.

Other strictures on reporters may be given only lip service. In at least one state, the police are expressly forbidden to give information to the press. Yet the top police command not only permits reporters to gather and publish police stories every day, but it provides a press room and unrestricted use of telephones. Elsewhere, it is a punishable offense for anyone, the press included, to listen to short wave police broadcasts. Yet the police know that press cars, press rooms and newspaper offices are equipped with receiving sets, tuned to police wave lengths, in order to insure speed and quality of coverage.

Such arrangements have their parallels in the U.S.

Seditious Libel

The Stuart case in South Australia, involving *The News* (Adelaide), points up other special legal problems that Australian newspapers have to live with.

The case began as rape and murder in a cave on a stretch of ocean beach 350 airflight miles northwest of Adelaide. Five days before Christmas, 1958, the dead body of a small girl was found there. South Australian police arrested a twenty-seven-year-old aborigine, Rupert Max Stuart, who had a brief police record; and soon after they announced his confession. Stuart, who understood little English and nothing about the law, was tried, convicted and sentenced to be hanged. The case was appealed to the South Australian Court of Criminal Appeal; to the High Court of Australia, the country's highest judicial body; then to the Judicial Committee of the Privy Council in London, supreme court of appeal in the British Commonwealth. The appeal was denied at each step. Stuart's execution was set for August 4, 1959. In the first phases of the case, the press's role was routine. There was little to set the story notably apart from other stories about sordid crimes of passion. Then a Catholic priest, who had first assumed Stuart to be guilty, took his doubts to South Australian government authorities who listened but took no action. The priest went to *The News,* Adelaide's afternoon tabloid. The key question was Stuart's whereabouts at 3:30 P.M. the day the child was murdered. Stuart worked in a traveling sideshow; and the only witnesses who would know his movements were itinerants, members of a part-gypsy band, who also worked with him. They were reported to be in Queensland. Five days before Stuart was to be hanged, *The News* published three statements from the troupe, the fruit of the priest's search, which put Stuart at the sideshow at the time of the crime. In front-page editorials, *The News* asked for postponement of execution. The next day the Premier of South Australia announced the creation of a Royal Commission, to inquire into the Stuart case. A Royal Commission is something like an American investigative grand jury.

The News and its editor, Rohan D. Rivett, criticized the membership of the Royal Commission, noting that two of its three judges had presided at Stuart's original trial and at one of the appeals. The commission began its inquiry. Three sideshow persons testified in Stuart's behalf. On the third day, J. Shand, Stuart's principal counsel, was stopped by Sir Mellis Napier, one of the judges, in his cross-examination of a police witness. The next day, after further interchanges with the judge, Shand suddenly withdrew from the case.

The walkout was big news and it broke on *The News'* time. The paper published two posters to advertise its top story: "SHAND QUITS 'YOU WON'T GIVE STUART A FAIR GO' " and "COMMISSION BREAKS UP. SHAND BLASTS NAPIER." The story was headlined: "MR SHAND INDICTS NAPIER 'THESE COMMISSIONERS CANNOT DO THE JOB.' "

The News and Rivett were instantly in deep trouble. Sir Thomas Playford, Premier of South Australia for more than twenty years, told the House of Assembly that to put into quotes words that "were never spoken" constituted "the gravest libel ever made against any judge in this State." *The News* thereafter published a leader called "Setting the Record Straight," which admitted the technical charge about the quote but suggested that readers exercise their own judgment about the fairness of the proceedings. The Royal Commission hearings continued. *The News,* after considerable effort, procured another barrister to represent Stuart who, his testimony given, departed the scene into jail, his sentence having been commuted to life imprisonment.

With Stuart out of the picture, the Playford government moved in against Rivett and *The News*. Nine charges were laid against the editor and his paper: three alleging seditious libel, three alleging defamatory libels knowing them to be defamatory, three involving plain defamatory libel. The heart of the matter, the summonses declared, was that *The News* had charged "the chief justice and judges were biased and unfair in carrying out their duties as Royal Commissioners . . . and that they were unfitted for judicial office." The only member of the South Australian Supreme Court who had not been directly involved in the Stuart trials heard the case against *The News* and Rivett.

In his statement to the court, Rivett spoke for the headline writers of the world when he said:

> The words in quotes, in accord with practice, contained what was considered a fair and accurate summary of what Shand said. Considerations of space often make it impossible to reproduce in a heading or poster the very words used, which here embraced both the statement about a thorough investigation and the statement that the Commission could not properly consider the matters before it. . . .
>
> I only intended in the posters and headings to give a fair and accurate summary and index of what happened at the Royal Commission and I think that's what I did. I am not guilty of the charges laid against me.

The jury was persuaded. Eight of the nine charges were dismissed and there was disagreement on the ninth. Later it, too, was dismissed. The jury's action may have extended the bounds of free expression in Australia, but not before the life of a newspaper and the freedom of its editor had been placed in jeopardy over an offense that could not possibly have been regarded as seditious libel by an American court.

10

The Australian
Journalists'
Association

Birth of The AJA

The letter was terse and to the point. It was dated at Melbourne, December 1, 1910. It read:

Dear Sir,—

A meeting of journalists, i.e. persons professionally and habitually engaged upon the staffs of newspapers or periodicals will be held at the cafe in the basement of the Empire Building, Flinders Street, Melbourne, on Saturday, December 10, 1910, at 8 P.M. sharp, for the purpose of considering the question of forming an organisation to secure registration under the Commonwealth Conciliation and Arbitration Act.

You are invited to be present and to extend an invitation to any other qualified person with whom you are acquainted.

Yours sincerely,
B. S. B. Cook,
(Melbourne 'Herald')
On Behalf of the Conveners.

That was the beginning.

The background was important. Australia's system of conciliation and arbitration, supervised by special federal and state courts, grew out of a long series of bitter industrial disputes beginning about 1890. By the end of the twentieth century's first decade, remarkable progress had been made in establishing and effectively using legal machinery to prevent or settle the type of fierce labor-employer warfare that had been enervating Australia.

In the Twenty-first Birthday Number of *The Journalist,* AJA's official newspaper (issue of April 24, 1931), the reason for the conveners' letter was set down this way:

> Bootmakers, bricklayers, miners, sea captains and officers, and other employees in widely varied avocations (sic), had taken full advantage of the new industrial legislation, and had been granted by the Commonwealth Arbitration Court substantial increases in pay and a shortening of hours. By collective bargaining the employees in the mechanical departments of newspapers had secured big improvements in their working conditions, and in many instances the salaries of journalists were less than those of other employees in the industry.
> Such was the state of affairs when Melbourne journalists decided that an effort should be made to improve the status of journalists by collective action.

About one hundred journalists attended the meeting called by B. S. B. Cook, federal roundsman for *The Herald*—Melbourne was then the federal capital. A motion that an organization be formed and registered "under the Commonwealth Conciliation and Arbitration Act" was carried 78 to 9. An eight-man committee was named to draft a constitution and rules. In the course of its work, the committee came up with a proposed name, which was quickly approved.

"The Australian Journalists' Association" applied at once for registration under the Commonwealth Conciliation and Arbitration Act. The application date was December 23, 1910. Notice thereof was printed in the *Commonwealth Gazette* of December 31, and registration was formally granted on May 23, 1911.

One of the Act's requirements was that a log of claims—a list of demands—for each disputant group be filed with the court as a basis for collective bargaining or for court decision if bargaining failed. The AJA served its first log on about fifty newspapers outside, and twelve within, the State of Victoria, on November 4, 1911. A month later a conference between AJA officials and representatives of daily newspapers in Melbourne, Sydney, Adelaide and Brisbane was held in Melbourne. From this series of meetings came the first agreement as to wages, hours and working conditions between the proprietors and the AJA.

The agreement ran for a year. It added an approximate £15,000 to the income of AJA members and, the twenty-first anniversary issue of *The Journalist* recalled, "for the first time in the history of Australian journalism, the principle that there should be some limit to the hours worked by journalists was recognized."

But this was not the only principle established. Before 1910, the journalist's lot was to work for a bare subsistence wage, six or even seven days and up to sixty or seventy or eighty hours a week, with no annual holiday, no overtime; under wretched working conditions; without sick or unemployment benefits and with none of the other perquisites now taken as a matter of course. The Australian pound was worth a great deal more then than now; but that first agreement of 1911, with its £7-a-week pay for senior reporters, was a prodigious increase over an average of about £3 a week.

It was small wonder that AJA grew steadily with the new century. From the first meeting of about one hundred founders, it increased in this fashion: 1911—593 members; 1920—1,017; 1930—1,817; 1940 —2,295; 1950—3,920; 1956—4,214.

New South Wales and Victoria Districts have by far the largest memberships. Totals as of June 30, 1960, were:

New South Wales	1,931
Victoria	1,240
Queensland	476
South Australia	360
Western Australia	383
N.S.W. Provincial	209
Tasmania	149
Canberra	107
Total	4,855

Negotiations and Court Awards

Most of the time since the founding year, the AJA and the proprietors have reached agreement without benefit of court decision. Agreements were voluntary in 1920, 1929, 1934, 1938, 1945, 1950 and (with an exception noted below) in 1958. The federal conciliators have settled disputed logs of claims only in 1917, 1927, and 1954–55.

The first time recourse to a court became necessary was in 1917. In that year, Mr. Justice Isaacs (later Sir Isaac Isaacs, who became Australia's first native-born Governor-General), made an award which the late Arthur Norman Smith, AJA General President in 1911, described as "the celebrated blue log, so called because it was printed on somewhat official-looking blue foolscap . . . [and] was the Magna Charta and Bill of Rights of the Association in one."

This award prescribed a format that is still followed. It set up a grading system, under which a journalist was advanced in salary as his experience and skill, therefore his value to his newspaper, increased. It ordered an apportionment of jobs according to grade, so that a substantial majority of employees would be in the best-paying brackets, set forth working hours and working conditions in meticulous detail for all editorial department employees, and provided for holidays. By raising wage and salary minimums, Smith declared, it raised "the professional status of journalists to something like what it should be."

In 1927, certain issues which the AJA and employers could not agree upon were arbitrated by Robert G. Menzies, then practicing law as a King's Counsel, and now Prime Minister of Australia.

A more recent major court intercession—and the worst, from the standpoint of time lost, energy and money expended—came as a result of a deadlock, in January, 1954, over logs of claims filed the previous June.

During 1954, Conciliation Commissioner A. S. Blackburn conducted hearings and took two million words of evidence from 121 AJA and eighteen proprietor witnesses in all six state-capital cities. He announced his decision on June 17, 1955. The eighteen-months' proceedings cost both sides thousands of pounds. Notably, when the Blackburn award expired, in 1958, a less intransigent mood prevailed, and agreement between AJA and metropolitan daily proprietors (with two Sydney exceptions) was quickly reached.

The Metropolitan Dailies Award is the basis for others in different media. Variations in schedules of work and pay rates are determined by such factors as cost of living, local working conditions, competitive strain and economics. Generally, minimum wages are higher in the metropolitan awards than in the others. These latter cover Newcastle dailies, the Australian Broadcasting Commission, public service, Australian Associated Press, Herald Gravure (Melbourne), press agencies, provincial dailies, provincial non-dailies, commercial broadcasting stations that operate independent news services.

In the metropolitan awards, rates of pay and certain other matters are often fixed lower or differently in Brisbane, Adelaide, Perth and Hobart than they are in Sydney and Melbourne, the two biggest capitals. Also, a wage differential is given morning paper employes when night work is required of them.

Details of Awards

In the machinery of settlement the AJA for employes, and a particular company (e.g., Associated Newspapers Ltd.) "and others" for the proprietors, file logs of claims that are in excess of what they expect to receive. This is not only accepted collective bargaining strategy—ask for the sun and settle for the moon—it is also insurance. The difference in detail between the opposing claims in each section of the log is known as "the ambit of dispute." In appeals for redress after the award is in effect, neither side is permitted to go beyond the limits of the ambit of dispute.

If, for example, the AJA is not happy about the ultimate decision on overtime pay rates for photographers, it cannot, upon appeal, ask for higher overtime rates than those it requested in its original log of claims. Nor may the proprietors, if they appeal the same rates as being too high, ask that overtime rates be set lower than they had proposed in their original log.

Because each group, through the court, makes demands that affect the other, each is simultaneously claimant and respondent. The final decisive document, ordered into effect by the court, is formally known as "The Journalists' (Metropolitan Daily Newspapers) Award."

After introductory matter, a section sets forth the schedule of "Salaries, Rates, Hours and Other Terms and Conditions" for "Members other than Cartoonists, Creative Artists, Press Artists and Press Photographers," i.e., the literary staff. This is done according to grade.

The grading schedule, like so many other phases of the award system, has no counterpart in U.S. journalism. The award sets up five grades or wage categories of journalists, the lowest being D grade. They progress upward through C, B and A and culminate in Special A grade. Special A minimum pay rates may be more than twice as much as D grade minimums.

Sydney and Melbourne journalists rate the highest pay, as noted. A second group is composed of Perth, Adelaide and Brisbane. Hobart, smallest of the capitals, is in a category by itself. In Australia, as elsewhere, it is a truism that the bigger the city the higher the living costs. Because of this, between each of the three divisions of metropolitan newspapers, grade for grade and job for job, there is an average drop in pay of about 5 per cent. Thus Hobart's scale is 10 per cent lower than Sydney's and Melbourne's. Morning paper pay rates are slightly higher—about ten shillings a week—than afternoon, because of the additional night work.

A comparison of the literary staff rates for all grades in the last three awards for Sydney and Melbourne metropolitan morning dailies suggests the pattern for all classifications:

TABLE 4.—LITERARY STAFF RATES, METROPOLITAN
DAILIES AWARDS

Grade	1950–55	1955–58 *	1960 **
Sp. A	£27/11/0	£39/15/0	£46/0/0
A	25/06/0	34/15/0	40/10/0
B	22/06/6	29/15/0	35/05/0
C	20/02/0	23/15/0	28/10/0
D	16/12/6	18/05/0	23/05/0

* Includes an increase of £1/05/0 ordered by the Conciliation and Arbitration Commission in the national basic wage in a 1956 decision.
** In 1958, two of three Sydney proprietors refused to accept wage settlements satisfactory to other metropolitan daily proprietors. Eventually, the AJA won its case against them. In 1960, after much bitterness and legal maneuvering the minimum Metropolitan Dailies Award rates for Sydney and Melbourne morning papers were set by a compromise at the amounts indicated.

The section of the award dealing with staff pay rates also covers miscellaneous related matters—rates for correspondents and bureau members who work outside the home state; rates for journalists employed on the company's periodicals, and so on.

Under "Classification of Members" the award prescribes these proportions for journalists by grade on metropolitan papers:

Not less than 15 per cent in A grade.
Not less than 50 per cent in B grade.
Not less than 17½ per cent in C grade.
Not more than 17½ per cent in D grade.

Grades A and B together thus account for 65 per cent of all staffers. If a paper has more staffers in any of the three top grades than the award orders, a corresponding percentage may be deducted from the requirement for next lower grade, e.g., if a paper has 25 per cent of its staffers in Grade A, it need have only 40 per cent in Grade B. In point of fact, most newspapers exceed minimum requirements in the top grades, keeping their best journalists on "margins"—pay rates in excess of the minimum for the pertinent grade.

The present grading system was begun with the Menzies award of 1927. Previously there were three grades with these percentage minimums for each: (1) Seniors—60 per cent; (2) Generals—20 per cent; (3) Juniors—20 per cent. Both sides, however, were unhappy about the classifications, so the present system was begun, with Special A grade for superior journalists entitled to special treatment.

Grading the Staff

Grading is the prerogative of the proprietor, exercised by the top editorial management, in practical effect at the news-editor and chief-of-staff level, subject to higher approval. There is no formula, rite or ritual in connection with a change of grade; and the AJA's only direct concern with administration of this part of the award is that the prescribed minimum percentages for each grade be maintained and that proper, up-to-date records be kept of all changes.

The individual journalist's concern, however, is constant and circumambient; for as he is graded so is he paid. The 65 per cent minimum allotment is evidence that most journalists, after they complete their cadetships, do not linger long in either D or C on the way up. It is only a special kind of young journalist who remains overlong in the two bottom categories—the kind whose difficulty is in adding performance to promise.

Grading is not done according to the nature of the job. Covering the courts, for example, is not A grade work per se and police rounds B grade, or vice versa. Grading is done according to the proficiency of the individual journalist and his value to the paper. Merit is declared to be the sole basis of upgrading; but it is not unusual for a C grade journalist, offered more pay by a rival proprietor, to find himself suddenly in B grade if he promises not to switch employers.

The time immediately after the signing of a new award is a period of some anxiety; for proprietors can downgrade as well as upgrade; and the increased cost of higher pay under a new award may be the gauge of how much a proprietor may wish to downgrade and to whittle margins (above-scale pay rates).

However, the AJA has effective weapons against such practices, beyond the built-in percentage minimums for each grade; and adjudication generally takes care of readjustments equitably.

Certain individuals are exempted from the award's pay provisions; notably, top editors and their deputies, chiefs of staff, news editors, chief sub-editors and editors of other publications issued by the same proprietor; also casual employes, district and country correspondents and members employed outside the Commonwealth.

Reporters' Rights and Responsibilities

Cadets or beginners rate a special section in the award.* Expense money for working journalists, travel fares, transport facilities and typewriter maintenance are prescribed by the award. Day-work and

* See Chapter 11.

night-work differentials are spelled out. Definitions of time worked are laid down, as are rules covering distant engagements, overtime, time off and special overtime. Use of the Duty Book which lists assignments, and the Time Book, for hours worked, is described. The rights, responsibilities, duties and pay of district correspondents, casuals, contributors, and country correspondents are specified.

The award directs how up-to-date records of staffers' grades, cadets' status and exemptions shall be kept. It details illness and accident compensation, death benefits, holiday leaves (four consecutive weeks at full pay for all classified journalists and cadets), notice for termination of services, employment at Darwin and Canberra, extra pay for duplication of work, rules about journalists who do photographic work and who broadcast, working accommodations in newspaper offices, the keeping of proper files of newspapers and making available copies of the current award to employers and employes, and the use of notice-boards for the AJA in reporters' rooms. The award specifies a closed shop, but permits certain exemptions.

One of the most significant of the provisions is also one of the shortest:

MALE AND FEMALE MEMBERS
"All provisions of this Award shall apply equally
to male and female members."

This includes, of course, rates of pay.

All the foregoing is covered by one section of the award. Another deals in similar, though briefer, fashion with "Cartoonists, Creative Artists, Press Artists and Press Photographers." A third and final section specifies the machinery for adjustment of wage rates and provides for a "Board of Reference" composed of three AJA and three employer representatives to deal with any matters that arise in connection with the administration of the award.

How AJA Works

Each of the six states of Australia is a district of AJA. In addition there is a New South Wales Provincial District; and a Canberra District, which until 1958 was a Division.

Every AJA member is affiliated with one of these eight units, each of which is autonomous. Ultimate authority is vested in popular vote of the membership. The governing body on the national level is the Federal Council (General President, two General Vice-Presidents, General Treasurer, General Secretary; two delegates from each district, one from each sub-district or division).

Federal Council holds annual and special meetings. When Federal Council is not in session, the Federal Executive administers AJA. This second body consists of the same general officers listed above, plus one representative from each district, one photographer representative and one artist-author representative. The practice is to designate Melbourne members as deputies for distant districts.

Except for a three-year (1933–36) switch to Sydney, Melbourne has been AJA headquarters ever since the association's inception. Periodically, Sydneysiders launch campaigns for a return to Sydney. A number of membership plebiscites have turned down the proposition—the latest, in 1958, by the almost irreducible margin of three votes—presumably because Melbourne is a city of less journalistic storm and stress than Sydney.

Federal Council has complete authority over policy, management and all AJA affairs. Federal Executive carries out general administration. Only three AJA officials are paid—the General Secretary, the Victorian District and the New South Wales District secretaries. The first General Secretary, S. E. Pratt, served thirty-seven years, bringing the organization through its adolescence and into maturity. His successor, Sydney Crosland, took over the office in February, 1955.

District units of the AJA present logs of claims for employees of various publishing units of their respective states. They help to administer sub-districts' affairs, hold membership meetings, keep books, collect dues, conduct social activities and do all other things necessary at the state level.

Each district publishes an "Annual Report and Balance Sheet," as of each June 30, which spreads upon the record all phases of AJA's activities for the year. It is prepared in time for the district's annual meeting, for which it serves as agenda and an accounting of stewardship. The policing of the award is reported therein; also the report of the Ethics Committee, which has the power to reprimand or penalize an offending member. It includes the dues standing of every member in pounds, shillings and unto the last pence. Few members are in arrears; many are not only "financial," i.e., in good standing, but are paid up in advance.

New South Wales and Western Australia permit only statewide unions to function. Thus, there co-exists in the New South Wales District of the AJA a New South Wales Journalists' Union, and in the WAAJA a West Australian Journalists' Union. Each, though, is a nominal matter, for the two unions in each state have the same officers and the same membership.

The AJA takes an active interest in matters other than wages, hours and working conditions. The instrument under which its District Ethics Committees operate is the AJA Code of Ethics, Article 49 in the Constitution, which reads:

> Each member of the Australian Journalists' Association shall observe the following Code of Ethics in his employment:—(1) He shall report and interpret the news with a scrupulous honesty. (2) He shall not suppress essential facts and shall not distort the truth by omission or wrong or improper emphasis. (3) He shall in all circumstances respect all confidences received by him in the course of his calling. (4) He shall observe at all times the fraternal obligations arising from his membership of the Association, and shall not on any occasion take unfair or improper advantage of a fellow member of the Association. (5) He shall not allow his personal interests to influence him in the discharge of his duties nor shall he accept or offer any present, gift or other consideration, benefit or advantage of whatsoever kind if such acceptance or offer is of a character which may have the effect of so influencing or benefiting him. (6) He shall use only fair and honest methods to obtain news, pictures and documents. (7) He shall reveal his identity as a representative of the Press before obtaining any personal interview for the purpose of using it for publication. (8) He shall do his utmost to maintain full confidence in the integrity and dignity of the calling of a journalist.

The Constitution sets forth detailed instructions for the application and enforcement of the code, and specifies procedures in the event of violation.

Press Council

Related to newspaper ethics is AJA's desire to create a "General Council of the Press" within each state. The annual meeting of the Federal Council in 1955, in Perth, endorsed the principle and the New South Wales District took leadership in seeking its establishment. The AJA proposes a board of able citizens to whom a person believing himself unfairly dealt with by the press might make appeal for redress. The New South Wales District of AJA has suggested a fourteen-man council—five to be named by newspaper management, two by the New South Wales Labor Council, two by the AJA District, one by the Sydney University Senate, one by state women's organizations, and one each from the state parliament's government and opposition members. An independent chairman would be the fourteenth member.

The AJA argues that there are numerous abuses short of actionable libel committed by newspapers, and that the proprietors and editors should not be the sole judges of whether mistakes should be corrected, erroneous implications set right and their other wrongful actions redressed. The Press Council would have some of the attributes of a court, a public letter box and an avuncular counsellor. Its chief means of granting relief to complainants and of rebuking offenders would be publicity and regular reports to the public.

Syndicated Imports

The AJA keeps up pressure to cut down on syndication imports from overseas, in such matters as comic strips, humor, fiction and features. Its understandable desire is that these be produced by Australians for use in Australian publications. It argues that such imports delay, or even stifle, the development of Australian talent. From the widespread use of overseas material—mostly from the U.S. and Britain—one must conclude that the AJA objective is a long way from being realized.

Golden Jubilee

In the Twenty-first Birthday number of the *Journalist,* published on April 24, 1931, B. S. B. Cook, who had sounded the call for the organizational meeting in 1910, wrote this brief wish:

> If only a portion of the original edifice endures and something more substantial is hereafter erected on its base, the conveners trust that it may be regarded as a monument to their labors to uplift journalism to that honored place in the professions which is its right and title to occupy.

The original edifice has endured. When in 1960 AJA celebrated its golden jubilee year, it was understandably extolled as one of organized labor's most remarkable organizations. Among working Australian journalists it holds close to 100 per cent membership. Only executives, persons with religious scruples against unions, and a few others, are not members.

Since its inception, AJA has been remarkably strike-free, although in recent years it became embroiled in two Sydney shutdowns which were not of its own making. One occurred in 1944, the other in 1955. Both left wounds and bitterness. Sydney, however, is the exception. Sydney proprietors and employee representatives sometimes behave as if they were mortal enemies instead of indispensable partners in a common enterprise. Tensions and ill-tempered brawls are not uncommon. Otherwise, relations with employers are generally good throughout the Commonwealth.

The remarkable record in amity which AJA and Australia's newspaper proprietors have made is not the least impressive part of Australia's newspaper story. To this, in some degree, the background of most of Australia's top newspaper executives has contributed. Practically all of them began as members of AJA. Many of the most powerful of today's press potentates were working journalists, and some were state or federal AJA officers, in their earlier years.

Occasionally, there is trouble though. The roughest time any district of the AJA has had during the last decade in its relations with proprietors occurred in July, 1955. A disagreement between the printers and management of the *Daily Mirror* (Sydney) began it.

The dispute took off in a number of directions; before a settlement was reached, all four Sydney dailies had suspended publication and were issuing a composite newspaper, and the AJA had become the proprietor of a short-lived (three days) daily: *The Clarion* appeared on July 13, 14, 15. But on Monday, July 18, *The Clarion* was a memory and *The Sydney Morning Herald*, the *Daily Telegraph*, *The Sun* along with the *Daily Mirror*, where it had all started, were back on the street again. The AJA had become embroiled when proprietors had ordered their editorial employees to work on the composite paper and AJA members had refused. But AJA was not a primary contributor to that shutdown.

The Australian Journalists' Association today is as much a part of Australian journalism as are the great presses that spread black ink from metal stereos onto newsprint in Australian newspaper press rooms. The association and the proprietors live together in harmony, not entirely because they are forced to do so, but because half a century of a relationship as intimate as marriage rests familiarly upon both.

One group respects the other. There is rancor, particularly at award-expiration time. There is hate here and there on one side for the other, and vice versa. But the absence of disastrous strikes, of vendettas by proprietors against the AJA, and vice versa, and the mutual respect that prevails are components of a situation that could profitably inspire close study by newspaper employers and employees in other lands, including the United States.

Since this is a comparative study, let one more judgment stand as conclusion to this section: the proprietors of U.S. daily newspapers and the American Newspaper Guild,* in their undivorceable relationship, lag behind the Australian press's labor relations in responsibility, maturity and performance.

* Close comparisons between the AJA and the American Newspaper Guild, its U.S. counterpart, are difficult to make. AJA membership is close to 100 per cent of all Australian journalists—4,855 for the six states. The ANG counted a total of 31,287 dues-paying members as of January 1, 1960—a steady growth from the January 1, 1950, total of 23,706, but still a long way from covering all of the U.S. Census estimated total of 63,000 newspaper, radio and television newsmen and newswomen in the United States. Altogether, the ANG has 214 contracts with employers, of which 147 cover 183 general-circulation daily newspapers of a total of 1,761 in the United States. The other 67 contracts are distributed in this manner: nine press association and news services, five weeklies, twelve magazines, two radio stations, nine foreign-language papers, twelve labor publications, three racing papers and fifteen miscellaneous agencies.

Thus, while the U.S. newsmen's union is many times larger in membership than the Australian, the percentage of daily newspapers organized in the United States—about 10 per cent—is far lower than in Australia. If other news media are included, the percentage gap becomes even greater.

The American Newspaper Guild, founded in 1933 by Heywood Broun, columnist and crusader, has concentrated its organization drives in the metropolitan centers, has tended to stay away from the smaller dailies and to do relatively little about weeklies and other media. Michigan, for example, has 53 daily newspapers, but the Guild has locals in only four Michigan cities. In Detroit, the state's largest city, the Guild had editorial department units at the *Detroit Free Press* and the *Detroit Times,* but not at the *Detroit News.* When the *Times* suspended publication on November 6, 1960, that reduced the Newspaper Guild of Detroit to the *Free Press* unit and a few miscellaneous units, covering labor, religious and certain specialized publications or groups.

In the United States, there is nothing comparable to the Australian award system or the training of cadets under awards. Disputes over collective bargaining and contracts are not automatically under court jurisdiction, as in Australia. However, the general structure of the AJA and the ANG, their use of state and regional divisions which pyramid into a national organization, their democratic methods, the practice of annual policy-making conventions and many other phases bear close resemblance one to another. General objectives are the same in both countries.

11
Cadet Training
for Journalists

Best of Its Kind

Among the most notable divergences between Australian and U.S. journalism is in methods of preparing young men and women for careers in journalism. Australia's system of cadet training is not only peculiarly Australian but is unique in many of its phases.

Moreover, it may be the best of its kind in the world; and its kind is four years of practical training in the mechanics of journalism, with exposure under skilled supervision to almost every type of news situation ever likely to confront a reporter. In this area, it does as a matter of course what no American journalism school would attempt to do with comparable thoroughness.

Against such judgment must be balanced a less happy conclusion. The cadet system trains young journalists, but fails to educate them. It does an excellent job mechanically. But despite certain acknowledgments, implicit and explicit in the journalists' awards about the value of higher education, the system does not do enough to educate young minds for the responsibilities of reporting, explaining and interpreting the news; and of helping constructively to shape the life of an increasingly complex world.

"The cadetship system," said one Australian editor, "is an excellent means of getting first-rate police reporters. But I am concerned about its failure to go beyond that."

His attitude and his criticism are unusual. In respect to university training, Australian editorial departments, with certain exceptions, compare with American city rooms of half a century ago, when editors held college graduates in scorn; and the man with an A.B. degree guarded his secret zealously, as if it were a loathsome disease or a sordid chapter from his past.

Beginning With AJA

The first (1911) agreement ever made between newspaper proprietors and the then one-year-old Australian Journalists' Association contained provisions for cadets. It declared that their weekly stipend would be £1/10 the first year of service, £2 the second year and £2/10 the third year.

There was early recognition by the AJA of the importance of education for journalism. The late Arthur Norman Smith, General President in 1911 (in whose honor the annual Arthur Norman Smith Lectureship in Journalism is held at the University of Melbourne) recalled in the Twenty-first Birthday Issue of the AJA's *The Journalist:*

> One of the most pleasant phases of the work was that connected with the education of journalists. Special efforts have been made in most States, Western Australia leading the way in a commendable manner. The Federal Executive [the A.J.A.'s chief administrative body] has always aided anything of the kind, and it drew up a scheme that was widely adopted. Most of the Universities have made provision for the issue of a Diploma of Journalism, an imprimatur that should be widely sought.

President Smith's hopes were not realized, for the AJA's scheme did not prosper generally.

Sydney University and the University of Western Australia set up curricula in journalism with a special diploma, but dropped them after a few years. By the mid-1950's only the Universities of Queensland and Melbourne, of Australia's institutions of higher learning, offered a Diploma in Journalism course. Moreover, the Diploma in Journalism —which equates to about three-quarters of a Bachelor of Arts degree —has had comparatively few takers among each year's new crop of cadet journalists and fewer finishers.

This academic deficiency is the worst that can be said of the cadet system. Since 1911, it has been improved and strengthened and has become an integral part of Australian journalism. Partly because most of them once were cadets themselves, editors and proprietors are actively aware that the quality of today's cadet training determines in good part the quality of tomorrow's newspapers. The pity is that devotion shown to training does not everywhere extend to higher education.

Cadet Provisions in Awards

Journalism awards follow a basic formula in defining the rights, duties, and other phases of cadet training. A summary of the provisions about cadets in a typical Metropolitan Dailies Award will illustrate:

A cadet is defined as an employee "constantly or regularly in training for journalism," or one who does the work of such an employee and who has not been engaged therein for four years.

The ratio of employees on metropolitan dailies is set at one cadet to every six graded journalists. This varies in non-metropolitan awards, and is a source of contention on small newspapers and periodicals with less than six staffers. They employ cadets as their circumstances warrant. Part of the AJA's purpose, of course, is to prevent the employment of cadets, at low rates of pay, to do the work of graded journalists.

Cadets usually work in their paper's city of publication.

Minimum wages for cadets are based on percentages of D grade morning newspaper pay scales of the state, according to this formula:

First year .... 37½ per cent
Second year 53   per cent
Third year .... 67½ per cent
Fourth year 85   per cent

In Sydney and Melbourne, the two largest cities, pay rates are highest. In Brisbane, Adelaide and Perth a slightly lower scale is in force. That in Hobart, the smallest capital city, is somewhat lower still. In the July, 1958, Metropolitan Dailies Award, cadet pay scales (which had not been benefited much by the 1954–55 Award) were increased up to £3/17/6 (about $8.68) a week. This was the decision about cadets' wages:

TABLE 5.—CADET PAY SCALE, METROPOLITAN DAILIES AWARDS

	A.M.'s Grade D. Weekly Pay	Cadet 1 yr.	Cadet 2 yrs.	Cadet 3 yrs.	Cadet 4 yrs.
Melbourne *	21/10/0	10/15/0	12/18/0	16/2/6	18/5/6 **
Brisbane, Adelaide & Perth	21/2/0	10/11/0	12/13/0	15/16/6	17/18/6
Hobart	20/14/0	10/7/0	12/8/6	15/10/6	17/12/0

* The disputed Sydney rate was settled in July, 1959, by Conciliation Commissioner J. H. Portus. Cadets were raised from £3/3/0 to £4/5/3 over the 1955 figure, for one to four years' service, or commensurate with the Melbourne scale above.
** The Australian pound is equivalent to about $2.25. Thus, in Melbourne, a

Cadetships usually are not longer than four years. Severance-of-employment pay arrangements are prescribed.

Cadets are to be "fully and thoroughly taught and instructed by the employer" in various phases of journalism, including continuous study "in practical journalism" under responsible instruction.

Cadets must acquire "full knowledge of the handling of news." They must learn shorthand and typing, attend lectures by senior journalists and others. They must be shifted from one type of work to another within their special fields. They "shall accompany classified graded journalists on assignments to receive practical instruction" in all kinds of news reporting.

Cadets are permitted four hours off each week to attend classes in shorthand, typewriting, or other instruction within the office; or to attend university or other approved classes. University fees are paid by the employer.

Cadets must be given two weeks' notice of termination of services. After the first forty-eight weeks of service, they are entitled to four consecutive weeks' annual holiday at full pay, and to the same sick benefits and other perquisites as journalists.

Awards designate three categories of cadets: journalist, artist and photographer. Each receives appropriate specialized training.

Recruitment and Training

With some variations, recruitment and training methods do not differ greatly among metropolitan newspaper offices.

Cadets are drawn from university freshman classes; from boys and girls who have passed the "Leaving" examination and have been awarded their "Leaving Certificates" (which approximate U.S. high school diplomas); and from employees working as copy boys or copy girls or in other junior capacities.

The Australian boy or girl attends school from about ages five to twelve in the primary grades; from about twelve to fifteen in the intermediate. Two years more to Leaving Certificate brings the youth to about age seventeen. If he wishes to attend a university, he goes to school another year for matriculation.

The pattern is to start the journalist candidate on his cadetship upon receipt of the Leaving Certificate. The month of decision is January, end of the school year which began the previous March.

There is anxiety among the youngsters as to whether or with what

---

fourth-year cadet would earn about the equivalent of $41.12. But the purchasing power of the pound in Australia is greater than that of commensurate dollars in the U.S.; ergo, Australian real wages are better than they seem.

distinction they passed. Among business and professional men and scouts for young talent there is competition for the brightest prospects as trainees. Many personnel managers for newspaper companies say they feel that if the youngsters are not induced to try journalism at that moment they are lost to the profession for good.

First recruitment step is a written application. Applicants must have passed English at the Leaving Certificate standard. Each candidate is interviewed by the newspaper's cadet counsellor—all metropolitan dailies surveyed had one (or more) full-time or part-time counsellors. Material about journalistic careers is distributed. Each candidate is interviewed by a staff committee who afterwards evaluate skill, personality, education and general background. Written quizzes are given to test general knowledge, news sense and writing ability.

Lectures are regularly held on the premises and cover a variety of subjects. Guided tours of the newspaper plant are frequent. Cadets are periodically examined by oral and written tests.

During a recent year, tours and lectures in one office averaged about three a month and covered a wide range:

Tours of the composing room, advertising department, mechanical departments; rights and wrongs of reporting; newspaper style; current affairs; sharpening copy; what gets into the paper; reading for journalists; history of British and Australian journalism (seven lectures); how to interview; how to summarize news; news quizzes; word usage; mechanics of grammar, layout and makeup.

In another office lectures were divided into two categories:

The first included magazine problems, pictorial journalism, picture layout, reportorial observation, radio and television news techniques, interviews and interviewing, news quizzes and news story exercises (writing of leads, story organization), sub-editing (copy-reading), court reporting, writing special articles.

The second group was mainly composed of background talks by staff members or others. Subjects included Indo-China, Burma, Thailand, Indonesia, the Colombo Plan, The Bandung Conference of Asian-African Powers (talks by press attaches from India, Pakistan and Indonesia), Formosa, the Japanese conquest of Malaya, the East Indies, Japan and the Far East. Other lectures dealt with state politics, Communists in the labor movement, and how to use reference books.

The cadet counsellor keeps an individual file on each cadet. A typical file contains interview reports, school records, comments by editors, roundsmen and other staffers; the cadet's edited copy and clips of his published stories.

The cadet counsellor, chief of staff and senior reporters criticize and discuss the cadet's work. All three categories of cadets—journalist, artist and photographer—report regularly to the counsellor, although technical instruction for the latter two groups is the responsibility of the art and photography departments. The counsellor is confidant as well as instructor.

Classes, Lectures and Exercises

All metropolitan papers regard their cadet programs with great seriousness. The cadet counsellors, full- or part-time, are men and women who enjoy teaching and who give without stint of their time, talent and devotion. Great care is exercised in selecting worthy cadet candidates, capable young men and women who will stay in the profession.

The final choice is usually made by a board composed of senior editors and executives. Since even the largest metropolitan papers take on only a small number of cadets each year, decisions are of considerable moment to the company as well as to the individuals chosen. It is noteworthy that there are few failures or drop-outs among the chosen few.

Some counsellors go beyond the award's requirements and offer counsel on cultivation of good taste in literature, music and theatre; and they often help the cadet with personal problems.

Attendance at shorthand and typing classes is compulsory. Classes are held regularly during the week. In shorthand a speed of 120 words a minute is the goal. Speed tests are frequent.

Classes conducted by newspapers for their own cadets took present form after World War II. Attempts had been made to get the proprietors to agree on a uniform cadet training program which would spell out the precise meaning of the "thorough" instruction specified in the award. Staff shortages were one reason for their failure. Another was that proposals favored the big papers and fell hard upon the small ones. There was no accord on standards. Thereafter, each company went ahead with its own training program.

The best of them are excellent. Lectures are cogent and authoritative. Care is taken with criticism of exercises and with actual assignments. Fundamentals of clear writing, organization, grammar, spelling, usage are stressed. Developing skills and knowledge are tested at intervals. Much time is spent in personal consultation.

In recent years, close attention has been given to training cadets in selecting and organizing news material and in summarizing it accurately. This has been a result of the dominance of tabloids, tighter newspapers and the mounting cost of newsprint.

In one office, the cadets meet for one hour twice a week before work in the morning. This is in addition to their shorthand and university classes, if they attend the latter. A senior staffer lectures on journalistic subjects. Stories are prepared and criticized. Skills in writing, in extracting information from people and other sources are examined. The vocabularies of science and other learned areas are explored. Meticulous care is given to criticism of individual cadet's work.

Lectures and other special events are divided so that the senior cadets (third and fourth years) will not have to repeat what the juniors are getting for the first time. The police roundsmen may set up a robbery situation in order to test a class's ability to observe closely. Lectures on photography deal with news picture-taking, photo editing, layout and related matters. Simulated interviews are held and the stories written from them are subjected to class criticism. News quizzes are given without previous announcement.

On-the-Job Training

The duties to which a cadet is assigned proceed from the easy to the difficult. A typical four-year cadet work pattern goes something like this:

First Year: Weather reports, market quotations, traffic courts, inquests, rewriting of news from country correspondents, minor meetings.

Second Year: Police courts, meetings of various societies, municipal and village councils, minor general assignments.

Third Year: Weekend police day rounds (males only), courts, a selection of other rounds, assistance to pictorial department, sports, women's departments, shipboard interviews.

Fourth Year: General reporting, including Parliament and Government rounds, consistent with the cadets' overall progress.

There are many variations, of course, in the general pattern.

Cadets on one morning daily start their reporting assignments on markets, compiling commodity prices. This is considered to be a stiff test because the state's primary producers (farmers and livestock men) are quick with protests about mistakes in price quotations; thus the cadet learns the importance of accuracy. On Saturdays, in the same office, the beginners are assigned to cover sports events by phone and in person.

Another paper requires its cadets to spend six months in the pictorial department. Later, some are assigned to its capital-city bureau in another state for an equal period.

Cadets are used as "ring around boys." They are assigned to call the rounds for the police report, listen to police radio, answer the telephone at the police press room, check police suburban stations, ambulance and fire brigade headquarters.

Cadets may spend limited periods in the non-editorial departments —(proof) reading room, composing room, process (photo-engraving) department, printing room, publishing (mail) room and so on. They are encouraged to find out why changes were made in their copy by the sub-editors or by the chief of staff. They learn the various steps copy passes through before it appears in the printed newspaper.

On the big dailies, cadets get style books, head-type books, guide books, and manuals of information. They edit house organs.

Cadets are not always started on the daily paper of a publishing firm. Of one company's eighteen cadets sixteen were with the daily—eleven on general news, five with the women's department—and two were with the firm's farm weekly.

A cadet may do his paper little good the first year. As one editor put it, "He's too green and frightened." But now and then one will blossom in as brief a time as six months. In some offices cadets are allowed one year off their cadetships for every year of University attendance.

Cadets are eligible for certain annual awards. Notable among these is the Montague Grover Memorial Prize competition, sponsored by the AJA, and named for an editor who helped to bring the North-cliffetype of journalism to Australia. In October, 1957, similar annual competitions were set up for cadet photographers and cadet artists by the AJA.

Diploma in Journalism

In Australia, a Bachelor of Arts (Ordinary) Degree, requires three years at full-time study; the Degree with Honours requires four years. For the Ordinary Degree, a total of ten credits must be earned: one each in English and a foreign language; six in two major studies of three years each—history, economics, political science or other; and two in electives—political science, history, psychology, physiology or other.

The Diploma in Journalism may be earned in two years at full-time—although it may take more than four, as it works out in practice. The student must acquire six pass credits at Melbourne University, seven at Queensland, from the Arts degree course. As noted earlier, only these two Australian universities offer this curriculum.

At the University of Melbourne, the Diploma in Journalism is administered by the Board of Studies in Journalism, whose chairman is W. Macmahon Ball, Professor of Political Science. The course may be summarized thus:

Candidates must pursue studies for at least two years after admission. A candidate must have matriculated, or be a cadet on a daily newspaper staff, or have had at least three years' newspaper experience.

First year subjects are English, either a study of literature or of writing forms; political science, a study of the nature of political institutions, constitutional problems and related matters; economics, a study of economic theory, economic organization and the economic structure of certain industries; Journalism A, a study of newspaper organization, production and management, newspaper ethics and practical aspects of journalism.

Second year subjects are one each from two groups: (1) British, modern or economic history, or international relations; (2) elementary jurisprudence and constitutional law or Australian history, or a continuation of English, or fine arts, or history and methods of science, or other approved elective.

Journalism B, taken the second year, was formerly called Law Affecting Journalism. It includes thirteen lectures on the history of law and laws concerned with journalism; freedom of speech and press; licensing; postal regulations; censorship; slander and libel; sedition, blasphemy, obscenity; right of privacy; contempt laws; electoral law; practical law for the journalist; rights of the press.

The journalism teaching staff at Melbourne is composed of lecturers in English, economics, political science, law and journalism. The degree of Diploma in Journalism is granted with satisfactory attendance at lectures and the satisfactory completion of prescribed examinations.

At the University of Queensland the requirements and procedures for the Diploma in Journalism are much the same. English, history and economics are prescribed subjects, the candidate having certain elective privileges. He takes Journalism A the first year and Journalism B the second; the ground covered is substantially the same as at Melbourne.

The Queensland course may be taken on a correspondence basis. During the year of this survey, thirty-five persons were enrolled, ten of them as correspondence students. A seven-man Journalism Advisory Committee oversees the journalism curriculum and is composed of the Dean of the Arts College, the professors of English, economics and history, one representative each from *The Courier-Mail, The Telegraph* and the Queensland unit of the Australian Journalists' Association.

The University of Western Australia's two-year course in technical journalism was offered from 1931 until World War II, of which it was a casualty. Sydney University's Diploma course was also short-lived.

Recent signs suggest, however, that change may be in store for cadet education. Australian journalists traveling in the U.S. visit schools of journalism. Fulbright, State Department, Smith-Mundt and Nieman (discontinued in 1959) fellowship programs include Australian journalists, who are also eligible for certain educational programs in Great Britain. John Bennetts, Canberra correspondent for *The News* (Adelaide), spent the school year 1957–58 in the U.S. teaching journalism classes at Michigan State University. U.S. newsmen traveling in Australia find there increasing interest in education for journalism.

More to the point, News Ltd., parent company of *The News* (Adelaide) recently announced a new program of potential significance. It goes beyond the Metropolitan Dailies Award's obligation to pay for tuition, fees and books of interested cadets.

Rohan D. Rivett, until 1960 editor-in-chief of News Ltd., wrote of the program before it went into effect:

> We are not restricting it to cadets. The scheme is open to all junior members of the staff. We are prepared to pay all University fees for any proposed course over a period of four, five or six years at Adelaide University. So far, nine members of the staff will be beginning their university studies this March [1959] but the number may grow rapidly. We are ready to spend up to £1,000 ($2,250) a year on the project.

If News Ltd.'s program should be adopted generally, Australian journalism will have taken a long step on the road to adequate higher education for journalists. However, much must be done before Australia is vigorously part of the worldwide trend toward university programs noted in UNESCO's recent volume, *Training for Journalists.*

An examination of that work, with its summaries of education for journalism in more than two-score countries, illuminates the unique quality of Australia's four-year cadetships. It is apparent that no other nation has a program of practical training as long and detailed, as closely integrated with the press, as carefully supervised by journalists and proprietors, as well-buttressed by the law, or as widely accepted by members of the newspaper profession. Australian academic preparation may leave something to be desired, but the practical training of cadets is as effective as it is indigenous.

Excellences and Deficiencies

The excellences of Australian cadet training are many. So, alas, are its weaknesses. U.S. journalism could benefit from many Australian practices. But U.S. journalism education has perhaps more to offer Australian journalism.

Among Australian editors are concepts about higher education which are puzzling to an American visitor. Nearly all consider a university degree to be desirable journalistic equipment, but they cannot see how it may be installed without wrecking the cadet system.

"After four years as a cadet," they say in effect, "a lad is about twenty-one; three or four more years at the University and he is in his mid-twenties. We can't afford to give him four years of cadet training and then wait for him to get an A.B.—or even a Dip. J., for that matter."

This concept is all or nothing—the present cadet program *vs.* a university degree program. Yet there is a rather obvious alternative— a blend of the two. A readjustment might revise or curtail certain phases of present cadet programs, transfer others to the university campus, provide more time and encouragement for university work.

A change of attitude is a basic requirement. Too much agreement is lip-service. There is little climate of acceptance as to the importance of academic studies. One of the first questions young U.S. job-seekers are asked: "Where did you get your A.B.?" is seldom heard in Australia. University education for journalists is not taken for granted. Few proprietors and editors preach its value. Not enough of them are university-educated.

The Australian cadet on a metropolitan daily lives and works within a short tram ride of a university. But the four hours off work his award gives him for classes each week are filled with shorthand and typewriting lessons, office lectures, examinations and consultations. There is not much time left for university attendance.

Even the free tuition and books provided by the award and paid for by his employer are not an irresistible inducement. Peaks of work at the office, unexpected assignments, the desire to hold the good will of his editors, and the fear that they regard his university classes as highly unimportant, may break both the university routine and the cadet's will to continue. The drop-out rate at the university is high among cadets who start; and not enough start.

The crux of the matter lies in the question, "Why is a university degree so important to the journalist?"

The city or town hall roundsman who knows the history, theory and practice of government in his own municipality is a better reporter of budgets, taxes, special services, capital expenditures, finance and other relevant problems than the roundsman who does not know. The best place to acquire such knowledge is in a university.

The reporter who investigates and reports slum conditions, community health, crime, traffic congestion and other metropolitan problems will do a better job if he has studied sociology and psychology. The labor roundsman who does not know the labor movement's history, its economics, its current status and function will be a less able reporter than his colleague who does know. The science reporter who has not acquainted himself with the sciences may be even worse than useless. He may make his paper ridiculous or the object of suits.

Another way to state it is that one of the urgencies of modern journalism is that editors can no longer be safely satisfied with the *who, what, when* and *where* of many news stories. The *why* and *how* too often overshadow all else.

In at least one field, Australian journalists need even more academic background than Americans. Because of Australia's isolation from the rest of Western society, of which she is such an important unit, Australian journalists should have solid grounding in Pacific area history. They should be close students of the politics, customs, aspirations and problems of the peoples of Southeast Asia and the Orient. They should know the ethnology of their part of the world; the economics of power politics; the history and dynamics of Communism, including its Oriental mutations; nationalism and motivations of neighboring peoples. The list is long and everything on it is basic.

It is perhaps more essential for Australian journalists to know all these things than it is for almost any other Australian group. The journalist reports, explains, analyzes and interprets, and no phase of the news budget is more important to Australia than that which comes from overseas. Australian newspapers need writers and editors who understand the cable news in all its meanings.

There ought to be diligent preparation for the day when the cadet will be next in line for sub-editing, picture editing, editorial writing, news analysis, news direction, column conducting, policy determination and other creative responsibilities. There ought to be a passion for learning, for the habit of study, for higher education. There is passion for shorthand, for typing, for covering a round competently; but little for these other matters.

In too many Australian editorial sanctums a brace of fetishes is worshipped to the continuing hurt of the Australian newspaper press: the fetish of cadet training in mechanics, with a special obeisance to shorthand; the fetish of the self-made reporter who began his cadetship at seventeen and is content to remain forever manacled by his Leaving Certificate.

The Australian universities are fountainheads of the kinds of knowledge and wisdom which Australian journalism must have. Yet the universities are being used to this purpose scarcely at all. There are many university-trained minds among the journalists of Australia, who are reporting and writing brilliantly. But there should be hundreds instead of scores. Australia is ill-served as long as present indifference and opposition to university training persist in the newspaper world.

An American observer is constrained to conclude that all this should not be regarded as a matter of choice by proprietors, editors, the Australian Journalists' Association, and others immediately concerned.

It ought to be considered a matter of commanding necessity.

Shorthand is not more important than survival.

12

Life-Blood: Advertising, Circulation and Promotion

The Business Office

Except that it bears the name of "counting house," the business office of a major Australian newspaper closely resembles that of an American metropolitan daily. The appearance it presents to the customer who comes in to insert an ad, pay for a subscription, buy a photograph, enter a contest or consult the files is about the same, and it has about the same kind of variations. Some newspaper counting houses are almost Dickensian; others are as bright, gleaming and contemporary as architects can make them. An American making a first business visit to one of them would feel at home.

The same is true for the divisions of the business offices. As a rule, there are more than in the U.S., for among the multiform activities of Australia's major newspapers there is more to be divided. The accounts, billings, subscription files and all else of their magazines, book clubs, job printing and so on must be kept up.

But in the daily newspapering phases, the divisions are the same. Under the business (or general) manager are the advertising department, with its display and classified units; and under the circulation department is the organization required to get today's paper to the consumer in the brief while before obsolescence sets in.

From All Over

Principal source of newspaper income is advertising. Over this important business the advertising manager presides. On the biggest papers he has assistants, and under him are the classified and display departments. Display draws from local retail and national sources, has its own salesmen and works closely with the advertising departments of local retail firms and with advertising agencies on national accounts.

In a typical month (April, 1961) column inches of advertising in the metropolitan dailies were divided this way: *

TABLE 6.—COLUMN INCHES OF ADVERTISING IN METRO-POLITAN DAILIES FOR A TYPICAL MONTH

	Total A.M.'s	Total P.M.'s	Combined Totals
Classified	290,576	21,912	312,488
Retail	116,243	152,871	269,114
Amusements	24,765	22,264	47,029
TOTAL LOCAL ADVERTISING	431,584	197,047	628,631
TOTAL ADVERTISING-NATIONAL	291,359	134,188	425,547
TOTAL ADVERTISING	722,943	331,235	1,054,178

Classified ads in the morning dailies lead all other categories. The tradition is strong for large classified ad sections on Saturday in the morning papers, with Wednesday a good runner-up. Also notable is that local retail display advertising is placed in greater volume with the afternoons.

The space ratio for all metropolitans runs about 55 per cent advertising to 45 editorial.** The figure may vary widely between papers,

* From *Newspaper News,* Friday, June 9, 1961. Tabulations prepared by the Bruce Tart Advertising Service. Figures are for 349 issues of the 14 capital city dailies. Total inches (editorial and advertising) for April, 1961, was 1,859,150.

** In Australia advertising is measured in inches, in contrast to the U.S. practice of measuring lines. Australian newspapers which carry the largest amounts of classified advertising have the highest proportion of advertising to news.

or vary in the same paper at different times. On an exceptionally heavy day for business, advertising may go as high as 70 per cent; during slack days it may go as low as 30 per cent or less. Some Saturday afternoon papers carry less than a page of advertising out of a slim total of twelve pages.

Friday night in the classified-ad department and composing room of an Australian morning metropolitan paper is a time of orderly confusion. A 12:30 A.M. printing deadline for a sixty-four-page paper means a succession of lesser deadlines and of mounting tensions. This is how the last hours pass:

A 4:00 P.M. check shows that 400 columns of classified are a certainty. At 10 columns per page, 40 pages are dummied for classified, with eight more pages held in reserve.

Copy and orders arrive by motorcycle messengers from district offices, by foot messengers, by mail, by phone, by train. Word comes that copy for a theater advertisement being flown in will be an hour late. As afternoon gives way to evening, attention centers increasingly on the telephone room.

Here thirty girls take care of last-minute customers. The department's staff of half a dozen classified salesmen, who deal as much in institutional good will as in the selling of space, can do little at this hour. Calls come through the main switchboard to a special panel which, by a system of lights, shows how heavy is the traffic and on which lines it is the heaviest.

Ads are set in 5-point type on a 5-point slug. A complex, but smooth-running system lands type for the ads in the proper classification and then arranges them in alphabetical order. At deadline, the ads are backed up into the last news page; necessary additions or subtractions to that page's news content are made. The final count comes out 430 columns, or 43 of the 64 pages, for classifieds.

It was an easy one to adjust this time; sometimes it is not.

A Student of Maps

The circulation manager of an Australian metropolitan daily is a dedicated student of maps of his home state, necessary aids in determining the shortest distance and shortest time between two points: the press room and the subscriber.

The circulation manager's problem of getting his paper to readers falls into two categories: 1) The metropolitan area; 2) The rest of the state. For both, he employs a system of news agents,* over which he keeps vigilant watch. In the U.S., through a network of district

* See Appendix F, "The Authorized News Agent System."

depots and newsboys, most dailies retain direct control of each copy of a home-delivered paper until it lands on the subscriber's doorstep. In Australia, the newspaper holds scores of contracts with news agents for home-delivery, and it is the news agent and his employees who assume responsibility for delivery.

Within the metropolitan area, the circulation manager's problem is basically similar to that of his U.S. counterpart. It is a matter of maintaining schedule on short truck runs, keeping a watchful eye on the performance of delivery personnel and so on. The problem outstate is a different matter entirely.

Whether his state supports many country dailies or none at all, the metropolitan circulation manager regards the whole state as his special preserve. Even in the two smallest states—Tasmania and Victoria—delivery to country towns and to faraway "bush" subscribers can present knotty problems. Tasmania, which approximates the area of West Virginia, and Victoria, which is about the size of Minnesota, are "small" only in comparison with their Australian sister-states. In the large states, the problems the circulation department must solve are formidable.

In point of fact, Brisbane newspapers are delivered regularly by air to Port Moresby, New Guinea, and to Rabaul, New Britain, though not every day. This, one Brisbane editor believes, may be the longest circulation "throw" in the world. It is, he said, the equivalent of regular delivery of *The Times* (London) to Moscow.

Outstate circulation is much greater for mornings than it is for afternoons, and is commensurately more important. Fast travel by night is easier than by day, and there are more night hours in which to make the runs. Conversely, because afternoons depend greatly upon street sales, weather affects them much more. There is a drop in sales for afternoons in agents' stores on wet days and at "open corners" where there is no overhead cover for a newsboy. *The Herald* (Melbourne), for example, normally makes upwards of 90,000 street sales a day. Even a light shower can have a serious effect; and a cloudburst at the wrong time of day—the five o'clock rush hour—can work a small disaster.

The Papers Go Through

In New South Wales, 685 news agents in the metropolitan area and 1,235 in rural centers get Sydney's four newspapers to readers. Bitter rivals in nearly everything else, the proprietors cooperate in the news agent system and in the means of delivery. *The Sydney Morning Herald* and the *Daily Telegraph,* whose proprietors occasionally assail one another on page one, share truck transportation to New South Wales country towns.

Six main truck routes fan out from Sydney like a gaunt outstretched hand with too many fingers. One goes northeast along the coast, 213 miles to Taree. A second goes north to Tamworth, 267 miles. A third travels northwest 263 miles to Dubbo. The fourth extends west and southwest through Bathurst and Cowra to Wagga Wagga, 302 miles from Sydney. The fifth goes southwest to Canberra, the national capital, 190 miles. The sixth follows the coast line south to Nowra, 100 miles. There is feeder service to smaller centers at various points en route to each destination.

First editions of the two Sydney morning papers start printing just before midnight. The papers are in Canberra by 7:30 A.M., in Dubbo by 8:00 P.M., Tamworth by 8:30 A.M., Wagga Wagga by 11:30 A.M.

Other New South Wales points between Sydney and the Queensland border, 600 miles north at its closest point, and between Sydney and the South Australia border, 900 miles west, are serviced by air. Population thins out according to the ratio of the distance from Sydney, but 7,000 copies of the *Daily Telegraph* are flown southwest into the Riverina district of the Murrimbidgee River Valley. Others are flown north to Coff's Harbor, on the coast. Farthest daily delivery point is to Broken Hill, New South Wales, which is near the South Australian border and is about twice the distance from Adelaide to Broken Hill. In the farthest reaches of these eastern circulation domains, Sydney's papers compete with Brisbane's to the north, with Melbourne's to the south, with Adelaide's to the west.

In South Australia, salt water compounds the problem. Ninety-eight per cent of the population lives in 14 per cent of the state's area, which means within 200 miles of Adelaide. But between Adelaide and readers to the west, at Port Lincoln and Whyalla, lie the Gulf of St. Vincent (Adelaide's sea front), the long crooked finger of the Yorke Peninsula and 200-mile-long Spencer Gulf. This makes South Australia among the most difficult states for deliveries. Trucks from Adelaide must go around the distant north ends of two great gulfs; or else papers must be sent by ship or by airplane, whose schedules are not always geared to press times. Yet, an 11:30 A.M. edition of *The News* is on sale 250 miles away at 4:20 P.M.; and subscribers in Mt. Gambier, 289 miles to the southeast, close to the Victorian border, can read one of *The Advertiser's* post-midnight editions at an 8:00 A.M. breakfast. To Australia's farthest-north city, Darwin, on the Timor Sea, transcontinental commercial airlines carry Adelaide's dailies.

Because it has the smallest circulation and is in the smallest state for both size and population, *The Mercury* (Hobart) has the least difficult time getting its editions to outstate subscribers. One edition starts by truck about 3:00 A.M. and arrives at Burnie on the north coast, 210 miles away, at 7:35 A.M. Another shipment gets into Launceston, 125 miles due north by 6:00 A.M. Trains take other papers up the Derwent Valley into the Central Highlands, starting at 4:00 A.M. Still another train shipment goes northward. Then comes home delivery for Hobart itself which, of course, is the principal circulation area.

The Mercury is the largest of Tasmania's three dailies—all of them morning papers. It competes with *The Advocate* (Burnie) and *The Examiner* (Launceston) on their home grounds. *The Mercury's* Launceston bureau sends a great deal of news to Hobart daily. *The Mercury* has upwards of 450 news agents, about 25 per cent of them in the Hobart metropolitan area. Home delivery accounts for about 50 per cent of *The Mercury's* sales therein. Papers are delivered by boys, who travel on foot or on bicycles. Three trucks making a total of ten runs service the local agents, last deliveries being made before 8:30 A.M. *The Mercury* is Tasmanian distributor for Melbourne and Sydney publications, many of which are flown from the mainland.

More than 100,000 copies of *The West Australian's* 156,006 daily circulation are delivered before 6:45 A.M. within the metropolitan and adjacent areas. Meanwhile, six long truck routes take most of the rest to Albany, 257 miles southeast by 5:00 A.M.; to Geraldton, 311 miles north by 5:25 A.M.; to York, 60 miles east by 4:30 A.M.; to Pemberton, 217 miles due south by 5:15 A.M.; to Margaret River, 178 miles southwest by 7:15 A.M.; and to Merredin, 165 miles east by 3:45 A.M.

In the northern half of huge Western Australia live only about 9,000 people. They read in the neighborhood of 2,000 *West Australians* and somewhat fewer copies of *The Daily News,* though all readers do not get both papers every day. Papers are flown into the far north on commercial flights about three times a week. Farthest point north is to Wyndham on a gulf of the Timor Sea. On two or three days a week, Perth papers get to Wyndham the day of publication.

To Kalgoorlie, which has West Australia's only daily outside of Perth—*The Kalgoorlie Miner*—bundles of *The Daily News* and *The West Australian* are flown each day at noon. Proportionately fewer copies of *The Daily News* are sold to country readers because it is an afternoon paper. *The Daily News'* agents are generally those who handle *The West Australian.*

Perth deliveries may be a little faster than elsewhere in Australia. Because of the mild sunny climate, what is known as "over-the-fence" delivery can be speeded up. News agents' delivery crews hold to the theory that the few times it rains it is better for the customer to have an early wet paper than a late dry one. An agent with one car can put about 1,400 papers per delivery over fences.

From Brisbane, papers are carried by plane, not only to New Guinea, but to Cape York, Australia's most northerly point and to coastal points between; to Normanton, near the base of the Gulf of Carpenteria; to Mt. Isa, the big mining center, close to the Northern Territory border; straight west to Cunnamulla; and more than half way across the continent, northwest to Darwin. Queensland Newspapers Ltd. spend thousands of pounds a year on air service alone. Every Sunday more than 45,000 copies of *The Sunday Mail,* sister publication to *The Courier-Mail* and *The Telegraph* are flown north on these routes.

To state what part of a newspaper's operation is "most important" is somewhat like trying to decide which link in a taut chain is the most important. Certainly, though, the best-edited newspaper in the world is not a newspaper if it is not read. To be read it must be delivered to its readers. There is little snow and less hail in Australia, but neither those, nor dark of night, nor accident nor much of anything else stays the various units of Australia's newspaper delivery system from their appointed rounds.

Promotion and Public Relations

Australian dailies, even in morning and afternoon monopoly situations, are acutely aware of the virtues of promotion and good public relations. All efforts in both are directed, as in the U.S., toward two groups: (1) business and industry, as potential advertisers; (2) the general public, as readers and subscribers.

It is impossible to measure good will and its opposite, ill will, toward newspapers. It can only be noted here that stereotyped attitudes toward the Australian press appeared to be similar to American views of American newspapers. There were the usual charges of bias: Newspapers are anti-labor; can't believe a thing you read in them; they do what the big advertisers tell them to do; they don't tell enough important news; they tell only one side of a story; not enough foreign news; not enough government news; not enough sports; too much foreign news, government news, sports.

These attitudes were based as much, or as little, upon emotion or insufficient evidence as in the United States. To combat the ill will and to build up good will, Australian newspapers appeared to be doing just about as much, or as little, in about the same ways, as American newspapers.

Every issue of *Newspaper News* contains stories of promotion and public relations practices that have proved themselves. Many bear New York, London and other datelines. The general field of public relations is expanding greatly in Australia and *Newspaper News* devotes much editorial space to it, not only in respect to newspapers but to public relations practices and techniques generally.

Toward the Potential Advertiser

Newspaper News itself is a favored medium for advertising promotion. The metropolitans use half- and full-page advertisements therein to note their sterling qualities as advertising media. Much is made of readership, retail-trading-area circulation, readers' buying power and so on. Advertisements are purchased in trade and specialized journals throughout Australia and as far away as Britain and the U.S. Brochures, charts, graphs are circulated to compare advertising effectiveness of the individual newspaper and its competitors.

Much thought and energy are expended in enticing buyers of classified advertisements. Because these are directed at the general reader-as-advertiser, the promotion thereof is on many fronts: in the paper itself; by spot commercials on the radio; by ads in theater, sporting, country show and other programs of public events; latterly by television. Institutional ads are published in the same media. Use is made of billboards, or hoardings, and of ads in other newspapers.

At least one morning paper found that faster delivery in distant places helped sell classified ads. By the use of timber carters (trucks), milk trucks and school buses it was able to cut down on delivery time. In many places where three or four days had been required for delivery the circulation department materially increased the number of families who get the day's paper before breakfast. Classified ads purchased in those areas began to rise.

Another morning paper publishes a four-page monthly summary of business conditions in its home state and circulates it among advertising prospects.

To Get and to Hold

The drumfire directed at the reader is loud, varied and continuous. He is beseeched, told, lured, enticed, beguiled, implored, promised, urged to buy a particular paper.

Most obvious, and most different from U.S. practices in promoting the day's sale of a metropolitan newspaper is the poster. Posters are not used in the U.S. The closest equivalent is the cardboard display on an honor box. But usually in the U.S. these advertise some department's work or some short-time special feature.

The Australian poster, on the other hand, advertises today's news today. It is a device which, like many another in Australia, came directly from Britain. (See illustration facing page 145.)

The poster is a sheet of newsprint that measures eighteen inches by twenty-six inches; it carries the paper's name prominently and a legend, printed as large as the space permits, that advertises the day's story most calculated to induce the passerby to buy a paper. It may be about anything in the paper:

HOSPITAL	ANOTHER	CABINET
CHARGES	ATTACK	CRISIS
TO DOUBLE	ON WOMAN	SHOCK

"Shock" and "Shocking" are words which recur in headlines and on posters, possibly because they are staples of Australian conversation in expressions of surprise or disapproval.

The posters are printed in time for insertion in bundles of newly-printed papers that are on the way to the news agent (See Appendix F). Posters are also used to advertise magazines and other publications. They are contained in frames made to size and are placed outside news agents' stores. One Sydney daily uses a buff paper to distinguish its own from posters of other papers. Poster letters may be four inches high.

Such activities as book clubs, dress patterns, cook books, picture books and other free or paid-for services all have a promotional value. They bring to readers' attention the merits of a paper as surely, though not as spectacularly, as the sky-writing which some papers use on a windless day.

There are also such other usual devices as window displays of special features or departments, booths at the Royal Show that each capital-city presents annually and which is comparable to a State Fair in the U.S. Prizes for excellence in surfing, football and other group competitions are given by many papers. Queens of this and that are popular with many promotion departments; finding and crowning the fortunate young female each season provides readers with a great deal of bikini and cheesecake art. A football contest drew 250,000 entries in a fortnight.

Quite often a fee—sixpence or a shilling—is charged for entering a promotion contest and some of the takings are prorated to a hospital, charity fund or other worthy cause. Motor cars, refrigerators, radios, movie and still cameras and other prizes, including cash, are distributed to winners.

In this same genre is a word-game based on crossword puzzle techniques which has also had quite a vogue in the U.S. In Australia, it is called "Wealthwords," "Gold Words" or something similar. It is laid out so that a majority of the ups and downs could be one of two or more words; the odds against a completely correct answer being, therefore, astronomical. This type of game, said A. H. Chisholm, in his article on "Newspapers" in *The Australian Encyclopedia,* "reached an extraordinary height" in 1955. One newspaper "was fined £50, under the Lotteries and Gaming Act, for conducting such a competition."

There are also such enterprises as "Learn-to-Swim" programs, surfing club, best garden, music, camera and other competitions, some with cash and other prizes of substantial value. One "Golden Baby Quest" was worth £3,000 in prizes.

Occasionally, illustrated books on newspaper production and a company's related activities are published. Tours bring the public into the plant itself. Book and cash prizes go to schools or to individual students for scholastic excellence. Direct mail is occasionally used for promotion. Here and there an informal speakers' bureau is maintained by a newspaper.

It does not take long for an idea in newspaper promotion to be born somewhere, be examined for its potentials, tried out and used until its usefulness is exhausted. The fecundity quotient for ideas in Australia is about what it is elsewhere; so proportionally about as many good promotional schemes are exported as are imported.

13

Conclusions
and Judgments

Aussie and Yank

A wry witticism has it that you can be an expert about a foreign country only if you stay less than ten days in it; thereafter, the longer you stay, and the more you learn, the less "expert" you become. Thus, only those visitors who have had the advantage of a superficial view of the Australian newspaper press can indulge the luxury of sweeping judgments. After my thirteen months of study, the need for careful summaries and cautious conclusions stands forth as a primary requirement.

Too, there is the matter of presumption. What right has a visiting American to pass judgment? None, except deep interest and the desire to complete a task to which considerable time and energy have already been devoted. That, plus the expectation, encountered nearly everywhere, that a study of this kind would attempt to draw conclusions. So presumption is justified, I hope, by the need to put an end in proper sequence to the beginning and the middle. There is no wish here to be definitive. What follows is one man's opinion.

The Fulbright award which made this study possible was granted so that the differences and similarities between Australian and American metropolitan newspapers might be examined. The similarities have far outweighed the differences: and that, perhaps, is the first conclusion.

An American visitor feels at home with Australian newspapers. The proportion of tabloids to standard-size dailies is much greater in Australia than in the U.S., but it is easy to find one's way around in both kinds. News is departmentalized the same way. Columns are narrower, headlines and typography dress are different, there is more "circus" makeup. Many headlines and stories use words, locutions and idiomatic phrases that puzzle. Stop-press and "fudge" boxes are unfamiliar. But these and other small differences detract little from the American reader's feeling that he is not far from home.

The language of newspapering is a little different, but in no important way. This is of far less consequence than that there is instant camaraderie, an immediately-established sense of freemasonry, among Australian and American newspapermen. Within seconds after meeting they are talking shop. In a newspaper sense, that means they are talking about everything underneath, beyond and inside the sun; for everything, at one time or another, concerns a newspaperman.

But there are much more basic similarities.

The press is free in both countries; it is independent of government control. Its right to print the news with impunity is guaranteed by the democratic society whose life it reports. Newspapers in both countries are owned by individuals or corporations. They profess to be dedicated to the public good; and similar dedications to the cash register and to the conservatism that is built-into big private enterprises cloud the zeal of the first dedication in Australia no more than they do in the United States.

As the poor man's encyclopedia, as mirrors of the world's day, as crusaders for rights against wrongs, as entertainment media, Australian newspapers may not do as superb a job as their proprietors claim; but they do a far better one than their most captious critics charge.

Indeed, in the last-named department—entertainment—they do an almost deplorably fine job, about which thoughtful journalists frequently become bitter and unhappy. As in the U.S., the entertainment function of newspapers in Australia has got shockingly out of hand. In one sense, because they take up so much space and are imports, in good part, from the U.S. and England—are not even home-grown —the comic-strip situation is worse in Australia than in the U.S. It helps to keep the frivolity content of the big journals noisomely high.

Against this may be balanced more fundamentals. The newspaper press of Australia is free from all subsidies. As in the U.S., decisive economic factors are at work on a business that is a profession, an art, a craft and a quasi-public institution with unique responsibilities and of unique performance.

The same problems of how to keep solvent are present. So are those of relationships with government, political parties, special interest groups; of dividing available space between advertising and editorial matter; of being fair, impartial and complete in coverage of news; of being enlightened, persuasive, fair-minded, cogent and lucid in opinions expressed; of being community leaders; of drawing a creditable line between giving the reader "what he wants" and "what he ought to have"; of "afflicting the comfortable and comforting the afflicted"; of interpreting readers to themselves; of keeping a firm control over the constant conflict between principle and expediency; in sum, of putting out good newspapers.

Australian newspapers also must show a profit in order to stay alive. Revenue is derived about 65-35 per cent from advertising and circulation. Tables of organization are much the same, though the names of comparable jobs vary a little. In both countries, newspapers seek to report the news objectively, dispassionately and completely in their news columns, reserving their views to the leader pages and opinion features. Both admit to responsibilities incapable of exact definition.

Australian and U.S. newspapers are subject to the same pressures of deadlines and the tyranny of "nowness." Both have only their editorial judgment as a checkrein—and it can slip badly—on the temptation to sensationalize for bigger circulation. The laws that restrict them are, in some areas, considerably different, as to kind and enforcement; but on balance they shape the end-product in about the same way.

Both newspaper presses have had to fight hard, bitter battles against government attempts to coerce or suppress, and the Australian combats of recent decades have been more vigorous than the American. Both presses are free from intimate ties with political parties, but both come home to conservatism when the chips are down.

Perhaps no Australian paper among them is as good as its proprietors and editors say it is; but if there are few to match those constants of absolute comparison, *The Times* of London and *The New York Times,* there are none as deliberately foul as the worst of the London papers. It is extremely pertinent to the similarities between U.S. and Australian newspapers that they share a common ancestor in the seventeenth and eighteenth century English press.

Traditions and Shortcomings

After such matters, the differences begin to show—traditions, for example. Not many U.S. newspapers seriously consider themselves as "newspapers of record," in the manner of *The New York Times.*

No paper in Australia does it as well as *The New York Times,* but proportionately more papers appear to have this sense of mission than have it in the U.S.

The Australian "newspaper of record" is found most notably among the broadsheets—*The Sydney Morning Herald, The Age* (Melbourne), *The Advertiser* (Adelaide), *The Courier-Mail* (Brisbane), *The Herald* (Melbourne); and in some tabloids, e.g., *The West Australian* (Perth) and the *Daily Telegraph* (Sydney).

In another category, there are papers with a crusading tradition, *The News* (Adelaide) for example.

There is also the tradition that afternoon papers should be edited more to amuse and entertain, while the mornings are "serious." The resulting concept, that afternoon papers are "feature papers" dealing chiefly in sin, sex and sensation is baffling to an American. Part of the bafflement derives from the tradition's absence in the U.S. If it were stronger, American readers would be grossly ill-served, for U.S. afternoons outnumber morning dailies five to one. (In the State of Michigan, the recent death of a morning paper left the state tally of dailies at 52 afternoons, *one* morning paper).

The reporting of hard news in Australia is done in a concise, efficient prose that is easy to read and to understand. This is true from Brisbane to Perth and in all capital points between. It is almost as if all writers had been taught in the same school, in which the usefulness of simple Anglo-Saxon-derived English and of lean-muscled working verbs were stressed. This survey is aware of no such study of readability of the Australian press as that made by Dr. Rudolf Flesch for the U.S. Associated Press. Such a study would doubtless show a creditable score.

This is no small merit, but a discussion of newspaper prose cannot be left there. On the debit side is the scarcity of deep, graceful, witty, allusive and evocative writing. It is there, but not in any quantity. *The Age* (Melbourne) and *The Sydney Morning Herald* probably produce as much as any other metropolitan daily. Again, name off the broadsheets and you have a good share of the best. Part of the reason is a simple matter of space: the broadsheets have more column-inches—for theme development, for reporting in depth, for exploration of subjects that are a bit apart from the ruck of the news. Inevitably they attract the kind of writer who can best do such tasks. There are such journalists on the tabloids, but not nearly as many. Much excellent newspaper writing in the U.S. is done by columnists—also a great deal of the worst—and this, as noted earlier, is a field Australian proprietors have rigidly limited.

John Douglas Pringle, editor (1951–57) of *The Sydney Morning Herald,* made a point of this in his Arthur Norman Smith Memorial Lecture at Melbourne University in June, 1957. Then he went a bit further. He said that "with a few honorable exceptions, Australian intellectuals are extraordinarily bad at expressing their thoughts in simple and vigorous English. . . . When you invite them to write an article they produce something so dull and unintelligible that it is guaranteed to frighten off readers in the first paragraph." *

This point may at first seem irrelevant to the main theme here, but it is not, for the English do much inviting of this sort. Their leading newspapers are full of excellent discussions of specialties by non-journalist specialists. Americans and Australians do little of it, and a leavening is lost to the press. To get a supply of adept "serious" scriveners—journalists well above the status of good police reporters—special efforts must be made. Australian editors seem not to be making enough effort. There is much room for improvement; in the "something for everyone" newspaper the Australian who likes the world of ideas often gets short shrift.

Bigness Again

Nothing (else) succeeds like success. The Australian capital-city newspapers exemplify the moss-grown maxim. Because they have succeeded so well, they not only dominate their respective states as newspapers, but by the relentless economics of success have made themselves dominant in other ways—in magazine and book publishing, radio, television, job printing and in a few non-communication fields.

Where these extra-curricular activities bear upon printing, the rationale is clear: It is uneconomic for huge presses to sleep statically between editions. Put them to work. In such fields as newsprint manufacture and overseas news importation the economic compulsion is equally plain.

When Ezra Norton became an ex-newspaper publisher, an interesting reason for the purchase was given by the new owners' financing agents, one of the three biggest newspaper proprietorships on the continent: They said they wished to keep Truth and Sportsman out of the hands of another member of the biggest three. Bigness had to grow bigger to protect itself. This reason for bigness, in altered phraseology, was encountered more than once in the course of this survey.

Surely, too, this is why Australian metropolitan newspapers, hav-

* Quoted from *Newspaper News,* July 1, 1957.

ing long been deep in radio, have gone heavily into television, although the monopoly trend there is held somewhat in check by the required inclusion of assorted non-newspaper associates in assignment of channels. The compulsion was economic in another way: The advertising pound was threatened. The way to nullify the threat was to do what had been done with radio. If the opportunity to lick 'em wasn't visible, join 'em—right at the start.

Another compulsion derives from the exceptions that prove our basic rule. The corporate newspaper psyche may be spectre-haunted by another aphorism, not conclusively demonstrable and not in quite as common coin: Get bigger or die.

The seven present proprietorships that control Australia's entire metropolitan daily press are evidence enough of the aphorism's potency.

More Light from Abroad

More than one Australian editor of the second or third echelon expressed regret that more overseas news was not published in the metropolitans. One even bitterly charged that sports and racing news, since the end of World War II, have steadily nibbled away the space allotted foreign affairs to its present deplorably small daily portion.

The AAP, within limits, does its job well. Incoming annual wordage is increased each year. But it is the view of many a cable editor that the biggest story of all for Australia—change in the Orient— is being badly neglected. There should be more special and press association personnel stationed in China, Japan, India, the countries of the southeast Asia mainland; in Indonesia, Formosa and in Oceania.

There is too much reliance upon London, Paris and New York for news, and not enough upon correspondents in middle and eastern Europe, in the U.S.S.R., in Africa, in the Mediterranean, in the mid-continent U.S. states. Australia, these editors say, still resists the World War II lesson that her future is bound up more with the Far Eastern half of the southern hemisphere than with the United Kingdom and Europe.

With all this I must agree; and I must echo one other sentiment widely encountered—that Australians should have more news about the United States. During my thirteen months in Australia, news from my homeland seemed mainly about violence and segregation; sex and adultery in café society and in Hollywood, and other ugly or nauseating trivia. One cable editor prized, above all other kinds, what he called "odd-ball four-par [paragraph] stories about Chic Sale hillbilly characters."

If Australia and the United States are to be cast in the world role of *fidus Achates* to one another—and they surely are—they must know each other better. And knowing each other, of course, is a two-way matter.

Leaders Should Lead

The starvation in the midst of plenty that afflicts many U.S. editorial pages is true of Australia's leader pages. Nothing is wrong with them that a keener respect for their purpose, more money for better staff, and more time for effective research and contemplation by the leader writers could not cure.

It was shocking for one conditioned to the Pulitzer concept of the editorial page as the newspaper's conscience to find in *The Sun News-Pictorial* (Melbourne), Australia's newspaper of biggest circulation, in *The Daily News* (Perth) and in the *Daily Mirror* (Sydney) no leader pages at all.* No amount of enlightened signed opinion can make up for the deficiency. The shock diminishes when one remembers the quality of editorials in many U.S. dailies, both large and small. Still, the visitor yearns for more Olympian thunder in the Australian press, more lightning bolts to smite the wicked, and much, much more light.

First-rate leader pages in Australia, in terms of leadership, of illumination, of crusading zeal, of broad vision and intellectual integrity are few and more than geographically far between. The U.S., with 1,750 daily newspaper and a metropolitan press numbering hundreds of units perhaps can afford a percentage of mediocre, stupid, troglodyte or even downright vicious editorial pages. Australia, with only fourteen metropolitan papers and an expanding population, cannot.

Perhaps the judgment is gratuitous, but this surveyor thought *The Sydney Morning Herald* leader page consistently the best of them all; and he found high but varying quality in the leader columns of *The Age* (Melbourne), *The Courier-Mail* (Brisbane), *The News* (Adelaide), *The West Australian* (Perth), the *Daily Telegraph* (Sydney), and *The Herald* (Melbourne). Familiar curses are at work in Australia, as in the U.S. Leaders that are insular, parochial, fence-straddling, stuffy, obscure, biased, heavily partisan are too

* One of News Ltd.'s innovations, after it purchased the *Daily Mirror* in 1960, was a leader page in a generally improved newspaper.

common. With one or two exceptions, there are not enough leader writers per paper.

Too often the views expressed are hag-ridden by old inter-colonial jealousies that should have been done in at Federation. Most leader writers are overworked; as the familiar charge goes, they have to write so much they do not have time to think. They ought to be permitted more time to contemplate and to investigate the issues with which they are expected to deal provocatively or definitively.

One reads about the fire and brimstone served up in the old days by the earlier editors of *The Age, The Argus, The Sydney Morning Herald* and *The Courier.* Time tends to glamorize forthright editors. But no great cause was ever led by newspapers dedicated to keeping boats on even keels. No worthy crusade was ever accomplished by a policy of not rousing the animals. Like the U.S., Australia has too much irrelevance, waspishness, worship of things-as-they-are in the published leaders of its major papers. A good leader page should be irascible, eternally contemptuous of sham, impatient with stupidity, volcanic against evil; it should not be predictable. The reader should not be permitted to believe that leader writers have only the courage of their employers' convictions and that these convictions are about the wrong things or in the wrong century.

Where Are the Informed Critics?

There are plenty of stereotyped, ideological and political blasts, but a visitor looks in vain for effective voices giving sustained, documented criticisms of the daily press, either from within or without. Representing, roughly, employee and proprietor viewpoints, neither the *Journalist* nor *Newspaper News* publishes much in criticism of the press beyond the doctrinaire and the expected.

There are reasons for the absence of criticism. The paucity of "serious" national journals of comment and criticism has long been a matter of concern to thoughtful Australians: In recent years, *Meanjin* (Melbourne), *Southerly* (Sydney) and the venerable *Bulletin* (Sydney),* have been more or less alone in the field. *The Observer* and *Nation* joined them in 1958. But seldom in these, or elsewhere, is there more than vagrant sniping, or an occasional probe of a specialized phase of journalism. Australia has few counterparts of the press criticism published in the English journals of comment or

* In November, 1960, Australian Consolidated Press, proprietors of *The Daily Telegraph* (Sydney), purchased *The Bulletin;* they merged it with *The Observer* early in 1961.

in the American *New Yorker* ("The Wayward Press" Department), *Harper's, The Atlantic, The Nation, The New Republic, The Reporter,* and in the "Press" sections of *Time* and *Newsweek,* among others.

Australia has few counterparts, either, of *Masthead, Nieman Reports, Journalism Quarterly,* the American Society of Newspaper Editors *Bulletin,* the Associated Press's and United Press International's weekly logs, the AP's *Red Books* and *Blue Books,* Sigma Delta Chi's *The Quill,* Theta Sigma Phi's *Matrix, American Editor, Grassroots Editor, Publishers' Auxiliary, American Press,* and similar journals concerned with journalism. There are too few Australian media for challenge of prevailing journalistic practices and concepts.

Finally, there is little information published in the general magazines about press institutions and newspaper personalities, famous or infamous. The reason for this last is not far to seek. Most of the general magazines are owned by the big newspaper companies. It would be poor taste to run stories about one's self or one's associates. And who wants to build up the opposition with publicity about them?

This does not mean that Australian editors are not aware of the need for improvement of product—nor does it mean, to be fair about it, that American newspapers have become paragons because of the greater flow of criticism in the U.S. Far from it. Newspapers go out of business when editors lose sight of this need, even briefly; and a visitor to Australia has only to sit in on editorial department conferences to know how strong and constant is the compulsion for better newspapers. But firing line concern is less with the larger, long term problems of newspaper ethics, improvement, and responsibility than with the way to improve the looks of today's page one or tomorrow's picture layout. There is, of course, much more self-criticism by the Australian press than is apparent to the outsider. There is also a great deal of vicious and petty criticism from outside. A. T. Shakespeare wrote about it in "After Fifty Years," a booklet issued for the golden jubilee conference, in 1949, of The New South Wales Country Press Association:

> One of the features of postwar years has been the extent to which the Press has found itself exposed to attack. Misunderstanding is not uncommon but there have been signs that criticisms and official attempts to undermine confidence in the Press have been much more serious. Much heart searching in the newspaper industry has sought to provide effective defence of the right and the means of free expression, and the newspaper industry in all branches has undergone a critical examination. (Page 35.)

Constant heart- and head-searching are *sine qua nons* of news-papering. Both kinds would be helped if Australia had more articulate practicing critics, and more media in which their criticisms could be published. If publishers and editors, at best, are notoriously thin-skinned about adverse judgment, in Australia they ought not to be subjected to so few chances to prove it. The sum of it is that the best newspapers on earth need informed criticism, for newspapers progress or deteriorate, they never stand still; only by intelligent criticism can they go forward. Australia's newspapers as a group are not exempt from this rule.

Still, fairness requires additional comment; for the newspaper press of a democracy is an obvious scapegoat. Its very form and nature make it vulnerable to attack for evils for which it is much less than totally responsible. It makes crime "attractive." It builds up hero-worship for mediocrity. It "glamorizes" unworthy men and women. It "encourages" immorality. It "loosens family ties." It does not encourage education, religion, right living, patriotism (finish the list yourself) strongly enough. And so on.

Charges like these are based on misconceptions about the nature and function of newspapers and about their ability to influence mass behavior. Some critics seem to expect newspapers to do better the tasks that parents, homes, churches, schools, government, labor unions, businesses and many other institutions and activities are supposed to accomplish. Such critics, basically, do not understand that the press is a *popular* institution, with all that implies of education levels, morality, family and individual interests, wisdom; and, perhaps most of all, with what it implies about reflecting the intellectual life of its readers.

Angus H. MacLachlan, general manager of *The Sydney Morning Herald,* stressed this point in the conclusion of his 1954 Arthur Norman Smith lecture, "Readability and Responsibility," * at the University of Melbourne:

> And now, at the end, I want to suggest to you that, in the long run, it is education that will decide the future standards of the Press, the radio, the films, and, before long, television. We call ourselves an educated nation because we have compulsory education, magnificent schools and a staggering educational budget. But is an educated nation one in which the great majority of its people are entirely withdrawn from any direct educational influence at the age of 15 and in which even those fortunate enough to have education after that age are taught much more about how to earn a living than about how to cultivate interests that will enrich their living. . . .

* Printed by John Fairfax & Sons, Pty. Ltd., 38 Hunter St. Sydney (1954).

218

And so I leave those questions with you—with this thought added: that while the Press must accept to the full its own responsibilities, its standards will more surely be raised when more of those who read it have been taught to read wisely and to read well, to prefer the better to the worse, to want to be informed as well as amused and to look on a free and responsible Press as evidence of their own freedom and a measure of their own sense of responsibility.

The Press's Public Relations

Australian readers don't seem to put a very high value on their newspaper press. In each capital, without exception, wherever there was more than one newspaper, I was asked in all seriousness, many times, whether I didn't think one of the papers was just about the worst in Australia. Sometimes the whole kit and boodle was consigned to the outer darkness.

"Lying rags," "Can't believe a word they say," "Nothing in them" —it was a familiar chorus. It was varied by another theme, also quite familiar, implied if not always spoken: that the critic, though he knew nothing about newspapering, would be a better editor than the editor. Here and there firm voices were raised in praise or approbation, but they were distressingly few.

Among members of certain specialized groups reactions were often identical. Much of labor's and of the Labor Party's canon is based upon the alleged iniquity of the press. Some labor leaders do what U.S. Southerners did to "damn Yankee"—blend their dislike into one word—"lyingcapitalistpress," varying it with "filthy," "bloody" or "lousycapitalistpress." It would be a terrible day for Labor solidarity if the rank and file were persuaded that the lying description was itself a lie or even as inaccurate and unfair as it palpably is.

There is the usual snob attitude toward the press among many university academicians and intellectuals. These people, having no accurate concept of what newspapers attempt to do, and obsessed by preconceived fixations about what they ought to be, attack the press with stereotyped criticisms that are often irrelevant, contemptible or absurd. The American press is similarly attacked by academic critics.

In sum, as in the United States, newspapers in Australia are astonishingly backward about public relations—their own. They attempt to catch big advertisers by praising themselves in full page ads in *Newspaper News* and NAARDS. They print institutional advertisements. They use plugs on the radio and on television. They indulge in all sorts of contests and premium offers to catch new subscribers and re-ensnare old ones.

But almost no attempts are made to tell the reading public what the proprietors conceive to be their mission in life. Little is printed about the staggering problems that face editors every minute of every working day, about the deadline decisions that must be made, why this was done instead of that, about the bona fides of the paper's management, about the long training and the wealth of experience required to make a dependable reporter or capable editor, about one thousand other matters that produce headaches, ulcers and good newspapers.

Australian and American editors have blind spots. They are stewards of an institution about which the public is avidly curious; yet almost never—except in anniversary editions, in occasional supplements or special sections—do the editors open the windows of their plants and their minds to the public. The complexity of the newspaper operation, the fallibility and humanity of the editorial staff, and the monumental difficulties that even the simplest story sometimes produces—if all these were more widely known, more understanding and appreciation of the newspapers of Australia would ensue.

Today and Tomorrow

The cliché runs that a country gets the kind of newspaper press that it deserves. This is only partly true, for another truth is that the press of a nation takes its character, direction and integrity from the men in the top newspaper positions. Still a third truth is that the worst of newspapers can become the best, and the best can degenerate into oblivion over the years. *The Denver Post* went from deplorable to excellent after its present editors took control. *The Sun* (New York) died of malnutrition after years of desperately trying to live on the memory of its brilliant reputation. These assorted truisms are another way of saying that the character and quality of today's newspapers are not necessarily the character and quality of tomorrow's. One of the challenges of newspapering is that any newspaper is always capable of improvement. This is as true in Australia as it is anywhere else on earth.

What, then, should be said here as a final word?

Certainly I can say nothing final about either Australia or its press; and even tentative conclusions are less important than the prospects for tomorrow and the day after.

This work is not a sociological study. I had neither means nor intent to assay the role of the press in Australian history or its impact upon current Australian life. Conclusions herein that seem to go in such directions are, lacking both a sociological and a scientific basis, more opinion than judgment. I made no special effort to turn up answers to questions about the metropolitan press's partisanship, the degree of its conservatism, attitudes of readers to their home newspapers, readership, apportionment of information and entertainment, newspapers' attitudes toward public evils and social ills. Here and there these matters were touched upon, but only incidentally because they were apart from my principal purpose. They had no proper place in this work—space limitations alone would rule them out. However, Australian newspaper proprietors ought to instigate research on these and many related matters so that the Australian press will know not only where it is now but where it is going.

There is much in the Australian metropolitan press of which every Australian may be proud. There is much for which Australian newspaper proprietors, editors and journalists may take great credit. Their enterprise and effectiveness in gathering and presenting much of the news is admirable. Their product—the newspapers themselves —must rank high in any evaluation of the world's newspaper press. But there are phases of Australian newspapering that are bad. Superficiality of reporting, sensationalism, entertainment at the expense of hard news, failure to provide adequate Asiatic news coverage, the scramble for cheap promotional gimmicks, too much concern with dividends and not enough with service and journalistic responsibility —these are some of the adverse factors which trouble the visitor and which should trouble thoughtful Australians even more.

It is true that the metropolitan daily press of Australia is a credit to the nation, a worthy supporter of the traditions of Western journalism, is frequently a bastion of strength, a noonday illumination and a staunch member of the all too small free press of the world.

But it must become increasingly better.

Its responsibilities are enormous. So must be its responses to challenge.

APPENDIX A

Acknowledgments

A special kind of gratitude goes to certain friends for their assistance: to these, for these reasons—

For endorsing my application when I submitted my Fulbright project proposal: President Clarence B. Hilberry, Wayne State University; Dean Victor A. Rapport, Liberal Arts College, Wayne State University; John S. Knight, president and editor, Knight Newspapers, Inc. (for which I worked for a decade); Dr. Ralph J. Casey, former director, School of Journalism, University of Minnesota.

For encouragement, assistance and counsel: W. Macmahon Ball, professor of political science and chairman of the Board of Studies in Journalism, University of Melbourne; Ian Maxwell, professor of English, University of Melbourne; Mrs. Margaret Sterne, associate professor of history, Wayne State University; Richard V. Burks, formerly associate professor of history, Wayne State University.

For shepherding the Holdens expertly and graciously in their Australian travels: Geoffrey G. Rossiter, executive officer, U.S. Educational Foundation in Australia; his capable staff; and Robert J. Boylan, until 1957 chief of the U.S. Information Service in Australia.

For assistance in gathering printed research material: C. A. McCallum, chief librarian, J. A. Feeley, assistant chief librarian, Phillip Garrett, research department, Public Library of Victoria, Melbourne; H. L. White, chief librarian, Commonwealth National Library, Canberra; and their respective staffs.

For permitting me the run of their newspaper plants and—to many of them—for adding the gift of continuing friendship: in Sydney— Vincent C. Fairfax, director, Angus McLachlan, general manager, John Fairfax Ltd.; John M. D. Pringle, editor, and Louis Leck, news editor, *The Sydney Morning Herald;* Lindsay Clinch, executive editor, and John Goodge, editor, *The Sun;* Sir Frank Packer, managing director, David McNicoll, editor-in-chief, Australian Consolidated Press Ltd.; J. Kingston

Watson, editor, *Daily Telegraph;* Eric Kennedy, former chief executive officer, Associated Newspapers Ltd.; John Briears, editor, *Newspaper News;* Lindsay Revill, *Pix Magazine;* in Melbourne—the late Sir Harold Campbell, editor, E. K. Sinclair, associate editor (now editor), Geoffrey Hutton, drama-music critic and feature writer, *The Age;* Sir John Williams, managing director, J. C. Waters, editor-in-chief, Archer Thomas, deputy editor-in-chief, The Herald and Weekly Times Ltd.; Frank Daly, editor, *The Sun News-Pictorial;* R. C. Edwards, editor, *The Herald;* Robert J. Nelson, last editor of *The Argus;* in Brisbane—T. C. Bray, editor-in-chief, *The Courier-Mail;* E. R. Jackson, editor, *The Sunday Mail;* John Wakefield, editor-in-chief, *The Telegraph;* in Adelaide— Rupert Murdoch, publisher, and Rohan Rivett, editor-in-chief, News Ltd.; John Bennetts, Canberra correspondent, *The News;* D. G. McFarling, managing editor, and Harry Plumridge, assistant editor, *The Advertiser;* in Perth—James E. Macartney, managing editor, and Malcolm J. L. Uren, assistant to the managing editor, West Australian Newspapers Ltd. (who also were hosts to me on their sixty-man, 3,000-mile, three-week tour of Western Australia's outback in July, 1956); in Hobart—G. F. Davies, chairman of directors, Davies Brothers Ltd.; R. E. Shone, editor, R. A. Fulton, chief of staff, Denis Hawker, feature and editorial writer, Bernard Gordon, chief, Launceston Bureau, *The Mercury;* R. W. Henry, manager, Australian Newsprint Mills Ltd.

For patiently typing and re-typing the manuscript: Mrs. Herman Stein and Miss Mary Scarlin, present and former Wayne State University Journalism Department secretaries. For invaluable work in preparing the final draft of this book for the printer: Mrs. Barbara Woodward, assistant editor, Wayne State University Press. For compiling the index: Sheila Holden, my wife.

Hundreds of Australians helped me to gather material for this book. They freely gave all they were asked to give; many gave much more. With nearly every one whose name is listed below I had a formal interview; with others I spoke informally and on social occasions. Not all those named continue in the positions which they held in 1956–57 when I knew them. Some of the persons listed have added promotions, honors, achievements and new chapters to their careers. Some have changed positions. Some have left the newspaper field. Some have seen their jobs become casualties of mergers and ownership changes. A few have died.

NOEL ADAMS, leader writer, *The Advertiser,* Adelaide; GORDON ANDREWS, acting cable editor, *The Age,* Melbourne; MURRAY ARCHER, picture editor, *The Argus,* Melbourne; MRS. MARY ARMITAGE, social editress, *The Advertiser,* Adelaide; HAROLD J. AUSTIN, news editor, *The Age,* Melbourne, JOHN ATHERTON, feature writer, *The Courier-Mail,* Brisbane.

ALAN BAILEY, finance editor, *The Advertiser,* Adelaide; NOEL BAILEY, police rounds, *The Sun,* Sydney; ERIC J. BALFE, parliament rounds, *The Mercury,* Hobart; NIGEL BALFE, sports editor, *The Argus,*

Melbourne; W. MACMAHON BALL, professor of political science and chairman of the Board of Studies in Journalism, University of Melbourne; ALLAN BARKER, reporter, *The West Australian*, Perth; J. F. BARKER, circulation manager, *The Mercury*, Hobart; JAMES BARNES, assistant editor, *The Sun News-Pictorial*, Melbourne; LEO BASSER, chief of staff, *Daily Telegraph*, Sydney; BRUCE BEAMER, Photography Department, *The Sun News-Pictorial*, Melbourne; MISS VICTORIA BECKINGSALE, *Australian Women's Weekly*, Melbourne Bureau; JACK BENGER, block room, *The Sydney Morning Herald*, Sydney; PETER BENNETT, sports editor, *The Sun News-Pictorial*, Melbourne; JOHN BENNETTS, Canberra correspondent, *The News*, Adelaide; DAVID BERRY, assistant editor, *The Sunday Mail*, Brisbane; I. T. BERTWHISTLE, cadet counsellor and book review editor, *The West Australian*, Perth; M. L. W. BEVAN, law courts rounds, *The Advertiser*, Adelaide; COLIN BINGHAM, leader writer, *The Sydney Morning Herald*, Sydney; JAMES BLAIKIE, deputy chief of staff, *The Courier-Mail*, Brisbane; HARRY BLAKE, editor, "Weekender" section of *The Argus*, Melbourne; KENNETH BLANCH, police rounds, *Telegraph*, Brisbane; DOUGLAS BOYES, deputy chief sub-editor, *Daily Telegraph*, Sydney; THE HON. HENRY E. BOLTE, Premier of Victoria, Melbourne; R. BOLAND, editor, *Sunday Times*, Perth; R. J. BOYLAN, United States Information Service, Canberra, A.C.T.; N. Q. BRADSHAW, circulation manager, *The Age*, Melbourne; T. C. BRAY, editor-in-chief, *The Courier-Mail*, Brisbane; JOHN BRIEARS, editor, *Newspaper News*, Sydney; A. C. BROOKE, manager, *The Advertiser*, Adelaide; DICKSON BROWN, production superintendent, *The Age*, Melbourne; STUART BROWN, news editor, *The Herald*, Melbourne; H. BROWNHILL, acting night editor, *The Advertiser*, Adelaide; JACK BRYANT, assistant editor, *The Sun*, Sydney; LAWRENCE BUCKLEY, manager, Syndication Office, John Fairfax Ltd., Sydney; A. V. BUCKLEY, night mechanical superintendent, *The Courier-Mail* and *The Sunday Mail*, Brisbane; MISS GWEN BURBIDGE, matron, Fairfield Hospital, Melbourne; ALLAN BURBURY, managing editor, *Woman's Day*, Melbourne; D. D. BURGESS, research officer, Trades Hall, Melbourne; JOHN BURKE, finance editor, *Telegraph*, Brisbane; GORDON BURLEY, teletype and cable room, *The Age*, Melbourne; DOUGLAS J. BURTON, head photographer, West Australian Newspapers Ltd., Perth; CHARLES BUTTROSE, leader writer, *Daily Telegraph*, Sydney.

J. CADE, copy taster, *The Argus*, Melbourne; THE HON. JOHN J. CAHILL, Premier of New South Wales, Sydney; KEITH S. CAIRNS, manager, Herald-Sun Television, Melbourne; BARNEY CAMPBELL, news editor, *The West Australian*, Perth; SIR HAROLD CAMPBELL, editor, *The Age*, Melbourne; ROSS CAMPBELL, feature writer and columnist, *Daily Telegraph*, Sydney; H. J. CANTWELL, cable editor, *The Sun*, Sydney; FRANK CARMODY, president of the Trades Hall Council, Melbourne; NOEL CARRICK, business-finance rounds, *The Herald*, Melbourne; REG CARTER, director, News Agency Control Board, West Australian Newspapers Ltd., Perth; KEVIN CASEY, columnist, *Daily News,* Perth; F. E. CHAMBERLAIN, federal president and general secretary, Western Australian Branch, Australian Labor Party, Perth; GEOFFREY CHINNER, chief sub-editor, *The Advertiser,* Adelaide; A. H. CHISHOLM, editor, *Australian Encyclopedia,* Angus & Robertson, Sydney; C. B. CHRISTESEN, editor, *Meanjin,* University of Melbourne; RON CHRISTIAN, Advertising Department, *The West Australian,* Perth; D. G. CHRISTIE, chief sub-editor, *The Argus,* Melbourne; THOMAS F. CHRISTIE, government rounds, *Daily News,* Perth; JACK CLARK, police rounds, *The News,* Adelaide; LINDSAY CLINCH, executive editor, *The Sun,* Sydney; STEWART COCKBURN, deputy chief of staff and feature writer, *The Advertiser,* Adelaide; H. GORDON COLEMAN, secretary, New South Wales District, Australian Journalists' Association; H. C. COLLINGWOOD, chairman, Stock Exchange, Melbourne; H. E. COLLINGWOOD, sports editor, *The West Australian,* Perth; JOHN COLLINS, cadet counsellor and deputy to the assistant editor (features), *The Advertiser,* Adelaide; MISS KATE COLLINS, assistant to chief of staff, *The Sydney Morning Herald,* Sydney; THE HON. ROBERT COSGROVE, Premier of Tasmania, Hobart; L. M. COTTON, features editor, *The Sydney Morning Herald,* Sydney; JACK COULTER, police rounds, *Daily News,* Perth; E. H. COX, Canberra correspondent, *The Herald,* Melbourne; P. G. CRAN, radio news editor, *The Courier-Mail,* Brisbane; SYDNEY CROSLAND, general secretary, Australian Journalists' Association, Melbourne; JAMES W. CRUTHERS, magazines editor, West Australian Newspapers, Ltd., Perth; DOREEN CULLEN, social editress, *The West Australian,* Perth; ALLEN CUMMINS, chief of staff, *The Courier-Mail,* Brisbane; WALLACE B. CUSACK, assistant editor for features and sports, *Daily News,* Perth.

GEORGE DALLY, circulation manager, *The Advertiser,* Adelaide; FRANK B. DALY, editor, *The Sun News-Pictorial,* Melbourne; L. V. DALY, features editor, *The Herald,* Melbourne; BARRY DARGAVILLE, parliament rounds, *The Age,* Melbourne; KARL DAVIDSON, radio news editor, *The Age,* past president, Victoria District, Australian Journalists' Association, Melbourne; G. F. DAVIES, chairman of directors, Davies Brothers Ltd., Hobart; JAMES DAVIES, industrial rounds, *The Sun News-Pictorial,* Melbourne; JOHN R. DAVIES, reporter, *Daily News,* Perth; W. B. DAVISON, assistant editor and columnist, *Telegraph,* Brisbane; ADRIAN DEAMER, chief of staff, *The Herald,* Melbourne; E. M. DEAN, reporter, Australian Broadcasting Commission, Melbourne; A. J. DeLANO, cable editor, *The Argus,* Melbourne; MRS. THELMA de TUETY, syndication manager, Consolidated Press Ltd., Sydney; GEOFFREY DICKSON, pictorial editor, *The News,* Adelaide; R. B. DORE, manager, Queensland Country Press, Brisbane; IRVINE DOUGLAS, leader writer, *Daily Mirror,* Sydney; HUME DOW, lecturer in rhetoric, University of Melbourne, Melbourne; SIR LLOYD DUMAS, chairman and managing director, Advertiser Newspapers Ltd., Adelaide; A. L. DUNN, news editor, *The Sun News-Pictorial,* Melbourne; MARK DUNNICLIFF, chief sub-editor, *The Sun,* Sydney; H. G. DUNNING, cable desk, *The Sun News-Pictorial,* Melbourne; DOUGLAS A. DUNSTAN, manager, Griffin Press, Adelaide; GLEN DUNSTAN, personnel manager, West Australian Newspapers Ltd., Perth.

RAY EASTWOOD, pictorial editor, *Daily News,* Perth; JACK EAVES, assistant chief of staff, *Daily News,* Perth; JOHN EDDY, economist, *The Herald,* Melbourne; R. C. EDWARDS, editor, *The Herald,* Melbourne; KENNETH ESAU, editor, *The Chronicle,* Adelaide; CLEM EMERY, circulation manager, News Ltd., Adelaide; S. L. ESKELL, director, *Newspaper News,* Sydney; MRS. BARBARA EVANS, assistant librarian, *The Argus,* Melbourne; PETER EWING, acting chief sub-editor, *Daily News,* Perth.

VINCENT C. FAIRFAX, director, John Fairfax Ltd., chairman, Australian Section, Commonwealth Press Union, Sydney; MRS. ESME FENSTON, editor, *The Australian Women's Weekly,* Sydney; MAURICE FERRY, makeup sub-editor, *The Sun,* Sydney; J. H. FINGLETON, bureau chief, Overseas Cable Service, Canberra; W. FITTER, chief sub-editor, *The Sydney Morning Herald,* Sydney; MICHAEL FITZGERALD, chief reporter, *The Argus,* Melbourne; THOMAS M. FITZGERALD, finance editor, *The Sydney Morning Herald,* Sydney; E. H. FITZHENRY, law courts rounds, *The Argus,* Melbourne; JOHN FLOWER, editor, *Sun-Herald,* Sydney; FRED C. FLOWERS, deputy chief of staff, *The Herald,* Melbourne; TOM FOLEY, race announcer and turf writer, *The Courier-Mail,* Brisbane; MISS JEAN FORRESTER, manager, teletype and cable room, *Telegraph,* Brisbane; DR. HANS FORST, librarian, John Fairfax Ltd., Sydney; ERIC FRANKLIN, government rounds, *The Advertiser,* Adelaide; R. A. FULTON, chief of staff, *The Mercury,* Hobart.

J. C. GAHAN, reporter, *The Sun News-Pictorial,* Melbourne; L. J. GAME, sales promotion manager, West Australian Newspapers Ltd., Perth; E. D. GARDNER, sports editor, *The Sydney Morning Herald,* Sydney; DUDLEY GILES, assistant editor, *The Herald,* Melbourne; KENNETH GILES, executive editor, Colorgravure, The Herald and Weekly Times Ltd., Melbourne; GEORGE F. GODFREY, president, Australian Journalists' Association, New South Wales District, Sydney; PETER GOLDING, columnist, *The Argus,* Melbourne; F. H. GOLDSMITH, research editor, West Australian Newspapers, Ltd., Perth; JOHN GOODGE, editor, *The Sun,* Sydney; BERNARD GORDON, Launceston Bureau chief, *The Mercury,* Hobart; K. B. GOYNE, general manager, *The Mercury,* Hobart; F. R. GRANT, assistant night picture editor, *The Argus,* Melbourne; MAX GRANT, business-finance cadet, *The Herald,* Melbourne; ALAN GREEN, chief of staff, *The Sydney Morning Herald,* Sydney; G. R. GREENLEES, assistant night editor, *The Sun News-*

Pictorial, Melbourne; T. STUART GURR, manager, Australian Audit Bureau of Circulations, Sydney.

NEIL R. HALL, cable editor, *The Herald,* Melbourne; RAY G. HAMILTON, business executive, Sydney; EFAN HANNAH, motor page editor, *The Courier-Mail,* Brisbane; ROY HANSON, deputy chief sub-editor, *Telegraph,* Brisbane; THE HON. A. R. G. HAWKE, Premier of Western Australia, Perth; DENIS N. HAWKER, feature and leader writer, *The Mercury,* Hobart; R. W. HENRY, general manager, Australian Newsprint Mills, Ltd., Boyer, Tasmania; FRED H. C. HESELWOOD, news editor, *The Courier-Mail,* Brisbane; S. J. F. HOCKING, managing director, Hocking & Co., Ltd., proprietors of *The Kalgoorlie Miner,* Kalgoorlie, W.A., and director, West Australian Newspapers Ltd., Perth; JOHN HOLDEN, features, *The Argus,* Melbourne; DUNCAN HOOPER, managing editor, *Australian Associated Press,* Melbourne; FRED HOWARD, leader and feature writer, *The Herald,* Melbourne; FRED HUBBARD, Australia Bureau chief, Time Inc., Brisbane; W. G. HUGHES, chief turf writer, *The Sun News-Pictorial,* Melbourne; MISS GRACE HUNTER, social editress, *The Age,* Melbourne; GEOFFREY HUTTON, drama and music critic, *The Age,* Melbourne; MISS JUNE R. HUXTABLE, business-finance rounds, *The Sun,* Sydney. S. RANDAL HEYMANSON, editor, Australian Newspapers Service, New York.

TONY INGLIS, business manager, Consolidated Press, Sydney; MISS FREDA M. H. IRVING, social editress, *The Argus,* Melbourne; E. W. IRWIN, Sydney correspondent, *The West Australian,* Perth.

E. R. JACKSON, editor, *The Sunday Mail,* Brisbane; MURRAY W. JAMES, chief of staff, *The News,* Adelaide; MISS PATRICIA JARRETT, social editress, *The Sun News-Pictorial,* Melbourne; LAWRENCE JERVIS, industrial rounds, *The News,* Adelaide; LAWRIE JERVIS, sports and general reporter, *The News,* Adelaide; L. C. H. JOHNSTONE, leader writer, *The Advertiser,* Adelaide; PHILIP F. JONES, general manager, Herald and Weekly Times Ltd., Melbourne; LAWRENCE M. JORDON, sports editor, *The News,* Adelaide; STUART K. JOYNT, editor, *Daily News,* Perth.

SIDNEY W. KELLEWAY, Australian Broadcasting Commission, government rounds, Melbourne; CLIVE C. KELLY, literary editor, *The Advertiser,* Adelaide; NEIL KELLY, assistant editor, *The Sunday Mail,* Adelaide; REGINALD H. KEMPTON, pictorial editor, *The Advertiser,* Adelaide; NEIL G. KENDRICK, pictorial editor, *The Sun,* Sydney; ERIC

KENNEDY, former chief executive officer, Associated Newspapers Ltd., Sydney; ROBERT KENNEDY, columnist, *Daily Telegraph*, Sydney; LAURIE KERR, deputy chief of staff, *The Argus*, Melbourne; MRS. ELEANOR KNOX, Town Hall rounds, *The Argus*, Melbourne; MRS. H. KNOX, law courts rounds, *Daily Telegraph*, Sydney.

MAX LAMSHED, assistant editor (promotion), *The Advertiser*, Adelaide; MISS LOIS M. LATHLEAN, social editress, *The Sun News-Pictorial*, Melbourne; K. B. LAURIE, secretary, Victorian Provincial Press Association, Melbourne; L. A. LAWLER, production manager, West Australian Newspapers Ltd., Perth; JOHN H. LAURENCE, finance and mining editor, *The West Australian*, Perth; LOUIS LECK, news editor, *The Sydney Morning Herald*, Sydney; SIR LANGLOIS LEFROY, K.B., M.C., chairman of directors, West Australian Newspapers Ltd., Perth; STUART LEGGE, deputy chief of staff, *The Sun News-Pictorial*, Melbourne; FRANK W. LEGGOE, news editor, *Daily News*, Perth; JOHN LILLIS, chief of staff for periodicals, John Fairfax Ltd., Sydney; J. LLOYD, cable desk, *The Sun News-Pictorial*, Melbourne; L. G. LOADER, government rounds, *The Argus*, Melbourne; DOUGLAS LOCKWOOD, Darwin Bureau chief, Herald and Weekly Times Ltd., Melbourne; W. G. LOH, leader writer, *The West Australian*, Perth; ROY A. LONG, director, West Australian Newspapers Ltd., Perth; D. LOVE, Canberra correspondent, *Daily Telegraph*, Sydney; GORDON LOVETT, assistant finance editor, *Daily Telegraph*, Sydney; K. A. LUKEY, Western rounds, City of Melbourne, *The Sun News-Pictorial*, Melbourne; J. G. LUSH, assistant chief sub-editor, *The Sun*, Sydney; FRED LYONS, manager, Feature Service, Herald and Weekly Times Ltd., Melbourne.

JAMES E. MACARTNEY, managing editor, West Australian Newspapers, Ltd., Perth; E. W. McALPINE, director, Consolidated Press, Ltd., Sydney; C. McCALL, classified advertising manager, *The Age*, Melbourne; W. R. MacDONALD, general manager, *Telegraph*, Brisbane; ALEXANDER MacDONALD, secretary, Queensland Trades and Labour Council, Brisbane; JAMES MacDOUGALL, columnist, *Daily Telegraph*, Sydney; COLIN G. McFARLAN, sports editor, *The Age*, Melbourne; D. G. McFARLING, managing editor, *The Advertiser*, Adelaide; PETER McGEORGE, police rounds, *The Mercury*, Hobart; NEIL McILLWRAITH, features editor, *Daily Telegraph*, Sydney; A. B. McKAY, advertising manager, *The Argus*, Melbourne; RT. HON. SIR WILLIAM JOHN McKELL, G.C.M.G., Governor-General of Australia 1947–1953, Sydney; ANGUS McLACHLAN, general manager, John Fairfax Ltd., Sydney; DAVID R. McNICOLL, editor-in-chief, Consolidated Press, Ltd., Sydney; MRS. DAVID R. McNICOLL, social editress, *Daily Telegraph*, Sydney; F. J. S. McNULTY, cable editor, *Daily Telegraph*, Sydney; MRS. E. M. McPHERSON, women's editor and cadet co-counsellor, *Daily News*, Perth; TONY McVEIGH, police and city courts rounds, *The Age*,

Melbourne; CHARLES MADDEN, special writer, *The Sun News-Pictorial*, Melbourne; MISS PATRICIA MANTON, women's editor, *The News*, Adelaide; F. KEITH MANZIES, theater and motion picture critic, *The Argus*, Melbourne; T. W. MARTIN, pictorial editor, *The Courier-Mail*, Brisbane; IAN MAXWELL, professor of English, University of Melbourne; KENNETH S. MAY, parliament-government rounds, cadet counsellor, *The News*, Adelaide; HENRY MAYER, senior lecturer in government, University of Sydney; T. F. MEAD, deputy chief of staff, *Daily Telegraph*, Sydney; C. MEEKING, bureau chief, National News Service, Canberra; GORDON MELVILLE, features editor, *The Age*, Melbourne; L. J. MILLER, editor, *Sunday Telegraph*, Sydney; L. W. MILLER, acting chief sub-editor, *The Mercury*, Hobart; ROBERT MILLER, United Press (U.S.A.), Southwest Pacific manager, Sydney; NORMAN MILNE, West Australian Petroleum Co., Perth; SIDNEY MITCHELL, chief sub-editor, *The Age*, Melbourne; S. V. MITCHELL, editor, *The Saturday Evening Mercury*, Hobart; R. J. MONKS, president, Australian Journalists' Association, South Australia District, Adelaide; RONALD MONSON, feature writer and foreign correspondent, *Daily Telegraph*, Sydney; MISS RHONA MOODY, acting chief, telephone room, *Telegraph*, Brisbane; DAN MORGAN, parliament rounds, *Telegraph*, Brisbane; P. CROSBIE MORRISON, wild life editor, *The Argus*, Melbourne; K. C. MOSES, sports writer, *The Argus*, Melbourne; NEIL MOODY, features editor, *The Sun News-Pictorial*, Melbourne; JOHN MOYES, news editor, *Daily Telegraph*, Sydney; LINDSAY V. MUDGE, assistant chief of staff, *The Argus*, Melbourne; THOMAS L. MUIR, literary editor, *The Age*, Melbourne; GEORGE MULCHINOCK, assistant to the night editor, *The Sun News-Pictorial*, Melbourne; B. R. MULLINER, secretary, Printing Industries Employees Union of Australia, Queensland Branch, Brisbane; C. C. MURDOCH, personnel superintendent, Australian Newsprint Mills, Boyer, Tasmania; RUPERT MURDOCH, publisher and director, News Ltd., Adelaide; HAL MYERS, Eric White Associates, Public Relations, Sydney; O. F. MINGAY, managing director, AARDS, Pty. Ltd. (Australian Advertising Rate & Data Service) Sydney; LEIGH MACKAY, AARDS, Pty. Ltd., Sydney.

R. R. NALL, features editor, *The Courier-Mail*, Brisbane; E. NEAL, Australian Broadcasting Commission, city rounds, Melbourne; ROBERT J. NELSON, editor and director, *The Argus*, Melbourne; BERNARD E. NETTERFIELD, personnel manager, Consolidated Press, Sydney; ALLAN NICHOLS, feature writer, *The Age*, Melbourne; J. L. NICOLL, circulation manager, *The West Australian*, Perth; KEITH W. NOUD, acting turf editor, *Telegraph*, Brisbane.

JACK O'CALLAGHAN, chief sub-editor, *The Courier-Mail*, Brisbane; JAMES A. O'CONNOR, secretary, Victoria District, Australian Journalists' Association, Melbourne; W. O'CONNOR, sports editor, *The Her-*

ald, Melbourne; RICHARD ODGERS, editor-in-chief and secretary, Australian United Press, Sydney; J. P. O'HARA, civic rounds, *The Sydney Morning Herald,* Sydney; ANDREW OLNEY, chief of staff, *The West Australian,* Perth; C. RONALD OLNEY, advertising manager, *The West Australian,* Perth; MISS JOSEPHINE O'NEILL, amusements editor, *Daily Telegraph,* Sydney.

SIR FRANK PACKER, managing director, Australian Consolidated Press Ltd., Sydney; F. L. PARSONS, circulation manager, *Daily News,* Perth; WILLIAM PATEY, leader writer, *The Argus,* Melbourne; J. D. PATIENCE, managing director, The Argus and Australasian Ltd., Melbourne; ROBERT W. PATON, editor, *Radio Call,* Adelaide; MISS JILL PATTEN, assistant librarian, *The Courier-Mail,* Brisbane; J. A. PATTERSON, chief of staff, *The Argus,* Melbourne; GEORGE R. PAYNE, sports editor, *Telegraph,* Brisbane; FRED PETERSON, features editor, *The Sun-Herald,* Sydney; THE HON. SIR THOMAS PLAYFORD, Premier of South Australia, Adelaide; HARRY PLUMRIDGE, assistant editor (features), *The Advertiser,* Adelaide; RAY POLKINGHORNE, deputy chief of staff and sports editor, *The Advertiser,* Adelaide; HARRY D. POTTER, chief of staff, *Daily News,* Perth; WILLIAM L. PRICE, Town Hall rounds, *The Sun News-Pictorial,* Melbourne; J. M. D. PRINGLE, editor, *The Sydney Morning Herald,* Sydney; SELWYN B. PRIOR, deputy news editor, *The West Australian,* Perth; NOEL PRISK, deputy chief of staff, *The News,* Adelaide; FRANK PROUST, aviation rounds, *The Sydney Morning Herald;* JERRY PYNT, sports editor, *Daily Telegraph,* Sydney; A. GILBERT PIKE, secretary, Audit Bureau of Circulations, Sydney.

JOHN QUINN, features editor, *The News,* Adelaide.

J. H. G. RAWLINS, civic rounds, *The News,* Adelaide; K. B. READY, news editor, *The Mercury,* Hobart; ALAN D. REID, Canberra correspondent, *Sunday Telegraph,* Sydney; ANDREW REID, leader writer, *The Mercury,* Hobart; LINDSAY REVILL, *PIX* Magazine, and cadet counsellor, *The Sun,* Sydney; H. E. RHODES, Printing Department, *The Age,* Melbourne; ARTHUR RICHARDS, leader writer, and assistant to the editor-in-chief, *The Courier-Mail,* Brisbane; W. T. G. RICHARDS, editor, *The West Australian,* Perth; JOSIAH RICHARDS, radio news editor and cadet counsellor, *The Argus,* Melbourne; ERIC RIEL, bureau chief, United Press (U.S.), Sydney; MRS. GWENATH RITTER, manager, Syndication Office, *The Argus,* Melbourne; W. RITTER, chief sub-editor, *The Sydney Morning Herald;* ROHAN D. RIVETT, editor-in-chief and director, News Ltd., Adelaide; MISS CONSTANCE RIX, librarian, *The News,* Adelaide; OSWALD ROBARTS, assistant features editor, *The Age,* Melbourne; MRS. CONSTANCE ROBERTSON, O.B.E., women's editor, *The Sydney Morning Herald* and *Sun-Herald,* Sydney; A. F. D. RODIE, public relations, Sydney; D. S. ROGERS, secretary, Melbourne Stock Exchange, Melbourne; HANS G. ROSENDORFF, librarian, West Australian Newspapers, Ltd., Perth; STANLEY ROSIER, manager, Perth News Bureau, West Australian Newspapers Ltd., Perth; GEOFFREY ROSSITER, executive officer, United States Educational Foundation in Australia, Canberra; HAROLD RUDINGER, Photography Department, West Australian Newspapers Ltd., Perth.

MISS IRENE SALVADO, chief librarian, *The Mercury,* Hobart; RICHARD H. SAMPSON, assistant business manager, *The Herald,* Melbourne; KEVIN SATTLER, turf editor, *The News,* Adelaide; ERROL E. SCHAEFFER, aviation and armed forces rounds, *Telegraph,* Brisbane; KENNETH SCHAPEL, Canberra correspondent, *Daily Telegraph,* Sydney; NORMAN SEWELL, news editor, *The News,* Adelaide; A. T. SHAKESPEARE, managing editor, *The Canberra Times;* FRANK SHAW, reporter, *The News,* Adelaide; MRS. A. V. SHELTON-SMITH; news editor, *The Australian Women's Weekly,* Sydney; H. E. SHOLL, law courts rounds, *The Age,* Melbourne; J. R. SHOLL, Western rounds, *The Argus,* Melbourne; R. E. SHONE, editor, *The Mercury,* Hobart; STANLEY SHERMAN, general manager, *The Courier-Mail,* Brisbane; CONRAD SIMONS, sports editor, *The Sun,* Sydney; E. K. SINCLAIR, associate editor, *The Age,* Melbourne; KENNETH SLESSOR, leader writer and literary editor, *The Sun,* Sydney; ROBIN SLESSOR, supplements editor, *Daily Telegraph,* Sydney; LOGAN SLIGO, government rounds, *The Courier-Mail,* Brisbane; J. T. SMITH, industrial rounds, *The Sun,* Sydney; ROBERT J. SMITH, chief sub-editor, *The Sun News-Pictorial,* Melbourne; E. LLOYD SOMMERLAD, secretary, New South Wales Country Press Association, and secretary, Australian Provincial Press Association, Sydney; PETER SPOONER, police rounds, *The Courier-Mail,* Brisbane; HARRY STANDISH, theater critic and feature writer, *The Herald,* Melbourne; IAN STEWART, chief of staff, *The Age,* Melbourne; MRS. LORRAINE STUMM, social editress and cadet counsellor, *The Sun,* Sydney.

GORDON TAIT, bureau chief, Associated Press (U.S.A.), Sydney; NORMAN D. TAYLOR, illustrations editor, *The West Australian,* Perth; T. C. TAYLOR, government rounds, *The Age,* Melbourne; GEOFFREY E. TEBBUTT, feature writer, *The Herald,* Melbourne; ROY E. TERRY, pictorial editor, *The Sun News-Pictorial,* Melbourne; ARCHER K. THOMAS, deputy editor-in-chief, The Herald and Weekly Times Ltd., Melbourne; MISS PATIENCE R. THOMS, society editress, *The Courier-Mail,* Brisbane; E. W. TIPPING, columnist, *The Herald,* Melbourne; DON TOOHEY, news editor, *The Sun,* Sydney; MISS MOLLIE V. TRAIT, women's editress, *The Advertiser,* Adelaide; W. TRAVERS, circulation manager, *Daily Telegraph,* Sydney; PETER R. TRUNDLE, City Hall roundsman, *The Courier-Mail,* Brisbane.

DR. CLIVE W. UHR, chairman, Brisbane Amateur Turf Club; MALCOLM J. L. UREN, assistant to the managing editor, West Australian Newspapers Ltd., Perth; MALCOLM C. UREN, Canberra correspondent, *The West Australian,* Perth.

JOHN VEITCH, features editor, *The Argus,* Melbourne; A. R. VICKERS, editor, *Telegraph,* Brisbane; JAMES E. VINE, turf editor, *The Courier-Mail,* Brisbane.

PETER WADLEY, attorney at law, Brisbane; JOHN WAKEFIELD, editor-in-chief, *Telegraph,* Brisbane; RAY WALKER, chief sub-editor, *Daily Telegraph,* Sydney; WILLIAM WALKER, cable editor, *The News,* Adelaide; CECIL WALLACE, night editor, *The Argus,* Melbourne; P. J. WALLACE, industrial registrar (retired), Queensland, Brisbane; DAVID W. WALLIS, assistant finance editor, *The Sun,* Sydney; C. M. WANMER, sub-editor, *Telegraph,* Brisbane; NOEL D. WANMER, leader writer, *Telegraph,* Brisbane; FREDERICK WARD, librarian, *Daily Telegraph,* Sydney; DENIS WARNER, feature writer, *The Herald,* Melbourne; MERVIN C. WARREN, chief of staff, *Telegraph,* Brisbane; J. C. WATERS, editor-in-chief, The Herald and Weekly Times, Melbourne; J. KINGSTON WATSON, editor, *Daily Telegraph,* Sydney; P. A. WATT, leader writer, *Telegraph,* Brisbane; S. D. WATT, features manager, West Australian Newspapers Ltd., Perth; PHILIP M. WEATE, business-finance editor, *The Argus,* Melbourne; N. K. WELSH, civic rounds, *The Mercury,* Hobart; H. L. WHITE, librarian, Commonwealth National Library, Canberra; OSMAR E. WHITE, feature writer and cadet counsellor, *The Herald,* Melbourne; L. L. WHITELOCK, pictorial editor, *Telegraph,* Brisbane; F. G. WHITING, chief of staff, *The Sun News-Pictorial,* Melbourne; W. FARMER WHYTE, bureau chief, Federal News Service, Canberra; D. G. WHYTE, business manager, West Australian Newspapers Ltd., Perth; DOUGLAS WILKIE, commentator and feature writer, *The Sun News-Pictorial,* Melbourne; GRAHAM WILKINSON, photo director, John Fairfax Ltd., Sydney; J. WILLES, deputy editor, *The Argus,* Melbourne; SIR JOHN WILLIAMS, managing director, The Herald and Weekly Times Ltd., Melbourne; B. A. WILLIAMS, chief of staff, *The Advertiser,* Adelaide; J. K. WILSON, associate editor, *The News,* Adelaide; NORMAN WILSON, assistant news editor, *The Herald,* Melbourne; A. R. S. WINDERS, Cable News Department, *The Courier-Mail,* Brisbane; VINCENT C. B. WRIGHT, parliament rounds,

The Sun, Sydney; PHILIP WYNTER, pictorial director, *Daily Telegraph,* Sydney.

LOU YARDLEY, parliament rounds, *The Age,* Melbourne; BARRY YOUNG, sports editor, *The Courier-Mail,* Brisbane; MRS. ROBERT BURNS YOUNG, assistant librarian, *The Advertiser,* Adelaide.

Most of the information and data in *Australia Goes to Press* are from the Australian men and women listed herewith. Whatever errors of fact, interpretation and judgment this book may contain are mine alone.

W.S.H.

Thumbnail Historical Sketches of Fifteen Australian Metropolitan Daily Newspapers

NEW SOUTH WALES: (Morning Papers) *The Sydney Morning Herald, Daily Telegraph;* (Afternoon Papers) *The Sun, Daily Mirror.*
VICTORIA: (Morning Papers) *The Age, The Sun News-Pictorial, The Argus;* (Afternoon Paper) *The Herald.*
QUEENSLAND: (Morning Paper) *The Courier-Mail;* (Afternoon Paper) *Telegraph.*
SOUTH AUSTRALIA: (Morning Paper) *The Advertiser;* (Afternoon Paper) *The News.*
WESTERN AUSTRALIA: (Morning Paper) *The West Australian;* (Afternoon Paper) *Daily News.*
TASMANIA: (Morning Paper) *The Mercury.*

NEW SOUTH WALES

The Sydney Morning Herald

The Sydney Morning Herald, oldest Australian metropolitan daily newspaper of continuous publication and the only metropolitan daily that proclaims its home city in its name, began life as *The Sydney Herald* on April 18, 1831. It commenced daily publication in October, 1840, and, in February, 1841, was sold by its founders to John Fairfax and Charles Kemp. For ten years it was the colony's only daily. In October, 1853, Kemp sold his interest to Fairfax; and the Fairfax family has continued in control through five generations. *The Sydney Herald* became *The Sydney Morning Herald* in August, 1842.

The Sydney Morning Herald has outlasted all opposition. In the 124th year of its life (1955) it signalized its endurance by moving into one of the most modern newspaper plants in the world. *The Sunday Herald* was established in 1949.

The most notable acquisitions by the Fairfax interests were fairly recent. *The Sun* and *The Sunday Sun* and a number of magazines were all that was left of Sir Hugh Denison's Associated Newspapers, as related below. In 1953, John Fairfax and Sons Pty. Ltd. acquired control of Associated Newspapers, continuing *The Sun* (an afternoon tabloid) and combining *The Sunday Sun* and *The Sunday Herald* into *The Sun-Herald*.

Another major change occurred in April, 1956, when the family company became a public company, John Fairfax Ltd. The Fairfax family retained one-half the shares of the new company. Twenty months later, in December, 1958, John Fairfax Ltd. arranged finance to enable an independent group to acquire the shareholding of Ezra Norton in Truth and Sportsman Ltd., which published four *Truths, Daily Mirror* and *Sunday Mirror* (Sydney), formerly the Sydney edition of *Truth*. The name of Truth and Sportsman, Ltd., was a few months later changed to Mirror Newspapers, Ltd. Early in 1960, these properties were purchased by News Ltd. of Adelaide (q.v.).

Besides *The Sydney Morning Herald, The Sun, The Sun-Herald* and periodicals of Associated Newspapers, the company publishes *The Financial Review,* a weekly founded in 1951, and has radio and television interests.

The Sydney Morning Herald, a morning broadsheet, is published every day except Sunday, from its offices, Broadway and Wattle St., Sydney. In 1959 its circulation was about 310,000.

Daily Telegraph (Sydney)

Under its flag on page one, the *Daily Telegraph* bears a volume number with a parenthesized "New Series" beginning in 1936. Its antecedents, however, go back to 1879.

A. H. Chisholm writes in *The Australian Encyclopedia,* under "Newspapers":

The most serious rival to *The Herald* (which became *The Sydney Morning Herald* and which enjoyed a morning monopoly in the 1870's), the *Daily Telegraph,* first appeared on 1st July 1879. Between 1927 and 1936 it had a variety of titles; all included the word "Telegraph" in some combination or another, except for the period 1st February 1930 to 15th February 1931, when it was called the *Daily Pictorial.* Since 23rd March 1935 it has been the *Daily Telegraph,* published by Consolidated Press. The *Daily Telegraph* of the 1890s was the spearhead of the opposition to Federation in New South Wales.

Another *Daily Telegraph* antecedent, *The Daily Mail*, underwent two name changes after it was founded in 1922—*Labor Daily* and *The Daily News*. It was incorporated in the *Daily Telegraph* in 1940.

Consolidated Press (now Australian Consolidated Press), began life in 1933 as publishers of *The Australian Women's Weekly*, the most phenomenally successful magazine in Australian history—its recent circulation was more than 800,000, or about one copy per 12.5 Australians, including infants and children.

Sydney Newspapers Ltd. was Consolidated Press's immediate predecessor. It was founded by Frank (now Sir Frank) Packer and E. G. Theodore, a former Queensland Premier.

Sydney Newspapers, Ltd., gained control of *The World*, a labor daily, but for a substantial consideration was dissuaded by Sir Hugh Denison from converting *The World* into an afternoon paper in competition with his *Sun* for a period of seven years. "E. G. Theodore, A Profile," published by Consolidated Press when Theodore retired as board chairman, puts the price paid by Denison for such abstention at £86,000.

Besides the *Daily Telegraph* and the *Australian Women's Weekly*, Australian Consolidated Press publishes the *Sunday Telegraph; The Bulletin and The Observer* (*The Bulletin* was purchased from the Bulletin Newspaper Co. Ltd. in November 1960; *The Observer* was founded by Australian Consolidated Press in 1958; the two were merged early in 1961); *Everybody's Weekly* (a 1961 merger of *Australian Woman's Mirror* and *Weekend*); *Modern Motor;* fiction and non-fiction books; children's books and text books; comic books; a variety of pulps and other specialized periodicals. It distributes the Pacific edition of *Time* and *Life* and is engaged in radio and television.

The *Daily Telegraph*, a morning tabloid, is published every day, except Sunday, by Australian Consolidated Press Ltd. from its offices at 168 Castlereagh St., Sydney. Its circulation in 1961 was about 324,000.

The Sun (Sydney)

In some ways, the history of *The Sun* has been more momentous, more involved with change, than that of any other extant Australian metropolitan paper.

Hugh Denison founded *The Sunday Sun* in 1903 and from it grew the daily *Sun*, which began, in 1910, by absorbing the protectionist *Australian Star*. Associated Newspapers, Ltd., was formed in 1929 to acquire Sun Newspapers, Ltd., and another newspaper company. From 1910 until his death in 1941, Denison was managing director of the two companies in succession. "These companies," wrote W. M. Corden, in *Meanjin*, "have been responsible for more newspaper deals and adventures than any other Australian firms." *The Sun*, said Corden, "has been described as Australia's first modern daily."

Denison's magic touch in Sydney worked for a time in Newcastle, N.S.W., but not at all in Melbourne. In the latter city he started another *Sun*, an evening paper to compete with *The Herald*, and then set up the morning *Sun News-Pictorial*. He lost them both to *The Herald's* proprietors. But in Sydney his good fortune was impressive for a time.

"By 1928," Corden continued, "there were six daily and five Sunday papers in Sydney" and, beginning that year, "Denison's company bought up one Sydney daily a year for three years, until he ended by running two competing morning dailies, two competing evening dailies, and three Sunday newspapers." Associated Newspapers, Ltd., was born with the first of these acquisitions.

By 1931 Denison's properties were in trouble, made deeper by the depression. *The Evening News* and *The Sunday Pictorial* were closed down. *The Daily Guardian* was merged with the *Daily Telegraph* and the *Sunday Guardian* with the *Sunday Sun*. The *Daily Telegraph* was sold to Consolidated Press in 1936. After the debacle, Associated Newspapers was left with only the *Sunday Sun*, *The Sun* and a number of magazines.

In 1953, *The Sydney Morning Herald* proprietorship gained control of Associated Newspapers. (See *The Sydney Morning Herald* above.) *The Sun* remained to compete with the *Daily Mirror*.

Sungravure, a wholly owned subsidiary of Associated Newspapers, Ltd., publishes a number of periodicals, including *Pix, People* and *Woman's Day with Woman* which combines *Woman's Day* (purchased from the Melbourne Herald and Weekly Times Ltd., in 1956) with *Woman*, which was first published by Associated Newspapers, Ltd.

The Sun, an afternoon tabloid, is published each day except Sunday, from its offices at Broadway and Wattle St., Sydney. Its 1960 circulation was about 295,000.

Daily Mirror (Sydney)

Youngest of Australian metropolitan dailies is the *Daily Mirror*. Volume I, Number 1 was published on May 12, 1941, by Truth and Sportsman Ltd. Its founder, and holder of the controlling interest until 1958, was Ezra Norton, son of John Norton, who acquired *Truth*, a Sydney Sunday paper in 1896. Truth and Sportsman Ltd. at one time published editions of *Truth* in all capital cities, though not all of them as Sunday papers. The West Australian *Truth* was suspended in 1931. In late 1958, Norton converted the Sydney *Truth* to the *Sunday Mirror*, then sold all his interests in Truth and Sportsman Ltd., which shortly afterwards changed its name to Mirror Newspapers, Ltd. In 1960, News Ltd., of Adelaide, purchased the former Norton properties. In May, 1961, the *Sunday Mirror* was re-designed and renamed the *Sunday Mirror News-Pictorial*. Besides four editions of *Truth*, Mirror Newspapers Ltd. publishes *Sportsman*, a weekly sports paper.

The *Daily Mirror*, an afternoon tabloid, is published daily except Sunday, by Mirror Newspapers Ltd., from its offices at Kippax and Holt Streets, Sydney. In 1960 its circulation was about 285,000.

VICTORIA

The Age (Melbourne)

The Age made its first appearance on October 17, 1854, three years after the new colony of Victoria had won separate status from New South Wales and during the excitement of the Victorian gold rushes.

Ebenezer Syme bought it on June 6, 1856, and took in his brother David, as partner, on September 27 of the same year. Ebenezer died in 1860 at the age of 34 and David, a year younger, became sole owner.

Under David Syme's proprietorship, *The Age* became the apostle of a high protective tariff which, made into law, materially forwarded the fortunes of Victoria's young industries.

In its centennial issue, October 16, 1954, *The Age* declared: "The paper struggled, flourished, commanded in the years when the thunder of the pen was needed to rouse public passion, and shape public opinion. . . . From 1860 to 1908 (the year of his death) the story of *The Age* was largely the story of David Syme, whose vision, determination and labors left a deep mark on the pages of Victoria's history."

The Age continued in the Syme family—David Syme was father of five sons—until 1948, when it became a public company, with shares sold on the open market. The family continued to be large shareholders and to maintain control. Oswald Syme, surviving son of David, became chairman of directors. H. R. Syme is general manager. In recent years, the company installed new presses and undertook an extensive building expansion and modernization program.

The company also published *The Leader,* farm and stock weekly, founded simultaneously with *The Age. The Leader* was discontinued, at the age of 102, in 1956.

The Age, a morning broadsheet, is published every day except Sunday, from its offices, 233 Collins Street, Melbourne. Its circulation in 1960 was 166,746.

The Sun News-Pictorial (Melbourne)

The most impressive success story in modern Australian daily journalism is that of *The Sun News-Pictorial.* It was launched on September 11, 1922, by Hugh Denison, Sydney newspaper proprietor, who followed this initial invasion of the Melbourne field with a second, *The Evening Sun,* in 1923. Neither paper prospered.

On April 27, 1925, The Herald and Weekly Times, Ltd., announced *The Evening Sun's* death and its own purchase of *The Sun News-Pictorial. The Evening Sun* went down permanently with the declaration that "the journal, as conducted," did not merit "any particular consideration." Of *The Sun News-Pictorial,* which was not an afternoon competitor, *The Herald* said its "natural home is with an evening newspaper whose plant and building and organization it can share." The sharing continues today.

In October, 1927, *The Sun News-Pictorial* absorbed *The Morning Post,* newspaper voice of the Country Party, which had been published for exactly two years. In 1928, *The Sun News-Pictorial* had 169,213 average daily circulation; in 1940, 250,000; in 1947, 375,973. Despite wartime restrictions and newsprint shortages (which cut it down to 12 pages at one time), it has continued to demonstrate that Australia is exceedingly hospitable to tabloids and to morning papers.

The Sun News-Pictorial, a morning tabloid, is published every day except Sunday, from the offices of The Herald and Weekly Times, Ltd., 44–74 Flinders Street, Melbourne. Its daily average net paid circulation for the six months ending September 30, 1960, was 563,153.

The Argus (Melbourne)

The first issue of *The Argus* came from the press on June 14, 1846; the last on January 19, 1957.

A colored plaque in its business office in downtown Melbourne proclaimed:

> *The Melbourne Advertiser* was first published (in manuscript) on January 1st, 1838 and made its appearance in print on March 5th, 1838. Its publication was suspended from April 23rd, 1838 until February 6th, 1839, when it re-appeared as *The Port Phillip Patriot*. On October 9th, 1848 it became the *Melbourne Daily News*. The second newspaper, the *Port Phillip Gazette,* was established on October 27, 1838. Its name was changed to *The Times* on March 18th, 1851 and on July 1st, 1851 it was merged into the *Melbourne Daily News. The Argus,* first issued June 2nd, 1846, absorbed the *Melbourne Daily News,* January 1st, 1852.

"Consequently," read the notice, "all the preceding newspapers are embodied in *The Argus.*"

In 1848, shortly after *The Argus* was launched, Edward Wilson bought it from its founder, William Kerr. Wilson became partner with Lauchlan Mackinnon, thereby beginning an association which built *The Argus* into a power in Australasian affairs. The same family ownership continued until 1936. *The Star,* an afternoon daily started by *The Argus* to compete with *The Herald,* lasted only three years.

In 1936, Wilson and Mackinnon became a public company. The *Daily Mirror* group of London purchased the property in 1949 and transformed the one-time vigorous crusader and arch-conservative among newspapers into a brash, chatty "broadsheet edited like a tabloid." But *The Argus* did not live up to the expectations of faraway owners and carried its own obituary notice on January 19, 1957.

The Argus' demise was ordered and carried through by its owners. As to the company's other effects, the death notice declared: "The Herald and Weekly Times Ltd. has agreed to pay for these interests by the allotment of £350,000 of shares of that company at par to the London companies which have a controlling interest in The Argus and The Australasian Post Ltd."

The properties purchased by The Herald and Weekly Times, Ltd., included *The Australasian Post,* a weekly general magazine, and *Your Garden,* a monthly. *The Argus* pioneered in color printing, with litho-offset four-color presses arranged in tandem with black-and-white letterpress.

The Argus, a morning broadsheet, was published every day except Sunday, Elizabeth Street, Melbourne. Its final issue stated that its circulation was 170,000.

The Herald (Melbourne)

The Herald is the parent publication of Australia's most extensive publishing and communications organization, The Herald and Weekly Times, Ltd.

The Herald traces its origin to January 3, 1840, in *The Port Phillip Herald,* which nine years later became *The Melbourne Morning Herald.*

Another twenty years later (1869) after difficult times and after being a bi-weekly for a period, it became an afternoon daily. It has remained so ever since.

The Daily Telegraph took over its place in Melbourne's morning field (also in 1869); but in 1892, *The Herald* took over *The Daily Telegraph*, which was then discontinued. The present company, The Herald and Weekly Times, Ltd., was formed in 1902. *The Herald* continued to out-live numerous afternoon rivals; and by the 1930's was in the dominant position in Melbourne.

Moreover, it could acquire and make profitable, as well as outlive. Hugh Denison's *Sun News-Pictorial* was purchased, as noted previously, by The Herald and Weekly Times, Ltd., in 1925. In 1929, under Sir Keith Murdoch, the company crossed state lines and secured control of *The Register,* and later *The Advertiser,* both of Adelaide. *The Advertiser* absorbed *The Register* in 1931. Advertiser Newspapers, Ltd., also acquired an interest in News, Ltd., of Adelaide.

Apart from all Herald and Weekly Times, Ltd., activities, Murdoch acquired *The Courier* and *The Mail,* both of Brisbane, and merged them, in 1933, into *The Courier-Mail.* By active development and the growth of the Australian population, The Herald and Weekly Times, Ltd., turned these acquisitions into the largest newspaper organization in Australia.

After Sir Keith's death in 1952, his holdings were divided between the company and his family, in the ways indicated by the brief sketches in this appendix, particularly in respect to News, Ltd., of Adelaide.

Today The Herald and Weekly Times, Ltd., a public company with about 10,000 shareholders, publishes *The Herald,* a broadsheet, and the only paper in the Melbourne afternoon field; *The Sun News-Pictorial,* morning tabloid; *The Weekly Times,* a rural newspaper; *Sporting Globe,* a bi-weekly. It also publishes books; maintains a book club; runs a huge gravure plant; republishes for Australasian sale *The New York Times'* Sunday supplement, *The Week in Review;* operates a radio station and a television station; publishes *The Australian Home Beautiful, The Listener-In, Aircraft,* and does job printing.

The Herald and Weekly Times, Ltd., owns a 37 per cent interest in Queensland Press, the public company which is proprietor of *The Courier-Mail, The Telegraph,* the only morning and afternoon papers in Brisbane, and *The Sunday Mail;* and 37 per cent of the shares of Advertiser Newspapers in Adelaide, which publishes *The Advertiser* and associated periodicals.

The Herald, an afternoon broadsheet, is published daily except Sunday, from its plant at 44–74 Flinders Street, Melbourne. Its daily average net paid circulation for six months ended September 30, 1960, was 466,407.

QUEENSLAND

The Courier-Mail (Brisbane)

The Courier-Mail's founding date was 1933, but the two component papers indicated by its name were much older. *The Moreton Bay Courier* was started on June 20, 1846, 13 years before Queensland became a new colony by separating from New South Wales. The paper began as a four-page weekly, became a bi-weekly in 1858, a tri-weekly in January, 1860, and, in May, 1861, acquired a new name and daily status—*The Brisbane Courier.* It had a succession of proprietors until 1933, when it was combined with its rival, *The Daily Mail.*

The Daily Mail was born soon after the turn of the century, on October 3, 1903. It changed owners twice in the next dozen years. The rivalry between *The Daily Mail* and *The Brisbane Courier* reached a climax in a defamation action instituted in 1915 by the older paper against the younger.

Both papers had published issues on Sundays during World War I, and in 1923 *The Daily Mail* established *The Sunday Mail* under separate editorial direction.

The Courier-Mail merger in 1933 was accomplished by Sir Keith Murdoch and John Wren, who had organized Queensland Newspapers Pty. Ltd., for the purpose. Wren had owned *The Daily Mail* since 1915. Murdoch controlled the new company. The Herald and Weekly Times Ltd., bought the interest of Murdoch's estate after his death in 1952. Queensland Newspapers Pty. Ltd., is now a wholly-owned subsidiary of Queensland Press Ltd., a public company in which The Herald and Weekly Times Ltd., owns a 37 per cent interest. Through Queensland Newspapers Pty. Ltd., the parent company also owns two radio stations, conducts an extensive book and magazine distribution service and a job printing business.

The Courier-Mail, a morning broadsheet, is published every day except Sunday from its plant at 288 Queen Street, Brisbane. In 1960 the paper's daily circulation was 235,697.

Telegraph (Brisbane)

The *Telegraph* began publication on October 1, 1872, in a period of newspaper proliferation in Queensland. Most of the new journals lasted only briefly. The *Telegraph* was a broadsheet for more than 75 years; it did not become a tabloid until 1948. It had no interstate ownership ties until 1955, when the Melbourne *Herald* group expanded its interests in Brisbane, adding control of the *Telegraph* to its control of the *Courier-Mail.*

The Herald and Weekly Times Ltd. today owns 37 per cent of the stock in Queensland Press Ltd. which owns the two papers. The balance is held thus: 33 per cent by general investors, mainly Queenslanders, and about 30 per cent by two Melbourne families without other publishing interests.

The *Telegraph,* an afternoon tabloid, is published every day but Sunday, from its offices in Queen St., Brisbane. In 1960 its circulation was 162,261.

SOUTH AUSTRALIA

The Advertiser (Adelaide)

In 1958, *The Advertiser* became the seventh metropolitan Australian daily newspaper to enter a second century of publication. It celebrated the occasion by constructing a handsome new home for itself. *The Advertiser* began (July 12, 1858) as *The South Australian Advertiser*, twenty-two years after the founding of the colony of South Australia, and after a succession of other papers had failed to survive for long. *The South Australian Weekly Chronicle*, still a weekly but now simply *The Chronicle*, a farm paper, was begun at the same time by the same proprietors. Adelaide's population in 1858 was about 60,000.

Since 1931, *The Advertiser* has been South Australia's only morning daily. On February 21 of that year, it absorbed *The Register*, which traced its beginnings back to 1836, the year the colony was founded. *The Register* was originally *The South Australian Gazette and Colonial Register;* its first issue (June 18, 1836) was published in London and its second in the infant community at Adelaide almost exactly a year later (June 3, 1837). *The Register* had become a daily in 1850.

Sir Langdon Bonython acquired *The Advertiser* in 1891 and was sole proprietor until January 10, 1929, when he sold it to Advertiser Newspapers Ltd., a public company, which is still the publisher. Thirty-seven per cent of the shares are owned by The Herald and Weekly Times, Ltd., of Melbourne.

Advertiser Newspapers, Ltd., publishes *The Advertiser, The Chronicle* and is half-owner of *The Sunday Mail* with News, Ltd. Its Griffin Press prints job orders and fine editions of books. The company owns one metropolitan and three country radio broadcasting stations and a 40 per cent interest in television station ADS-7.

The Advertiser, a morning broadsheet, is published every day, except Sunday, from 121 King William Street, Adelaide. In 1960 its circulation was 184,040.

The News (Adelaide)

The News, South Australia's only evening newspaper, published by News Ltd., is one of the youngest papers of the Australian metropolitan group. It first appeared on July 24, 1923, as a broadsheet.

J. E. Davidson was managing director of News Ltd., which also owned *The Barrier Miner* (Broken Hill, N.S.W.) and *The Port Pirie Recorder,* then South Australia's only provincial daily. In 1925, News Ltd., purchased its competition—the two other Adelaide dailies in the afternoon field. Its growth in circulation has been steady ever since. By 1939, it had passed 41,000, reaching 100,000 in 1951.

Davidson launched an afternoon daily in Hobart. It was also named *The News,* but it died after eighteen months. In 1926, he purchased the *Daily News* of Perth and held it and his other properties until News Ltd., 'was acquired by Sir Keith Murdoch. Today News Ltd., continues in Murdoch family control, under Rupert Murdoch, Sir Keith's son.

News Ltd., with Advertiser Newspapers Ltd., holds joint ownership in the Weekend Publishing Company, which produces *The Sunday Mail* on News Ltd., presses. News Ltd. has a substantial interest in a major metropolitan radio station and controls South Australia's first television station, NWS-9. It still owns *The Barrier Miner* and a radio station at Broken Hill. In Melbourne, News Ltd., owns the Southdown Press, which publishes *New Idea,* a woman's weekly; *The Australian Journal,* a fiction magazine; and several periodicals, including *TV Week*. In 1955 News Ltd. purchased Western Press in Perth. This company publishes *The Sunday Times,* only Sunday newspaper in Western Australia. News Ltd. owns a number of small country newspapers in Western Australia and also controls the Wimmera *Mail-Times,* a tri-weekly in Western Victoria. News Ltd. entered the Sydney publishing field in late 1959 with a group of suburban weeklies and early in 1960 bought the *Daily Mirror* (Sydney) and other former Norton properties from the Fairfax group (q.v.).

The News, a tabloid, is published every afternoon except Sunday, from its plant in North Terrace, Adelaide. Its 1960 circulation was 120,140.

WESTERN AUSTRALIA

The West Australian (Perth)

Perth's only morning newspaper, *The West Australian,* has been in continuous publication since January 5, 1833, only four years after Western Australia was proclaimed a colony (1829). The parent paper was a weekly, *The Perth Gazette and Western Australian Journal,* edited and printed by Charles Macfaull, who had been associated with earlier Perth papers.

The West Australian's present proprietors believe there is a possibility of extending the paper's accepted birthdate back to February, 1831, when another Macfaull (manuscript) newspaper, *The Western Australian Chronicle and Perth Gazette,* was launched. If continuity can be established, *The West Australian* can claim to antedate *The Sydney Morning Herald,* acknowledged longevity champion.

After a number of changes of names and ownerships, *The West Australian* appeared under its present name as a bi-weekly in 1879. It has been a daily newspaper since 1885. Among its proprietors was Sir Winthrop Hackett K.C.M.G., M.A., LL.D., M.L.C., who was managing director, editor and sole owner of *The West Australian* from late in the nineteenth century until his death in 1916. He was also first chancellor of the University of Western Australia.

After Sir Winthrop's death, *The West Australian* became the property of the university. West Australian Newspapers Ltd., bought it in 1926 and has owned it ever since. One lasting educational consequence is that the university is now so splendidly endowed, as a result of the sale, that students are admitted tuition-free.

Other publications of West Australian Newspapers Ltd., are the *Daily News, The Weekend News, The Countryman* and a series of handsomely illustrated annuals. The company does some job printing and owns a one-half interest in one metropolitan and three country radio stations and a substantial interest in TVW/Limited, the only commercial television station in Western Australia.

The West Australian, a tabloid, is published every morning except Sunday from Newspaper House, 125 St. George's Terrace, Perth. Its 1960 circulation was 156,006.

Daily News (Perth)

Perth's only evening newspaper, the *Daily News,* also owned by West Australian Newspapers Ltd., was founded on July 26, 1882, as Western Australia's first daily paper. It was a broadsheet until 1939 when it adopted its present tabloid format.

The *Daily News* was begun by the proprietors of *The Inquirer and Western Australian Journal of Politics and Literature* (first published on August 5, 1840), who wished to put an evening newspaper into the Perth field. In 1886 it absorbed two other papers. In 1896 the proprietors started *The Morning Herald. The Inquirer* died in 1901, *The Morning Herald* in 1909. Arthur Lovekin, associated with the *Daily News* since 1886, became its owner in 1916. Ten years later he sold the paper to News Ltd., of Adelaide, then a subsidiary of The Herald and Weekly Times Ltd., of Melbourne. On August 6, 1935, West Australian Newspapers Ltd. purchased the *Daily News* and began the daily newspaper monopoly the company still enjoys in Perth.

The *Daily News,* a tabloid, is published every afternoon except Sunday from Newspaper House, 125 St. George's Terrace, Perth. Its 1960 circulation was 95,504.

TASMANIA

The Mercury (Hobart)

Hobart Town, capital of Tasmania which was proclaimed a colony in 1825, had seen its first newspaper born fifteen years earlier, in 1810. Hobart Town was second only to Sydney in acquiring papers of general circulation and by 1854 had seen many of them come and go. In that year, on July 5, John Davies began publishing *The Hobarton Mercury.*

The paper was launched as a bi-weekly, became a tri-weekly on January 1, 1858, and a daily on January 1, 1860. Over the years it absorbed the older *Colonial Times, The Tasmanian, The Tasmanian Daily News, The Daily Courier, The Advertiser* and *The Tasmanian News.* "Hobarton" was dropped from the title and the paper continues today as *The Mercury,* Hobart's only daily newspaper.

Besides its long life, *The Mercury* is notable for having been continuously under one family ownership. From John Davies, editor and owner from 1854 to his death in 1872, the succession passed to his two sons, J. G. Davies (1872–1916) and C. E. Davies (1872–1921); to C. R. Davies, a grandson of the founder (1921–1926); to C. B. Davies, another grandson (1926–1946); to Charles Davies, a third grandson (and cousin to C.R. and C.B.) (1946–1954); to G. F. Davies, a great-grandson, present Chairman of Directors.

In 1957 *The Mercury* acquired the presses of the late *Argus* (Melbourne) and reverted to a broadsheet. The proprietors of *The Mercury* also publish *The Saturday Evening Mercury.*

The Mercury, a broadsheet, is published every morning except Sunday by The Mercury Newspaper Pty. Ltd., at 93 Macquarie Street, Hobart. Its 1960 circulation was 47,343.

APPENDIX C

Australian Periodicals

Newspaper Statistics. From compilations in the 1961 NAARDS the Australian newspaper press by states may be tabulated this way:

AUSTRALIAN NEWSPAPER PRESS BY STATES*

Figures Taken to Sept. 1961	New South Wales	Victoria	Queensland	South Australia	Western Australia	Tasmania	Northern Territory & Pacific Area	Canberra, A.C.T.	Totals
TOTAL NEWSPAPERS	258	197	77	62	44	11	5	1	655
Capital-City Dailies	4	3	2	2	2	1	0	1	15
Capital-City Weeklies	3	1	2	2	1	2	0	0	11
Suburban Dailies	2	0	0	0	0	0	0	0	2
" Twice Weeklies	2	0	0	0	0	0	0	0	2
" Weeklies	73	56	7	8	5	0	0	0	149
" Fortnightlies	0	0	1	4	3	0	0	0	8
" Monthlies	0	0	0	4	5	0	0	0	9
Country Dailies	13	6	9	0	1	2	0	0	31
" 5 Days a Week	6	0	2	0	0	0	0	0	8
" 3 Days a Week	12	9	4	2	1	0	1	0	29
" 2 Days a Week	47	25	8	4	3	1	1	0	89
" Weeklies	96	97	39	34	23	5	3	0	297
" Fortnightlies	0	0	3	0	0	0	0	0	3
" Monthlies	0	0	0	2	0	0	0	0	2

* Table Courtesy AARDS PTY. LTD., Sydney, publishers of NAARDS: Newspaper Advertising Rate and Data Service.

The preponderance of country newspapers is noteworthy. The country press—in contrast to the capital-city and suburban press—accounts for about two-thirds of all newspapers in the tabulation. "Country" in the Australian sense includes all population centers separate from the capital cities, and at a distance from them. Most are small. The term "suburban" relates to a characteristic of the big population centers not apparent from the word itself. Of the capital cities, only Brisbane (area: 385 square miles) includes in its corporate limits the populated metropolitan area. The cities of Sydney, Melbourne, Adelaide, Perth and Hobart are actually minute patches—some as small as a square mile. But in each instance the name of the capital includes by implication up to or more than a score of separate municipalities, each with its own municipal administration, and all of them suburban to the capital. Woollahra, Randwick, Waverley, Hunter's Hill, Leichhardt, Mosman, Manly and a number of others are separate local governmental units that make up metropolitan Sydney. Among Melbourne's clustering suburbs are Kew, St. Kilda, Brighton, Caulfield, Toorak, Footscray, Malvern, Prahran, Port Melbourne.

The model is English—as with London City and its many suburbs. The fact is significant here because the pattern affords ready-made circulation areas for suburban newspapers, most of them small in circulation and of free distribution.

Australian papers also die, and in 1955–56 eighteen papers ceased publication. Most were country weeklies.

Sunday Newspapers. Seven publications clearly fall within the category of Sunday newspapers. A number of others fall short because their emphasis is not as strong upon news as it is upon features, or because emphasis on news is non-existent.

These are the seven Sunday newspapers and the dailies with which they are most closely associated:

SYDNEY:	1. *Sunday Telegraph* (*Daily Telegraph*).
	2. *The Sun-Herald* (*The Sydney Morning Herald* and *The Sun*).
	3. *Sunday Mirror News-Pictorial* (*Daily Mirror*).
BRISBANE:	4. *The Sunday Mail* (*The Courier-Mail*).
	5. *Sunday Truth* (*Daily Mirror*, Sydney).
ADELAIDE:	6. *Sunday Mail* (*The News* and *The Advertiser*).
PERTH:	7. *The Sunday Times* (*The News*, Adelaide).

No Sunday papers are published in Melbourne or Hobart. Of the seven, *The Sunday Mail* (Brisbane) is the only broadsheet. *Truth*, a weekly with four state editions, is published on Sunday in Brisbane, for Queensland distribution, but *Truth* appears on Thursdays in Melbourne (where the three Southeastern Australia editions are printed) and in Hobart, and on Fridays in Adelaide, for distribution in Victoria, Tasmania and South Australia respectively. The *Sunday Mirror News-Pictorial* (Sydney) was metamorphosed from the New South Wales edition of *Truth*.

Because an important part of the criteria for Sunday papers is hard news, a number of periodicals do not quite fall within the category. Their emphasis is upon features. Much smaller than the Sunday papers, but closer to the category are *The Saturday Evening Mercury* (Hobart), published by *The Mercury* (Hobart); and *The Saturday Evening Express* (Launceston), published by *The Examiner* (Launceston). Others might be mentioned but not included, for varying reasons.

With the exception of *The Sunday Times* (Perth), and the Brisbane edition of *Truth,* Sunday newspapers are produced and published in close physical association with a daily newspaper, as suggested in the foregoing list. *The Sunday Times* (Perth), far western outpost of News Ltd., publishers of *The News* (Adelaide), is relatively a next door neighbor to News Ltd.'s stable of 26 small weeklies in Western Australia.

The Sun-Herald (Sydney), which advertises that it "has the highest circulation of any newspaper (DAILY or SUNDAY) in Australia," is an amalgam of *The Sunday Sun and Guardian* and *The Sunday Herald.* Since its founding in 1953, it has drawn on the resources of John Fairfax Ltd. publications, principally *The Sydney Morning Herald,* to assist the labors of a core of full-time editors and staffers. Similarly with its opposition, the *Sunday Telegraph* (Sydney), which draws upon the *Daily Telegraph. The Sunday Mail* (Brisbane) borrows staff from *The Courier-Mail,* with which it shares a building.

The *Sunday Mail* (Adelaide) is unique in Australia. For the most part *The News'* staff produces the paper under guidance of a full-time echelon of editors, although *The Advertiser* and *The News,* strong rivals in the daily field, share the ownership evenly.

General news comes to each Sunday paper from the parent organization, with certain added special arrangements. Australian Associated Press furnishes much of the overseas news budget. Interstate stories are filed through correspondents and bureaus, or are obtained by arrangements similar to those among the dailies; e.g., *The Sunday Mail* (Brisbane) gets part of its Queensland news from the Queensland Country Press Association, in the same building. Rounds for local stories are manned in the same manner as for the dailies.

Because there are few Sunday papers, the circulation drive is intense. Editions are run for special areas. Victoria and Tasmania, where Sunday papers are not published, are prime targets for the Sunday papers of Sydney and Adelaide. *The Sunday Mail* (Brisbane) fights the Sydney Sunday papers for circulation in the New South Wales–Queensland border areas. The *Sunday Mail* (Adelaide) disputes Sydney supremacy in Broken Hill and other western New South Wales towns. Sydney's Sunday papers ship by air, not as many as *The Sunday Mail* (Brisbane), but several thousand papers, to northern Queensland, New Guinea and Papua. Alone among the Sundays, *The Sunday Times* (Perth) has had no competition except *The Western Mail,* since *The Mirror,* a Saturday paper, and the Western Australia edition of *Truth,* ceased publication.

Circulations in the Sunday field are impressive, as these September 1960 figures declare:

The Sun-Herald (Sydney)	631,722
Sunday Telegraph (Sydney)	598,000
Sunday Mirror News-Pictorial (Sydney)	365,322
The Sunday Mail (Brisbane)	299,281
Sunday Truth (Brisbane)	198,236

Sunday Mail (Adelaide)	213,121
The Sunday Times (Perth)	124,764
	2,430,446

The total circulation figure means that there is about one Sunday newspaper for every four Australians.

A notable fact of Sunday newspaper life anywhere is that as magazines strain to become more timely in the newspaper sense, Sunday papers work hard to become more like magazines. This is also the sum of things in Australian Sunday publication.

Magazines and Other Periodicals. The Press Directory of Australia and New Zealand, published by Country Press Ltd., of Sydney, goes beyond the newspaper field to include periodicals of all sorts. A summary of its classifications suggests the wide variety of Australia's reading matter.

By states, once more, the latest (1958) *Press Directory* listings, exclusive of newspapers, may be summarized thus:

SUMMARY OF AUSTRALIAN PERIODICALS
(EXCLUDING NEWSPAPERS)

TYPE OF PUBLICATION *	New South Wales	Victoria	Queensland	South Australia	Western Aust.	Tasmania	Australia
Broadcasting and Radio	8	5	1	1	1	0	16
Foreign Community	14	8	0	0	1	0	23
Motion Pictures and Photography	11	4	0	0	0	0	15
Motoring and Aviation	17	12	3	1	2	0	35
Religious	20	29	8	10	3	2	72
Scientific, Technical, Educational and Professional	37	41	7	6	2	2	95
Sporting	18	12	2	2	1	1	36
Stock, Farm and Garden	38	24	9	8	13	3	95
Trade and Commerce	81	57	21	10	11	9	189
Unions, Association, Organizations, Etc.	113	58	23	23	19	2	238
Women, Fashions, Etc.	14	6	3	4	1	1	29
Miscellaneous	57	46	8	5	3	5	124
TOTALS	428	302	85	70	57	25	967

* No non-newspaper periodicals are published in the Australian Capital Territory or in the Northern Territory.

The chart indicates how Australians are served with a wide choice of magazines and other periodicals. Many of them, including the national magazines, are published in Sydney and Melbourne, richest and most populous capitals of the two richest and most populous states.

Several matters are noteworthy.

One is the dominant role played in the national field by women's magazines. They are largest in circulation and in business volume. During the thirteen-month period of this survey, the third largest-circulation women's magazine bought out the second largest so that it could more effectively compete with the largest of all. Picture magazines, trade magazines, children's magazines, pocket-magazines and many another kind appear for a time and then as suddenly disappear. The big publishers—mostly newspaper proprietors—are fluid in their periodical publishing practices.

Another is that not only magazines but books, special periodicals and job printing of all kinds are produced by newspaper companies.

A third is that the newspaper and magazine business in Australia is extensive, lively, fiercely competitive, vulnerable to adverse economics and change. Many publications are long-lived: Seven metropolitan dailies have celebrated their centennials. The oldest country daily continues in good health—*The Maitland Mercury* (N.S.W.) which was begun in 1843. And *The Bulletin* (founded in 1880), the Sydney weekly, though recently purchased by Australian Consolidated Press (Sydney), still irascibly plays the critic to politics, poetry, literature and almost everything else Australian.

The Labor Press. The Press Directory names 238 publications in "Unions, Associations, Organizations." Because Australia is so heavily unionized and because the Australia Labor Party is a powerful force in both state and federal politics, it is no surprise to find many union and labor publications among the 238; however, no major daily newspaper in Australia is owned and published by any segment of labor.

The only labor daily extant is *The Barrier Daily Truth* of Broken Hill, N.S.W. (population 37,000), of which the proprietor is the Workers Industrial Union of the Barrier District. Its circulation is about 7,000, somewhat less than that of its afternoon opposition, *The Barrier Miner,* owned by News Ltd., of Adelaide. *The Barrier Daily Truth,* a morning paper, advertises that "Every miner receives a copy." But important as it is as a mineral producer, Broken Hill is not a metropolitan area and its papers do not circulate widely.

In his course on "The Popular Press" at the University of Sydney, Henry Mayer, senior lecturer in government, has this to say about labor papers:

In this century there have been Labor dailies, sometimes short-lived, in all capitals except Perth. There was the *Daily Herald* (Adelaide) from 1910 to 1924; Brisbane had an evening paper—*The Daily Standard* from 1912 to 1936; Hobart had *The World* from 1918 to 1924. Sydney had the famous *The Labor Daily* from 1922 to 1938. In all of these papers, Trade Unions and the Labor Movement had some capital. In Melbourne a short-lived *People's Daily* existed from 1903 to 1904 and generally supported the Australian Labor Party (ALP), though it was not officially supported by it. . . . In general, it is agreed that three causes were responsible for the failure of Labor papers: lack of capital, insufficient support from ALP voters as readers; and a struggle for control over the papers by factions within the Labor Movement.

Besides the reasons mentioned by Mr. Mayer, labor's failure in the daily field may be also partly ascribed, as in the U.S., to refusal of big advertisers to do continuing business with labor publications, and to the labor papers' special-interest approach to the news.

Many papers serve as news and discussion media for their memberships: notably the fortnightly *Australian Worker* (Sydney), official organ of the Australian Workers Union and the Australian Labor Party; *The Worker,* Queensland AWU–ALP weekly; *The South Australian Worker,* published by the United Trades and Labour Council of South Australia and the Australian Council of Trade Unions; *Journalist* (Melbourne), monthly tabloid published by the AJA; the monthly *Railways Union Gazette* (Melbourne); and *Labor News* (Sydney), Ironworkers' monthly tabloid.

APPENDIX D

Radio and Television

There are two types of radio stations in Australia—National Broadcasting Service (federally owned and operated) and Commercial Broadcasting Service. In June, 1959, according to the Commonwealth Bureau of Census and Statistics, there were 66 National and 108 Commercial radio stations in the states and territories.*

AUSTRALIAN RADIO BROADCASTING STATIONS

TYPE OF STATION	*N.S.W.*	*VIC.*	*QLD.*	*S.A.*	*W.A.*	*TAS.*	*N.T.*	*A.C.T.*	*PAPUA-N.GUIN.*	*TOTAL*
National:										
Medium-Frequency	16	5	12	8	7	4	2	2	1	57
High Frequency	1	3	2	0	2	0	0	0	1	9
Commercial:	37	20	20	8	14	8	0	1	0	108
								TOTAL		174

Licenses are granted commercial stations for three-year periods and for renewals of one year. The three-man Australian Broadcasting Control Board is under the Postmaster-General, and there is a seven-man Australian Broadcasting Commission.

* Call letters for stations include a number indicating the home state: e.g., 2BL Sydney (N.S.W.), 3AR Melbourne (Victoria), 4QR Brisbane (Queensland), 5AN Adelaide (South Australia), 6WN Perth (Western Australia), 7ZL Hobart (Tasmania), 9PA Port Moresby (Papua-New Guinea). Canberra stations use the figure 2—the Capital Territory is within the New South Wales boundaries.

The National Broadcasting Service—or ABC, for Australian Broadcasting Commission—is operated much like the United Kingdom's BBC, on public money. Commercial stations and networks sell time and advertising and are more or less of a pattern with the commercial stations in the U.S.

Markedly different from the U.S. practice is the licensing of listeners. In Australia it is illegal to own or operate a radio without a license from the Postmaster-General's Department. These cost £2/15 a year for a Zone #1 license (the area within 250 miles of an ABC station) and £1/8 for a Zone #2 license ("the remainder of the Commonwealth"). In 1958–59, there were 2,263,712 licenses in force throughout Australia.

Television is the latest arrival in Australian communications. It began operating in Sydney and Melbourne in late 1956, in time for telecasts of the Olympic Games at Melbourne. Since then all states have acquired television stations. As with radio, government and commercial stations compete with one another. Television viewers' licenses cost £5 per year for one or more receivers at a single address.

As of December 1960, more than a million (1,121,000) viewers' licenses had been issued—about 75 per cent of them in New South Wales and Victoria.

In a land as vast and—over most of it—as lightly populated as Australia, electronic communications, particularly radio, are vitally important. In the lonely central areas, government and commercial radio, supplemented by the wonderful Flying Doctor two-way pedal-radio network, are the closest tie station families have with the outside world.

APPENDIX E

Professional Associations, Trade Services and Publications

Numerous associations among the Australian press seek to promote the special interests and objectives of their membership.

Largest numerically is the Australian Journalists' Association (AJA), which includes practically every employed newspaperman and woman in Australia. (See Chapter 10.) Other groups include proprietors, business, circulation and advertising managers and agents, among others.

The Australian Newspaper Council. The Australian Newspaper Council (ANC), an association of metropolitan newspaper proprietors, represents the recent merger of two groups: the Australian Newspaper Proprietors Association and the Australian Newspaper Council. Their former separate existence symbolizes the frequently rugged intransigence and individualism of Australia's newspaper proprietors.

The first proprietors' association was the Australian Newspaper Conference, Melbourne-born in the 1920's. It worked, after a fashion, despite interior frictions, but not well enough for the war years of the 1940's. The Australian Newspaper Proprietors Association (ANPA) was its successor, and it continued from 1939 to 1945. Then, as *Newspaper News* reported in its Twenty-Fifth Anniversary Edition, "As horizons for peacetime production widened there was a drive for plant, increased output and therefore more newsprint." On the rock of newsprint shortage the

ANPA split. A dissident group calling itself the Australian Newspaper Council was formed on February 19, 1948. Newsprint did not remain a torrid issue beyond the 1940's, but for more than a decade the two groups continued their separate ways. Each had its own rules and each had its separate bureau for accrediting advertising agents until the recent reunion. In 1958, the two associations merged, except for two holdouts, into the Australian Newspaper Council.

The same proprietors determine Australian Associated Press policy, and some of them are associated in the manufacture of newsprint in Australian Newsprint Mills Ltd. But they maintain their individuality and independence of action on other matters.

ANPA included these newspaper companies: *The Sydney Morning Herald, The Argus* (Melbourne), *The Age* (Melbourne), *Telegraph* (Brisbane), *The Mercury* (Hobart). Other papers were members of the accrediting bureau only: *The Sun* (Sydney), *The Newcastle Morning Herald, The Newcastle Sun.*

The new ANC is composed of the foregoing and these: Australian Consolidated Press (Sydney), Herald and Weekly Times (Melbourne), the *Sun News-Pictorial* (Melbourne), Advertiser Newspapers Ltd. (Adelaide), Queensland Newspapers Pty. Ltd., Western Press Ltd. (Perth).

Australian Provincial Press Association. The Australian Provincial Press Association (APPA) is a federal association of state organizations of small newspapers of less-than-daily publication. It includes the New South Wales Country Press Association, the Victorian Provincial Press Association, the South Australian Provincial Press Association, the Provincial Press Association of Western Australia, and the Tasmanian Provincial Press.

The APPA was founded in 1906. Among its special concerns are agreements between unions and managements covering hours, wages, and working conditions; newsprint, advertising, legislation affecting the press. A code of ethics governs the professional and business conduct of members.

The APPA holds annual conventions and conducts other business through the secretary, the officers and a committee of management. Most of the common purposes of country newspapers are also served on the state level, by the state associations listed in the foregoing paragraph. Queensland papers similarly served by the Queensland Country Press Association remained unaffiliated with the APPA.

New South Wales Country Press Association; Country Press Ltd. Oldest of the state groups—indeed, the oldest newspaper organization in Australia —is the New South Wales Country Press Association, founded in 1899. Its Sydney offices are also the home offices for the APPA.

Affiliated with the New South Wales Country Press Association and sharing the same offices is Country Press Ltd., which publishes at intervals of about three years *The Press Directory of Australia and New Zealand.* Country Press Ltd. also maintains an extensive advertising service and one of the major clipping bureaus of Australia.

The other state associations of small less-than-daily publication hold to similar purposes and allegiances. Each has its home office in the capital city. None of the country press associations which are members of APPA gather or transmit news to member papers. An exception is the Queensland Country Press. (See Chapter 7.)

Australian Provincial Daily Press Ltd. The Australian Provincial Daily Press Ltd. (APDP) is composed of twenty-six newspapers from five states (South Australia has no provincial dailies), members being the proprietors or their representatives. Its aims and objectives are those of the two similar metropolitan-paper organizations. Its secretary-managing director is also secretary to the Provincial Press Accreditation Bureau, and the two share the same Melbourne address.

The Bureau acts as the advertising accrediting authority for the APDP, the APPA, and the state, provincial, or country press associations. Accreditation affirms the bona fides of advertising agencies, firms and individuals.

Australian Association of Advertising Agencies; Australian Association of National Advertisers. Relative newcomers to Australian publishing are the country's advertising associations. The two leading groups are the Australian Association of Advertising Agencies—known as the four A's —and the Australian Association of National Advertisers. With the expansion of Australian business and industry each is playing an increasingly important role in the field of publications.

Printed advertising, principally in newspapers and magazines, accounts for about three-fourths of an Australian advertising expenditure estimated at upwards of £40,000,000 annually. The relationship among these associations, agents, agencies, clients and newspapers is close and continuous.

Commonwealth Press Union. About seventy Australian newspaper executives are members of the Commonwealth Press Union (Commonwealth here meaning not Australia, but the British Commonwealth of Nations). About forty members are from the metropolitan papers.

The union's most notable activity is its series of Commonwealth Press Conferences, held when possible every fifth year. The first conference met in Great Britain in 1909, its founding year. Australia and New Zealand were co-hosts in 1925, and Australia was host in 1955 for the eighth conference in the series. In 1959, golden jubilee year, it met again in Britain. The union's membership includes more than three hundred British Commonwealth newspapers.

The Commonwealth Press Union has achieved many notable goals. It was instrumental in establishing the penny-per-word flat rate for press telegrams throughout the Commonwealth. It has hastened news transmission between Britain and Australia. It has fought the continuing battle for freedom of information on many fronts throughout the world. It helps arrange for news transmission on special events (coronations, international parleys, etc.); and is the court of appeal for London correspondents who find themselves in conflict with government over news coverage.

The Australian Section of the Commonwealth Press Union maintains offices in Sydney.

International Press Institute in Australia. The International Press Institute, a world-wide association of newspaper editors, founded in 1951, has an active Australian section. Among I.P.I.'s more than 900 members are editors and publishers from 18 Australian newspapers. All but two metropolitan companies—Sydney's John Fairfax, Ltd., and Truth and Sportsman (*Sydney Morning Herald, Sun* and *Daily Mirror*) are affiliated. Australian editors have attended international conferences, arranged by the Institute in Asia, Europe and North America. Each conference includes extensive tours of the host country.

In 1957, I.P.I. instituted a program of Commonwealth Exchange Fellowships. The fellowships give five selected U.S. journalists an opportunity to work and travel for three months in each of the five major countries of the British Commonwealth; and one each from these five countries to travel for three months in the United States.

Audit Bureau of Circulations. To the Australian newspaper, magazine and advertising world "A.B.C." means Audit Bureau of Circulations. This "watchdog of circulations," founded in 1932, took its genesis from the U.S. Audit Bureau of Circulations and its United Kingdom equivalent. It was begun, like its overseas models, from the understandable wish of proprietors, advertisers and advertising agents for a dependable, impartial, continuing summary of circulation statistics.

Membership is open to all types of publications, the only stipulation being that the candidate-periodical have a paid circulation capable of verification. There are 890 members of the Audit Bureau of Circulations: 245 advertisers, 314 advertising agents, 304 publishers, and 27 branch offices.

The A.B.C.'s silver jubilee celebration, in May, 1957, marked the retirement of T. Stuart Gurr, secretary of A.B.C. since its inception.

A.B.C. auditors certify net paid circulation of member-publications every six months. Summaries are issued privately and confidentially to members. Stereo labels for masthead publication and special certificates indicate membership. Audit costs are borne by the publisher. Annual subscriptions vary from £1/10/0 for country publications with less than 1,000 circulation, to a maximum of £20/0/0 for publications with circulations of more than 90,000. Advertisers pay £7/0/0 per year and advertising agents £20/0/0. Published circulation figures carefully designate whether they are A.B.C.-audited or "publisher's statements."

Control is vested in a committee of twenty-three members, divided according to field: six publisher members from the metropolitan daily and/or Sunday newspapers; three publisher-members from the country press; two publisher members from the weekly and national press; two miscellaneous publisher members; five advertiser members; five advertising agent members. The executive committee consists of six members—one from each field.

In the metropolitan daily field, all Australian newspapers but one belong to the Audit Bureau of Circulations. The lone holdout is *The Sydney Morning Herald.*

"*Newspaper News.*" This periodical is the trade journal of the Australian communications field. It plays a role in Australia comparable to that of *Editor and Publisher* in the U.S., and to that of *World's Press News and Advertisers' Review* in the United Kingdom. It is read by newspaper, magazine, advertising, circulation, graphic arts, radio, television and business people. It is tabloid size and printed on coated paper.

In 1957 the proprietors changed *Newspaper News* from a monthly to a fortnightly periodical and brightened it typographically. In the same year they began publication of a new fortnightly periodical, *Radio Television News,* which had been the radio and television section of *Newspaper News.*

Newspaper News keeps abreast of trends and developments in newspaper areas, in advertising inchage, advertising accreditations, printers and printing, paper supply, personnel changes in communications industries, photography, type and typography, color printing, packaging and display, printing machinery, and all else that pertains to communications.

Not the least of its interest to readers is the occasional exchange of irascible compliments in large advertisements between rival newspapers or executives. Besides its news function, it is the best market-place Australian newspaper and magazine proprietors have in which to win space-buying friends and to influence advertisers.

Newspaper News was founded in 1928 by David Yaffa, who died in 1947. Along the way it absorbed other trade publications, including *Advertising in Australia* and *Advertisers Monthly.* In 1953 it published a Coronation Year Twenty-Fifth Anniversary Edition that is valuable source-material about Australia's publishing past. *Newspaper News* also produces other specialty publications, notably *Graphic Arts and Printers Handbook.*

Advertising Rate and Data Service. Chief Australian advertising compilations are published by AARDS Pty. Ltd. and its associated firm, Mingay Publishing Co., Pty. Ltd. of Sydney. AARDS publishes advertising rates and data service for various media under these designations: BAARDS (radio and television broadcasting stations), NAARDS (newspapers), GAARDS (general media, including non-newspaper publications). Mingay publishes trade magazines in the radio-television and electric appliance field. A Supplement Service enables AARDS subscribers to keep up-to-date records on all notable changes in the advertising data of individual publications.

APPENDIX F

Authorized News
Agent System

Throughout Australia the system of authorized news agents is the means by which readers receive most of their newspaper and periodical reading material.

To explain its details and illuminate its operations, *The Age* (Melbourne), is used here as an example. Points differ from state to state, but essentials are identical. *The Age,* a morning broadsheet, was chosen because its home city, Melbourne, at the time of this study was the only metropolis where three papers were being published in either the morning or the afternoon fields. As such, it well illustrates the basic cooperation accorded the system by competitors. Now, of course, with *The Argus* gone, there are only two morning dailies in Melbourne.

The physical act of transporting newspapers throughout Melbourne and Victoria is accomplished by truck, mail, train, airplane, and newsboy, much as in the U.S. But the structure and operation of the system are different. The authorized news agents and sub-agents, who are the principal functionaries, are not employees of individual newspapers, as in the U.S. They work under separate contracts with the Australian papers.

In 1956 all three Melbourne morning newspapers—*The Age, The Argus* and *The Sun News-Pictorial*—published their first editions about the same time, close to midnight. All three used the same method of delivery of bundled papers for each edition. All four dailies (including the afternoon *Herald*) used the same authorized agents in Melbourne and throughout Victoria, with few exceptions.

The top authority controlling news agencies, including their sale and purchase, is a Board of Valuers, composed of circulation managers of the dailies, plus a chairman-assessor.

It is the circulation manager's job to see that the reader gets his paper when he expects it, to see that authorized agents and sub-agents are dependable and that the news agents who do the actual daily delivery adhere to rigid standards and schedules.

Three hundred or more authorized agents distribute newspapers in the Melbourne area. There are about six hundred sub-agents. The principal job of the first group is to get the papers to the individual subscribers. They do this principally through teams of newsboys peddling regular routes. An agent may employ as many as 30 boys—the average is 12— each boy delivering between 80 and 120 papers.

The boys carry all morning dailies on their routes. One house may subscribe to only one paper. The next house may take more than one. The boy will also deliver, on the various days of publication, other periodicals —Victorian, Australian or overseas.

For these last, the authorized agent has delivery arrangements with such organizations as Gordon and Gotch, Australian wholesale distributors. The subscriber can get *Time* magazine or *London Economist, Punch* or *New York Times Week in Review* delivered to his home.

There are two kinds of sub-news agents. Neither kind delivers daily papers or periodicals to homes. The *full* sub-news agent deals only in newspapers, magazines, cards, stationery and tobacco. The *mixed* sub-news agent may sell all sorts of sundries, be an agent for various services or run other small businesses on the side. His principal activity is not necessarily the sale of newspapers and magazines.

The area of an authorized news agent is not allotted by a set formula or by population count; but the maximum number of houses an authorized agent's area may contain, to insure satisfactory service, is about two thousand. A new residential area, where the lots are big and the houses are widely spaced, may have only two or three sub-agents. Sections that are more crowded may have as many as seven or eight.

The Melbourne telephone directory, under City and Suburban News Agents, lists forty-three authorized agents for thirty-five districts—six with two agents, one with three, the others with one. Outside Melbourne's metropolitan area, cities and towns on the circulation routes of the Melbourne newspapers have their own authorized agents and sub-agents.

Still another city group, an exception to the exclusive nature of circulation areas, is composed of about forty-two semi-authorized news agents —once known as "cash agents." They have the same rights and privileges as authorized news agents, but do not work within well-defined boundaries. They act as a check on the delivery system. If a customer is dissatisfied with the service he gets, he can request the semi-authorized agent to make the delivery.

If a news agent wishes to sell his business, he must follow a set procedure.

Every agency has a good-will valuation. This is determined by the Board of Valuers after the assessor has collated all relevant material for the Board: the news agency's accounts for all publications for the past year, its sales from all sources—local, state, national and foreign; its costs and operating expenses—wages, maintenance, furnishings, overhead; profits, good will, the growth or decline of the area. The assessor makes up a schedule by which the Board of Valuers determines the good-will valuations of the business and sets the sale price. Once the business has been valued it is advertised for sale by the assessor.

Meanwhile the assessor accepts applications from prospective purchasers of the authorized agency. These go to each of the daily papers' circulation managers, who study them and divide them into three groups: rejects, possibilities and probabilities. There may be as many as fifty applications for one agency. Preference is accorded "returned soldiers" —veterans of World War II who served overseas or north of a line drawn between Brisbane and Western Australia, where men usually saw combat service.

The likeliest half-dozen or more are chosen from this group by the circulation managers of the Melbourne dailies. Their choices go to the assessor, who reduces the list further. The remaining applicants are given the privilege of going over the books of the agency up for sale, and of making a thorough investigation of the area, the agency's selling points and of the methods of delivery. Each may also write a statement of how he will operate if he is the successful buyer.

The Board of Valuers then makes its selection of a successor to the retiring agent. Generally the choice is unanimous. But if one circulation manager wishes to reject the majority choice and name another man or a partnership to be his paper's authorized agent, he may do so. Disputes are submitted for settlement to the general managers of the dailies.

Restrictions on the buyer are rigidly enforced. He must, for example, be able to put up cash or securities equivalent to at least 75 per cent of the agency's good-will valuation. Banks may not advance him more than 35 per cent of the sum. He can, however, borrow money for his stock and fittings. The buyer pays over only that amount fixed by the Board of Valuers and by the expert stock valuers for the good will of the agency.

After the buyer has made his deposit for purchase of the business, the assessor holds it in escrow for one month. This gives the new agent a chance to check sales to determine whether they coincide with the sales schedule upon the strength of which he bought the business.

If a sales statement claims a sale of 400 papers a day and only 380 are moved, the buyer may challenge the schedule. Such protests must be lodged with the assessor within seven days after the first month of his operation of the business. So numerous are the checks and balances, and so careful are the assessor and the Board of Valuers that, over the years, only two purchasers have protested. Under the system, too, there is no chance for bribery or hidden premiums paid to secure news agency business.

The authorized agent may ask for the appointment of particular sub-agents, who are also chosen by the newspaper circulation managers. In rapidly growing areas a sub-agent may become an authorized agent, a process which requires redistricting of established areas: e.g., the valuation of one agency area went from £1,100 ($2,475) to £14,000 ($31,500) in ten years.

Generally, a new agency gets a start with the petition of a sub-agent that he be advanced to the higher rank. Since he can be advanced, in established areas, only at the expense of the agent operating there, he must pay for the privilege, under a formula administered by the Board of Valuers. If his new agency is cut from the areas of two or more established agents, he pays a sum of money to each of them, thereby acquiring the exclusive right to distribute in the new area. The price may run as high as £1,000 ($2,250) to each of four authorized agents for a small corner of the territory of each.

Delivery Procedures. The actual delivery of daily newspapers by the publishers to authorized agents is a six-times-a-week operation which, for morning papers, commences at 12:30 A.M. and continues until 5:45 A.M.

The Age's presses roll for the first edition at 12:30 A.M. Thereafter, delivery trucks must meet a schedule in which seconds count. The breakdown of a press, or stoppage for adjustment or repairs, can throw off the entire system.

From day to day, newspapers may vary widely in size. *The Age's* biggest day, in terms of pages, is Saturday, when its huge classified section and Literary Supplement are published. Wednesday's editions are also fat. On these two days, as many as twenty-three trucks carrying papers to authorized agents and common carrier terminals (trains, busses, mail or airplanes) may be required. On other weekdays, sixteen or less may be all that are needed.

In the publishing (mailing) room, papers are wrapped in bundles which vary according to the number of pages in a single copy.

The bundles—each containing 250, 200, 150, 100, 75, or 50 copies, depending on the size of the paper—are prepared by the publishing room crew. Simultaneously, an odd number of copies, representing the excess number over the even bundles an agent is to get, is being wrapped. Into this smaller bundle go two other items. One is the display poster, printed earlier in the evening, which the dealer will use to advertise a top news story of the day. The other is an addressographed slip of paper bearing the agent's name, address and the number of papers and posters he is to get. One of these labels may read:

Mr. Kinsey,
Royal Road,
West Kew.

Alongside, in heavy crayon, is written:

$$\frac{30-1}{2}$$

On the reverse of the label will be written in heavy crayon the figure "230."

This label will be wrapped, address-side out, with 30 copies of that day's *Age* and one of the day's display posters. This is the "pilot parcel" for Mr. Kinsey's delivery.

The driver of Truck No. 11, due to leave *The Age* loading dock at 4:10 A.M. knows he has 16 stops to make on his route, including Mr.

Kinsey's agency. At each of the 16 places a different number of papers is to be left. Driver No. 11 will be given 16 bundles, each with a different address and each containing as many papers as the first crayoned number above the crayoned line. The second number above the line is the number of posters in the bundle.

The Age's crew of markers know before they commence marking the labels that the edition will be a 32-page paper. Each bundle, therefore, is destined to contain 100 papers, for that is the most convenient number per bundle for editions running from 24 to 32 pages. Because the driver knows that the number below the crayoned line is the number of bulk bundles the dealer is to receive, he knows that Mr. Kinsey of Royal Road, West Kew, is to receive 230 papers that morning—the 30 papers and one poster in his pilot package and two others of the bulk wrapping of 100 copies each.

When Mr. Kinsey of Royal Road, West Kew, receives his morning delivery he will count his two bundles of 100 copies each, and the pilot bundle containing 30 copies and get the correct total of 230. He will check this with the number marked on the inside of the address label. If his count and the crayoned figure there do not coincide, he will call *The Age's* circulation department.

Before the driver starts on his delivery run to the 16 agents, he refers to a record in the car dock indicating the total number of bulk bundles of 100 he is to load. He may carry upwards of 6,200 copies of *The Age,* plus the 16 addressed parcels.

He is provided with a typewritten list of his deliveries—each agent's name, address, number of addressed bundles (one to each) and number of bulk bundles to be left at each address. As the driver makes each drop he checks off the agent's name. At the end of his run his truck is empty.

The morning papers have an agreement with news agents that trouble at one plant will not impede delivery of editions for all. Bundles for delivery to individual subscribers must be in the hands of authorized agents by 5:45 A.M. If they are not, the agents must commence delivery of the papers on hand and not be required to deliver the tardy papers— even if they arrive at 5:46 A.M.—until after they have completed delivery of those at hand.

Hobart is an exception among the capitals. It has no liaison between circulation managers or need for a Board of Valuers, because *The Mercury* has no competition. If an agent wishes to sell his business, he simply puts it up for sale. However, *The Mercury* will help out with an evaluation of the business if help is requested.

Glossary

Most of the newspaper terms defined below are used in the text of this book. A complete glossary—if one could be compiled—would run much longer. Many familiar words used interchangeably by newspapermen of Australia and the United States are omitted. Others without apparent relationship to journalism are included because they appear in the text. Within both countries there are certain regional differences in journalistic terms. In the U.S., for example, *red pepper* is used in the Middle West to denote *time copy*—filler stories in early editions that may be thrown out in favor of live news later on.

Australian Newspaper Terms

AAP—Australian Associated Press.

ABC—Australian Broadcasting Corporation; Audit Bureau of Circulations.

AJA—Australian Journalists' Association.

ALP—Australian Labour Party.

ANC—Australian Newspaper Council; proprietors' group.

ASHES—Non-existent symbolic trophy which goes to the winner of the Test Cricket matches between England and Australia.

AUP—Australian United Press.

AUTHORIZED NEWS AGENT—A merchant who contracts to deliver to subscribers, or to sell over the counter, copies of newspapers and magazines.

AWARD—Court-sanctioned agreement between AJA and media proprietors governing wages, hours and working conditions of employees.

BASH—To strike, hit, assault physically.

BASIC WAGE—Minimum wage set by Australian courts.

BLOCK—Engraving, cut.

BLOCK ROOM—Storage room for engravings.

BROADSHEET—Newspaper with large page size—15"–17" x 21"–23".

CABLE EDITOR—Editor in charge of overseas news.

CADET—Apprentice reporter; cadetship is four years of prescribed work.

CADET COUNSELLOR—A seasoned journalist in charge of cadet training for a newspaper.

CASUAL—A part-time employee hired for a particular service; e.g., *casuals* cover minor sports contests for a newspaper.

CHIEF OF STAFF—Editor in charge of local, state and national news; somewhat comparable to United States *city editor,* although his responsibility for news coverage is more extensive.

CHIEF REPORTER—Top journalist who is given special assignments, often of an investigative nature; term is falling into disuse.

CONVENER—Person who calls a meeting.

COPY TASTER—Editor who scans all news copy and advises news editor on play and treatment.

COUNTING HOUSE—Business office.

COUNTRY PRESS—Newspapers in cities and towns outside the metropolitan areas of the six capital cities.

CUTTING—Clipping from a newspaper.

DINGO—Australian wild dog.

DIP. J.—Diploma in Journalism; awarded upon completion of a university curriculum in journalism.

DIVISION—Vote in a legislative body; a *division* of the federal House of Representatives is a record of the votes for and against an issue.

DROP COPY—Delivery of an item in one city with copies sent from there to other delivery points, e.g., a photograph is delivered in Melbourne and *drop copies* are sent to Sydney and Adelaide.

DROP-ON—A replate made during an edition's run.

DUTY BOOK—Schedule of reporters' assignments.

EDITOR-IN-CHIEF—Chief editor of a publishing house which may publish books, magazines and other matter, besides newspapers.

EDITRESS—Woman editor; head of women's or society departments.

FEDERAL COUNCIL—Policy making and governing body of an organization, e.g., *Federal Council of the AJA.*

FEDERAL EXECUTIVE—Officers of a national organization, e.g., *Federal Executive of the ANC.*

FIFTY-FIFTY LETTERS—Brief letters to the editor; one *fifty* refers to the limit on number of words; the whole term indicates half *pro* and half *con.*

FINANCIAL—Member of an organization in good standing in respect to dues payment; to be *not financial* is to be in arrears.

FLONG—Papier-mâché sheet on which is impressed image of type and engraved plates in preparation for stereotype casting.

FOOT PATH—Sidewalk.

FUDGE—Late news or bulletin matter.

FUDGE BOX—Place reserved on page one, varying from one-fourth to three-fourths of a column, for publication of late news, printed by means of a small roller which eliminates needs for recasting whole front page.

FUTURE BOOK—Record of upcoming foreseeable news events.

GOVERNOR—Principal officer of state government, appointed by the British monarch; has great prestige but little political power.

GOVERNOR-GENERAL—Principal officer of the Commonwealth government, also appointed by the British monarch; also has great prestige, not much political power.

GRADE—Rank, assigned by management to a journalist, which governs his pay; *D grade* is lowest, *A* and *Special A grades* are highest.

GRAND FINAL—Decisive matches in championship football.

GRAZIER—Cattle or sheep raiser in eastern Australian States; cf. *pastoralist* in Western Australia.

GRIZZLE—Argument.

HANSARD—Verbatim account of debate and proceedings kept in all British legislative bodies; *see U.S.* Congressional Record.

HIGH COURT—Highest judicial tribunal of the Commonwealth of Australia; *see U.S.* Supreme Court.

HIRE-PURCHASE—Installment buying.

HUMP YOUR BLUEY—Carry your luggage; cf. *waltzing Matilda.*

INCHAGE—Advertising measure; Australian advertising is measured by the column inch, not by the column line as in the U.S.

INTERSTATE—Across state lines; to sell a feature story *interstate* is to sell it in other states.

INTRO—Introductory paragraph of a story; *see U.S.* Lead.

JOURNALIST—Newspaper man or newspaper woman.

LATE STOP—Last press run of the day.

LATE STOP MAN—Editor in charge of late stop period.

LAY-BY—A layaway purchase.

LEADERS—Editorial comment by a newspaper on events, issues, men; *see U.S.* Editorials.

LEADER PAGE—Page reserved for leaders, columns, letters to editor, cartoons, background stories, etc.; *see U.S.* Editorial Page.

LEAVING CERTIFICATE—Certificate awarded at graduation from secondary school, comparable to a U.S. *high school diploma.*

LITERALS—Typographical errors.

LORD MAYOR—Elected chief executive officer of a capital city.

L.S.D.—Slang for money; pounds, shillings, pence.

LTD.—Limited; designation of a company which sells shares to outside buyers; all metropolitan newspapers are owned by such public companies.

MANAGING DIRECTOR—Executive in active charge of the company; in newspaper firms, the ultimate authority in editorial and business operations; usually second only to chairman of directors.

MARGINS—Pay rates in excess of the minimums for any grade of journalist.

METROPOLITAN DAILIES AWARD—Court-sanctioned or court-ordered agreement between management and the AJA for the capital-cities dailies; on this agreement all other AJA-management awards are based.

MONEY-SPINNER—A profitable enterprise, e.g., a publication rich in advertising and subscriptions is a *money spinner*.

NEW AUSTRALIAN—Immigrant to Australia; a *new chum*.

NEWS AGENT—A merchant who contracts to deliver to subscribers, or to sell over-the-counter, copies of newspapers and magazines; short for *Authorized News Agent*.

NEWS EDITOR—Editor in charge of positioning and play of news.

NIGHT EDITOR—On a morning paper, editor in direct charge of editions; may also be news editor.

NOTICE BOARD—Bulletin board.

NOTICE PAPER—Agenda for a legislative or other formal group.

OFFSIDER—Lieutenant; relief man; assistant; stand-in for an executive.

O.T.C.—Overseas Telecommunications Commission.

OUTBACK—The dry deserted interior of Australia; the country "beyond the black stump."

PAR—Paragraph.

PASTORALIST—West Australian term for cattle and sheep raiser.

PETROL—Gasoline; *See U.S.* Gas

PICTURE-SALES OFFICE—Department where prints of news pictures may be purchased by the public.

PICTUREGRAM—Photograph transmitted by telephone or wireless.

POSTER—Printed sheet used by the newspapers to advertise the top news story of the day; posted on sandwich boards outside news agents' stores.

PREMIER—The principal elected political executive of a state; *see U.S.* Governor.

PRIME MINISTER—The principal political executive of the Commonwealth government; cf. *President of the United States*.

PROCESS—Photoengraving procedure.

PROCESS DEPARTMENT—Photoengraving department.

PTY. LTD.—Proprietary limited—a designation used after a firm's name to indicate a family or closely-held ownership; shares not sold to the public.

PUBLISHER—Foreman of the publishing room; cf. *foreman* of U.S. mailing room; sometimes, officer of the company; but not usually paper's owner or owner's representative as in the U.S.

PUBLISHING ROOM—Place where printed newspapers are delivered by conveyer belt from the press; *see U.S.* Mailroom.

PUNTER—Better; a person who wagers on the outcome of a horse race or other unpredictable event.

QUESTION TIME—First order of business at sessions of Federal and State Parliaments; the prime minister, premier or other ministers are asked to answer questions which are printed and distributed to members in advance.

QUESTIONS WITHOUT NOTICE—Questions asked ministers at *Question Time* which are not printed in advance.

RAR—Rules all around; a story set off by borders or by a box.

REPORTERS' ROOM—Workroom for the literary staff of a newspaper.

RESPONSIBLE GOVERNMENT—Government by majority or coalition of parties exercising administrative and legislative leadership; derives from the British form, which requires that failure to pass major legislation proposed by the government shall result in a no-confidence vote and new elections.

RING-AROUND-BOYS—Cadets who call the rounds of police stations, various markets, bureaus, agencies, etc., for the day's news developments.

ROSTER—Reporting tasks to which members of the literary staff are assigned each day.

ROUND—An activity or area regularly assigned to a reporter; *see U.S.* Beat.

ROUNDSMAN—A reporter assigned to a *round* or *beat*.

ROYAL SHOW—Annual exhibition of agricultural and manufactured products staged by each state at a specific time; cf. U.S. *state fairs*.

ROYAL TOUR—Official state visit by the monarch or member of the royal family.

SAVAGE—To wound cruelly, mutilate, maim or dismember: e.g., "Dingos had *savaged* the body of the dead station hand."

S.P.—Starting price; the amount a horse will pay if it wins a race.

SPORTS SUB—Sub-editor for sports; there are also social *sub-editors,* leader page *sub-editors,* etc.

SQUATTER—Large landholder of the early days.

STATION—Large holding of pastoralist or grazier; cf. U.S. *ranch*.

STOP-PRESS NEWS—Story important enough to stop the presses and remake page one; or to insert in a fudge box.

SUB-EDITOR—Journalist charged with the responsibility of preparing copy for the printer; *see U.S.* Copy Reader.

SUB-EDITORS' ROOM—Copy reading department; *see U.S.* Copy Desk.

TABLOID—Half-size newspaper; same as U.S. tabloids.

TELEPHONE ROOM—Department where girls are stationed who take stories dictated over the telephone by reporters covering distant events.

TENDER—Formal estimate of cost, with offer to undertake project; cf. U.S. *Bid*

TEST CRICKET—Championship match staged between countries of the British Commonwealth.

TIME BOOK—Record of time spent on job by journalists.

TRAM—Streetcar.

VENUE—Site of an event, especially a sporting event, e.g., the Melbourne Cricket Grounds was the *venue* for track events at the 1956 Olympic Games.

VET—To scan a piece of copy quickly: i.e., a chief of staff *vets* a reporter's story to insure that it is satisfactory before he turns it over to the sub-editors.

WHINGE—Complaint; to *whinge* is to complain or grouse.

U.S. Newspaper Terms

ALIBI COPY—Carbon copy of a story retained by a reporter to show how he wrote the original.

A-MATTER—Material sent out to the composing room in advance of a predictable news event, e.g., text or story about a speech to be delivered later on a newspaper's time; background story on a public function.

ANG—American Newspaper Guild.

AP—Associated Press.

APME—Associated Press Managing Editors, an organization of AP newspapers' news executives.

ASSIGNMENT—An event to be covered.

ASSISTANT CITY EDITOR—Second in command at the city desk; keeps close tabs on reporters working on assignments.

BEAT—A reporter's continuing assignment, e.g., police *beat*, labor *beat*; *see Australian* Round.

BEAT OR NEWS BEAT—An exclusive story, only one paper has it.

BEAT REPORTER—Reporter who covers a *beat*.

BID—Formal estimate; *See Australian* Tender.

BLOW-UP—To enlarge a photo or other piece of art.

BODY TYPE—Font in which most of the news-editorial text of a paper is set; usually 8-point.

BREAKING STORY—A news event that changes swiftly—a big fire, a trial, a legislative debate, etc.

BULLETIN—A brief story, with only meager details; if it is received just before press time it may be printed prominently on page one under a *Bulletin* slug.

BUSINESS OFFICE—Department that supervises advertising, circulation and other business phases of a newspaper; *see Australian* Counting House.

CABLE-ESE—Words compressed to save double rates, e.g., "ongo Paris," "upcheck outstraighten Britgovernment budget rumor."

CHASER—News story or correction in a story changed or made during the run of an edition.

CHEESECAKE—Pictures of pretty girls in beguiling poses and not much else.

CIRCUS MAKEUP—Bold use of large headlines, splashy art and white space.

CLIPPING—A clipped news story; *see Australian* Cutting.

CITY ROOM—Editorial department of a newspaper; *see Australian* Reporters' Room.

COLUMN—A peculiarly overdone American phenomenon; regularly published comment or report on almost every kind of activity, e.g., opinion *column,* "Inside" Washington *column,* general chatter or gossip *column,* bridge *column,* astrology *column;* there have even been obituary editors who claimed to be columnists with their news-obituary reports.

COMPOSITE STORY—A news event of wide and complex proportions covered by two or more reporters, e.g., tornado, blizzard, other disaster.

CONGRESSIONAL RECORD—Verbatim official reports of proceedings of the United States House and Senate; *see Australian* Hansard.

COPY DESK—Horseshoe-shaped desk for copy-readers who sit at its "Rim" and are supervised by a "Slotman," or head copy-reader, who sits inside the U.

COPY READER—Edits copy for good English, writes headlines; *see Australian* Sub-Editor.

CROP—To cut out unnecessary areas or figures in a photograph.

CUB—Young, green inexperienced reporter; *see Australian* Cadet.

CUT—A photo-engraving plate of a halftone or line drawing.

DEPTH REPORTING—Coverage that goes below surface news, probing into the "why" or background causes of a news situation.

D.O.A.—Dead on arrival, usually at a hospital.

DOPE STORY—Story that deals with possibilities, e.g., the possible outcome of tomorrow's election or today's athletic contest.

DOUBLE TRUCK *or* DOUBLE SPREAD—Two pages of a newspaper made up as a unit at the center fold of a section; either an advertisement or a long illustrated story.

EDITORIALS—The anonymous opinions of a newspaper on issues, people and events of the day, published in a specially-reserved place on the editorial page; *see Australian* Leaders.

EDITORIAL PAGE—Besides editorials, it may carry editorial paragraphs, letters to the editor, signed correspondence, various kinds of columns, cartoons, other opinion and background stories; *see Australian* Leader Page.

FILE—To send to a newspaper by telegraph or cable a story from a distant point.

FUTURE BOOK—Record of upcoming news events kept by city editor or other editors.

F.Y.I.—For your information.

GAS—Gasoline, motor fuel; *see Australian* Petrol.

"GEE-WHIZ NEWS"—News of exciting nature; opposite to *So-What News.*

GENERAL-ASSIGNMENT REPORTER—He covers no special beat but is available for reporting any event that is newsworthy.

GOVERNOR—The popularly-elected chief executive officer of an American state; but not necessarily the leader of the majority party in the state's legislature.

GRAF—Paragraph; *see Australian* Par.

HARD NEWS—News of major importance; likely to be consequential to the shape of coming events on a local, state, national, international or interspacial level.

HELL-BOX—Dump for used type.

HIGH SCHOOL DIPLOMA—Printed proof of four completed years of secondary education; cf. Australian *Leaving Certificate.*

HONOR BOX—Receptacle on street corners for vending of newspapers; money is dropped in coin slot on the customer's *honor.*

INSTALLMENT BUYING—Buy it now, pay later at intervals; *see Australian* Hire-Purchase.

JUMP STORY—Story that begins on one page and breaks over to another; usually the break is from page one to an inside page; also called *Break Story.*

LABEL HEAD—Headline without a verb, e.g., "President's Message to Congress."

LAY-AWAY—Merchandise reserved for a customer; *see Australian* Lay-by.

LEAD (lĕd)—Thin type-metal, used between lines and paragraphs to space out short columns.

LEAD (lēed)—First words or sentences of a story or other newspaper piece; may contain the five W's; *see Australian* Intro.

LEGMAN—Reporter on the scene of a news event who telephones facts for a story to a rewrite man stationed in the newspaper's city room.

LINAGE—Number of lines in an advertisement; total lines of advertising in an issue or during a given period, e.g., total *linage* for March.

LINERS—Classified advertisements.

LOBSTER WATCH—Midnight shift; nightside duty.

MAILROOM—Department where printed and folded newspapers are received by conveyer belts from the printing presses; point from which bundled newspapers start their journey by truck, newsboy, railroad train, etc., on their way to the ultimate consumer—the reader; *see Australian* Publishing Room.

MANAGING EDITOR—Top executive for news and features.

MARKER—Slip of colored paper sent to makeup editor in composing room by copy desk to indicate length of a story or to tell him of changes to come in a story.

MAT—Short for *matrix;* a small metal mold for casting letters, figures, etc., in a line of type; also a papier mâché sheet used to impress type faces and engravings from a form or chaise of type as first step in stereotyping process; *see Australian* Flong.

MINIMUM WAGE—Law that sets lowest legal level of pay; *see Australian* Basic Wage.

MOBILE PICTURE UNIT—Apparatus for transmitting news pictures by telephone.

MORGUE—A newspaper company's library, reference room, storeroom for clippings, mats, engravings, pictures, reference books.

NEWSBOY—Young male who sells newspapers on the street or who delivers them to subscribers' homes.

NEWS EDITOR—Executive in charge of the use, play and positioning of news; may be next in command under managing editor.

NEWS HOLE—The space available for news and features in an edition; based upon the advertising total, which governs number of pages.

NEWSPAPERMAN, NEWSPAPERWOMAN—Reporter, editor or person otherwise concerned in the newspaper business, especially with the news-editorial phases; *see Australian* Journalist.

NICKEL-PLATER—A story that is "longer than the Nickel Plate Railroad."

OPEN PAGE—Page to which stories are jumped from page one or other pages; kept open for changes in running stories from edition to edition.

OUTSTATE—The rest of the state beyond the metropolitan circulation area of a newspaper's home city; much of the news for the state edition originates *outstate*.

PAPER TO BED—The last stereotyped plate has been cast and put on the press; the edition, put to bed, is ready to roll.

PHOTOG—Photographer.

PIX—Pictures.

PONY WIRE—A press association service to small papers. The news budget is sometimes dictated over the telephone, sometimes dispatched to the paper by bus or other conveyance.

PRIVILEGE—Constitutional or legal protection against libel suits: e.g., news of government is generally *privileged* matter.

PUBLISHER—Top executive of a newspaper company; may be the owner of the owner's designated representative; contrast with *Australian publisher*.

QUERY—A correspondent *queries* a newspaper about coverage of an event in his home area.

RAILROAD—To send a story to press without usual editing or proofreading because of deadline pressures.

RED PEPPER—Filler stories; to be discarded in later editions in favor of live news.

REPLATE—To remold a stereotype plate after additions or other changes have been made on the page.

ROP—Run-of-the-paper; a display advertisement slugged *ROP* may run anywhere the advertising department orders.

SECTIONAL STORY—News story with many phases which must be covered by two or more reporters, i.e., blizzard, big fire, a big political convention, etc.; *see* Composite Story.

SEVERANCE PAY—Wages given to an employee who has been discharged; may be as much as a week's pay for every six months worked for the paper.

SIDEBAR—A story that tells a related phase of a major news event.

SIDEWALK—Continuous strips of concrete reserved for pedestrian travel; *see Australian* Foot-Path.

SLOTMAN—Chief copy-reader who sits in copy desk "slot."

SLUG *or* SLUG-LINE—Reporter's last name and subject of story, used in upper left-corner to identify all copy and material pertinent to story, e.g., *Jones-Fire*. Also a standing head, e.g., *Bulletin*.

"So-What News"—A routine news story; opposite to *Gee-Whiz News*.

Space Rates—The rate per line or per inch a newspaper pays a *space writer*.

Space Writer—Reporter paid by the inch or line of published material.

Spiked Story—Story not used; thrown away; put on a desk spike.

Staffer—Member of a newspaper's editorial staff.

Standard Size—Newspaper format with page that measures approximately 17″ x 22″.

Stereo—Stereotype plate.

Streetcar—Electrically-powered public conveyance; now almost obsolete; *see Australian* Tram.

Stringer—Part-time correspondent paid by the length and number of his stories that are published.

Supreme Court—Supreme Court of the United States is the highest court of appeal in the U.S.; each state also has a *Supreme Court*.

Take *or* Short Take—A few words or lines of a story written on one sheet of paper and sent out to the composing room for quick processing; written thus because deadline is near.

Telegraph Editor—Editor who chooses and edits stories from press association dispatches and work of other agencies transmitting by teletype or telegraph.

Thirty—End of story; written *30*.

Time Copy—Feature stories and material to be set into type in slack periods in the composing room.

Turtle—Metal-wheeled table used to transport forms or chaises of type from point to point in the composing room; surface accommodates standard-size newspaper pages.

Wire Desk—Telegraph desk.

Wired Photo—Photograph transmitted by telephone or wireless.

Selected Bibliography

Listed below are books and other materials from which I have quoted, which were useful to me, or which might prove useful to the reader in pursuing phases of the subject further. I have made no attempt to be complete in the listing, or even comprehensive.

BOOKS

A Century of Journalism: "The Sydney Morning Herald" and its Record of Australian Life. Edited by Warwick Fairfax. Sydney: John Fairfax and Sons Ltd., 1931.

Ball, W. Macmahon. *Nationalism and Communism in East Asia* (Revised). Melbourne: Melbourne University Press, 1956.

Bonwick, James. *Early Struggles of the Australian Press.* London: Gordon and Gotch, 1890.

Chisholm, A. H. *The Making of a Sentimental Bloke: A Sketch of the Remarkable Career of C. J. Dennis.* Melbourne: Georgian House Pty. Ltd., 1946.

Crusade for Journalism: Official History of the Australian Journalists' Association. Edited by Geoff Sparrow, General President 1939–43. Published for the Association's Jubilee (1960). Melbourne: Federal Council of the AJA, 1960.

Courtney, Victor. *All I'll Tell.* Sydney: Shakespeare Head Press, 1956.

Fairfax, J. F. *The Story of John Fairfax.* Sydney: John Fairfax & Sons Pty. Ltd., 1941.

Ferguson, J. A.; Foster, Mrs. A. G.; and Green, H. M. *The Howes and Their Press.* Sydney: Sunnybrook Press, 1936.

Fletcher, C. B. *The Great Wheel: An Editor's Adventures.* Sydney and London: Angus and Robertson Ltd., 1940.

Lamshed, Max. *The South Australian Story.* Published to mark the centenary of *The Advertiser.* Adelaide: Advertiser Newspapers Ltd., 1958.

Mander, A. E. *Public Enemy: The Press.* Sydney: Currawong Publishing Co., 1944.

News Agencies, Their Structure and Operation. Paris: United Nations Educational, Scientific and Cultural Organization, 1953.

Pearl, Cyril. *Wild Men of Sydney.* London: W. H. Allen, 1958.

277

Penton, Brian. *Censored!* Sydney: Shakespeare Head Press Pty. Ltd., 1947.

Pratt, A. *David Syme: Father of Protection in Australia.* London: Ward, Lock & Co., Ltd. 1908.

Pratt, George H. *The Press in South Australia—1836 to 1850.* Adelaide: The Wakefield Press, 1946.

Press, Radio and World Affairs. Edited by W. Macmahon Ball. London and New York: Melbourne University Press in association with Oxford University Press, 1938.

Sommerlad, Ernest C. *Mightier Than the Sword.* Sydney: Angus and Robertson Ltd., 1950.

Sawer, Geoffrey. *Guide to Australian Law for Journalists, Authors, Printers, and Publishers.* Melbourne: Melbourne University Press, 1949.

Year Book of the Commonwealth of Australia. No. 41. Canberra, A.C.T.: Commonwealth Bureau of Census and Statistics, 1955.

Year Book of the Commonwealth of Australia. No. 45. Canberra, A.C.T.: Commonwealth Bureau of Census and Statistics, 1959.

MAGAZINE AND OTHER ARTICLES

Chisholm, A. H. "Newspapers," *The Australian Encyclopedia.* Sydney: Angus & Robertson Ltd., 1958.

——. "Periodicals," *ibid.*

Corden, W. M. "Towards a History of the Australian Press," *Meanjin,* June, 1956, pp. 171–84.

——. "The Australian Press: A Note," *ibid.,* December, 1956, p. 444.

Curthoys, Roy L. "The Press and its Critics," *The Australian Quarterly,* September, 1936, pp. 55–61.

Davies, A. G. "Queensland's Pioneer Journals and Journalists," *Journal Historical Society of Queensland,* III (1945).

Dixon, M. F. "Bold Experiment in Nationally-Owned News Service," *Meanjin,* March, 1955, pp. 115–20.

"Early Struggles of the Colonial Press," *Newspaper Press Directory.* Sections on Australian colonial newspapers. London, 1905.

Grover, M. "Held Over: Reminiscences of a Newspaper Man," *Lone Hand,* July–October, 1914.

Horne, D. B. "A 'Breathing Space' for the Press? (Elections and the Press)," *The Australian Quarterly,* September, 1949, pp. 15–20.

McKay, Claude. "Soliloquy on the Australian Press," *The Australian Quarterly,* March, 1939, pp. 74–78.

Norman, Albert. "Australian Press Has Popular Support," *Monthly Bulletin of the International Press Institute,* IV, No. 9 (January, 1956), 5–6.

"On Duty With the A.A.P.," *Newspaper News,* Twenty-fifth Anniversary Number, March, 1953, p. 74.

Pringle, John M. D. "Intellectuals and the Press," *Meanjin,* September, 1957, pp. 299–300. (Extracts from Arthur Norman Smith Memorial Lecture in Journalism delivered at the University of Melbourne.)

Scott, Winifred. "The Growth of the Australian Press," *Journal of the Society of the Arts* (London), LII, No. 2,702 (September 2, 1904), 775–80; No. 2,703 (September 9, 1904), 785–92.

Truman, T. C. "The Press and the 1951 Federal Elections," *The Australian Quarterly,* December, 1951, pp. 33–44.

PAMPHLETS, BROCHURES AND LECTURES

Banner, Franklin C. *A Study of the Australian Press.* Pennsylvania: Pennsylvania State College, 1950.

Heaton, Herbert. *The Early Tasmanian Press and Its Struggle for Freedom.* Issued March 17, 1916, pp. 1–25.

Lack, Clem. *History of Australian Journalism.* Lectures at the University of Queensland. Brisbane, 1956. (Mimeographed).

Mayer, Henry. *The Popular Press.* Ten lectures at University of Sydney. Sydney, 1956. (Mimeographed.)

McLachlan, A. H. *"Readership and Responsibility."* The 18th Arthur Norman Smith Lecture in Journalism at the University of Melbourne. October 27, 1954. Melbourne, 1954.

Shakespeare, A. T. *A Brief History of the Australian Provincial Press Association, 1906–1956.* Canberra: Federal Capital Press, 1956.

——. *After Fifty Years: New South Wales Country Press History.* Sydney: New South Wales Country Press, 1950.

Sommerlad, E. Lloyd. "Evolution of the Australian Press—1919–1952." Unpublished Manuscript.

NEWSPAPER SUPPLEMENTS

The Advertiser (Adelaide). *Centennial Edition,* July 12, 1958.

The Age (Melbourne). *Centennial Edition Supplement,* October 16, 1954.

The Clarion (Sydney). Complete file of the newspaper published on behalf of Australian Journalists' Association (N.S.W. District) and the Printing Industry Employees' Union (N.S.W. Branch) during the 1955 Sydney strike. (1) July 13; (2) July 14; (3) July 15, 1955.

The Herald (Melbourne). *Centenary Edition,* January 3, 1940.

The "Herald's" New Building. Supplement to *The Sydney Morning Herald,* December 21, 1955.

Heralds of the News. Supplement to *The Advertiser* (Adelaide), September 1, 1936.

The Mercury Centenary Magazine. Supplement to *The Mercury* (Hobart), July 5, 1954.

The News (Adelaide). *Thirtieth Anniversary Edition,* July 24, 1953.

NEWSPAPER TRADE AND PROFESSIONAL PUBLICATIONS

Audit Bureau of Circulations. Semi-annual tabulated statements of member publications and their latest circulations. Audit Bureau of Circulations, Sydney.

Australian Journalists' Association. Annual Reports of AJA Districts; AJA Constitution and By-Laws (Revised to 1953); Metropolitan Dailies and other Awards; files of *Journalist* (AJA monthly paper).

Commercial Radio and Television. Edited by John Briears. Sydney: Newspaper News Pty. Ltd., 1956.

Directory of Metropolitan and Provincial Daily Newspapers. Sydney: Commonwealth Press Union, 1955.

1961 NAARDS—Newspapers: Australian Advertising Rate and Data Service. Sydney: Mingay Publishing Co., 1961.

Newspaper News. Semi-monthly journal of the Australian newspaper, advertising and graphic arts industries. (Files and Twenty-fifth Anniversary number.)

Press Directory of Australia and New Zealand. 13th ed. Edited by E. L. Sommerlad. Sydney: Country Press Ltd., 1954.

Press Directory of Australia and New Zealand. 14th ed. Edited by E. L. Sommerlad and N. L. Roberts. Sydney: Country Press Ltd., 1958.

Index

Aborigines: 85, 87; Stuart case, 167–69

Adelaide. *See* South Australia

Advertiser, The (Adelaide): character of, 10, 161; editor, 28; use of stringers, 41; judging space requirements, 46; leader page, 52; sports department, 62; women's pages, 74; files, 81; at Canberra, 104, 105; courts coverage, 108–09; AAP member, 121; London address, 127; cable news, 132; teletype machines, 136; list of features, 148–49; book page, 153; and Herald and Weekly Times Ltd., 105, 136, 157, 241; circulation problems, 203, 261; history of, 242–43; address and circulation, 243; and *The Sunday Mail,* 249

Advertiser, The (Hobart), 245

Advertiser Newspapers Ltd. (Adelaide), 23, 241, 243, 256

Advertisers' Monthly, 259

Advertising in Australia, 259

Advertising Rate and Data Service (NAARDS, BAARDS, GAARDS), 260

Advocate, The (Burnie), 122, 204

Afternoon Dailies: procedures on, 1, 39–40; sports, 71; business-finance coverage, 76, 77, 78; Parliament coverage, 84; police coverage, 87–88; Canberra coverage, 106; foreign news, 122, 125, 130; Sydney coverage, (AUP), 138; Perth news, 142, 143; syndicate material, 157; use of light material, 160–61; as "feature" papers, 212

Age, The (Melbourne): character of, 8, 160–61; page one change to news, 13; division of each pound spent, 23; editor, 28, on AUP circuit, 41, 138; chief sub-editor, 44; leader page, 52, 215, 216; letters, 52; at Canberra, 104, 106; courts coverage, 109–10; AAP member, 121; London address, 127; cable news, 131–32; teletype machines, 136; daily features, 149; "Junior Age" department, 152; book page, 153; writing in, 212; history of, 238–39; address and circulation, 239; ANC member, 256; news agent system, 261–65

Agence France Press, 143

Aircraft, 241

Alice Springs, N.T. *See* Northern Territory

"Ambit of dispute," 175

American Newspaper Guild compared to AJA, 182–83

Anti-labor charges, 54, 116–17

Argus, The (Melbourne): reasons for including, viii–ix; death of, viii–ix, 9, 240; character of, 9; presses purchased by *The Mer-*

Argus, The (Melbourne) (*continued*)
cury, 11, 245; change to page one
news, 13; 1956 contempt of court
case, 59, 166; at Canberra, 106;
fiction, 150; comic strips, 159;
leaders, 216; history of, 240; address and circulation, 240; ANPA
member, 256; news agent system,
261–65
Arthur Norman Smith Lectures: 1954
quoted, 218–19
Asia news. *See* Far East
Australasian Post, The, 240
Australian Associated Press (AAP):
at Canberra, 105, 106; as chief
source of foreign news, 121–26;
in New York, 128; accredited to
U.N., 128; daily list of stories,
130; expansion of services, 131;
and U.S. integration story, 134;
newspapers with AAP teletype ma-
chines, 136, 137; Perth service,
142; Journalists' Awards for, 174;
control of, 256
Australian Association of Advertising
Agencies, 257
Australian Association of National
Advertisers, 257
Australian Audit Bureau of Circula-
tions, 15, 258–59
Australian Benefit Society, 114
Australian Broadcasting Commission
(ABC), 105, 107, 128, 139–41, 253–
54
Australian Broadcasting Control
Board, 254
Australian Capital Territory (A.C.T.),
5, 101–02, 104–08, 203
Australian Consolidated Press Ltd.
(Sydney): publications of, 20, 57,
62, 157, 237; related enterprises,
20, 237; editor-in-chief, 28; N.Y.
office, 128; as syndicate, 157, 158;
216n; purchases *The Bulletin,* 251;
ANC member, 256. *See also Daily
Telegraph* (Sydney), history of;
Sun, The (Sydney), history of
Australian Constitution, 53
Australian Council of Trades Unions,
115

Australian Gallup Poll, 21
Australian Home Beautiful, 241
Australian Journal, The, 243–44
Australian Journalists Association
(AJA): 155; 159; membership and
growth, 172; and Awards, 171–78;
organization and administration,
177–80; Jubilee Year, 181; dispute
with proprietors, 182; 255
Australian Labor Party (A.L.P.), 53,
93, 113–17, 251–52
Australian National University, 102
Australian Newspaper Conference,
255
Australian Newspaper Council, 255–
56
Australian Newspapers Service, 128
Australian Newspaper Proprietors As-
sociation, 255
Australian Newsprint Mills Pty. Ltd.
(ANM) (Boyer), 23, 24, 25, 256
Australian Press Association, 122
Australian Provincial Daily Press Ltd.,
257
Australian Provincial Press Associa-
tion, 256
Australian Star, 237
Australian United Press (AUP): in-
ternal circuits, 41; at Canberra,
105; and AAP, 122; newspapers
with AUP teletype machines, 136;
as source of domestic news, 137–
38; Perth news, 142
Australian Women's Weekly, 20, 57,
157, 160, 237
Australian Worker (Sydney), 252
Australian Workers Union (A.W.U.),
115
Associated Newspapers Ltd. (Sydney),
18, 19, 23, 237–38
Authorized News Agent system, 261–
65
Automobile Clubs, 79
Awards, Metropolitan Dailies', 171–
78

Ball, W. Macmahon, 133, 193
Ballarat, 8, 14, 114
"Bamboo Curtain," 131

Barrier Daily Truth, The (Broken Hill), 251
Barrier Miner, The (Broken Hill), 41, 136, 243
Baseball in Australia, U.S., 65
Basketball, 66
Bays Transport Service Ltd., 21
Beats. *See* Rounds and roundsmen
Beeden, George W., 112
"Ben Boyang," 159
Bennetts, John, 194
Ben Roth, N.Y. syndicate, 158
Betting. *See* Punting
"Bigness" in Australian newspapers, 213–14
Blacktrackers. *See* Aborigines
Blackburn, A. S., 174
Block rooms. 79, 81
"Blue Log" Award, 173
"Bluey and Curley," 155, 159
Board of Valuers, 261–65 *passim*
Boldrewood, Rolf, 149
Bonython, Sir Langdon, 243
Book Clubs, 21
Books and book reviewing, 149–50, 153–54
Bowling and bowling clubs, 66
Boxing, 65
Boyer. *See* Tasmania
Brisbane. *See* Queensland
British origins of Australian journalism, 11–13
Broadcasting. *See* Radio broadcasting; Television broadcasting
Broadsheets, 34–36 *passim*, 48, 78, 131–33 *passim*, 146, 156. *See also The Advertiser* (Adelaide); *The Age* (Melbourne); *The Argus* (Melbourne); *Courier-Mail* (Brisbane); *The Herald* (Melbourne); *The Mercury* (Hobart); *The Sydney Morning Herald* (Sydney)
"Broker to Client," 77
Burnie. *See* Tasmania
Business and finance departments, 75–78
Bureaus, newspaper, 136, 137, 141–43
Business offices, Australian newspaper, 199–200

By-line column writing, 53, 61–62
Bulletin, The (Sydney), 128, 149, 216, 216n, 237, 251
Bulletin Newspaper Company Ltd., 237

Cabinet, Prime Minister's, 94, 102–103, 107
Cable and Wireless Ltd. (London), 124
Cable charges, 126, 128, 130
Cable editor. *See* Editors
Cable news. *See* Foreign news
Cablese, lack of, 130, 143
Cadet Counsellors, 189–97 *passim*
Cadets: 72, 77, 80, 138, 142, 163; training system, 185–97; and 1911 Awards, 186; provisions in Awards, 187–90; recruitment and training, 188–92; shorthand and typing, 190, 197; classes for, 190; four-year training, 191; prize competition for, 192
Calwell, Arthur A., 115
Camera Press (London), 158
Canberra. *See* Australian Capital Territory
Canberra correspondents, 104–108
Capital cities of Australia, 4–11, 97. *See also* Australian Capital Territory, Canberra; New South Wales, Sydney; Queensland, Brisbane; South Australia, Adelaide; Tasmania, Hobart; Victoria, Melbourne; Western Australia, Perth
Capital-city journalism: effects of population distribution on, 4–5; description of, 5–15; London offices, 127–28; and radio, 139. *See also* New South Wales; Queensland; South Australia; Tasmania; Victoria; Western Australia
"Captain Yonsson," 159
Carr, B. J., 123
Cartoonist, Editorial, 29, 55. *See also* Comic strips
Casuals. *See* Correspondence by stringer
Cattle, 139

Censorship, World War II, 54
Central Intelligence Bureau, 90
Changes in Australian newspapers, 13, 32
Chief of Staff (C.O.S.), 36–40, 129
Chief sub-editor. *See* Editors
Chisholm, A. H., 154
Christmas season, 150
Chronicle, The (Adelaide), 128, 243
Cinema. *See* Films
Circulation of Australian newspapers; 2, 5; circulation manager's problems, 201–202; news agent system, 201, 261–65; delivery difficulties, 202–205, 211; Sunday newspapers, 249–50
"Circus" makeup, 210
City Council, 98, 99
Civic roundsmen, 97–100
Civil Libel, 163
"Clancy," 79
Clarion, The (Sydney), 182
Classified advertisements, 73, 206
Cleary, Jon, 149
Climate, effect on sports, 61
"Club, The," 106
Code restricting name-calling, 108
Code of Ethics, AJA, 180
Collective bargaining, 172
Colonial Times (Hobart), 245
Color printing, 155
Columns and columnists, 53, 147–48
Comic strips, 154–55, 158–59
Commerical radio-television, and ABC, 139–41 *passim*
Commonwealth Arbitration Court, 172
Commonwealth Conciliation and Arbitration Act, 171, 172
Commonwealth Gazette, 172
Commonwealth press cable rates, 126, 128
Commonwealth Press Union, 257–58
Commonwealth Scientific and Industrial Research Organization (CSIRO), 102
Communism and the Communist Party, 93, 116

Competition, Australian newspaper, 18, 33
Compulsory voting, 53–54, 93
Conpress Printing Ltd., 20
Consolidated Press Ltd. *See* Australian Consolidated Press Ltd.
Constitution, Australian, 53
Contempt of Court, 59, 112, 163, 164, 166, 167–69
Cook, B. S. B., 171, 172, 181
Copyright laws, 165
Copy taster, 47
Corden, Dr. W. M., 17, 237
Correspondence by stringer: 40–42; in sports, 63; use of casuals, 63, 109; at Canberra, 105; AUP, 137; ABC, 140
Costs of publishing, 22–24
Counter-attack in self-defense, 164
Country correspondents. *See* Correspondence by stringer
Countryman, The (Perth), 244
Country Party, 53, 54, 93, 239
Country press of Australia, 41, 122, 137, 138–39, 158, 256, 257
Country Press Ltd., 257
Courier, The (Brisbane), 216, 241–42
Courier-Mail, The (Brisbane): character of, 9, 160–61; published by Queensland Newspapers Pty. Ltd., 20; division of each pound spent by, 23; employees, 24; editor-in-chief, 28; on AUP circuit, 41; reference department, 80; at Canberra, 104, 105; court stories, 109; AAP member, 121; London address, 127; overseas news, 132; teletype machines, 136; and Herald and Weekly Times Ltd., 105, 136, 157, 241; and Queensland Country Press, 138; feature editor, 146; book page, 153; and Queensland University Journalism Committee, 194; plane deliveries, 202, 205; syndication arrangements, 158; leader page, 215; history of, 241–42; circulation and address, 242; 249
Court procedure, 164
Courts coverage. *See* Rounds and roundsmen

Courts of Australia: Land and Valuation Court, 108; Federal High Court, 108, 110, 164, 167; State Supreme Courts, 108, 109, 110, 111, 164, 167; municipal courts, 110, 111; Court of Criminal Appeal, 167; Commonwealth Arbitration Court, 172

Courts rounds. *See* Rounds and roundsmen

Crane, Clare, 74

Cricket, 65, 68

Criminal Investigation Bureau, 87, 88

Criminal libel, 163

Criticism of newspapers: Australia and U.S. compared, 216–18; of Australian, by Australians, 217, 218, 219

Crosland, Sydney, 179

Crown appointees, 53

Cumberland Newspapers Ltd., 18

Dailies, Provincial: Journalists' Awards for, 174

Daily Courier, The (Hobart), 245

Daily Guardian, The (Sydney), 238

Daily Herald (Adelaide), 251

Daily Mail, The (Brisbane), 241–42

Daily Mail (London), 158

Daily Mail, The (Sydney), 237

Daily Mirror (Sydney): not included in study, viin; 7, 28, 51, 104, 105, 110, 122, 128, 133, 137, 154, 182, 215; history of, 238; bought by News Ltd., 244; and IPI, 258

Daily News (Perth): character of, 10; publishers of, 21; managing editor, 28; mobile picturegram unit, 60; Saturday sports editions, 67; form guide, 70; women's and social pages, 74; business-finance news, 76; reference departments, 80; AAP member, 122; London office, 127; overseas news, 133; teletype machines, 136; and Perth News Bureau, 142–43; film reviews dropped, 152; and syndication, 157; and Herald and Weekly Times Ltd., 157–58; Rigby and Ward on, 159; circulation system, 204; no leader page in, 215; 1926 purchase by Davidson, 243; West Australian Newspapers Ltd. and, 244; history of, 245; address and circulation, 245

Daily News, The (Sydney), 237

Daily Pictorial (Sydney), 236

Daily Standard (Brisbane), 251

Daily Sun, The (Sydney), 236

Daily Telegraph (Melbourne), 241

Daily Telegraph (Sydney): character, 7; news on page one, 12; and Rupert Murdoch, 18; published by Australian Consolidated Press Ltd., 20, 236; editor, 28; style book, 49; leader page, 52, 55; attempt to censor, 54; pictorial department, 57; sports, 62; racing coverage, 71; women's and social pages, 74; "Broker to Client," 77; "Clancy," 79; reference department, 81; rounds and roundsmen, 83, 109; at Canberra, 104, 105; courts covage, 109; AAP member, 121; London address, 127; N.Y. office, 128; accredited to U.N., 128; Suez crisis coverage, 128; overseas news, 132–33; teletype machines, 137; features, 146; supplements, 150; book page, 153; comic strips, 155, 159; syndicated material, 157, 158; 1955 shutdown, 182, 216n; delivery system, 202–03; 212; leader page, 215; history of, 236–37; address and circulation, 237; and Sunday papers, 249. *See also The Sun,* history of

Darling Downs, 139

Darwin, N.T. *See* Northern Territory

Davidson, J. E., 243

David Syme and Company Ltd., 28

Davies Brothers Ltd., 19, 20, 23, 24

Davies family: C. B., C. E., Charles, C. R., G. F., J. G., John, 245

Deakin, Alfred, 114

Decisions, court, 164–65, 166, 167, 168, 169

Defamation suit, 241–42
Defamatory libel, 169
Defense against libel, 164
Denison, Hugh: 17; and Sydney
 Newspapers Ltd., 237; and *The
 Sun*, 237–38; invades Melbourne,
 237; sells *The Sun News-Pictorial*,
 241
Deputy Chief of Staff, 37, 39
Dictation system, 118–120
Diploma in Journalism: 163; at
 Queensland and Melbourne Uni-
 versities, 186; compared to A.B.
 degree, 186; requirements for, 192–
 94
Dixon, M. F., 141
Domestic News. *See* Australian United
 Press; Bureaus, Capital-City; Cor-
 respondence by stringer; Perth
 News Bureau; Queensland Country
 Press
Drama. *See* Films
Drop-on (replate), 50
Dunne, Sarah, 74

Edition changes, 31–33
Editorial research. *See* Morgues, newspaper
Editors: the editor, 28–29; night, 29;
 news, 33–36; table of organization
 of, 34; no state editors, 36; sub-
 editors, chief sub, 43–50, 63, 125,
 129; leader page, 52, 147; picture,
 56, 57–58; sports, 60–68; turf,
 68–71; social editress, women's
 editress, 72, 74–75; business-finance,
 75; motor, 78–79; cable, 125, 129–
 34; no telegraph editors, 129; features editors, 145–46. *See also* News
 conferences
Eight-hour day, 114
Eisenhower, Dwight D., 134
Elizabethan Theatre Trust, 153
Engravings. *See* Block Rooms
Eucalyptus, source of Australian
 newsprint, 24
Euphemisms, lack of, 109
Eureka Stockade battle, 8, 14, 114
Evatt, Dr. H. V., 135
Evening News, The, 238

Evening Sun, The (Melbourne), 239
Everybody's Weekly, 237
Examiner, The (Launceston), 106,
 128, 249
Exchange arrangements: photographs,
 56; business-finance news, 78; east-
 west news, 142; syndicated material,
 158
Exmouth Gulf. *See* Oil search
Export of Australian news, 143, 157,
 159, 160
Exchange Telegraph and Press As-
 sociation, 140
Express, The (London), 158

Fair comment and criticism, 164
Fairfax, John, 236. *See also* John
 Fairfax Ltd., John Fairfax Pty.
 Ltd. and *The Sydney Morning
 Herald*
"Family Man," 159
Far East news coverage, 128, 130–31
Fatchen, Max, 149
"Fatty Finn," 159
Features editors. *See* Editors
Features: business and finance, 77;
 145-61; books, 149–50, 153–54;
 fiction, 149–50; films, 152–53; his-
 torical, 154
Federal High Court, 108, 110
Federal News Service, 105
Federal Parliamentary Press Gallery,
 104
Federation, Australian: 101; opposed
 by *Daily Telegraph* in 1890's, 236
Fellowships: for Australian journal-
 ists, 194; IPI Commonwealth Ex-
 change, 258
Ferber, Mary, 74
Fiction, 149–50
Fifty-Fifty letters, 52–53
Films, 152–53
Finance. *See* Business and finance
 departments
Finance editor. *See* Editors
Financial Review, The, 236
Fire companies, 87
First newspaper in Australia, 14, 85;
 illustration, facing page 144
Fisher, Andrew, 114

Flying Doctor, 254
Foreign correspondents, 125, 126–29, 140
Foreign news: 121–38; emergency transmission, 124; per cent printed, 130; from Asia, 130–31, 214; in the broadsheets, 131–32; in the tabloids, 132–33; from the U.S., 133–35, 214–15; more needed in Australian papers, 214. *See also* Australian Associated Press, Australian Broadcasting Commission
Foreign Policy, Australian, 54
Football, 32, 61, 63–65
Form Guides, 69, 71
"Frisky," 159
Fudge-box, 31, 210
Fulbright grants, 194

Geelong. *See* Victoria
General Motors-Holden, 79
Geography, effects of, 2–4, 6
"Ginger Meggs," 159
Gold mining. *See* Eureka Stockade
Golf and golf clubs, 66
Government: local, 36–37; state, 93–94; houses of Parliament, 93–94, 102; premier, 94, 117, 168–69; prime minister, 94, 102, 103, 106–07; federal, 102, 103
Government rounds. *See* Rounds and roundsmen
Government and Opposition, 107
Governors: Governor-general, 94, 102; state, 94
Grading system, 173–77
Graphic Arts and Printers Handbook, 259
Graziers, 53
Griffin, Walter Burley, 101
Griffin Press (Adelaide), 243
"Gunn's Gulley," 159
Guns, not carried by police, 90–91
Gurr, T. Stuart, 258

Hackett, Sir Winthrop, 244
Hansard, 80, 81, 107
Hardwood, newsprint from, 24–25
Headlines, 48–49, 50
Hearst papers (U.S.), 22

Herald, The (Melbourne): character of, 8, 212; distribution, 21; editor, 28; editions, 31; "The Herald Saturday Review," 52; photography department, 56; Saturday sports editions, 67, 68; Sarah Dunne on, 74; at Canberra, 104, 105; court stories, 109; AAP member, 121; London address, 127; overseas news, 132, 157; teletype machines, 136; not on AUP circuit, 138; feature writers, 146; book page, 153; syndicated material, 154, 157, 158; B. S. B. Cook and, 171, 172; street sales, 202; leader page, 215; history of, 240–41; address and circulation, 241; news agent system, 261
Herald and Weekly Times Ltd. (Melbourne): 18, 19, 132; its publications and activities, 21, 24, 241; division of each pound spent, 23; 1955 income, 23; editors, 28; style book, 49; photography department, 56; at Canberra, 105; teletype machines, 136–37; as syndicate, 157; overseas news, 157, 158; buys *The Evening Sun* and *The Sun News-Pictorial,* 239; history of, 241; and Brisbane papers, 241; shareholder in *The Advertiser,* 243; and News Ltd., 245; ANC member, 256
Herald Gravure, Journalists' Awards for, 174
Herald Tribune, The (N.Y.), 158
"Herman Wizzer," 159
High Court of Australia. *See* Courts of Australia
History of Australian Journalism, 13–14, 235–45
Hobart. *See* Tasmania
Hooper, Duncan, 123
Horse racing. *See* Sports departments
Hours of work, 172–73
Houses of Parliament, 93–94, 102
Howe, George, 85
Hungerford, T. A., 150

Iddon, Don, 149
Immigration, 54

Incomes of Australian newspapers, 23
Industrial Awards. *See* Awards, Metropolitan Dailies
Industrial rounds. *See* Rounds and roundsmen
Inquirer and Western Australian Journal of Politics and Literature, The (Perth), 245
Integration, U.S. racial, 134
Internal news agencies, 32, 41–42. *See also* Australian United Press; Perth News Bureau; Queensland Country Press Association
International Press Institute, 128, 258
"Investors Notebook," 77
Irish, R. A., 18
Isaacs, Sir Isaac: 1917 Award, 173–74
Isolation as national policy, 54
Israel, 134

Japan, 121
Jefferis, Barbara, 150
Job, Mrs. E. M., 150
Job printing, 20–22 *passim*
John Fairfax and Sons Pty. Ltd. (Sydney): publishers of *The Sydney Morning Herald*, 19, 236; and Australian Newsprint Mills Pty. Ltd., 24; buys Associated Newspapers Ltd., 236, 238; becomes public company, 236
John Fairfax Ltd. (Sydney): ixn; finances purchase of Truth and Sportsman, 18, 236; subsidiary companies, 19; directors, 19, 28; picture department, 57; library-morgue, 81; syndication, 157, 158; publications of, 236; *Sun-Herald* and, 249; and IPI, 258
Joliffe cartoons, 159
Journalist, The: AJA monthly, 15; on AJA founding, 172; 21st anniversary issue quote on 1911 award, 172–73; B. S. B. Cook quoted, 181; A. N. Smith quoted, 186; and employee viewpoint, 216; as union paper, 252
Journalists' situation before 1910, 172

Judicial Committee of the Privy Council (London), 110, 167–68
Jump Stories, 50
Jurisdiction of Australian courts, 164, 166

Kalgoorlie Miner, The, 136, 138, 204
Kelly, Ned, 9, 87, 89
Kelly-Rainier wedding, 59
Kemp, Charles, 236
Kerr, William, 240
Kind, A. W. V., 123
King Features (N.Y.), 158

Labor Daily, The (Sydney), 237, 251
Labor disputes: 114, 117; journalists', 171–73
Labor-management relations, 181–83
Labour Party. *See* Australian Labour Party
Labor News (Sydney), 252
Labor Press, 251–52
Landy, John, 66
Law and the press, 163–69
Law courts. *See* Courts of Australia; Rounds and roundsmen
Lawler, Ray, 152
Law lists, 108
Leader, The, 239
Leader of the Opposition, 107
Leaders and leader pages, 51–55, 130, 145, 147, 215–16
Leaving Certificate: cadets and, 188–89; shortcomings, 197
Leads, 48–49
Legislative Assembly. *See* Parliament, state
Legislative Council. *See* Government
Lending Libraries. *See* Libraries, newspaper
Letters to the Editor, 52–53, 63
Libel laws and decisions: British origins, 12, 163; *Argus-Sun News-Pictorial* case, 59, 166; use of photographs, 59, 166–67; defamation, 163; civil vs. criminal, 163; use of names, 166; seditious libel, 167–69
Liberal Party, 53, 54, 93
Libraries: viii, 13; newspaper, 78-82

Licenses, radio and TV listeners', 139, 253–54
Life Magazine (U.S.), 81, 158, 237
Listener-In, The, 241
Literary sections and editors. *See* Books and book reviews
Literary competitions, 149–50
Local government authorities, 36–37
Logs of Claims, AJA, 111, 172, 173–75
London Illustrated News, 81
London offices of Australian newspapers, 127–28
London Planet, 158
London Standard, The, 158
Look Magazine (U.S.), 158
Lord Mayors, capital city, 98, 99
Lotteries, 84
Lovekin, Arthur, 245
Low, David, 159
Lower House. *See* Houses of Parliament

Macartney, James E., 152
Mace, The, 95, 107
Macfaull, Charles, 244
McGhee, John, 149
Mackinnon, Lauchlan, 240
MacLauchlan, Angus H., 218–19
Macquarie, Lachlan, 113
Magazines, Australian, 145, 147, 250–51
Mail-Times, The, 244
Maitland Mercury, The, 251
Makeup, Australian newspaper, 48–50
Managing Director, 28
Margot, 74
Mayer, Henry, 251–52
Meanjin, 17, 141, 216, 237
Melbourne. *See* Victoria
Melbourne Advertiser, The, 240
Melbourne Cricket Ground (MCG), 65
Melbourne Cup, 60–61, 71
Melbourne Daily News, The, 240
Melbourne Herald Cable Service, 158
Melbourne University Diploma in Journalism, 186, 192–94
Memorandum of Association, AAP, 122, 123

Menzies, Prime Minister Robert G., 54, 102–03, 135, 174, 176,
Mercury, The (Hobart): 4; character of, 11, 22, 161; parent company of, 20; editors, 28; chief-of-staff, 37, 62; Tasmanian correspondents, 40; Launceston bureau, 40, 204; Margot on, 74; business and finance, 75, 76; library-morgue, 81; civic rounds, 99; at Canberra, 106; AAP member, 122; London address, 127; book page, 153; comic strips, 155; news agents circulation system, 204, 265; history of, 245; address and circulation, 245; ANC member, 256
Mercury Board Containers Pty. Ltd. (Hobart), 19
Mercury Newspapers Pty. Ltd. (Hobart), 19, 245
Mercury Press Pty. Ltd., 19
Michigan (U.S.), daily newspapers in, 212
Mirror Newspapers Ltd., 18–19. *See also Daily Mirror* (Sydney), history of
Mobile units, newspaper, 60, 71, 89
Modern Industrial Destructors, 20
Modern Motor, 237
Molnar, editorial cartoonist, 159
Monopoly trends, 17–18, 21–22
Montague Grover Memorial Prize, 192
Moreton Bay Courier, The, 241–42
Morgues, newspaper: picture, 59–60; reference, 79–82
Morning dailies: edition times, 1, 2; procedures on, 38, 39; business and finance pages, 78; police coverage, 88; Canberra coverage, 106; foreign news, 122, 125, 130; AUP news, 138; and Perth News Bureau, 142, 143; syndicate material, 157; light features, 160–61; as "serious" papers, 212
Morning Herald, The (Perth), 245
Morning Herald and Miner's Advocate (Newcastle), 4
Morning Post, The, 239
Moses, Charles, 140
Motor editor. *See* Editors
Motor news, 78–79

Movies. *See* Films
Municipal government, 36–37, 97–100
Murdoch, Rupert, 18
Murdoch, Sir Keith, 17, 18, 122, 241, 242, 243

NAARDS, 4, 15, 247, 260
Name-calling prescribed, 108
Names, use of in reporting, 112, 166–67
Napier, Sir Mellis, 168
National News Service, 105
Negro-white relations, U.S., 134
Newcastle. *See* New South Wales
Newcastle Morning Herald, The, 256
Newcastle Sun, The, 256
Newhouse Organization (U.S.), 22
New Idea, The, 160, 243
News, The (Adelaide): character of, 10; editor, 28; stringers, 40–41; leader pages, 55; stand on Suez crisis, 55, 135; library, 81; Parliament coverage, 84; at Canberra, A.C.T. 104n, 105; AAP member, 122; London address, 128; foreign news, 133; teletype machines, 136; feature editor, 146; book page, 153; syndicate arrangements, 158; the Stuart case, 167–69; circulation problems, 203; as crusader, 212; leader page, 215; history of, 243–44; address and circulation, 244; and *The Sunday Mail,* 248–49
News, The (Hobart), 243
News Agents, Authorized: in Sydney and rural centers, 202; how system works, 261–65
News budgets, 125, 139, 142
News conferences, 29–30
News editor. *See* Editors
Newsgathering, early, 126
News Ltd. (Adelaide): Norton properties acquired 1960, ixn, 18, 236, 238; executive head, 19, 28; 1956 profits, 23; at Canberra, 104n; owns *Barrier Miner,* 136; and journalists' education, 194; history of, 243–44; publishes weeklies, 249

New South Wales: Sydney, 3, 6–7, 76, 77, 97, 99; Sydney journalism, 7, 55, 83, 89–90, 99, 138; Newcastle, 4, 174, 256. *See also* Associated Newspapers Ltd.; Australian Consolidated Press, Ltd.; *The Barrier Miner; The Bulletin; Daily Mirror; The Daily Sun; Daily Telegraph;* John Fairfax and Sons Pty. Ltd.; John Fairfax Ltd.; Mirror Newspapers; *Sportsman; The Sun; The Sun-Herald; Sunday Mirror News-Pictorial; Sunday Telegraph; The Sydney Gazette and New South Wales Advertiser; The Sydney Mail; The Sydney Morning Herald; Truth;* Truth and Sportsman Ltd.
New South Wales Country Press Association, 256–57
Newspaper boards of directors, 19
Newspaper executives, 19–20
Newspaper circulation, 2, 21, 261–65
Newspaper House, 142
Newspaper News: News on page one of dailies, 12; 25th Anniversary issue quoted, 12, 22, 23, 151, 259; as reporter for Australia press, 15; quoted on publishing costs of metropolitan papers, 22; on division of each pound spent by six newspaper companies, 23; on Far East cable rates, 128; on ABC news service, 139, 140; on supplements, 151; and Yaffa Syndicate, 157; on promotion-public relations news, 206; as advertising medium, 206; J. D. Pringle quoted in, 213; employers' viewpoint and, 216; proprietors groups, 255; history, 259
Newspaper ownership, 5, 17–22 *passim*
Newspapers: Australian Advertising Rate and Data Service (NAARDS), 4, 15, 247, 260
Newspapers, Australian: kinds and totals, 4; compared to U.S., 209, 211; by states (chart), 247; Sunday, 248–50
"Newspapers of Record," 72, 211–12
Newspaper terms: Australian, 267–72; U.S., 272–76

Newsprint, 22, 23, 24, 25
News transmission: 124, 125, 126; pre-cable, 126; volume percentages, 130
Newsweek (U.S.), 158
New York Times, The (U.S.), 123, 211–12, 241, 262
New Zealand, 122, 124, 158
Night editor. *See* Editors
Niland, D'Arcy, 150
Non-dailies, provincial, Journalists' Awards for, 174
Northern Safari, viii
Northern Territory: Darwin, 3, 139; Petrov case, 89, 159; AUP news, 138; Alice Springs, 139; Port Moresby, 139
Norton, Ezra, viiin, ixn, 18, 19, 213, 238
Norton, John, 238
"Now-ness," 52, 147, 211

Observer, The: criticism of newspapers in, 216; merged with the Bulletin, 216n, 237
O'Connell Pty. Ltd., 19
Oil search, 60, 77, 159
Olympic Games (1956), 6, 11, 66, 159
Overseas Cable Service, 105
Overseas correspondents. *See* Foreign correspondents
Overseas Telecommunications Commission (OTC), 56, 58, 124, 136
"Over-the-fence" newspaper delivery, 205

Packer, Sir Frank, 237
Pacific area news: 123, 124, 128–29, 130–31
Page make-up: tabloid, 34–35; for cable news, 129; broadsheets, 131; foreign news on *Daily Telegraph,* 132–33
Paris-Match, 158
Park, Ruth, 149
Parliament, Federal: 93; early, in Melbourne, 97; in Canberra since 1927, 101–03; operations of, 106–08; and labor, 115. *See also* Rounds and roundsmen
Parliament rounds. *See* Rounds and roundsmen
Parliament, State: 92–97. *See also* Rounds and roundsmen
Parrott, W. E., 123
Pastoralists, 53
Paterson, A. B., 79
Paul Popper, 158
Pay, rates of under grading system, 175–76
Payrolls, 23–24
People, 238
People's Daily (Melbourne), 251
Periodicals, Australian, 250–52
Perth. *See* Western Australia
Perth Gazette and Western Australian Journal, 244
Perth News Bureau, 141–43
Perth Newspapers Ltd., 21
Petrov case, 89, 159
Photo Editor. *See* Editor
Photographers, Staff, 56
Photography, photojournalism. *See* Pictures, News
Photo sales and offices, 160
Pictures, News: use of, 48, 55–60; on morning and afternoon papers, 57; from overseas, 56, 57, 58; costs of wired, 58; racecourse, 59, 71; filing of, 80; from half-tones, 80; police round, 89, 90, 166, 167; in tabloids, 133; sales to public, 160. *See also* Editor
Pix, 238
Playford, Sir Thomas, 168, 169
"Pogo," 155
Police personnel, 86–87, 88–89; no firearms, 90–91; crime news, 91–92, 108–09, 166–67
Police rounds. *See* Rounds and roundsmen
Politics in Australia, 53, 104, 107
Political Parties, 93–94, 107, 117. *See also* Australian Labour Party; Liberal Party; Country Party; Communism and the Communist Party
"Popular Press, The," lectures by Henry Mayer, 251–52

Population, effects on Australian journalism, 3–5
Port Moresby. *See* Northern Territory
Port Phillip Gazette, The, 240
Port Phillip Herald, The, 240
Port Phillip Patriot, The, 240
Port Pirie. *See* South Australia
Port Pirie Recorder, The, 243
Portus, J. H., 1959 Conciliation Commissioner, 187n
Posters, newspaper use of, 168, 206–07
Postmaster General's Office (PMG), 56, 58, 124, 135
"The Potts," 155, 159
Pound, value of Australian, 23
Pratt, S. E., former AJA general secretary, 179
Premier. *See* Government
Press Agencies, Journalists' Awards for, 174
Press Association (England), 158
Press Council, proposals for, 180–81
Press Directory, Australia and New Zealand, 250, 251
Press Gallery: State Parliaments, 93; city councils, 99; Federal Parliament, 104, 107, 136–37
Press runs of dailies, 15
Price Boards and Quotations, 78
Prime Minister. *See* Government
Pringle, John Douglas, 213
Privilege, 164, 166, 167
Privilege Books, 21
Profits, newspaper, 23
Promotion, newspaper, 21, 205–06, 207–08, 218–19
Proprietors, newspaper, 17–25
Provincial Press: Australian Provincial Press Association, 256. *See also* Country Press
Public benefit, 164
Public companies, 18–20
Public relations. *See* Promotion
Public service, Journalists' Awards for, 174
"Published by Authority," 12, 14
Publishing costs, 22–24
Punting, 61, 68, 71

Queensland: Brisbane, 3, 9–10, 97; Brisbane journalism, 9–10, 84, 88; police, 88; government, 93; courts, 111; sugar news, 125, 139; Rockhampton, 139. *See also The Courier-Mail* (Brisbane); *The Sunday Mail* (Brisbane); *Telegraph* (Brisbane); Telegraph Newspaper Company (Brisbane)
Queensland Country Press Association, 41, 122, 138–39, 256, 257
Queensland Literature Board of Review, 164
Queensland Newspaper Pty. Ltd., 20, 242, 256
Queensland Objectionable Literature Act, 164
Queensland Press Ltd., 20, 24, 241
Question Time, Parliament, 95, 107

Race horse summaries, files of, 70
Racing Clubs, 71
Radio: receiving sets, 61; and Parliament sessions, 107; stations, 137, 139, 253–54; ABC, 139–41; listeners' licenses, 139, 253–54; Broadcasting Act, 141
Radio broadcasting interests: of John Fairfax Ltd., 236; of Australian Consolidated Press, 237; of Herald and Weekly Times Ltd., 241; of Queensland Press Ltd., 242; of News Ltd., 243; of Advertiser Newspapers Ltd., 243; of West Australian Newspapers Ltd., 244
Radiograms, 61
Radio news. *See* Australian Broadcasting Commission
Radioteletype overseas channels, 124
Radio Television News (Sydney), 15, 259
Railways Union Gazette (Melbourne), 252
Reciprocal services. *See* Exchange arrangements
Reference rooms, 79–82
Register, The (Adelaide), 241, 243
Related enterprises of newspaper companies, 20–22, 235–45 *passim*

Reporters. *See* Rounds and rounds-
men
Reporting methods: no rewrite, 47,
118–19; typing of copy, 48; for
sports, 68; for horse racing, 71;
dictation, 87. *See also* Mobile units;
Telephoned news stories
Reprints in newspapers, 150, 156, 158
Responsibility, newspaper, 164
Restrictions on news: 109, 140–41:
163–69 *passim*
Reuters, 105, 122, 123, 124, 128, 140,
158
Revealing news sources, 165
Rewrite system, absence of, 47, 118–
19
Rigby and Ward, 159
Rivett, Rohan D., 168, 169, 194
Rockhampton. *See* Queensland
Ross, Lloyd, 114
Rounds and roundsmen: principal
rounds, 83–84; police, 85–92; state
government, 92–97; Town Hall, 97–
100; Federal government, 101–08;
courts, 108–13; industrial, 113–18;
miscellaneous, 118; coverage by
AUP, 138
Royal Commission, 168, 169
Royal family (British), 59, 159, 160
Royal Show, 136, 160

Salaries and wages, 22, 23, 172–78
passim
Saturday Evening Express, The
(Launceston), 249
Saturday Evening Mercury, The
(Hobart), 245, 249
Sawer, Geoffrey, 112, 165
School sports, 66
Sectarianism, 93
Seditious libel, 167–69
Serials and serial rights, 149–50, 160
Shakespeare, A. T., 217
Shakespeare Head Press, 20
Shand, J., 168, 169
Sheep, 139. *See* Wool market
Shorthand: reporters use of, 107,
118–19; in cadet training, 185–
97 *passim*

Smith, Trevor, 148
Social Editress. *See* Editors
Social and Women's: news, 72–75
Socialism in Australia, 115
South Australia: Adelaide, 3, 10, 84,
97, 98–99, 116; Mt. Gambier, 41;
Port Pirie, 41; unions in, 116;
supreme court, 109; Stuart case,
167–69. *See also Advertiser, The*
(Adelaide); Advertiser Newspa-
pers Ltd.; *Chronicle, The* (Ade-
laide); Griffin Press; *News, The*
(Adelaide), News Ltd.; *Sunday
Mail, The* (Adelaide)
South Australian Advertiser, The,
243
*South Australian Gazette and Colo-
nial Register, The,* 243
South Australian Provincial Press
Association, 256
*South Australian Weekly Chronicle,
The,* 243
South Australian Worker, The (Ade-
laide), 252
Southdown Press, The, 243
Southeast Asia, 123, 128, 130–31
Southerly, 216
Smith, Arthur Norman, 173, 186;
lectureship, 186, 213, 218–19
"Speewa Jack," 159
Sporting Globe (Melbourne): 61,
68, 157, 160, 241
Sports: weekend coverage, 32–33,
67–68; importance to Australians,
60–61, 65; cf. with U.S., 61; columnists and specialists, 62–63; department personnel, 63; women
and, 66; interstate, 68; horse racing, 68–72; overseas, 127; sections,
156
Sportsman (Sydney), 61
Standing heads: vice-regal, personal,
53; women's pages, 74; court coverage, 108–09; cable news, 132
State government: rounds and
roundsmen, 92–97; U.S. and Australian capitals compared, 92;
Houses of Parliament, 93, 94, 95,
96, 97; U.S.–Australian constitutions compared, 93; party system,

State government (*continued*)
93, 95; compulsory voting, 93; administrative responsibilities, 96; heads of, 94; cabinet ministers, 94, 95; Question Time, 95; States' rights, 95
State news coverage: Australian and U.S. compared, 36–37
States' rights issue, 95
Stawell Gift, 66
Stephens, J. S., 44
Stevenson, Adlai, 134
Stewart, Douglas: *Ned Kelly,* 152
Stock exchanges, 75–77
Strikes. *See* Labor disputes
Stringer, correspondence by. *See* Correspondence by stringer
Stuart, Rupert Max: aborigine tried for murder, 167–69
Style and style books, 49, 112
Sub-editors. *See* Editors
Subbing problems, 48–50
Suez crisis (1956), 55, 128, 129, 134–35
Suffrage, universal, 53
Sugar production, 125, 139
Sun, The (Sydney): character of, 7; published by Associated Newspapers Ltd., 19, 237, 238; editors, 28, 33; procedures on, 33–34, 49–50, 84; no Saturday leader page, 52; photo department, 57, 59, 90; sports columnists, 62; radio equipment, 84, 90; police coverage, 90; at Canberra, 104; AAP member, 121; London address, 127; cable news, 132; teletype machines, 136–37; fiction in, 150; syndicated material, 157; 1955 shutdown, 182; acquired by Fairfax, 236; history of, 237–38; address and circulation, 238; ANC member, 256; and IPI, 258
Sunday features, 155–57
Sunday Herald, The (Sydney), 236, 248
Sunday Mail, The (Adelaide): Canberra coverage, 105; AAP service, 122; London office, 128; ownership, 243; 248, 50

Sunday Mail, The (Brisbane): employees, 24; editor, 28; Canberra coverage, 105; AAP service, 122; colored comics, 155; only Sunday broadsheet, 156; "Sunday Mail Magazine" section, 156; "Uncle Joe's Horse Radish," 159; circulation problems, 205; owned by Queensland Press Ltd., 241, 248–50
Sunday Mirror (Sydney), 238
Sunday Mirror News-Pictorial (Sydney), 238, 248–50
Sunday Newspapers, 142, 143, 145, 155–57, 248–50
Sunday Pictorial, The (Sydney), 238
Sunday Sun, The (Sydney), 237, 238, 249
Sunday Telegraph (Sydney): pictorial department, 57; sports editor, 62; at Canberra, 105–06 *passim;* AAP service, 122; "Today" section, 156; comic strips, 159; 237, 248–50
Sunday Times, The (Perth): at Canberra, 105; AAP service, 122; 244, 248–50
Sunday Truth (Brisbane), 248–50
Sungravure Ltd., 19, 238
Sun-Herald, The (Sydney): picture department, 57; at Canberra, 105; AAP service, 122; London office, 128; "Fact" feature, 156; Australian comic strips, 159; 1953 combination, to form, 236
Sun-Herald Cable Service, 122
Sun News-Pictorial, The (Melbourne): character of, 8; distribution, 21; editor, 28; stringers, 41; no leader page, 51, 215, 239; photo department, 56, 59, 60; contempt case (1956), 59, 166; women's department, 73, 74; at Canberra, 105; courts coverage, 109; AAP member, 121; London address, 127; cable news, 132; teletype machines, 136, 137; fiction in, 150; "Young Sun," 152; syndicate material, 157; founded, 239; history, 239; address and circulation, 239; purchased by

Herald and Weekly Times Ltd., 241; ANC member, 256; and authorized news agent system, 261–65
Superior Features (New York), 158
Supplements and supplements editors, 150–51, 156
Supreme Court. *See* Courts of Australia
Surfing, 66
Sydney. *See* New South Wales
Sydney Gazette and New South Wales Advertiser, 14, 85
Sydney Herald, The, 236
Sydney Mail, The, 149
Sydney Morning Herald, The (Sydney): character of, 7, 161; change to page one news, 13; competition with Murdoch, 18; and John Fairfax Ltd., 18, 19, 57, 236; editors, 28, 34; leader pages, 52, 55; letters to the editor, 52; stand on Suez crisis, 55, 135; picture department, 57, 59; sports coverage, 62, 71; women's and social news, 74; business and finance, 75; library-morgue, 81; at Canberra, 105, 106; courts coverage, 108, 109; AAP member, 121; pre-cable newsgathering, 126; London address, 127; in New York, 128; cable news, 132; teletype machines, 136, 137; fiction in, 149, 150; book page, 153; syndicated material, 157, 158; editorial cartoonist, 159; 1955 shutdown, 182; N.S.W. circulation, 202–03; quality of writing, 212; leaders, 215, 216; history of, 235–36; 244, 249; address, 236; circulation, 236; and IPI, 258; not in ABC, 259
Sydney University journalism curriculum, 186, 194
Syme Family: David, Oswald, H. R., 239
Syndicates and Syndication, 148, 157–60; AJA opposition to imports, 181

Table-of-organization, average newspaper, 34

Tabloids: character of, 27; compared with broadsheets, 27, 34–36, 48, 59, 109, 131–33, 146; court coverage, 109–10; overseas news, 129, 131–33; typical Sunday, 155–57. *See also Daily Mirror, The* (Sydney); *Daily News, The* (Perth); *Daily Telegraph* (Sydney); *News, The* (Adelaide); *Sun News-Pictorial, The* (Melbourne); *Sun, The* (Sydney); *Telegraph* (Brisbane); *West Australian, The* (Perth)
Tasmania: 3, 24–25, 76; Hobart, 3, 4, 11, 40, 89, 97, 99, 245; Boyer, 24–25; Launceston, 11, 40, 122; Burnie, 11, 40, 122. *See also* Davies family, *Mercury, The* (Hobart)
Tasmanian, The (Hobart), 245
Tasmanian Daily News, The (Hobart), 245
Tasmanian News, The (Hobart), 245
Tasmanian Provincial Press, 256
Taxes, 61, 98
Tea-break, 44
Telegraph (Brisbane): character of, 10; ownership, 20, 242; staff, 24; editors, 28; "break-up conference," 31; sports coverage, 67; at Canberra, 105; AAP member, 121; in London, 127; teletype machines, 136, 137; syndicated material, 157; picture sales, 160; and Queensland University journalism committee, 194; circulation problems, 205; history of, 242; address and circulation, 242; ANC member, 256
Telegraph Newspaper Company (Brisbane), 20
Telephoned news stories, 68, 71, 118–20
Telephone room, 118–20
Teleprinters and operators, 124–25, 136–138
Teletype room, 135–37
Television: broadcasting, 61, 140, 254; why newspaper companies went into, 213–14; stations, 243, 244; listeners' licenses, 254

Television interests: of John Fairfax Ltd., 236; of Australian Consolidated Press Ltd., 237; of the Herald and Weekly Times Ltd., 241; of Advertiser Newspapers Ltd., 243; of News Ltd., 243; of West Australian Newspapers Ltd., 244
Telex, 135, 136, 137
Tennis, 61, 66, 124
Theatre reviewing, 152–53
Theodore, E. G., 237
Time Magazine (U.S.), 81, 156, 237
Times, The (London), 123, 211
Times, The (Melbourne), 240
Town Hall. *See* Rounds and roundsmen
Track, 66
Trades Unions, 115, 116
Trash vs. solid features, 160–61
"Trial by Newspaper," 164, 165, 166
Trials and trial reporting, 163–69
Trial testimony, publication of, 165
Trotting races, 66
Truth: Capital-city editions, ix; Sydney edition becomes *Sunday Mirror,* then *Sunday Mirror News-Pictorial,* ixn; Melbourne edition becomes *New Truth,* ixn; sports coverage, 61; at Canberra, 105; London office, 128; acquired by News Ltd., 236. *See also Daily Mirror* (Sydney), history of
"Truth and Public Benefit," 164
Truth and Sportsman Ltd.: sold to John Fairfax Ltd. company, becomes Mirror Newspapers Ltd., viiin, 18, 19, ?36; competition as factor in sale of, 21; purchased by News Ltd., 236; and IPI, 258. *See also Daily Mirror,* history of
Turf reporting, 68–72
Turnbull, Clive, 12
TV stations: ADS-7, 243; NWS-9, 243; TVW/Limited, 244
TV Week, 244
Type-books, 50
Typing of copy, 48

"Uncle Joe's Horse Radish," 159
UNESCO, 194

Unicameral parliament: Queensland, 53, 93–94
Unions: in newspaper industry, 32; in Australia, 115–18
United Nations, 128, 134
University of Queensland: Diploma in Journalism course, 186, 192–94 *passim*
University of Western Australia: curriculum in journalism, 186, 194; 244
Upper house of Parliament, 93, 94. *See also* Houses of Parliament
U.S. Associated Press, 122, 123, 125, 137, 143
U.S. columnists, 148
"Us Girls," 159
U.S. news, 133–35
U.S. newspapers compared with Australian: editors, 32, 36, 37; sports coverage, 61; civic rounds, 97; beats and rounds, 83; state capital coverage, 92; courts, 110; labor, 117; reporting methods, 118–20; AAP and U.S. AP, 125; wire news, 129; magazine pages, 145; columning, 147–48; supplements, 151; syndicates, 157
U.S. United Press and U.S. United Press International, 122n, 123, 132, 137, 140, 143, 158

Vacation (holiday) leaves, 32
Vice-regal (Personal) column, 53
Victoria: Melbourne, 3, 7–9, 97; Geelong, 4; Melbourne journalism, 7–9; Stawell, 66; rivalry with Sydney, 78; rounds, 84, 89; courts, 111; Trades Union Hall, 115–16; AAP, 138; Perth News Bureau, 142–43; murder trial, 166–67; AJA beginnings, 171–72; news agent system, 261–65. *See also Age, The* (Melbourne); *Argus, The* (Melbourne); David Syme and Co., Ltd.; *Herald, The* (Melbourne); Herald and Weekly Times Ltd.; *Suns News-Pictorial, The* (Melbourne)

Victorian Provincial Press Association, 256
Volunteer Life Saving Clubs, 66
Vote, compulsory, 53–54, 93

"Wally and the Major," 155, 159
Ward and Rigby, 159
Watson, John C., 114
Weather and overseas news, 124
Weather news on police round, 86
Weekend (Sydney), 62, 237
Weekend News, The (Perth), 244
Weekly Times, The (Melbourne), 128, 241
West Australian, The (Perth): character of, 10, 161; customer services, 21; owned by West Australian Newspapers Ltd., 21; production costs, 23; editors, 28; stringers, 41; photo department, 60; racing coverage, 70; business-finance, 76–77; library-reference department, 80; at Canberra, 105; courts coverage, 109; AAP member, 122; in London, 127; cable news, 133; teletype machines, 136; and Perth News Bureau, 142–43; no film reviews, 152; syndicated material, 157, 158; circulation system, 204; leader page, 215; history, address, circulation, 244
West Australian Newspapers Ltd. (Perth): "Northern Safari," viin; managing editor, 19, 28; publications, 21; owns trucking firm, 21; paper supply, 23; employees, 24; photography department, 57; mobile picturegram unit, 60; reference department, 80; AAP news, 142; Perth News Bureau, 142; syndication and, 157; history, 244–45; ANC member, 255–56
West Australian Petroleum Ltd. ("Wapet"), 77
Western Australia: Perth and journalism in, 3, 4, 10, 84, 85, 89, 126, 127, 148; size of, 3, 5, 86. *See also Daily News, The* (Perth); *Kalgoorlie Miner, The; West Australian, The* (Perth); West Australian Newspapers Ltd.
Western Australia, Provincial Press Association, 256
Western Australian Chronicle and Perth Gazette, The, 244
Western Mail, The (Perth), 244, 256
Western Press Ltd., 256
Wheat, 139
"White Australia" policy, 114
Williams, Sir John, 128, 130, 131
Williamson, H. D., author "The Sunlit Plain," 149
Wilson, Edward, 240
"Witchetty Tribe," 159
Wollongong, 4
Woman, 238
Woman's Day, 19, 160; merged with *Woman,* 238
Women's and social departments: 72–75
Women's Editress. *See* Editors
Women's Magazines, 251
Wool market: brokers, 77; sheep, 78, 139
Worker, The (Brisbane), 252
Working conditions, journalists' early, 172–73
World, The (Hobart), 251
World, The (Sydney), 237
World's Press News and Advertisers' Review, 259
Wren, John, 242
Wrestling, 66
Writing quality in Australian newspapers, 212–13
Wynne, A. Watkin, 123

Yaffa, David, 157, 259
Yaffa Syndicate, 157
Young, Chic, 154
Young readers, 151–52
Your Garden, 240